BURGESSES AND BURGESS LAW IN THE LATIN KINGDOMS OF JERUSALEM AND CYPRUS (1099–1325)

Burgesses and Burgess Law in the Latin Kingdoms of Jerusalem and Cyprus (1099–1325)

MARWAN NADER

ASHGATE

Published by
Ashgate Publishing Limited
Gower House
Croft Road
Aldershot
Hampshire GU11 3HR
England

Ashgate Publishing Company
Suite 420
101 Cherry Street
Burlington, VT 05401-4405
USA

Ashgate website: http://www.ashgate.com

British Library Cataloguing in Publication Data
Nader, Marwan
Burgesses and burgess law in the Latin Kingdoms of Jerusalem and Cyprus (1099-1325)
1.Freemen – Jerusalem – History – To 1500 2.Freemen – Cyprus – History – To 1500 3.Europeans – Jerusalem – History – To 1500 4.Europeans – Cyprus – History – To 1500 5.Law – Jerusalem – History – To 1500 6.Law – Cyprus – History – To 1500 7.Jerusalem – History – Latin Kingdom, 1099–1244 8.Cyprus – History – To 1500 I.Title
956.9'4032

Library of Congress Cataloging-in-Publication Data
Nader, Marwan.
Burgesses and Burgess law in the Latin Kingdoms of Jerusalem and Cyprus, 1099–1325 / Marwan Nader.
p. cm.
Includes bibliographical references and index.
ISBN 0-7546-5687-X (alk. paper)
1. Justice, Administration of—Cyprus—History. 2. Courts—Cyprus—History. 3. Middle class—Legal status, laws, etc.—Cyprus—History. 4. Justice, Administration of—Palestine—History. 5. Courts—Palestine—History. 6. Middle class—Legal status, laws, etc.—Palestine—History. I. Title.

KJ945.N33 2006
347.5693—dc22

2005034775

ISBN-13: 978-0-7546-5687-6
ISBN-10: 0-7546-5687-X

Printed and bound in Great Britain by MPG Books Ltd. Bodmin, Cornwall.

Contents

Acknowledgements

I am very grateful to all those who made possible the completion of this book. The staff of Cambridge University Library, the Institute of Historical Research and the Jafet Library of the American University of Beirut helped patiently with my queries and gave generously of their time. I wish also to express my gratitude for the financial aid which I received at the time of my research both from Fitzwilliam College and the Ian Kharten Trust.

Above all, I owe a great debt to Professor Jonathan Riley-Smith. Without his guidance and constant encouragement this book would have remained unwritten. I must also mention the kindness and generosity of Mrs Louise Riley-Smith.

Finally, I dedicate this book to my parents Anthony and Alexandra, and sisters Myrna and Rania. They have supported me every step of the way.

Marwan Nader

Abbreviations

AOL	*Archives de l'Orient Latin*
BIHR	*Bulletin of the Institute of Historical Research*
BJRL	*Bulletin of the John Rylands Library*
BF	*Byzantinische Forschungen*
DOP	*Dumbarton Oaks Papers*
ECQ	*The Eastern Churches Quarterly*
EHR	*English Historical Review*
HPM	*Historiae Patriae Monumenta*, ed. iussu Regis Caroli Alberti, 20 vols (Turin, 1836–)
JMH	*Journal of Medieval History*
Kausler	*Livre des assises de Jérusalem*, ed. E.H. Kausler (Stuttgart, 1839)
LA	*Liber Annus*
MAHEFR	*Mélanges d'Archéologie et d'Histoire de l'Ecole Française de Rome*
MHR	*Mediterranean Historical Review*
RAO	*Recueil d'Archéologie Orientale*
RB	*Revue Biblique*
RBe	*Revue Bénédictine*
REB	*Revue des Etudes Byzantines*
RHC	*Recueil des Historiens des Croisades*, ed. Académie des Inscriptions et Belles-Lettres (Paris, 1841–1906)
RHC Lois	*RHC Lois. Les Assises de Jérusalem* (2 vols, 1841–43)
RHC Occ.	*RHC Historiens Occidentaux* (5 vols, 1844–95)
RHC Or.	*RHC Historiens Orientaux* (5 vols, 1872–1906)
RHDFE	*Revue Historique de Droit Français et Etranger*
ROL	*Revue de l'Orient Latin*
RRH	*Regesta regni Hierosolymitani, 1097–1291*, ed. R. Röhricht (Innsbruck, 1893); *Addit-amentum* (Innsbruck, 1904)

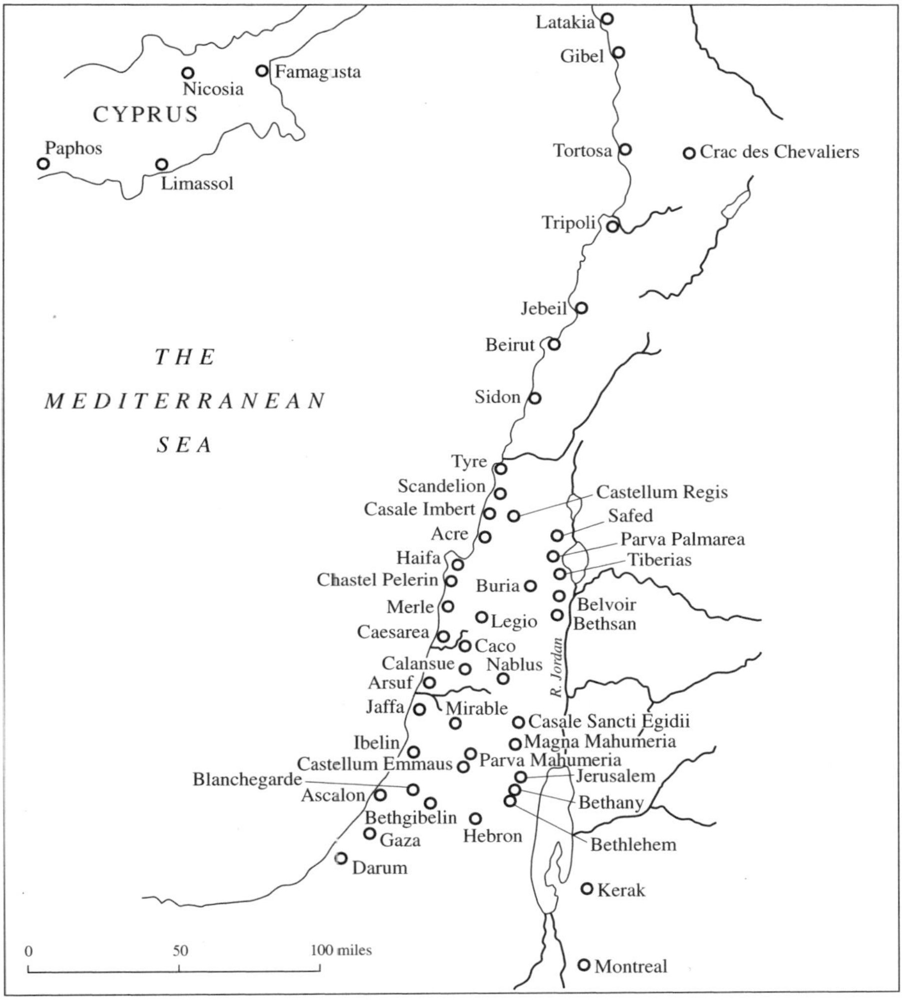

- Acre
- Arsuf
- Ascalon
- Beirut
- Belvoir
- Bethany
- Bethgibelin
- Bethlehem
- Bethsan
- Blanchegarde
- Buria
- Caco
- Caesarea
- Calansue
- Casale Imbert
- Casale Sancti Egidii
- Castellum Emmaus
- Castellum Regis
- Chastel Pelerin
- Crac des Chevaliers
- Darum
- Famagusta
- Gaza
- Gibel
- Haifa
- Hebron
- Ibelin
- Jaffa
- Jebeil
- Jerusalem
- Kerak
- Latakia
- Legio
- Limassol
- Magna Mahumeria
- Merle
- Mirable
- Montreal
- Nablus
- Nicosia
- Paphos
- Parva Mahumeria
- Parva Palmarea
- Safed
- Scandelion
- Sidon
- Tiberias
- Tortosa
- Tripoli
- Tyre

Map: Sites in Syria, Palestine and Cyprus to which reference has been made in this study

Introduction

Put simply, burgesses were Latin non-feudatories who arrived in the Holy Land either as crusaders, pilgrims, or colonists, and settled in the cities or rural villages. They appear in sources of the twelfth and thirteenth centuries as merchants, market tradesmen, craftsmen, artisans, investors, money-changers, translators, fishermen and farmers. To date, however, no satisfactory explanation has been given as to how these people, who originated from diverse regions of Europe, and were accustomed to their own laws and institutions, were able to organize themselves into a class whose status, as legally defined in royal, seigneurial and ecclesiastical domains, set them apart from native non-Latin Christians and Muslims. It has not been sufficiently determined what contributions were made by burgesses – the largest non-native population in the kingdom – to the formation of the Latin states. What position early on did burgess representatives assume in the decision-making assemblies convened by the monarch? Moreover, what developments relating to burgess legislation and jurisdiction took place in the twelfth century? Inevitably, a study concerned with finding answers to such questions draws comparisons between eastern burgesses and their western counterparts – particularly those in France about whom more is known. It considers whether the basic burgess laws and institutions of the kingdom of Jerusalem originated in certain regions of Europe, and ascertains the extent to which jurisdictional developments in the East mirrored those in the West. It also highlights any significant differences and emphasizes the unique elements of burgess society in the Latin states.

The starting point of this study is Europe in the second half of the eleventh century. The decades preceding the First Crusade were marked by significant demographic changes. The population of western Europe was growing at a faster rate than ever before, cities were flourishing, and rural settlements expanding into hitherto unpopulated regions. So too discernible was the emerging and increasingly privileged class of freemen. In the latter part of the eleventh century, the commercial and jurisdictional rights which they enjoyed may be perceived as manifestation of an emerging concept of 'public power'.[1] The principles of public power, namely the degree of authority a lord, or *seigneur justicier*, could yield, and the extent to which a community could administer its own affairs, elect its own representatives, and judge by peers the misdemeanours of its members, occupied the minds of lawmakers and legal writers alike. Issues concerning person and property were also recurring in charters of liberties of this period. Documents, in general, served as written proof of the communal rights which lords bestowed on

---

1 Y. Bongert, *Recherches sur les cours laïques du Xe au XIIIe siècle* (Paris, 1948), p. 115.

their tenants, especially as traditionally practised customary laws were rarely codified.

The principles of public power may be further linked to the growth of trans-European migration in the eleventh century. I return to this subject at a later stage when assessing the impact medieval migratory patterns may have had on the creation of the kingdom of Jerusalem. One suggestion is that crusading extended migration to the Holy Land. But is there evidence to substantiate such a theory? An equally relevant question to ask is what persuaded non-feudatories to join the crusade armies of 1096. Were they driven by materialism or spiritual motivation? Were they recruited at centres of preaching as pilgrim-soldiers, or did they join the crusade movement as migrating settlers? Were they drawn from the ancient cities where preachers such as Peter the Hermit actively sought followers, or predominantly from the rural villages and especially the *burgi*? Though there has been much written on the incentives of the nobility, the motives of the non-knightly classes have been less scrutinized. This is somewhat surprising bearing in mind the many references in contemporary chronicles and annals to their involvement in crusading.

It is generally agreed that the First Crusade evolved into a popular movement. Indeed, the majority of people who participated as soldiers or non-combatants belonged to the classes of serfs or freemen. The perception is that all classes of people responded enthusiastically to the widely preached crusade message. Yet, regardless of this fact, the mass appeal of the enterprise, and the involvement of Latin non-feudatories in the foundation of the kingdom of Jerusalem, has been largely ignored. Understandably, most studies have focused on the knightly crusade and the establishment of a feudal system in the Latin states of Palestine and Syria, in particular the constitutional and political role of the nobility during almost two hundred years of the kingdom's existence. By comparison, no comprehensive history of non-feudal crusading and eastern burgess settlement has been written. The objective of this present study is to address this historical imbalance.

The summer of 1097 marked the arrival of the first crusaders in Asia Minor en masse, and the capture of Antioch on 3 June 1098, while important strategically, further represented the beginning of significant European urban settlement in the East. Jerusalem fell to the crusaders on 15 July 1099. The goal to liberate the Holy City, first preached by Pope Urban II at Clermont almost four years earlier, had been achieved, and many crusaders their vows fulfilled returned home if they had the means to do so.[2] Others, however, remained. They had set off from Europe either as serfs who had been granted permission to go on crusade by their lords, or as free inhabitants who had been recruited at centres of preaching. To contemporary chroniclers they had with their enthusiasm and fervour swelled the ranks of the crusade armies. Significantly, at some point in the East – and possibly

---

2 J.S.C. Riley-Smith, *The First Crusade and the Idea of Crusading* (London, 1986), p. 42.

during the actual crusade campaign – all members of this class of non-nobles, who had served the cause of crusade so ably and loyally, were granted free and equal status. Hierarchically, they formed themselves into a new 'middle class' that stood between the European nobility and the lower indigenous peoples.

Joshua Prawer was particularly interested in the origins of burgesses, arguing that the class of *burgenses* in Palestine and Syria originated from among the *pedites* of the First Crusade. His opinion was that these *pedites* were peasants who arrived in Palestine from European villages situated in centres of crusade recruitment. They were not, he maintained, city-dwellers as the population of western towns at the end of the eleventh century was very small.[3] I would agree the *pedites* were some of the first burgess settlers in the East, but Prawer's argument that they were peasants recruited from villages in Europe is only partially accurate. First, cities were very important centres of recruitment for crusade preachers who could expect to attract large local audiences to their oratories, apart from the men and women who were drawn from the surrounding countryside. Secondly, the remark that all *pedites* were peasants is rather sweeping and fails to distinguish between crusade serfs and freemen – including those presumably of burgess status – who headed East. It is also important to understand that in western Europe in the latter part of the eleventh century, there was significant growth in the creation of rural *burgi* and *castra*. These settlements of freemen were broadly situated within the catchment areas of crusade preaching.

Prawer further addressed the issue of whether the first crusade represented the beginning of a large-scale movement of European peoples to the Levant. He theorised that migration in the twelfth century was mainly from regions in southern France.[4] More recently, this supposed influx of non-noble Latin settlers into the kingdom of Jerusalem, was viewed by Ronnie Ellenblum as part of a more general process of migration in contemporary Europe. In the 'Frankish castra, as in the European ones,' he has written, 'heterogeneous societies, consisting of settlers who had arrived from distant places, were created'. His opinion was that the kingdom of Jerusalem like southern France, Spain or Sicily, was an attractive destination to those wishing to settle there and take advantage of whatever opportunities it had to offer. In this context, the class of burgesses did not necessarily originate from crusaders, but rather from settlers in 'search for places of residence which would give them better social status and better economic conditions'.[5] Initial confinement of Europeans to the urban conglomerations for reasons of security was followed by

---

[3] J. Prawer, *Crusader Institutions* (Oxford, 1980), pp. 240–62; and J. Prawer, 'Social Classes in the Crusader States: The Burgesses', in N.P. Zacour and H.W. Hazard (eds), *A History of the Crusades: The Impact of the Crusades on the Near East* (Wisconsin, 1985), vol. 5, pp. 146–8.

[4] Prawer, 'Social Classes in the Crusader States: The Burgesses', p. 154; R.C. Smail, *Crusading Warfare, 1097–1193* (Cambridge, 1956), pp. 40–63.

[5] R. Ellenblum, *Frankish Rural Settlement in the Latin Kingdom of Jerusalem* (Cambridge, 1998), p. 78.

widespread rural settlement. Ellenblum's research convinced him that these places of settlement – particularly in south-eastern Transjordan and western and lower Galilee – were in districts populated by a majority of native Christians.[6] Favourable economic conditions in the villages, including the freedom to buy and sell property, elevated the status of Latins above that of Muslims, Jews and native Christians (Orthodox, Monothelite Maronites, and Monophysite Jacobites) who as villeins could be tied to the land. However, a premise of this study is that European mass migration to the kingdom of Jerusalem was unlikely to have taken place. Many parts of the crusader states, and in particular the south-eastern territories around Muslim Ascalon, were not conducive to Latin settlement. It is difficult to believe that in the first decade of the twelfth century large numbers of people would have chosen to migrate to the Levant when equally favourable conditions for settlement and commerce existed in *burgi* and *castra* in various regions of Europe.

Once the crusaders established some form of military control over their newly-acquired cities in the East, the formation of a new middle class was a requisite tool of occupation. The forging of a new system of burgess jurisdiction strengthened the social standing of Latin settlers above natives who had limited rights. But the precise contribution made by burgesses to the process of settlement has often been misinterpreted.[7] Dodu viewed the creation of the burgess class by the kings of Jerusalem as a counter-balance to the growing powers of the feudatories.[8] This is a theory which seems to place the formation of a burgess class at a much later date than the one proposed in this study. In my opinion burgess communities, laws and juridical institutions were established from the first years of settlement at a time when the class of feudatories, still recovering from a crusade which had severely depleted its ranks, was incapable of perpetuating the kingdom's existence merely as an occupying force. As lords and landowners they required the communities of burgesses to administer their cities and villages and the economies of their domains.

There have been other notable theories regarding eastern burgesses. Cahen, writing about burgesses in the principality of Antioch, suggested that the class of Latin non-feudatories had naturally evolved because the indigenous peoples of the

---

6 Ellenblum, *Frankish Rural Settlement*, pp. 282–3.

7 A.A. Beugnot, Introduction to *RHC Lois*, II; H. Prutz, *Kulturgeschichte der Kreuzzüge* (Berlin, 1883); E. Rey, *Les Colonies franques de Syrie aux XIIe et XIIIe siècles* (Paris, 1883); G. Dodu, *Histoire des institutions monarchiques dans le Royaume de Jérusalem, 1099–1291* (Paris, 1894); C.N. Johns, 'The Crusader Attempt to Colonise Palestine and Syria', *Journal of the Royal Central Asian Society*, 21 (1934), 288–300; C. Cahen, *La Syrie du nord à l'epoque des croisades et la principauté franque d'Antioche* (Paris, 1940); J. Richard, *The Latin Kingdom of Jerusalem*, trans. J. Shirley (Amsterdam, New York and Oxford, 1979), pp. 121–9; Prawer, *Crusader Institutions*, chapters 5, 9, 12 and 13.

8 Dodu, p. 271.

principality were already organised into communities.[9] I would agree to an extent with this idea, but would not propose that this development was natural or organic in any way, certainly not in the kingdom of Jerusalem. There was rather a planned and deliberate process of settlement from the very beginning. The burgess court of justice, for instance, effectively discriminated between Europeans and non-Europeans, and between Latin Christians and non-Latin Christians. The reinforcement of essential differences, particularly religious ones, ensured that the indigenous Christians and Muslims who did indeed have their own courts, could not qualify as subjects of burgess jurisdiction. And in a similar way, the alienation of property set aside ostensibly for possession by burgesses was strictly regulated.

Attention has been drawn to the fact that the class of burgesses never developed the independence associated with those who lived in European communes. Jean Richard emphasised the point that whereas members of a western commune swore fidelity to the commune itself, burgesses in the kingdom of Jerusalem 'never ceased to be their lords' men'. Depending on where in the kingdom they resided, they swore fealty to the king, a secular lord or an ecclesiastical institution with rights of jurisdiction.[10] Further interest in the organisation of burgesses led Hans Mayer to suggest the class was founded on the principle that a man should be judged by his peers.[11] It was a principle widely practised in Europe in the eleventh century, and formed the bedrock of jurisdiction in the kingdom of Jerusalem where the king and his tenants-in-chief were increasingly willing for their burgess communities to judge themselves in matters of criminal and civil law. I accept Richard and Mayer's opinions because it would be a mistake to underestimate the rate of development of burgess justice in the early twelfth century. In recent years the debate surrounding the existence of the *Letres dou Sepulcre* – the written general legislation of the kingdom supposedly lost after the fall of Jerusalem to Saladin (1187)[12] – has led some historians to question the veracity of the thirteenth-century jurists who ascribed well-formed courts of burgesses with wide-ranging legal competence to the reign of Godfrey of Bouillon (1099–1100), and, therefore, to underrate the achievements of burgess jurisdiction and legislation. The jurists and in particular John of Ibelin should be read with a modicum of scepticism, but their histories should not be dismissed as complete fabrication.

Legislation in the kingdom was formulated in different ways, either by means of common consensus, as at the general assemblies which established secular or ecclesiastical laws; by the king in royal domain or the *seigneurs justiciers* in their lordships; by Church institutions in the rural Latin settlements over which they had jurisdiction; or by jurors of *Cours des Bourgeois* who set precedents in their

9 Cahen, *La Syrie du nord*, p. 547.

10 Richard, *The Latin Kingdom of Jerusalem*, p. 127.

11 H.E. Mayer, *The Crusades*, trans. J. Gillingham (Oxford, 1988), p. 176; Richard, *The Latin Kingdom of Jerusalem*, p 127; J.L. La Monte, *Feudal Monarchy in the Latin Kingdom of Jerusalem, 1100–1291* (Cambridge, Mass., 1932), pp. 104–105.

12 John of Ibelin, *Le Livre des assises*, ed. P.W. Edbury (Leyden, 2003), p. 624.

judgement of test cases. In basic terms, laws enacted by rulers were known as *assises*, *dreit* or *leis*.[13] In the twelfth century some royal legislation was definitely written down. For instance, copies of the twenty-five decrees issued at the Council of Nablus (1120) were, according to William of Tyre, preserved in the archives of many churches.[14] But it has been argued that law was based not so much on any legislative work undertaken by the kings of Jerusalem, as on the precedents set by the Jerusalem courts.[15] Certainly, in Acre in the second half of the thirteenth century, the *Cour des Bourgeois* kept a register of the judgements which it made and possibly the precedents it set.[16] Notably, in an oath sworn by jurors in the *Cour des Bourgeois* in Nicosia, they promised to resolve cases according to the *assises* of the kingdoms of Jerusalem and Cyprus where such laws existed. Otherwise, they were to reach decisions reasonably based on their good judgement.[17]

In the sources burgess laws were occasionally referred to as 'customs'. The distinction between *costumes* and *assises* is not fully clear,[18] although in some twelfth-century charters customs were specifically associated with a city or village where they were in common usage. This study will demonstrate that in spite of local differences there was uniformity at least between certain burgess laws in the kingdom of Jerusalem. The evidence illustrates how similar, for example, were laws of tenancy and basic court procedure throughout the land. There is, nevertheless, little evidence to support La Monte's view that many of the laws of the kingdom were based on the 'customs of eleventh century Europe as brought to the East by the men of the first crusade',[19] even though there were some similarities in the twelfth and thirteenth centuries between legislation in the Latin East and western Europe. Cahen highlighted the influence of Norman law on aspects of burgess jurisdiction in the principality of Antioch,[20] and Prawer argued that the 'Livre de la Cour des Bourgeois' of Acre incorporated passages from a twelfth-century law-book of Provençe, *Lo Codi*.[21] This though seems to contradict

---

[13] E.H. Kausler (ed.), *Livre des assises de Jérusalem* (Stuttgart, 1839), pp. 75, 141–2, 269, 341–2 and 350–51; cf. A.A. Beugnot (ed.), 'Livre des assises de la Cour des Bourgeois', in *RHC Lois*, II, pp. 42, 86, 170, 218 and 225. See also Philip of Novara, 'Le Livre de forme de plait', in *RHC Lois*, I, p. 547.

[14] William, Archbishop of Tyre, *Chronique*, ed. R.B.C. Huygens with H.E. Mayer and G. Rösch (Turnhout, 1986), pp. 563–4.

[15] Richard, *The Latin Kingdom of Jerusalem*, p. 69.

[16] 'Abrégé du livre des assises de la Cour des Bourgeois', in *RHC Lois* II (hereafter, 'Livre contrefais'), p. 246. Kausler, p. 271 (cf. Beugnot 'Livre des assises', p 172).

[17] 'Livre contrefais', p 238. They promised to make judgements 'par assise ou usage...et de ce où il n'auroit assize ou usage, au plus près de la raizon, celon lor conoissance'.

[18] P.W Edbury, 'Law and Custom in the Latin East: *Les Letres dou Sepulcre*', *Mediterranean Historical Review*, 10 (1996): 72, 78.

[19] La Monte, *Feudal Monarchy*, p. 97.

[20] Cahen, *La Syrie du nord*, pp. 550–55.

[21] Prawer, *Crusader Institutions*, p. 362.

his other argument that *borgesie* tenure and the legal procedures which shaped it originated in the north of Europe.[22]

As regards the status of eastern Latin non-feudatories, previous definitions have followed certain logic in arguing that burgesses were characterised solely by their location – whether they were urban or rural settlers – by their rights as tenants, or by their legal standing. None of these definitions, however, is sufficient. Cahen argued that to be a burgess in the principality of Antioch 'il faut posséder un immeuble, une "bourgeoisie"'.[23] This definition could not be applied to the kingdoms of Jerusalem or Cyprus where knights held *borgesies*, as well as native Christians who, because they were not Latins, did not belong to the class of burgesses. Prawer, on the other hand, defined the status of a burgess as a Frank who did not belong to the class of feudatories.[24] But the fact that burgesses were not fief-holders was only one aspect of their standing. Prawer further argued that the establishment of *Cours des Bourgeois* in the early twelfth century defined the legal standing of the class of non-noble Latin freemen,[25] but it ought to be remembered that these courts also exercised justice over non-Latins in serious cases including high justice. So merely being subject to this court did not make a person a burgess. It is my contention that the status of burgesses who lived among a predominantly non-Latin population in royal and seigneurial cities and in the *villes neuves*, was defined by a combination of three factors: religion, jurisdiction and property. Burgesses were Latin Christian men or women of European or native origin, tenants of *borgesies*, and subject to *Cours des Bourgeois* in civil and criminal matters, or in certain cases Church courts vested with authority over them. Nothing less than all of these characteristics combined defined a person as a burgess.

As in Europe at this time, the generic term *burgenses* was denotative not just of residence in a city or a *burgus*, but of all types of settlements including merchant quarters. Interestingly, the earliest reference to burgesses as a distinct class is a document of 1110.[26] Other charters are more revealing. The charter of 1123 granting the Venetians a quarter in Acre, described *burgenses* as persons who were 'in uico et domibus Venetorum habitantes'.[27] Possession of property was a pre-requisite as all those who possessed houses were expected to swear an oath of

---

[22] Prawer, *Crusader Institutions*, pp. 252, 255–6, 350–51.

[23] Cahen, *La Syrie de nord*, p. 548.

[24] Prawer, *The Latin Kingdom of Jerusalem. European Colonialism in the Middle Ages* (London, 1972), p. 77.

[25] Prawer, *Crusader Institutions*, pp. 148–9, 350–51.

[26] R. Röhricht (ed.), *Regesta regni Hierosolymitani, 1097–1291* (Innsbruck, 1893), no. 59, p. 13.

[27] G.L.F Tafel and G.M. Thomas (eds), *Urkunden zur älteren Handels und Staatsgeschichte der Republik Venedig: Mit besonderer Beziehung auf Byzanz und die Levante* (3 vols, Vienna, 1856–57), vol.1, p. 88.

fealty to the commune and the doge of Venice.[28] When in 1187 Conrad of Montferrat confirmed Pisan possessions and jurisdiction in their quarter in Tyre, a distinction was drawn between merchants and burgesses. The Pisans were granted a court over all their compatriots in their quarter 'whether merchants (*scapuli*)[29] or burgesses'.[30] And in Cyprus in the thirteenth century a royal decree concerning rules of marriage also distinguished between 'borgois' and 'marchant'.[31]

One of the criteria which defined burgess status was property. Burgesses were tenants of *borgesies*, usually houses, curtilages, shops or arable lands in the cities and rural settlements, but, as we shall see, this did not exempt other non-burgesses from holding such tenancies. A *borgesie* could be alienated or transferred temporarily, and its tenant owed some kind of service including, usually, the annual payment of *cens* or *rente*. Previous studies of this type of property have not, generally-speaking, distinguished between the different types of *borgesie*. Apart from houses and plots of arable land, there were also whole villages which were *borgesies*. And the *heritage de fié*, another type of city *borgesie* which formed part of a fief, has been overlooked by historians. Prawer argued that burgage-tenure was a 'European institution imported wholesale' into the kingdom of Jerusalem. He stressed the alienability of *borgesies* which could be sold, exchanged, donated and pledged by tenants, and contended that the yearly rent paid by tenants to their lords was only nominal.[32] There is, however, a counter-argument demonstrating that payment was not merely symbolic but proportional to the size and value of a *borgesie*. The rents received by secular lords and ecclesiastical institutions from the lease of their *borgesies* in perpetuity and for a short-term were an important source of income. On the subject of alienation, it was suggested by Prawer that a *borgesie* could be alienated in private, and that the intervention of a *Cour des Bourgeois* was simply to publicise the transfer of property.[33] He also asserted that a *borgesie* could be granted 'in alms' to an ecclesiastical institution privately.[34] Again, there are grounds to dispute this theory. Evidence does show that the alienation of a *borgesie* had to be authorised by the court under whose jurisdiction the property was located, and that a donor required the permission of a *Cour des Bourgeois* when making an eleemosynary donation. The charitable gift 'in alms' modified the legal standing of a *borgesie* by removing it from royal or seigneurial

---

[28] O. Berggötz (ed.), *Der Bericht des Marsilio Zorzi: Codex Querini-Stampalia iv3 (1064)* (Frankfurt, 1991), p. 143.

[29] On the meaning of *scapuli*, Prawer, *Crusader Institutions*, p. 246, note 88.

[30] J. Müller (ed.), *Documenti sulle relazioni delle città Toscane coll'oriente Cristiano e coi Turchi fino all' anno 1531* (Florence, 1879), nos 23 and 27.

[31] 'Bans et ordonnances des rois de Chypre, 1286–1362', in *RHC Lois* II, p. 359.

[32] Prawer, *Crusader Institutions*, pp. 252, 255–6, 350–51; Prawer, *The Latin Kingdom of Jerusalem*, pp. 78–9; Prawer, 'Social Classes in the Crusader States: The Burgesses', p. 153.

[33] Prawer, *Crusader Institutions*, pp. 282–6.

[34] Prawer, *Crusader Institutions*, pp. 324–5.

jurisdiction and placing it under the authority of an ecclesiastical court. Subsequently, its tenant was subject to the laws of burgess tenancy as exercised by this legal body. The military orders, particularly the Hospitallers, received many *borgesies* by way of charitable donations.

Prawer maintained that the first properties in the kingdom were created through the 'law of conquest', this being the right of a person to claim ownership of a property he acquired when a city was captured. Arbitrary seizure of land, referred to in contemporary accounts of Latin conquest and settlement, was, he believed, the basis of allods or freeholds.[35] This contention accorded with his belief that the occupation of territory, which was to become the kingdom of Jerusalem, was haphazard. Prawer's interpretation has been challenged by Jonathan Riley-Smith who views settlement in Palestine and Syria as much more ordered; the encompassing hierarchies of jurisdiction and tenancy did not allow for the existence of *allodia*.[36] Mayer accepts both these theories as plausible, arguing that while, generally-speaking, Latin settlement was a systematic and ordered affair, this did not rule out arbitrary seizure of land.[37] It is my belief that allodial property probably did not exist in the kingdoms of Jerusalem and Cyprus, and that the possessor of a *franc borgesie*, which was exempted from the payment of rent but remained subject to a *Cour des Bourgeois* when being alienated, was not the tenant of a freehold.

The other characteristic which defined a burgess was that he came under the jurisdiction of a *Cour des Bourgeois*. The court was the legal, administrative and financial arm of a lord. The composition of the *Cour des Bourgeois*, some of its legal procedures and its authority over transactions has been the subject of study,[38] although not enough attention has been paid to its competence in other matters such as marriage, inheritance, illegitimacy, debt – including the pledging of *borgesies* – and manumission. In addition, while emphasis has been placed on the powers of royal and seigneurial *Cours des Bourgeois*, the authority of other courts with jurisdiction over burgesses and *borgesies* has been largely ignored. All in all, historians have defined the role of *Cours des Bourgeois* without demonstrating fully the complexities of burgess jurisdiction in the kingdom of Jerusalem. We should avoid looking for clues as to the development of the court of burgesses in the usual places. There is strong evidence that in the first decades of the twelfth century, the secular courts which were established by ecclesiastical institutions and the 'customs' they formulated, influenced generally the way *borgesies* were leased,

---

35 Prawer, *Crusader Institutions*, pp. 240–62; Prawer, 'Social Classes in the Crusader States: The burgesses', pp.145–70.

36 Riley-Smith, 'The Motives of the Earliest Crusaders and the Settlement of Latin Palestine, 1095–1100', *EHR*, 98 (1983): 734–5.

37 Mayer, *The Crusades*, p. 153.

38 La Monte, *Feudal Monarchy*, pp. 106–107; Prawer, *The Latin Kingdom of Jerusalem*, pp. 145–51; Riley-Smith, *The Feudal Nobility and the Kingdom of Jerusalem, 1117–1277* (London, 1973), pp. 85–7.

alienated and transacted. When tracing the history of jurisdiction in the twelfth century, consideration should be given to these Church courts which though concerned with burgess matters were in their composition and competence fundamentally different to the *Cours des Bourgeois*.

The objective of this book is to define the status of burgesses in Palestine, Syria and Cyprus in the twelfth, thirteenth and fourteenth centuries (1099–1325). My intention is to illustrate as precisely as possible the subtle social gradation which was at work, and part of this investigation involves discounting factors which I believe did not affect status. I do not think, for instance, that the status of burgess was reserved for wealthier individuals – status was based principally on legal and not economic stratification. Neither is there sufficient evidence to contend that as in some French cities status was conditional on residence for a minimum period of time, for example a year and a day.[39] I would further dispute the contention that only the residents of a city or a village which was fortified or resembled a *burgus* came to be described as *burgenses*. I earlier explained how in western Europe the etymological link between *burgus* and *burgensis* was gradually loosened to the point that *burgenses* became a general description of inhabitants of all types of settlements. A final issue concerns the theory that status was determined by self-perception.[40] But are we to believe that in eastern Latin society where social stratification was rigidly based on religion, jurisdiction and property-possession, burgess status was ultimately no more than a matter of choice or self-designation? This study proves that there are no grounds for such an argument.

---

39 The law books of the kingdoms of Jerusalem and Cyprus are silent as to whether minimum term of residency was a precondition of burgess status.

40 P.W. Edbury, 'Famagusta Society ca. 1300 from the Registers of Lamberto di Sambuceto', in *Kingdoms of the Crusaders: From Jerusalem to Cyprus* (Aldershot, 1999), p. 93.

Chapter 1

Burgess Origins and the First Crusade

The development of European non-feudal society and institutions in the eleventh century is an immense subject, but in the context of this study it is important to describe briefly the social and legal status of *liberi homines*, freemen – more specifically the class of *burgenses* – and their standing above the lowest order of men, the *servi* – unfree serfs who were tied to the land – before proceeding to consider their participation in the crusading movement. For etymological reasons which may begin to explain the origins of the class of burgesses, discussion centres on a type of territorial unit known as a *burgus*, and draws particular attention to its function as a rural domain of freemen, and its obvious resemblance to the *ville neuve* of the kingdom of Jerusalem. It is a comparative approach further adopted when considering certain juridical and administrative aspects of *burgi*. An overall objective is to try and describe conditions of property and person in western Europe on the eve of the First Crusade. Of particular interest is the extent to which society in the kingdom of Jerusalem developed in the twelfth century as a result of or parallel to changes in western Europe.

The dissemination of the crusade message coincided in the second half of the eleventh century with exponentially demographic growth, economic prosperity – particularly trade in the Mediterranean and North Sea – and unparalleled juridical and institutional developments in many parts of France. It was also a time marked by significant migrations of people. An ever-expanding population was supported by both spontaneous and planned agrarian expansion through the clearing and cultivating of forests and fallow land.[1] The cities were centres of gravity where a growing merchant class was drawn to trade, but although urbanization began taking hold in this period, the agrarian economy remained a mainstay of medieval life. One may even make a connection between a widening crisis of rural overpopulation in areas of increasingly redundant labour and deficient agricultural production – a pattern most apparent in regions of southern France – with the effort of landowners to construct villages *ex nihilo* away from centres of concentrated settlement.

Symptomatic of agrarian expansion was a settlement-type known variously as a *bourg* (Lat. *burgus*, perhaps of Germanic origin), *sauveté* or *ville neuve*. Such was the popular and widespread appeal of *burgi* to commercial migrants that contemporary and near-contemporary commentators attested to the growth of this

---

1 D. Herlihy, 'The Agrarian Revolution in Southern France and Italy, 801–1150', *Speculum*, 33 (1958): 26, 34–5.

type of settlement.[2] It is known that *burgi* were created both by secular and ecclesiastical lords, and their free inhabitants were defined collectively not simply by the physical boundaries of their community, but more importantly by the unique rights which they were granted by their lord. Intrinsically, these rights centred round the freedom and alienability of their property.

In a study of rural *burgi* in eleventh-century Normandy, Lucien Musset categorised the various settlement-types founded predominantly in the vicinity of monasteries and castles, and demonstrated how they served an economic as well as defensive function.[3] Far from spontaneous, they were carefully planned and conceived, and their boundaries clearly delineated. Newly created villages, moreover, which were fortified, were known as *castra* or *castella* and afforded their inhabitants greater security than *burgi*. Increased fortification was particularly evident in Languedoc in the eleventh century, although this process – described by Toubert as '*incastellamento*'[4] – was, it has been argued, quite often a sign of wealth than of any real or perceived external dangers.[5] Nevertheless, some form of military duty (*servicium*) was often a condition of residence in both *burgi* and *castra*.[6] Even in ecclesiastical *burgi*, as was the case in Maine, infantry obligation fell on the local inhabitants, and more specifically on the adult male population.[7] All in all, these were preconditions of settlement. The rules of residency were rigidly applied and exemption from certain obligations, such as military service, required special seigneurial dispensation.[8]

The existence of *burgi* or *castra* had demonstrable impact on the countryside. It is worth making the point that as these nucleated communities drew settlers and grew in size, they had the contributory effect of diminishing or eliminating completely pre-existing smaller villages. They constituted a 'regrouping' of the rural population and a new 'social dimension' in the sense that they redefined the collective standing of residents subject to the same rules of tenancy. There is

---

2 On this point, see W. Colette (ed.), *Les Deux rédactions en vers du Moniage Guillaume* (2 vols, Paris, 1906–11), vol. 1, p. 273

3 L. Musset, 'Peuplement en bourgage et bourgs ruraux en Normandie du Xe au XIII siècle', *Cahiers de Civilisation Médiévale*, IX (1966): 178–89.

4 P. Toubert, *Les Structures de Latium médiéval. Le Latium méridional et Sabine du IXe siècle à la fin du XIIe siècle* (2 vols, Rome, 1973), vol. 1, pp. 303–447.

5 E. Magnou-Nortier, *La Société laïque et L'église dans la province ecclésiastique de Narbonne de la fin du VIIIe à la fin du XIe siècle* (Toulouse, 1974), p. 251.

6 Musset, p. 203; M. Bourin-Derrau, *Villages médiévaux en Bas-Languedoc: Genèse d'une sociabilité Xe–XIVe siècle* (2 vols, Paris, 1987), vol. 1, p. 64.

7 R. Latouche, 'Un Aspect de la vie rurale dans le Maine au XIe et au XIIe siècle: l'Establissement des bourgs', *Moyen Age*, 8 (1937): 54–6.

8 F. Vercauteren, 'Les Libertés urbaines et rurales du XIe au XIV siècle', in *Les Libertés urbaines et rurales du XIe au XIV siècle. Colloque internatio*nal (Brussels: Pro Civitate, 1968); E. Glasson, *Histoire du droit et des institutions de la France* (6 vols, Paris, 1882–83), vol. 5, pp. 90–95; E Chénon, *Histoire générale du droit français public et privé des origines à 1815*, (2 vols, Paris, 1926–29), pp. 736, 738–9.

certainly evidence of the regrouping of scattered settlements in Gascony in the second half of the eleventh century,[9] and a comparable process in Biterois where the topographical reorganization of loosely connected rural villages into a more compact and enclosed *castra* can be traced from the ninth to the twelfth century.[10]

Of course this form of physical and social reordering was not peculiar to the countryside. In urban settings, *burgi* (or *suburbia)* arose on the fringes of ancient cities as self-contained commercial and jurisdictional entities. In such developments the inhabitants of the urban *burgus* were set apart from the *cives* of the longer-established city community,[11] and as in the rural *burgus*, the inhabitants were distinguished by the institutional and commercial incentives accorded to them by their lord.

In fact, so significant were these free communities in defining the status of burgesses, that it has been suggested the term *burgenses* (other related terms include *burgarius* and *burges*), in Normandy at least, may have originally denoted any freeman who lived in a *burgus novus*.[12] The apparent flaw in this argument is that although *burgi* were, besides Normandy, very evident in places such as Anjou, Tourain and Poitou, in others like Picardy, this settlement-type was by strictest definition rare.[13] Similarly, in Berry rural settlements in the eleventh century grew around pre-existing villages and were seldom created *ex nihilo*.[14] More importantly, the term *burgus* appears but infrequently in charters relating to Berry. Does this discrepancy mean that an alternative etymological explanation for *burgensis* needs to be sought? There is a compromise solution, namely that in regions like Normandy, *burgenses* did to begin with specifically denote inhabitants of *burgi*, but that gradually this generic term came to signify the status of a class of people who lived in all manner of places, a term which was adopted in regions where *burgi* were not in evidence.

The freemen of the *burgi* were vested with special tenurial rights and exemptions in return for payment of rent in money or in kind.[15] The property they possessed was above all else characterized by its alienability, a house or area of farmable land which though subject to certain restrictive conditions of tenure,

---

9 C. Higounet, 'Structures socials: Castra et castlenaux dans le sud-ouest Aquitain (Xe–XIIIe siècles)', in *Structures féodales et féodalisme dans l'occident méditerranéen (Xe–XIIIe siècles)* (Rome, 1980), p. 116.

10 Bourin-Derrau, vol. 1, p. 50.

11 Schneider, J., 'Les Origines des chartes de franchises dans le royaume de France (XIe–XIIe siècle)', in *Les Libertes urbaines et rurales du XIe au XIVe siècle. Colloque international* (Brussels, 1968), p. 39.

12 Musset, p. 183.

13 Musset, pp. 203–204.

14 G. Devailly, *Le Berry du Xe siècle au milieu du XIIIe. Etude politique, religeuse, sociale et economique* (Paris, 1973), pp. 303–305.

15 The lord of the *burgus* of Saint-Rémi of Reims, to take one example, offered new migrants exemption from tax on all their transactions, as well as the common use of a marketplace. See Schneider, p. 39.

could be freely bequeathed, leased, mortgaged, or pledged. The concomitant right of a wife, moreover, to equal share of possession with her husband, was widely regarded by later jurists as idiosyncratic.[16] But what term was commonly used to describe this tenancy? Its increasing popularity is attested in charters of the eleventh century where occasionally it was described as *burgagium* (Fr. *borgesie*). It should be pointed out, however, that defining *burgagium* as a property found solely in a *burgus*, is as inaccurate as defining *burgensis* as simply a resident of a *burgus*. Whilst certainly not inconceivable that there existed an etymological link between the two, the fact remains that this peculiarly alienable property was widely found in *burgi* as well as cities and other types of rural settlements.[17]

Certainly in Normandy and regions of western France, a *burgagium* could not be sold without the express permission of a *seigneur justicier*.[18] Property transfer requiring no seigneurial approval was, it may be gathered from the *Summa de Legibus Normannie*, an innovation of the mid-thirteenth century. The point to make is that in the preceding century and a half, the alienation of *burgagium* had gradually evolved from a public to a private procedure. Significantly, over a similar period in the kingdom of Jerusalem, the transfer of property always required the approval and legal authority of the lord in whose domain it was located. And contrary to Prawer's assertion regarding property ownership, it may be ascertained from documentary evidence, that private alienation was practiced at no time in royal, seigneurial or ecclesiastical domain.

Although the distinctive alienability of property encouraged fluidity in agricultural holdings, in other words an increase in the rate of land transference, concern must have been raised from some quarters that in certain cases such a free movement of property could prove counter-productive. There may have been anxiety that alienation of more scattered holdings contributed to less efficient agricultural production.[19] Equally, there may have been objection that alienation served to undermine the stability and cohesion of the family unit by allowing land to pass outside the control of its immediate members. This latter concern possibly explains why familial right of pre-emption was applied to the sale or exchange of *burgagium*. It was a condition of tenure not untypical of the general re-emphasis in the eleventh century on the right of close relatives to pre-empt, endorse, or revoke the transfer of family property (to avail oneself of the legal ruling of *revocatio*).[20]

---

16 J. Yver, 'Le Droit privé des villes de l'ouest de la France, spécialement villes normandes', *Recueils de la Société Jean Bodin*, VIII (1957): 134–5, 148–53, 160.

17 R. Génestal, *La Tenure en bourgage: Etude sur la propriété foncière dans les villes normandes* (Paris, 1900), p. 88.

18 Yver, 'Le Droit privé des villes de l'ouest de la France', 141, 142.

19 Herlihy, pp. 24–6.

20 On this point cf. G. Duby, *La Société aux XIe et XIIe siècles dans la région mâconnaise* (Paris, 1971), pp. 136–7, 272–81. I further discuss the parallel development of familial pre-emption or revocation – the conveyance of divided or undivided *burgagium* – in the kingdom of Jerusalem, below, pp. 104–106, 114–16.

A *burgagium* was not allodial property and as such a possessor could not be classed as an absolute owner but rather as a tenant. He paid rent (*census*) each year on a particular feast day and did so in perpetuity or until such time as when he sold his property. Whether it may be argued that *census* was merely a token payment is a moot point, though Génestal was firmly of the opinion that in Normandy, in the majority of cases – and those most probably where the proprietor of the land was *seigneur justicier* – this was no more than a peppercorn rent. In fewer cases was the amount owing proportionate to the true value of the property.[21] It is in this respect that the rules prevailing in the kingdom of Jerusalem seem to have differed, and as argued in a later chapter, more typically rental payment reflected the market value of the *burgagium,* and the collection of *census* was for a lord an important source of income.

Laws and Customs

A secular or ecclesiastical lord imposed certain conditions of habitation which over a certain period of time came to be described as *consuetudines* or 'customs'. A custom was defined as a rule that was not part of any written legislation, and which in the prevailing opinion of medieval authors had been in existence for at least ten years.[22] The diversity of customs was regional and even in some cases local. Eleventh- and twelfth-century documents are replete with examples of localized customs – those of Paris, Amiens and Reims for example – whilst more regionally the customs of Brittany, Anjou, Poitou and Berry, to name but a few, were particularly well known. Diversity was especially true in the north and north-east of France. Localized customs in Normandy, for instance, shaped rules of alienation,[23] but this did not, as one may initially assume, contribute in any way to an amorphous concept among contemporaries as to the status of property and person in a *burgus*. The opposite was in all evidence true, as from the latter part of the eleventh century there was beginning to evolve a cohesive definition. Notwithstanding local and regional differences in basic conditions governing inhabitants of *burgi*, there were essential similarities. This is an especially germane observation when comparing regional laws and institutions in England and Normandy. To explain, as *burgi* developed they became synonymous with certain rules of settlement. Thus, for example, the customs of Breteuil (*Leges Britolienses*), dating from the second half of the eleventh century, were extensively practised in Normandy, and according to the Domesday Book adopted in a *burgus* in Cheshire.[24] The foundation of the village of Auffai in Normandy, observed Orderic Vitalis, was modelled on Cormeilles and its customs (*Leges*

21 Génestal, p. 98.

22 Chénon, vol. 1, pp. 490–91.

23 Génestal, pp. 122–4, 126–7, 168; Chénon, vol. 1, p. 500

24 Schneider, p. 43.

Cormelienses).[25] The customs of Loiret, moreover, were in the twelfth century propagated in the Loire region, whilst the influential customs of Avesnes were replicated in at least thirty other places throughout Hainault and Vermandois. The regional proliferation of the customs of Beaumont (*Leges Bellimontis*) in the twelfth and thirteenth centuries has also been well documented.[26]

The customs of Breteuil and Cormeilles were, among others, not written down, and yet they remained unforgotten and influential many decades after their initial introduction. Not least, the implementation of French local practices in a *burgus* in England betrays a far-reaching influence of certain tried and tested customs. This phenomenon strongly intimates that the adoption of essential *consuetudines burgi* contributed to a commonality of judicial, commercial and tenurial practices. Indeed, spontaneous convergence of the basic rules of tenancy may partly account for the development of a more general definition of the status of *burgenses* and of *burgagium* in many parts of Europe in the eleventh century.

Non-Feudal Juridical Institutions and Administration

The following discussion focuses attention on certain developments in justice and administration particularly relevant in the context of this study. There is an obvious need to avoid making unsuitable comparisons between different regions of France where the various components of judiciary – for example, the jurors, judges, competence, and sentencing powers of non-feudal courts – evolved at different rates. Nevertheless, the intrinsic notions which are of most interest to us, those of freedom, common agreement, legal and administrative representation and judgment by peers, may be generally remarked upon. These were essential building blocks of juridical institutions whether in France or the newly created kingdom of Jerusalem.

The theme of public power is frequently recurring in charters of the eleventh century, in particular charters of liberties. What authority should a lord, *seigneur justicier*, have over the freemen in his city or rural *burgus*? He may choose to bestow on them greater freedoms, but to retain control through his representatives, namely the *baillus*, *castellanus* or *vicecomes*, officials whom he personally appointed. What, however, were the collective rights which inhabitants should expect? And how should they participate in the administration and jurisdiction of their community? In a legal context, judgement by peers was more widely practised, and appointed jurors were frequently referred to in documents as *scabini*. This type of institutional development was nourished by a sense of communal cohesion and of identity, and in the latter part of the eleventh century, it has been noted, a growing and wealthier burgess population was

---

25 Génestal, pp. 234, 236–7; Schneider, p. 43.

26 C.J. Joset, *Les Villes au pays de Luxembourg (1196–1383)* (Brussels, 1940), pp. 100–101.

increasingly vociferous in its demands.[27]

It may be evinced from a select reading of eleventh-century French documents that the role of the *scabini* did not differ widely from region to region. It is another aspect of this institutional uniformity which I have already highlighted when discussing the formulation of law and custom. Election was carried out either by selective or universal suffrage – involving, perhaps, only the lord, the existing *scabini*, or the consent of the whole community – and the number of elected varied from place to place. In order to qualify as a *scabinus*, a person had to be permanently resident in his locality – meaning usually for at least a year and a day – and on being chosen had normally to swear an oath of office. The essential duties of the *scabini* were to bear witness – when authorizing the transfer of property for instance – to hear criminal cases, and, in resolving dispute, to apply the most apposite law or custom. Where local legislation appeared lacking or defective in any way, they were also charged with adopting what they considered to be the most relevant custom from neighbouring regions. As a legal body they were entrusted with serving their community with the approval of the lord whose authority they carefully complemented rather than diminished or impeded. However, though engaged principally in a legal capacity, the responsibilities of the *scabini* were quite evidently more wide-ranging, including, for example, the collection of revenue needed for the upkeep of fortifications.[28] They may, therefore, be more aptly described as community leaders, inasmuch as they assumed more than a purely legal position, and especially if we are to believe they were commonly elected representatives. As was befitting, their approval was sought by a lord in matters which had direct bearing on the community, and their written consent provided in accompanying documentation.[29] This decision to consult the *scabini*, and in turn involve the greater burgess community in the processes of legislation, was not merely a token gesture on the part of a lord. General agreement, on the contrary, became a robust and enduring principle.

This sketch of the *scabini* though brief is, nevertheless, revealing of some of the ways in which non-feudal society evolved in the latter years of the eleventh century. So significant were institutional changes that a correlation has even been drawn between the growth of a more prosperous urban burgess community with increasing influence on its lord, and the appearance of *scabini*.[30]

---

27 R. Monier, 'L'Administration et la condition juridique des habitants de la ville d'Arras au XIIe siècle', in *Mélanges Paul Fournier* (Paris, 1929), p. 553; F.L. Ganshof, 'Les Transformations de l'organisation judiciaire dans le comté de Flandre', *Revue Belge de Philologie et d'Histoire*, 18 (1939): 51.

28 Monier, pp. 553–7.

29 Monier, p. 555.

30 Ganshof, p. 51

European Burgenses – A General Definition

I have ascribed to the eleventh century important societal and institutional changes among the class of free non-feudatories. The piecing together of disparate clues sufficiently serves to highlight the underlying significance of greater individual as well as collective autonomy vis-à-vis the community lord. I am wary of the pitfalls of generalization and, accordingly, it has been necessary to take into consideration the rate and variability of change in regions of France both in developmental and terminological terms. For example, the building of *burgi* was particularly notable in Normandy in the eleventh century, while the process of *incastellamento* was most intense in Languedoc in approximately the same period. The word *burgensis*, furthermore, appears in charters originating in Normandy, Macon, Loire and Rhône regions in the first part of the eleventh century, whereas it does not appear in text of the Dauphinois until much later on, possibly as late as the thirteenth century.[31]

And yet, irrespective of linguistic disparity, and what may appear on the surface contradictory evidence, a cogent theory arises. The construction of *burgi* was a European and in particular a Norman phenomenon. It was within the spatial and legal boundaries of *burgi* that the elements of rural life and the rudiments of urban institutions and commerce converged. From the original description of the inhabitants of a *burgus* was derived the term *burgensis*, although this came progressively to denote a class of people who lived in all manner of settlements both rural and urban. Equally, a type of property known as a *burgagium* was found commonly although not exclusively in *burgi*. The possessor of a *burgagium* had the essential freedom of alienation, and a wife enjoyed equal share of property acquired jointly with her husband. I should add that of all regions of France it was in Normandy that the categorization and codification of this type of tenure was most advanced.[32]

By the end of the eleventh century the term *burgensis* began to acquire a more legal dimension. We may accept a broad definition of the European *burgensis*: a Christian – and never a Jew – who did not belong to the class of *rustici*, and lived either in a city or a rural village. He may have been, as was commonly the case, a merchant or a farmer, but never a knight or a churchman.[33] There were other defining traits of this social gradation; for instance, the children born of burgess parents were automatically considered burgesses. Beyond this set of criteria, which firmly established status, legal language defined a *burgensis* as a person with certain rights recognized by written laws or unwritten and widely practised

---

31 M. Vital Chomel, '"Francs et "rustiques" dans la seigneurie dauphinoise au temps des affranchisements', *Bulletin Philologique et Historique* (1965): 286; Génestal, pp. 218–19; Duby, p. 270.

32 Yver, 'Le Droit privé des villes de l'ouest de la France': p 157.

33 These criteria form the basis of Duby's definition of a burgess; Duby, *La Société aux XIe et XIIe siècles dans la région mâconnaise*, p. 271.

customs upheld by special courts in urban and rural communities. Evidently, besides the classes of knights and serfs, a middle class of freemen, to whom belonged *burgenses*, began in this period to appear in stronger relief.

Non-feudal Society and the Preaching of the First Crusade

Against this backdrop of developments in eleventh-century Europe the First Crusade was preached. Recruitment was aimed ostensibly at those financially able to undertake such a long journey, but the crusade message was universally preached and responded to by serfs and freemen alike. Ecclesiastical preachers acknowledged the mutability of society whilst at the same time cautioned against its excesses. There was particular concern that broader freedoms loosened the ties traditionally established between lord and subject. Freedom and wealth, therefore, could be perceived as synonymous with corruption and vice, and crusade was to be preached as an undertaking to cleanse all men of sin.

Chronicles, annals and letters furnish evidence of the recruitment of non-feudatories in the propaganda campaigns of 1095 and 1096. Entries were often brief although no less a valuable record of the manner of people who were recruited and the reasons for their participation. On the whole, judging from references to crusade propaganda, preachers were so enthusiastically received by large audiences that within a few months of Pope Urban II proclaiming the expedition to Jerusalem at the council of Clermont (18–28 November 1095) the message had spread far and wide.[34] For contemporary commentators the crusade message was encompassing of all social classes. At Clermont Pope Urban urged all people to take the cross if they were able, but proscribed against the participation of a select group including old men, unaccompanied women, and clerics who did not have the consent of their superiors.[35] On his arrival in Anjou at the beginning of Lent 1096, he again made a general appeal to help eliminate the 'heathen race' which had occupied Jerusalem.[36] The pope, wrote Fulcher of Chartres, desired that both 'rich and poor' go on a crusade,[37] whilst according to the chronicle of Saint-Maixent, there was widespread response from people 'noble and base, rich and poor' who wished to join the movement.[38] Albert of Aachen wrote in his chronicle

---

34 H.E.J. Cowdrey, 'Pope Urban II's Preaching of the First Crusade', *History*, 55 (1970): 177–88.On crusade recruitment and the response of lay people, see Riley-Smith, *The First Crusade and the Idea of Crusading*, pp. 31–57.

35 Robert the Monk, 'Historia Iherosolimitana', in *RHC Occ.*, III, p. 729.

36 L. Halphen and R. Poupardin (eds), *Chroniques des comtes d'Anjou et des seigneurs d'Amboise* (Paris, 1913), pp. 237–8.

37 Fulcher of Chartres, *Historia Hierosolymitana (1095–1127)*, ed. H. Hagenmeyer (Heidelberg, 1913), pp. 134–5.

38 P. Marchegay and E. Mabille (eds), *Chroniques des églises d'Anjou*, (Paris, 1869), p. 412.

that Peter the Hermit, soon after attending the council of Clermont, preached in Berry – the first city in his propaganda campaign – to nobles as well as commoners of 'all professions'.[39] Whilst Guibert of Nogent reported in his chronicle the drive for recruitment in other French cities.[40] Though such accounts of preaching and response seem somewhat exaggerated in tone, the rhetoric and turgid language so often employed by writers does not in any way detract from contemporary perception of crusade as a movement of monumental importance among the non-knightly classes.

The involvement of the lower classes of people in crusade elicited from chroniclers both condescension and approbation. The idea that a movement of noblemen and poor alike could be driven towards a single unifying objective seemed wrong, but less so when viewed as a fundamentally Christian undertaking whose participants were rewarded with remission of their sins. In a time when famine and disease could be interpreted in highly biblical and apocalyptic terms, crusade propaganda conveyed the message of remission for the sins of all men. The 1096 annal of Bernold of Constance emphasized in similar language the popular appeal of crusade penance and absolution to the most destitute of people. Many, he remarked, however, were ill-equipped to cope with the exacting conditions of the journey East, and not long after setting out abandoned their march and returned home.[41] The 1096 entry of the Rosenfeld Annals also recorded how large numbers of people in rural communities had been moved by Peter the Hermit's preaching to join the crusade.[42] In all likelihood, for a significant number of people, pilgrimage to Jerusalem was from the outset an opportunity to escape the general conditions of poverty and hardship.[43] But to judge from the tenor of some contemporary chroniclers highly enthused by the magnitude and passion of preaching and response, many non-feudatories took the cross because they were also spiritually driven. Serfs were so overcome by spiritual zeal, wrote one chronicler, that no lord could stop them leaving their homes, and such was their 'fear and love of God' that everyone was free to set out on the journey.[44] As measure of the success of crusade propaganda, entire villages, it was reported, were 'emptied' of their inhabitants.[45] It is interesting at this point to reflect on two seemingly conflicting notions: the freedom of all men and women, with few exceptions, to take the cross and leave their homes with no guarantee of return, as opposed to the prevailing conditions of servility which tied serfs to the land and severely restricted their movement. The

[39] Albert of Aachen, 'Historia Hierosolymitana', in *RHC Occ.*, IV, p. 272.

[40] Guibert of Nogent, 'Historia qua dicitur Gesta Dei per Francos', in *RHC Occ.*, IV, p. 142.

[41] Bernold, 'Chronicon', *MGH SS*, 5, p. 464.

[42] Rosenfeld Annals', *MGH SS*, 16, p. 101; 'Annales Magdeburgenses', *MGH SS*, 16, p. 178.

[43] Ekkehard of Aura, 'Hierosolymita', in *RHC Occ.*, V, p. 17.

[44] 'Historia Peregrinorum euntium Jerusolymam', in *RHC Occ.*, III, p. 174.

[45] 'Rosenfeld Annals', p. 101.

suggestion is that so important was this spiritual endeavour that a master should not stand in the way of his serf if he wished to go on crusade.

Although rural villages including *castra* became meeting-points or stop-off points along the journey,[46] the densely populated cities were the most popular places for crusade propaganda. It is most interesting that rhetoricians such as Peter the Hermit sought to focus their preaching on the urban centres. The essentially 'urban character of [Peter's] ministry'[47] is quite revealing. In the early years of the twelfth century stories surrounding his exploits and his association with the poorer elements of the cities began to circulate. Peter is an enigmatic figure and the true extent of his role as a propagandist and as one of the leaders of the so-called Peasants' Crusade remains a source of contention among modern historians, but it is generally agreed that he was a central figure of influence in the crusade movement post-Clermont. If the evidence is to be believed, the charismatic appeal of this rabble-rousing preacher from Picardy, helped spread the crusade message further and with greater speed than any other individual of the time including the pope.[48] Peter's conspicuous success in the cities may be measured not only in terms of the numbers of people he recruited to go on crusade, but also, if stories are to be believed, the considerable sum of money which he raised for the expedition.[49] The Peasants' Crusade, composed it would seem of a large number of non-feudatories and knights, set out in March 1096 about five months before the official date of departure of the main armies.[50]

By choosing urban centres preachers widened their appeal and targeted as broad a number of people as possible. They were greeted by a captive audience of men and women. Albert of Aachen noted that when Peter the Hermit preached at Berry, the mass of poor people were so moved by his oratory, that even the adulterers, murderers and robbers among them took the cross.[51] Apart from being the administrative and judicial hub of medieval life, cities were rallying-points for the rural *rustici*,[52] as well as home to the relatively prosperous merchant class.[53]

---

46 'Historia Peregrinorum euntium Jerusolymam', p. 174.

47 E.O Blake and C. Morris, 'A Hermit Goes to War: Peter and the Origins of the First Crusade', *Studies in Church History*, 22 (1985): 82.

48 The most recent book on Peter the Hermit is J. Flori, *Pierre l'Ermite et sa croisade* (Paris, 1999), although still useful is H. Hagenmeyer, *Peter der Ermite* (Leipzig, 1879). On Peter's contribution to crusade propaganda, see C. Morris, 'Propaganda for War. The Dissemination of the Crusading Ideal in the Twelfth Century', *Studies in Church History*, 20 (1983): 79–101.

49 According to Albert of Aachen, during the march through Hungary, the beleaguered Christian army was fiercely assaulted and Peter's treasure-chest of gold and silver plundered; Albert of Aachen, p. 281.

50 F. Duncalf, 'The Peasants' Crusade', *American Historical Review*, 26 (1920–1921): 440, 443.

51 Albert of Aachen, p. 272.

52 Blake and Morris, p. 82.

There was obvious preference for recruits with some source of wealth like property which they could sell or pledge so as to finance their journey. Few would have underestimated the cost of crusading, although an equally small number were adequately prepared for the challenges ahead. But whether they planned to return or settle in the Holy Land, crusade was a measure of their commitment.

The conclusions I have drawn are based on the theory that the First Crusade was made up of both classes of serfs and freemen. The crusaders constituted a cross-section of eleventh-century society. Admittedly, serfs were in the majority, but it has been too readily assumed that they were solely the *pauperes* alluded to in the chronicles. Prawer, most notably, found it convenient to argue from the premise that the *plebs* of the First Crusade were mostly peasants.[54] The tendency has been to lump together all non-knightly crusaders. Indeed, what is termed as the Peasants' Crusade is in itself a misnomer. For these reasons we should not overlook the predisposition of chroniclers to describe in indiscriminate terms the non-knightly classes simply as *pauperes*, *minores*, or *plebs inferior*. Equally, we should note those rare occasions when their language is more precise and distinction is made between the social standing of the poor. Thus, for example, one author remarked that *liberi* as well as *servi* were moved to join the crusade,[55] whilst Orderic Vitalis differentiated between the free city dwellers (*urbani*) and the *rustici*.[56] Ekkehard of Aura distinguished between the *turmae peditum*, the foot-soldiers, and the *catervae ruricolarum, feminarum ac parvulorum*,[57] the large body of poor non-combatants accompanying the main armies of crusaders, the majority of whom may have been serfs. The *turmae peditum*, it is also reasonable to assume, included freemen of the cities and rural *burgi*, who, as I have already noted, had some military experience.

Crusade or Migration?

In summary, large numbers of non-feudatories took the cross, and of those who headed East in 1096 a significant number served in the main crusader armies as *pedites*. Others with no allegiance to any particular lord on the journey may have accompanied as non-combatants. Others still, followed immediately in the wake of crusade as migrants. Certainly at a time when there was no general word for crusade, some chroniclers were more disposed to view the events of 1095–1096 as

---

53 Though migrants were often drawn to cities by commercial incentives, the desire for social enhancement was no less a consideration.

54 Prawer, *Crusader Institutions*, pp. 384–5.

55 'Notitiae duae Lemovicenses/De Praedicatione Crucis in Aquitania', in *RHC Occ.*, V, p. 350.

56 Orderic Vitalis, *The Ecclesiastical History of Orderic Vitalis*, ed. and trans. M. Chibnall (6 vols, Oxford: Clarendon Press, 1969–1980), vol. 5, p. 16.

57 Ekkehard of Aura, pp. 111–12.

a great migration of people. For Orderic Vitalis, apart from a 'journey', a holy war undertaken by an army of pilgrim-soldiers, this crusade was a *transmigratio populorum*.[58] Whilst in the words of another near-contemporary historian, it was a *maxima commotio* of men and women.[59] A similar impression was left on chroniclers who regarded crusade and the taking of the cross as a core military campaign within a larger-scale movement of people.[60] Of course chroniclers were prone to hyperbole, nevertheless, the unprecedented participation of such large numbers of non-knightly people characterized crusade as a mass movement, and warranted in the eyes of some its description as a migration.

The word *migratio* reflected accurately the scale and impact of crusade, but to what extent was migration a continuous phenomenon? In searching to answer this question, Ellenblum sought to incorporate the movement of people East within the greater 'social and cultural' context of European migration. 'It is doubtful whether in the minds of the Lombards or Burgundians', he has written, 'there was any great difference between settlements in Languedoc and Catalonia or the Frankish east. Settlement in the East was, perhaps, somewhat more dangerous and more distant ..., but it also had many inducements'.[61] Let us, however, consider Ellenblum's hypothesis. In the eleventh century there was in Europe, it would not be amiss to suggest, a notable degree of movement away from centres of overpopulation and correlative underemployment, to regions of lesser settlement and greater opportunity. In economically depressed rural areas which suffered from poor productivity, efforts were made by landlords to drive away redundant labour by buying up and reorganizing land in a way that would be beneficial to the agricultural efficiency of more compact communities.[62] Add to this factors of famine, pestilence and internecine wars, and the decision to relocate was often a compelling one.[63] Conversely, long distance migrants were drawn by the commercial incentives to be found in some cities and rural villages. In particular, *burgi* and *castra* could accommodate the influx of migrants by offering land to cultivate and even greater rights of settlement.

Bourin-Derruau's toponymic study of *castra* is attestation of the geographical extent and complexity of European migratory patterns.[64] Emigrants to Languedoc, for instance, were, for whatever reasons, drawn from regions as far away as Aquitaine, Massif Central and Catalonia.[65] Additional evidence points to migration

---

58 Orderic Vitalis, vol. 5, p. 8.

59 Historia Peregrinorum euntium Jerusolymam', p. 174.

60 'Cronica S. Petri Erfordensis Moderna,' *MGH SS*, 30, p. 357.

61 Ellenblum, *Frankish Rural Settlement*, pp. 79–80.

62 Herlihy, pp. 34–5.

63 F. Vercauteren, 'Marchands et bourgeois dans le pays mosan aux XIe et XIIe siècles', in *Mélanges Félix Rousseau. Etudes sur l'histoire du pays mosan au Moyen Age* (Brussels, 1958), pp. 661–2.

64 Bourin-Derruau, vol. 1, pp. 255–6.

65 Bourin-Derruau, vol. 1, pp. 255–6, 267.

from Spain and England to cities in the south-west of France including Montpellier. In the opposite direction, French immigrants from Toulouse and Limoges settled in central and northern Spain in the late eleventh and early twelfth century.[66] However, I do not accept the theory which incorporates the kingdom of Jerusalem within this complex network of European migration. The inducements or pressures on people to migrate must be strong enough to overcome a natural reluctance to do so. Even the decision to join the First Crusade was underscored by strong spiritual motivation. And whilst I would agree Europeans did migrate to the Holy Land in the wake of crusade, I have found no evidence to support the premise that in the twelfth century they continued to do so spontaneously in any significant numbers, or that they viewed settlement in the East as no more risky than, say, settlement in southern France or Spain. Admittedly, in the sources we occasionally come across stories of men who sacrificing the little they had, sought a better life in the East. In the 1140s, for instance, Constance, a shoemaker, left the village of Châlons-sur-Marne to go to Jerusalem in order to escape the punitive taxes of the local bishop.[67] But such examples are few and far between. I am more inclined to think that the bulk of settlers came with the First Crusade and subsequent crusades. Not even the capture of Jerusalem in 1099 seemed to encourage more migration from Europe. Writing in 1100, Fulcher of Chartres bemoaned the fact that only a small number of Latins remained to defend the kingdom, whilst only a few of the pilgrims who arrived in the East chose to settle permanently.[68]

Non-Feudatories on the First Crusade

The First Crusade has been described as chaotic, but there were efforts by secular and ecclesiastical leaders to instil some semblance of order and discipline among the foot soldiers and non-combatants who accompanied the knightly ranks. Evidence of their involvement is slender, but the picture is not as clouded as it seems initially. It is possible to piece together the clues from a close reading of eye-witness accounts as well as later narrative sources. The histories of Fulcher of Chartres and Raymond of Aguilers, to mention but two, describe the involvement of non-feudatories, both soldiers and non-combatants, in the siege of Muslim cities and the capture of property. In first-hand accounts can also be found evidence of the participation of non-feudatories in the ad hoc meetings that were called by crusade leaders. Later historians, in particular William of Tyre – who seems to

---

[66] C. Higounet, 'Mouvements de population dans le Midi de la France du XIe au XVe siècle', in *Paysages et villages neufs du Moyen Age* (Bordeaux, 1975), pp. 418, 419, 423, 429, 436.

[67] *AOL*, I, p. 536.

[68] Fulcher of Chartres, pp. 387–8.

have had at his disposal narrative sources which have not survived[69] – cast further light on the *secunda classis* or *plebs inferior*.[70]

Although the First Crusade is considered to have been a largely Frankish enterprise, its members were drawn from many parts of Europe. In fact the generic term 'Frank' incorporated in its meaning a broad spectrum of people both French and non-French.[71] Setting out East in the spring and summer of 1096 with the intention of capturing Jerusalem, crusaders were united by their Catholic faith and bound by the strong spiritual desire to liberate the Holy City from Muslims. Judging from Fulcher of Chartres's account, the largest force of the crusaders was made up of *pedites* (excluding non-combatants), an essential military component of the First crusade.[72] He gives no indication of their status, whether they were peasants or freemen, but mentions on more than one occasion that they participated in military sieges and were rewarded with confiscated properties.[73]

Jerusalem fell to the crusaders on 15 July 1099. Many crusaders their vows fulfilled returned home, whilst others remained. In the lands of Syria and Palestine, Europeans naturally drew more closely together; Muslims were a common enemy. It may be tentatively suggested that after the capture of Jerusalem the first crusaders were very few in number relative to the size of the native Christian and Muslim populations. It may be broadly stated, bearing in mind the unreliability of narrative accounts, that throughout the history of the kingdom of Jerusalem, the Franks constituted a minority of the total population.[74] More certain is that from departing western Europe in the summer of 1096 to the fall of Jerusalem almost three years later, the overall number of crusaders was decimated. Along their march they had borne the brunt of battle, starvation, disease and desertion.[75] From

---

69 P.W. Edbury and J.G. Rowe, *William of Tyre: Historian of the Latin East* (Cambridge, 1988), pp. 45–6.

70 William, Archbishop of Tyre, *Chronique*, ed. R.B. Huygens with H.E. Mayer and G. Rösch (Turnhout, 1986), pp. 227, 417.

71 Riley-Smith, *The First Crusade and the Idea of Crusading*, p. 86.

72 Fulcher of Chartres, pp. 408, 430.

73 Fulcher of Chartres, pp. 304, 403. Many of those who eventually settled in the cities, it may be further gleaned from Fulcher's account, remained obligated to military service; Fulcher of Chartres, pp. 408, 430.

74 For a discussion as to the possible size of the Frankish population in Palestine, see J. Prawer, *Histoire du royaume latin de Jerusalem* (2 vols, Paris, 1969–71), vol. 1, pp. 568–76; M. Benvenisti, *The Crusaders in the Holy Land* (Jerusalem, 1970), pp. 26–8; J.C. Russell, 'The Population of the Crusader States', in N.P. Zacour and H.W. Hazard (eds), *A History of the Crusades*: *The Impact of the Crusades on the Near East* (Wisconsin, 1985), vol. 5, pp. 295–314; Ellenblum, *Frankish Rural Settlement*, p. 31.

75 For accounts of starvation at Antioch following the fall of the city to the crusaders on 3 June 1098, see Hill, R. (ed.), *Gesta Francorum et aliorum Hierosolimitanorum* (London: 1962), pp. 33, 62; Peter Tudebode, *Historia de Hierosolymitano Itinere*, eds J.H. Hill and L.L. Hill (Paris, 1977), p. 68, 104; Albert of Aachen, p. 412, Fulcher of Charters, p. 246. See also Riley-Smith, *The First Crusade and the Idea of Crusading*, pp. 58–90.

a logistical point of view, crusade manpower engaged in occupying, settling and consolidating Syrian and Palestinian cities had been severely stretched. I would cautiously draw attention to the figures given by contemporaries. According to Raymond of Aguilers, there were 12,000 crusaders at the siege of Jerusalem, the overwhelming number of whom were *pedites*.[76] Fulcher of Chartres reported that in 1100 there were only 300 knights and the same number of foot soldiers left to guard Jerusalem, Jaffa, Ramle and Haifa.[77] He also mentioned that in 1101 the king could only muster an army of 260 knights and 900 foot soldiers from Jerusalem, Tiberias, Caesarea and Haifa.[78]

The crusade leaders cultivated settlement. Having suffered the privations of a long military campaign, the *pedites* were rewarded with plunder, land and housing. Under the rules of conquest it was usual practice to grant the general *populus* the right to possess freely and in perpetuity property – and movables – they managed to appropriate from Muslims and, it would seem, indigenous Christians. But of course it was not a free-for-all even if the wide-scale slaughter and expulsion suggests otherwise.[79] The frenzied pillaging was certainly uncontrollable[80] but as William of Tyre stressed, somehow in the midst of this chaos, legal constraint, what he termed as the *jure proprietatis*, was imposed on the appropriation of property. This was law in the sense that the right of possession had first to be conceded by crusade leaders, and if, as mentioned in eyewitness accounts, crusaders marked property which they seized with the sign of the cross, their claim of rightful possession remained dependent upon a lord's approval. This theory of orderly conquest leaves little room for suggestion that the sudden displacement of the indigenous population led to the allocation of allodial property and the creation of absolute ownership.

Crusade leaders promoted settlement in other ways. Attached to the law of possession were basic rights of alienation. It is not impossible that at this early stage certain aspects of tenancy which would later be associated with the type of property defined legally as *borgesie* were applied. The properties set aside in Jerusalem, for instance, were to belong exclusively to the European *populus* who were free to sell, lease or exchange them. They were of course prohibited from alienating to Muslims and perhaps even native non-Latin Christians – discrimination in the latter case, though subsequently surviving under the customs governing *borgesie* tenancy in royal, seigneurial and ecclesiastical lordships, was, judging from the documentary evidence, largely overlooked in actual practice. The establishment of a property market was of paramount importance as it encouraged settlement, and a house in particular could be regarded as a profitable asset.

---

76 Raymond of Aguilers, *Le 'Liber' de Raymond d'Aguilers*, eds J.H. Hill and L.L. Hill (Paris, 1969), p. 148.

77 Fulcher of Chartres, p. 389.

78 Fulcher of Chartres, p. 408.

79 Fulcher of Chartres, pp. 266–7.

80 Fulcher of Chartres, pp. 234–5.

Agreement, Law-making and Jurisdiction (1096–1099)

As was characteristic of later royal and seigneurial governance in the kingdom of Jerusalem, the advice and consent of the non-knightly classes was sought whenever it was deemed appropriate by crusade leaders. General assemblies were convened it would appear on an ad hoc basis to agree upon a common course of action, for example matters of military strategy, clerical elections or even the division of property subsequent to the capture of a besieged city.[81] At one general assembly, for instance, Stephen of Blois was elected commander-in-chief with the consent of the princes and of the 'common counsel of the whole army'.[82] General assemblies, however, may have served another purpose, perhaps even in a judicial context.

An examination of eyewitness accounts reveals some of the earliest rules imposed by Church and secular leaders on the mass of non-feudatories. The lawless behaviour of crusaders is a recurring theme in the anonymous *Gesta Francorum*, and the histories of Peter Tudebode, Raymond of Aguilers and Fulcher of Chartres. Certain violations of Church stricture were particularly deserving of censure. Fulcher of Chartres excoriated crusaders for having sexual liaisons with 'lawless' Muslim women.[83] On the issue of miscegenation – that is sexual relations between European Christians and non-Christians – the position of churchmen in the Holy Land was unequivocal and such unions were judged morally reprehensible. Denunciation of other forms of deviancy was no less severe. The presence of European women among the crusaders elicited particularly condemnatory language from contemporaries concerned that men were being easily led astray by forbidden desires. Though accepting of women as providers of succour in times of need,[84] crusade leaders sought to re-establish order and discipline by segregating all married and unmarried women from the ranks of soldiers.[85] Coupled with adultery and fornication the vices of drunkenness, gambling, rowdiness and swearing were perceived as symptomatic of a general breakdown in normative behaviour. Underhanded commercial practices, theft and pillage seem also to have caused consternation.[86]

The response of crusade leaders, the upholders of moral rectitude and social order, was to introduce a set of laws and condign punishments for immoral and criminal behaviour. As a result, any person accused of wrongdoing would be tried in a court of law. I use the word court loosely in the sense of a body of chosen

---

81 Riley-Smith, *The First Crusade and the Idea of Crusading*, pp. 86–7.

82 Hill, *Gesta Francorum*, p. 63; Peter Tudebode, pp. 104–105.

83 Fulcher of Chartres, p. 243; Hill, *Gesta Francorum*, p. 337.

84 Riley-Smith, *The First Crusade and the Idea of Crusading*, p. 63; Hill, *Gesta Francorum*, p. 19; Peter Tudebode, p. 106.

85 Fulcher of Chartres, p. 223. Prince Bohemond of Antioch adopted a similar policy and barred all women from his army (Fulcher of Chartres, p. 521). See also William of Tyre, pp. 264–5.

86 William of Tyre, pp. 264–5.

individuals – *judices* as they were referred to in the sources[87] – entrusted with legal duties, who met at certain times to hear cases and to pass sentences. In the words of William of Tyre, they dispensed justice *juxta legum*, according to law, and were vested with special powers to investigate a case and to enforce a judgement.[88] It was agreed, continued William, to introduce the new laws with the common consent of people, although from where these laws were adopted is not known. Neither is it possible to determine from the available evidence how *judices* were appointed or their number. William simply states that wise and loyal men were chosen to become judges. There are also no clues as to their actual status. They may conceivably have been churchmen, although, as I explain in a later chapter, in the kingdom of Jerusalem the *judex* was a non-feudatory learned in legal matters who presided over the *Cour des Bourgeois* in place of the viscount.[89] In Europe by this time, the role of the *judex* as presiding head of a secular court was also well established.

The *judices* of the crusade armies had the authority to administer both low and high justice and justice of blood, which rules out that they were judges in a Church court. Sentencing was draconian. They were within their powers to sentence to death (*sub poena mortis*) any person caught committing an adulterous or illicit sexual act. They had also the option of issuing a verdict of corporal punishment for any of the miscellaneous infractions listed above. According to William of Tyre, the judges were so successful in punishing offenders that others were deterred from breaking the law.[90]

It may be conjectured this was a court of all non-feudatories, as the narrative accounts do not suggest courts were created to deal separately with matters concerning freemen or serfs. It may simply have been the case that common law was the beginning of an abiding principle in the East which held that all non-feudal Latin Christians were of equally free status. This embryonic judicial body was, it may even be argued, a forerunner of later courts of burgesses in the kingdom.

An Overview of Eastern Burgess Settlement

Invariably, a study which attempts to trace the history of burgesses in the kingdom of Jerusalem is faced with certain difficulties. For the most part there is little evidence regarding the formative years of the twelfth century, at least in terms of the inception of burgess settlement in the Frankish kingdom. It is of course necessary throughout to adopt a guarded view when dealing with the law books of thirteenth-century jurists who attributed the creation of burgess courts to the

87 Robert the Monk, p. 262.

88 William of Tyre, p. 188.

89 See below, pp. 144–5. ‘L’Estoire d’Eracles Empereur et la conqueste de la terre d’outremer’, in *RHC Occ.*, I, p. 150.

90 William of Tyre, pp. 264–5.

kingdom's first ruler Godfrey of Bouillon (1099–1100). Nevertheless, putting to one side the proclivity of jurists to myth-making, I shall demonstrate how early burgess settlers were able to organize themselves into a recognizable community within the first decade of the twelfth century.

The history of early settlement is rather vaguely understood, and it is a necessary consequence to consider sources which augment first-hand accounts of the role of Latin non-feudatories in the period of transition from crusade to settlement. The treatises of the thirteenth-century Latin Syrian jurists, in particular John of Ibelin and Philip of Novara, seem to recount incontrovertibly how non-feudatories in Jerusalem were, from as early as the reign of the kingdom's first ruler Godfrey of Bouillon, organized into a class of burgesses with its own laws and court of justice, the royal *Cour des Bourgeois*. John of Ibelin explains that the laws attributed to Godfrey and his successors were written down, but that the legislation of the kingdom, the *Letres dou Sepulcre*, were lost after the fall of Jerusalem to Saladin in 1187.[91] Historians have been understandably reluctant to accept this interpretation of the kingdom's history *prima facie*, and it has been suggested the treatises of the thirteenth-century jurists were at times biased and self-serving.[92] It has even been claimed their subjectivity was underscored by a broader political agenda. Peter Edbury has argued that the existence of the *Letres dou Sepulcre* was a myth concocted by Philip of Novara and John of Ibelin in response to the challenge posed by an influx of French nobles and knights in the thirteenth century, and their insistence that the customary laws of the kingdom should conform to those in France.[93] By fabricating the existence of the *Letres dou Sepulcre* the jurists could claim the rulers of Jerusalem had already issued legislation but that these laws had been lost in 1187.[94] I am certainly in agreement that the histories of the jurists should not be accepted automatically, and not least because their treatises were written several decades after the events which they describe. But whether there is sufficient evidence to support Edbury's assertion that the treatises were apocryphal rather than historically inaccurate is open to debate. A compromise perhaps would be to contend that John of Ibelin and Philip of Novara's accounts of the kingdom's jurisdiction and legislation were more precisely an embellishment of the truth instead of total fabrication. I am inclined to this latter opinion as I am convinced that in an effort to explain the existence of the *Letres dou Sepulcre* as mere myth-making and propaganda, and to discredit jurists' ascription of a well-formed legal system to the reign of Godfrey of Bouillon, there

---

91 John of Ibelin, p. 624.

92 Riley-Smith, *The Feudal Nobility and the Kingdom of Jerusalem*, p. 136.

93 That John of Ibelin incorporated into his work material he had found in Philip of Novara's, detracts from the overall value of his treatise which was written nearly eighty years after the fall of Jerusalem, and cannot be viewed as an independent and reliable account. On this latter point, see P.W. Edbury, 'Law and Custom in the Latin East: *Les Letres dou Sepulcre*', *Mediterranean Historical Review*, 10 (1995): 72.

94 Edbury, 'Law and Custom in the Latin East', 71–9.

is a danger, at least as far as the class of burgesses is concerned, of underestimating the actual rate of development in jurisdiction and written legislation during the first years of the twelfth century. The strong likelihood is the *Letres dou Sepulcre* did not exist but there is evidence, nonetheless, to support the view that certainly from the reign of Baldwin I (1100–1118), and possibly from as early as the reign of Godfrey of Bouillon, Latin non-feudatories had established a court of justice in Jerusalem, whose basic function and the duties of its officials resembled in several respects those of the *Cour des Bourgeois* described in the law-books of the thirteenth century.

An effectual system of jurisdiction was a priority. It was previously discussed how the crusade leaders concerned by general lawlessness among their followers chose to enforce order through an ad hoc court of law and arbitration. It may be surmised that in a similar vein a system of justice was immediately necessary to implement the laws (*assises*) enacted by the king, and to meet the requirements of every significant burgess community. The creation of a special court was requisite in ensuring that only Latin non-feudatories subject to its jurisdiction could belong to a class distinct from the indigenous population. It is important, furthermore, to bear in mind that the superimposition of a discriminatory system of jurisdiction afforded the Latin rulers greater control over the division of property. In this regard, the importation of the alienable but conditional leasehold of the European *burgagium* (*borgesie*) met all requirements. It was of paramount importance that apart from the allocation of fiefs, non-feudal properties like *borgesies* should remain exclusively and perpetually in the hands of Christians. The aim of such a policy enforced rigidly by a system of jurisdiction which oversaw the alienation of *borgesies*, and applied consistently throughout secular and ecclesiastical territories, was to exclude Muslims from possessing property in certain city areas and Latin rural villages.

There is an equally strong case to argue that from the first decade of the twelfth century there existed in Jerusalem a body of non-feudal legislation. In basic terms, the broad range of laws enacted by rulers were known as *assises*, *dreit* or *leis*. There were *assises* particularly associated with the ruler who decreed them. In the 'Livre de la Cour des Bourgeois', the burgess law-book of Acre, there is reference to the *assises* of King Baldwin I regarding criminal assault and street cleaning.[95] To these early laws were added the *assises* of King Baldwin II (1118–1131) concerning matters of disinheritance,[96] and the *assises* of King Amalric (1163–1174) concerning maritime law and cases of adultery.[97] In the first quarter of the twelfth century, moreover, there was already developed a practice of writing down legislation. For instance, copies of the twenty-five decrees issued at the Council of Nablus in 1120 were, according to William of

[95] Kausler, pp. 141–2, 350–51 (cf. Beugnot, 'Livre des assises', pp. 86, 225). See also Philip of Novara, 'Le Livre de forme de plait', p. 547.

[96] Kausler, p. 269 (cf. Beugnot, 'Livre des assises', p. 170).

[97] Kausler, pp. 75, 341–2 (cf. Beugnot, 'Livre des assises', pp. 42, 218).

Tyre, preserved in the archives of many churches.[98]

Turning our attention to the actual process of settlement, we may consider how European Christians were widely dispersed in their new kingdom. In all important respects, the Frankish population may be described as territorially fragmented, as in the light of recent research we are no longer compelled to subscribe to the theory Frankish settlers were almost exclusively confined to urban living. It has been convincingly demonstrated that networks of Frankish rural communities were created in certain regions of the kingdom, like for example the south-eastern territory.[99] European settlers were divided between the cities and rural communities situated either in royal domain or in the lordships of the king's tenants-in-chief. Foremost they swore fealty to the monarch, but owing to the political and legislative structure of the kingdom of Jerusalem, they also swore allegiance to the controlling authority under whose jurisdiction they resided – whether a great lord or an ecclesiastical institution – and were bound to abide by the laws of their locality as there was it seems no general legislative code for the whole kingdom.

The growth of urban settlement in the first decades of the twelfth century may be measured in terms similar to those which applied in Europe. City burgesses had their own jurors (*jurati*), equivalent to the European *scabini*, who were well-known and respected figures of society, usually members of prominent families or the business community. The twin principles of general agreement – the approval of a lord – and judgement by peers were strongly in place. As in urban France,[100] the idea of public solidarity was further enhanced by the appointment of jurors increasingly more representative of the interests of their community. The changes in judiciary were of course progressive in the twelfth century, and the impression of a near-fully evolved burgess court is first derived from the law books of the thirteenth century. But this rate of development does not compare unfavourably with the general picture in Europe over a similar timescale. The social and legal position of jurors, the responsibilities they had towards their community, and the accountabilities towards their lord, developed only slowly.[101]

The foundation of the Frankish village of Magna Mahumeria (al-Bira) is further illustrative of the pattern of rural development in the kingdom. The *casale* had originally been granted to the church of the Holy Sepulchre by Godfrey of Bouillon and sometime after 1100 a community of Franks had been established by the canons. A document of 1156 reveals that the village was at this time composed of settlers from several regions of Europe, particularly from central and south France, Italy and Catalonia.[102] The canons were it seems vested with a certain

98 William of Tyre, pp. 563–4.

99 Ellenblum, *Frankish Rural Settlement*, pp. 15–19.

100 Bourin-Derruau, vol. 1, p. 324.

101 J. Duesberg, *Les Jurisdictions scabinales en Flandre et en Lotharingie au moyen-âge* (Louvain, 1932), pp. 24ff..

102 G. Bresc-Bautier (ed.), *Le Cartulaire du chapitre du Saint-Sépulcre de Jérusalem* (Paris, 1984), no.117, 237–9. Benvenisti, pp. 75–80.

degree of legislative power and court authority over settlers in secular – principally tenurial – matters. As a condition of settlement villagers were required to swear allegiance to the church of the Holy Sepulchre. The example of Magna Mahumeria is a significant indicator of the level of legal and juridical subsistence to be found in Latin rural communities in the kingdom.

As in contemporary Europe, unwritten custom was without question a bedrock of Latin society in the kingdom of Jerusalem. Jurisdiction, furthermore, was based to some extent on an analogous practice of adopting well known customs. In the case of Magna Mahumeria, this new settlement seemed to acquire from early on in the century a reputation as the archetypal Latin *ville neuve*, and its influential customs were, judging from charters of privileges, adopted in other villages in the kingdom. This practice does in part explain why there existed a degree of jurisdictional, administrative and commercial uniformity in the rules governing eastern burgesses. The important customs of *villes* neuves were perpetuated in this manner and as in Europe were probably never codified. It is a subject which I return to in a later chapter.

Arguably, therefore, by the early part of the twelfth century the typical European *burgus* – the general layout of farm land and houses, and the basic customs of tenancy and jurisdiction uniformly shaped over the preceding decades – served as a template for Latin settlement in Palestine and Syria. In the kingdom they successfully recreated European settlement types. It is a point worth making bearing in mind that early Latin settlers had from the outset to adjust to life in rural areas as well as cities. From the beginning they probably had in their minds the ideal type of village, and the most suitable customs, system of jurisdiction and administration. It is even plausible to suggest that in the early stages there was similar adoption in rural *villes neuves* of well known, tried-and-tested customs long associated with certain European *burgi*. Immigrants may even have brought with them their own customs.

This interpretation of the transitional period of Latin settlement in the East differs somewhat to the one advocated by Prawer. A principle tenet of his argument is that European institutions and property types, such as *borgesie* tenancy, were ‘part of the process of urban evolution’, which were ‘imported wholesale’ into the kingdom of Jerusalem. It would be reasonable, he added, to look to ‘elements of city life’ in order to explain adequately this type of tenure.[103] For Prawer, moreover, the eastern Latin kingdom was predominantly an urban society where new immigrants had out of necessity to adapt to city life.[104] In my assessment, Prawer’s theory *a propos* the type of society in the East, is intrinsically flawed because it is based upon an erroneous interpretation of the origins and popularity of the European *borgesie*. It is important to reiterate the point made earlier, that in the eleventh century the rules of tenancy of the type of property usually described as *borgesie* were not confined to the cities, but generally

---

[103] Prawer, *Crusader Institutions*, p. 252.

[104] Prawer, *Crusader Institutions*, p. 384.

practised in the rural villages. In the light of evidence, the assumption that we should look solely to city life in order to explain this tenure – and more specifically to the vocabulary of northern France when defining its basic features[105] – seems mistaken. Society in the East was far from confined to the cities. I would go so far as to suggest the success of the kingdom of Jerusalem was, right from the outset, largely dependent on a society able to adapt to life both in the cities and the countryside.

European Freemen, Crusade and Eastern Settlement – A Conclusion

The intention of this chapter was to offer a brief history of European, essentially French, non-feudal society in the latter half of the eleventh century. The lines of investigation into the formation of burgess settlements, laws and institutions in the kingdom of Jerusalem were traced back to this earlier period. The evidence strongly supports the contention that on the eve of the First Crusade there was in the regions of France a growing class of freemen, predominantly made up of merchants and farmers, who lived both in urban agglomerations and rural villages, and were, relatively speaking, wealthier and more socially cohesive than ever before. This class of people was quite often referred to in charters and chronicles as *burgenses* – regardless of the agreed origin of the word – and prospered due mainly to three factors: greater demographic growth, intensive settlement and increased migration. Moreover, we have seen how the rules governing the lease of *burgagium* differed from one locality to another, but that at the same time paradoxically there were certain aspects of essential uniformity. Well known customs carried to new destinations by word of mouth and migration, went some way to promoting a more homogenous concept of property and person. All this took place in a period of unprecedented levels of jurisdictional and institutional developments.

The growth of the class of *burgenses* coincided with the emergence of a popular crusading movement. The principles of inclusiveness were part-and-parcel of crusade propaganda and preachers were able to appeal successfully to serfs and freemen in the cities and rural villages. On crusade secular and ecclesiastical leaders worked concertedly to root out misdemeanour and more serious criminal offences. Their crude but effective system of justice included a court which had competence in criminal and commercial matters over crusaders. Significantly, this appears to have been one of the earliest examples of Latin law-making in the Holy Land.

The capture of Jerusalem marked the beginning of a new social and legal order fundamentally different to that existing in Latin Christian Europe. The thirteenth-century jurists, seemingly tendentious in ascribing the establishment of a burgess legal system to the first year of the kingdom of Jerusalem's existence, were more

---

105 Prawer, *Crusader Institutions*, p. 252.

accurately reflecting the unique and remarkable circumstances of a century and a half earlier. By the time of the creation of the kingdom of Jerusalem, European – if not native Latin – *servi* had ceased to exist in the Holy Land. Jurisprudence held fast the fundamental principle that all European Catholics and their descendants were free. The true extent of this statement may be gauged from charters and law books which reveal that the term *burgenses* came to denote all permanent residents in the kingdom whose status matched precisely a set of criteria legally defined and strictly applied.

Chapter 2

Burgess Law-Making and Legal Institutions

We have seen how European settlers in Palestine and Syria superimposed a system of justice which strengthened the burgess class at the expense of a weak indigenous population. The king and lords in their domains wished to create courts of justice for their burgess communities, and from what we know of later practices, the laws they issued would have been written down – even the precedents which were set by the courts – and collected, possibly over successive generations. In the beginning, however, the writing down of laws did not necessarily mean the compilation of law books per se. The existence of the *Letres dou Sepulcre* may have been apocryphal, but the story is, nevertheless, revealing of the way in which individual laws, including those of other nations, were copied and preserved in a single place for common consultation.

It is my contention that there was probably no general law book for the whole kingdom of Jerusalem, and that instead there was in place a complex system of justice, a characteristic feature of which was the development of local 'customs'. It is for this reason doubt should be cast on the accounts given by thirteenth-century jurists John of Ibelin (writing in the 1250s and 1260s) and Philip of Novara (writing in the mid-1260s) as to the origin of legislation, and their belief that in the early years of the twelfth century the king and leading members of the nobility and Church had agreed on the authority of the collection of laws known as the *Letres dou Sepulcre*. Whilst we may be inclined to question the existence of the *Letres dou Sepulcre*, there is evidence, nevertheless, to suggest certain laws did have general application throughout the kingdom of Jerusalem in the twelfth and thirteenth centuries. These laws may have been formulated at general assemblies attended by the king, his tenants-in-chief, churchmen and burgesses to deliberate on matters of common interest. Furthermore, a premise underlying this study is that alongside this general legislation, secular lords, ecclesiastical institutions and the European merchant communities, vested with rights of jurisdiction over inhabitants in their cities, quarters or *villes neuves*, established their own laws or 'customs' over burgesses resident in their domains. The fact that cities and *villes neuves* adopted each other's 'customs' contributed to the uniformity of laws in the kingdom. It will also be seen how jurors of *Cours des Bourgeois* had the authority to set precedents and even amend legislation in cases they saw fit.

Jurisdiction was divided among secular lords and ecclesiastical institutions, but paradoxically, there was a significant level of legal uniformity. The charters often describe a particular Latin community as having its own *consuetudines* or 'customs'. Whereas a law, or *assise*, was basically a piece of written legislation, a custom was a seigneurial decree or court precedent of which there was no existing record, but had been in use for a lengthy period of time. Apart from the *consuetudines civitatis Acconensis*[1] or the *usus et consuetudines patrie seu civitatis Accon*,[2] there can be found reference to the *usus et consuetudines civitatis Jerusalem*[3] and the *consuetudines terre Tripoli*.[4] Besides the *consuetudines Mahumeria*, adopted by the Church of the Holy Sepulchre in the settlement known as Nova Villa in 1160,[5] the rules of tenancy in the settlement of Parva Palmarea were shaped by the *usus et consuetudines burie*.[6] The settlement of Bethgibelin provides further evidence of the adoption of 'customs'; the court of the Hospitallers adopted the *consuetudo Lithde* (Lydda) – because it was the most apt for dealing with the crime of plunder committed by their inhabitants – as well as certain *consuetudines* of Jerusalem.[7] At Nova Villa the Holy Sepulchre adopted tried and tested rules of tenancy, and the same was probably true in Parva Mahumeria, Bethsuri and other settlements managed by the canons. The success of these villages, which were well-planned in advance,[8] can be gauged from this repeated adoption of their 'customs'. It is worth bearing in mind that custom may have been favoured by courts and legal practitioners over other forms of written law because in the twelfth century memory was valued more greatly than written record. At any rate, according to the 'Livre de la Cour des Bourgeois', it was expected of a king that he maintain 'les bons hus et les bones coustumes dou reaume'.[9]

Eid ?

The Letres dou Sepulcre

Accounts of the origin of the first laws of the kingdom of Jerusalem, the *Letres dou Sepulcre*, were based on a tradition that Godfrey of Bouillon (1099–1100), with the agreement of feudatories and burgesses, inquired into the laws of other lands before deciding on the most suitable *assises*. Godfrey established a legal system for

---

1 E. Strehlke (ed.), *Tabulae Ordinis Theutonici* (Berlin, 1869), no. 91, p. 73.

2 Strehlke, no. 86, p. 69.

3 J. Delaville Le Roulx (ed.), *Les Archives, la bibliothèque et le trésor de l'Ordre de Saint-Jean de Jérusalem à Malte* (Paris, 1883), no. 34, p. 120.

4 J. Delaville Le Roulx (ed.), *Cartulaire général de l'Ordre des Hospitaliers de St.-Jean de Jérusalem (1100–1310)*, no. 754, p. 479.

5 Bresc-Bautier, no. 126, p. 253; Ellenblum, *Frankish Rural Settlement*, pp. 68–9, 82, 92.

6 Delaville Le Roulx, *Cartulaire général*, no. 19, p. 909.

7 Delaville Le Roulx, *Cartulaire général*, no. 399, p. 273.

8 Ellenblum, *Frankish Rural Settlement*, pp. 92–4; A.J. Boas, *Crusader Archaeology: The Material Culture of the Latin East* (London, 1999), pp. 63–8.

9 Kausler, p. 62 (cf. Beugnot 'Livre des assises', p. 33).

the whole kingdom and according to tradition lords with rights of *cours et coins et justise* governed Latin Christians in their lordships by these laws.[10] The collection, according to Philip of Novara, was made up of 'toutes les assises et bons us et bones costumes', issued or established by later rulers and came to be known as the *Letres dou Sepulcre* because it was kept in a box in the church of the Holy Sepulchre in Jerusalem.[11] This collection of individual laws written down on separate pieces of parchment, was accessible to the jurors of both the High Court and the *Cour des Bourgeois* to consult whenever they needed to know what law to apply in a particular case. The *Letres*, it was further recounted, were the fulcrum of the kingdom's legal system, but when Jerusalem was captured by Saladin in 1187 they mysteriously disappeared, and though a few wise men such as Ralph of Tiberias and the burgess Raymond Anteaume knew the laws from memory, they were not rewritten.[12] It is puzzling why an attempt was not made in the following decades to reproduce this important collection of laws, and why there were no copies deposited in the archives of other cities. In Philip of Novara's account, King Aimery (1197–1205) requested from Ralph of Tiberias and other legally-minded men to reconstruct the lost laws of the kingdom, but that when Ralph refused, citing his unwillingness to work with men who were of a lower class than him, the idea was abandoned.[13] It seems peculiar that this was the end of the matter especially as the loss resulted in uncertainty as to what the actual laws of the kingdom were. Philip even admitted knowledge of past legislation depended on hearsay and that, generally speaking, there was a poor understanding of the laws.[14] In fact, no sources of the twelfth century mention the *Letres dou Sepulcre*. It is true, admittedly, that the two principal chroniclers of the kingdom of Jerusalem, Fulcher of Chartres and William of Tyre, had a tendency to under-report or even totally ignore events of significance.[15] But though we must be wary of misinterpreting what authors chose not to include in their chronicles, it is, nevertheless, difficult to explain adequately why Fulcher of Chartres would omit to mention the *Letres dou Sepulcre* particularly as he was always eager to paint the kingdom in a favourable light. The same could be asked of William of Tyre who would have been chancellor and would not have missed the opportunity of crediting the kings of Jerusalem with formulating legislation and strengthening the political cohesion of the kingdom. Adding further to the argument the *Letres dou*

---

10 John of Ibelin, pp. 54–5.

11 Philip of Novara, 'Le Livre de forme de plait', pp. 521–3.

12 Philip of Novara, 'Le Livre de forme de plait', pp. 521–2.

13 Philip of Novara, 'Le Livre de forme de plait', p. 523.

14 Philip of Novara, 'Le Livre de forme de plait', p. 521.

15 The reasons why William of Tyre and Fulcher of Chartres omitted to mention some significant events in the history of the kingdom of Jerusalem have been discussed by B.Z. Kedar, 'On the Origins of the Earliest Laws of Frankish Jerusalem: The Canons of the Council of Nablus, 1120', *Speculum*, 74 (1999): 327–8; and H.E. Mayer, 'The Concordat of Nablus', *Journal of Ecclesiastical History*, 33 (1982): 541–2.

Sepulcre probably did not exist, is the fact that they were not mentioned in the 'Livre de la Cour des Bourgeois' which did otherwise make several references to twelfth-century royal acts of legislation. Even the author of the 'Livre contrefais', who makes manifold allusions to law books of the kingdom of Jerusalem, hints nowhere at the establishment of such an important collection.

John of Ibelin's account of the origin of the *Letres dou Sepulcre* is doubtful in certain respects. He was eager to stress the principle of legislation by agreement, first with regard to Godfrey's legislative assembly of leading nobles, churchmen and burgesses, and, secondly, with respect to the work carried out by successive rulers who with the counsel of their wisest men made amendments and additions to the laws. John claimed that these assemblies were held in Acre so that visitors arriving on the general passages could be questioned about laws in foreign lands.[16] Yet, there are no records of these meetings in other sources and only once in the twelfth century is there evidence that the knowledge of a visitor to the Holy Land was used to decide a point of law.[17]

The existence of the *Letres dou Sepulcre* has also been doubted because, it is claimed, the degree of legislative development attributed by the jurists to the reign of Godfrey of Bouillon seems unrealistic. Grandclaude sought to traverse this argument by pointing out that the *Letres dou Sepulcre* was supposed to include not simply those laws compiled under the rule of Godfrey, but also the legislative work carried out by successive kings of Jerusalem in the twelfth century.[18] In support of his ideas Grandclaude went on to show that twenty-five *assises* could be dated from the period before 1187, and suggested the immense legislative activity the jurists attributed to the twelfth century was not exaggerated.[19] This is a cogent argument and Grandclaude proved overwhelmingly significant legislation was enacted before 1187. There are grounds, however, to differ with Grandclaude on two points. First, doubt may be cast on the existence of a single collection for the whole kingdom of Jerusalem known as the *Letres dou Sepulcre*. And, secondly, John's history of twelfth century legislation should not be dismissed out of hand. His was not a work of complete fiction, and for this reason the degree of legislative development attributed to the early years of the kingdom should not be viewed as wholly unrealistic. The reasons behind this argument are set out below, demonstrating how in this period the rate of formal legislation in the towns and cities was more advanced than previously thought.

---

16 John of Ibelin, p. 54.

17 Riley-Smith, *The Feudal Nobility and the Kingdom of Jerusalem*, p. 195.

18 M. Grandclaude, *Etude critique sur les livres des assises de Jérusalem* (Paris, 1923), pp. 99–102; G. Recoura, 'Les Assises de Jérusalem. A Propos d'un livre récent', *Le Moyen Age*, 26 (1924–25): 151–65; J.L. La Monte, 'Three Questions Concerning the Assises de Jerusalem', *Byzantina Metabyzantina*, I (1946): 204–208.

19 M. Grandclaude, 'Liste d'assises remontant au premier Royaume de Jérusalem 1099–1187', in *Mélanges Paul Fournier* (Paris, 1929), pp. 329–45.

The Process of Law-Making

Laws were issued in the first years of the kingdom's existence, and some legislation reflected the circumstances of the day. We may begin by considering how defensive weaknesses prompted the establishment of one of the earliest laws. William of Tyre records in his history that a general *edictum* was passed in 1100 instructing that if a person abandoned his property and another held it for a year and a day without being challenged, then the new tenant could acquire it permanently and legitimately. This had been done, wrote William, because many Latin settlers were abandoning the kingdom in times of danger only to return when there was guarantee of greater security.[20] Presumably, if this precautionary law had been introduced in 1100, it must have served as a strong disincentive to those who may have wished to re-migrate. Proprietorial legislation was thus agreed and applied throughout the kingdom, and, once again, the implication is that from early on non-feudatories held property not as freeholders but as leaseholders subject to rules of tenancy. The nobility determinedly tackled problems by legislative means and in so doing enforced settlement as much as encouraged it. It is worth noting that vestiges of this *edictum* are identifiable in the legislation of Antioch in the twelfth century, Acre in the thirteenth century – when the law of a year and a day had widespread influence on rules of *borgesies* leasehold – and Nicosia in the fourteenth century.[21] Arguably, however, by this time, the principle underscoring the rule of a year and a day, that is in the interest of greater security men should be forbidden from abandoning property, had become less significant or totally redundant. Yet, it remained for sub-leaseholders a means of acquiring total possession of their property should opportunity arise.

The fact that in the twelfth century the *edictum* of a year and a day had common application was not unique. The twelfth-century law of shipwreck, for example, issued by king Amalric (1163–1173) seems also to have applied generally in the kingdom. 'Quar le roy Amauri, de bonne memoire', it is written in the 'Livre de la Cour des Bourgeois', 'donna ceste franchise par *tout le reaume de Jerusalem*'.[22] I understand this to mean the whole of the kingdom both inside and outside royal domain. The law set out the rules governing shipwreck and personal

[20] William of Tyre, p. 446.

[21] Kausler, p. 124 (cf. Beugnot, 'Livre des assises', p. 76). In Acre, if a lessor did not collect *cens* from his lessee for a year and a day, he forfeited his *borgesie* and his sub-tenant acquired it legally. Indeed, a parallel law of the principality of Antioch held that if in a legal dispute over a *borgesie* a defendant could prove that he had had possession of a property for a year and a day without challenge from the plaintiff, it was his to keep in perpetuity; L.M. Alishan (ed.), *Assises d'Antioch* (Venice, 1876), p. 66.The law similarly applied in Nicosia in the fourteenth century, as according to the author of the 'Livre contrefais', it had been established in the early years of the kingdom and applied to all tenants of *borgesies* whether burgesses, fief-holders, churchmen or members of the merchant communities; 'Livre contrefais', p. 311.

[22] Kausler, p. 81 (cf. Beugnot, 'Livre des assises', p. 47).

property, including the rights of burgesses to possess merchandise recovered from sunken vessels. Other 'asises dou reaume de Jerusalem' concerned servants, slaves and enfranchisement;[23] alienation of *borgesies* and disputes in court arising from the transfer of property;[24] the making of pledges and the sale of collateral;[25] the court testimony of Muslims, Jews and indigenous Christians,[26] and their rights to judicial duel in cases of murder or treason;[27] aspects of marriage, inheritance, intestacy and the education of children;[28] and crime and punishment.[29] This is a long list but it is important to include because it highlights the process of law-making in the kingdom as a whole. Detailed and wide-ranging laws could be issued centrally by the king and adopted by *seigneurs justiciers* in their domains.

There were of course laws which applied specifically in royal domain. The author of the 'Livre de la Cour des Bourgeois' attributed the origin of several laws to legislation carried out by the kings of Jerusalem in the twelfth century. King Baldwin I (1100–1118), we are informed, established the laws of *cop aparent*, that is to say physical assault against another person.[30] His successor King Baldwin II (1118–1131) introduced laws on inheritance and disinheritance, setting out twelve reasons why parents could disinherit their children legitimately and seven reasons why children could disinherit their parents.[31] King Fulk (1131–1142) ordained a law on the ownership of hunting birds.[32] And King Amalric made legislation on the jurisdictional competence of the *Cour de la Chaine*.[33] He also established a law relating to adultery and murder within a burgess marriage.[34] This legislation applied, foremost, to burgesses living within the boundaries of royal jurisdiction. The fact that these laws were described in the 'Livre de la Cour des Bourgeois' of Acre, suggests they were in force in this royal city and elsewhere when the law book was being written in the mid-thirteenth century. It is, furthermore, an indication of both the continuity and endurance of royal legislation that laws issued in the early decades of the twelfth century should remain in use almost a century

---

[23] Kausler, pp. 68–9, 222–4, 225–6, 228–9, 231–2, 239–40 (cf. Beugnot, 'Livre des assises', pp. 38, 138–9, 139–40, 141–2, 143, 148–9).

[24] Kausler, pp. 242–3 (cf. Beugnot, 'Livre des assises', p.152).

[25] Kausler, pp. 70–71, 87–8, 255 (cf. Beugnot, 'Livre des assises', pp. 39, 52–3, 162–3).

[26] Kausler, pp. 90–91 (cf. Beugnot, 'Livre des assises', pp. 54–6).

[27] Kausler, p. 327 (cf. Beugnot, 'Livre des assises', p. 209).

[28] Kausler, pp. 149, 179–80, 182–3, 202–203, 204, 205, 211–12, 217–18, 240, 269–70 (cf. Beugnot, 'Livre des assises', pp. 91, 111–12, 113, 125, 126, 127, 131–2, 135, 149–50, 170).

[29] Kausler, pp. 289–90, 290–91, 314–15, 323–4, 332–3 (cf. Beugnot II, pp. 184, 185, 200, 206, 212).

[30] Kausler, p. 311 (cf. Beugnot, 'Livre des assises', p. 198).

[31] Kausler, pp. 266–70 (cf. Beugnot, 'Livre des assises', pp. 169–70).

[32] Kausler, pp. 305–307 (cf. Beugnot, 'Livre des assises', pp.194–5).

[33] Kausler, p. 75 (cf. Beugnot, 'Livre des assises', pp. 42–3).

[34] Kausler, pp. 341–2 (cf. Beugnot, 'Livre des assises', pp. 218–19).

later. The preservation of individual laws and perhaps compilation of royal legislation in the latter half of the twelfth century may have been the basis of the law book of Acre.

The point should be made that the kings of Jerusalem did not require the consent of their subjects when formulating laws. Nevertheless, in the twelfth century the drawing up of royal legislation developed essentially as a dual process involving the king, or his officials, and representatives of the burgess class, who collectively conceived, amended and executed law, and tacitly agreed that this form of law-making was preferable to any other. This facet of public power drew the burgess community within the sphere of seigneurial decision-making as advisors and co-signatories. The author of the 'Livre de la Cour des Bourgeois' could look back to this period as important in shaping the legislative basis of the burgess community in Acre. But this dual process was transgressed when King Baldwin[35] issued a law without the advice of his burgesses, instructing that those who did not keep clean the street outside their houses were liable to a fine of seven and a half *solidi*. The substance of the law itself was inconsequential, but the manner in which this royal ordinance was passed 'sans le conseill de ses homes et de ses borgeis de la cité', was symbolically significant.[36] It is not entirely clear, however, why the king should set such a legislative precedence, unless following some kind of disagreement he wished to demonstrate through his actions that the involvement of burgesses in the process of law-making was not mandatory but merely by invitation. In other words, the king chose to seek advice (*conseill*) and burgesses became accustomed to giving it. When in 1120 King Baldwin II desired to exempt the burgesses of Jerusalem from tax they paid at the city gates when bringing in foodstuffs, he drew up a written document of the privilege counter-signed by representatives of the burgess community, and according to William of Tyre, sealed with the royal seal and proclaimed to have validity in perpetuity.[37] *Conseill* in this respect had become an intrinsic part of the process of legislation in Jerusalem.

Notably, the law on street cleaning remained in use in thirteenth-century Acre. It was still a duty of the viscount to proclaim it publicly, although he had freedom whether or not to enforce the fine: the author of the 'Livre de la Cour des Bourgeois' advised pardoning anyone infringing the law from paying the seven and a half *solidi*.[38] Evidently, the *Cour des Bourgeois* did not have the right to overturn a royal ordinance once it had been issued. Thus, on the one hand, the

---

35 The law book does not state whether the king was Baldwin I (1100–1118), Baldwin II (1118–1130), Baldwin III (1146–1160), Baldwin IV (1173–1182), or Baldwin V (1183–1186).

36 Kausler, pp. 350–51 (cf. Beugnot, 'Livre des assises', p. 225).

37 Bresc-Bautier, no. 27, p. 89; William of Tyre, p. 565; Fulcher of Chartres, pp. 636–7.

38 Kausler, pp. 350–51 (cf. Beugnot, 'Livre des assises', p. 225).

continued implementation of a contentious twelfth-century ordinance may be interpreted as meaning burgesses could object to its retention, but voiced their objection from a position of weakness, because ultimately it was the decision of the king whether to seek their advice or not. But, on the other hand, this allusion to the development of legislation by a reliable source, hints at the relative influence of burgesses in their relationship with the king in the first years of the kingdom's existence. Additionally, the perceived violation of dual process seems to have been exceptional and was cited by the author of the 'Livre de la Cour des Bourgeois' because it reflected the self-confidence of the burgess community in reasserting its legislative authority. It was reaffirmation of the powers of the *Cour des Bourgeois*. A law may have carried the weight of royal authorization, but it was the court which interpreted the legislation as it saw fit.

There are strong indications the legislative process in the lordships mirrored that in royal domain. But we should not assume legislation was primarily urban in character. On the contrary, law-making coexisted in the much smaller rural Latin villages. In the *ville neuve* of Bethgibelin, to take one example, the Hospitallers acted as legislators over their settlers and were described as having their own 'customs'. It would, therefore, be a mistake to place sole emphasis on the city burgesses because from the inception of the kingdom this class of people was never only under the jurisdiction of secular *Cours des Bourgeois*. Incontrovertibly, the courts of the Church contributed significantly to the management of land and to the jurisdiction of *borgesies*. Church institutions such as the Holy Sepulchre settled some of the earliest rural settlements, established their own courts and formulated their own laws to deal with matters concerning the burgess tenants of their *borgesies*. A Latin community was established in Magna Mahumeria in the 1120s, or perhaps as early as 1115.[39] And so widespread was the influence of the rules prevailing there that they came to be known as the 'customs of Mahumeria'.

Whether in the city or rural village, a *seigneur justicier* possessed the right of *justise*, meaning that he both exercised jurisdiction over fief-holders and burgesses living in his domain as well as legislated. On this point of legislative activity there are intriguing references in the fourteenth-century Nicosian law-book, the 'Livre contrefais', to the existence of several Latin 'livres des Assizes' of the kingdom of Jerusalem.[40] The inference is that the author had knowledge of, or direct access to, not only the *assises* of Acre but also of other cities. When precisely these laws were compiled or copied remains a mystery, but their existence is testimony of legislative activity throughout the kingdom. After all, from the twelfth century cities regularly based their burgess laws on precedent, and the charters they issued often cited the well known customs of other cities and Latin villages in the kingdom. This contributed to an exchange in legal ideas, a diffusion of law and

[39] Ellenblum, *Frankish Rural Settlement*, p. 73; Fulcher of Chartres, pp.731–2. See also C. Kohler (ed.),'Chartes de l'abbaye de Notre-Dame de la Vallée de Josaphat en Terre Sainte (1108–1291). Analyse et extraits', in *ROL*, VII (1899), p. 30.

[40] On this point, see below, pp. 59–60.

custom either in written form or by word of mouth. We should not readily assume that in almost two hundred years of Latin rule, only Acre managed to compile a *livre* of its laws. Naturally, the city has attracted most attention among historians, but its development in legislative terms, and its formulation and codification of laws, should not be interpreted as unique, but rather as a model of what was probably taking place in other Latin cities. The general impression is that legally and institutionally, if perhaps not commercially, the thirteenth century was a period of unprecedented burgess achievements which compared favourably, if not surpassed, developments in burgess jurisdiction and legislation in contemporary Europe.

Law-Making and General Assemblies

References to burgesses are progressively more common in sources of the twelfth century. They are more involved in the legal processes which shape their communities. They manage to exert greater public power on the way their lordships are administered. The overall impression is of a class more assertive of its rights. At ad hoc gatherings burgesses continued to advise the king or lord in the drawing up of legislation, and to give *consilium* when property was being conceded. A general assembly, also described as a *concilium*, *parlement* or *conventus publicus*, summoned secular and ecclesiastical legislators from all Latin communities to discuss matters of common interest and to pass laws. It was usual for the king or regent to attend – as suzerain over all subjects inside and outside the boundaries of royal domain – as well as his tenants-in-chief, fief-holders, representatives of the military orders and confraternities, churchmen and burgesses.[41] The communities of fief-holders and burgesses were also represented by members of the High Court and the *Cour des Bourgeois* of the city in which the assembly was convened. The decisions of these assemblies, as those agreed at Nablus in 1120 and Jerusalem in 1183, were written down and copies made. As the kingdom's inhabitants, they agreed a common course of action and endeavoured to unify their objectives and ideals. Of course on the finer points of law, the decisions of these assemblies were not binding on the *seigneurs justiciers*, as each lordship had its own laws which took primacy. Nevertheless, there were matters which affected them all. In the general tax of 1183, King Baldwin IV stressed that agreement over taxation had been reached with the acquiescence of all Latin

---

[41] Riley-Smith, *The Feudal Nobility and the Kingdom of Jerusalem*, pp. 194–8; J.S.C. Riley-Smith, 'A Note on Confraternities in the Latin Kingdom of Jerusalem', *BIHR*, XLIV (1971), 303–304. For other general assemblies, see William of Tyre, p. 853 (Nazareth, 1160); p. 882 (Nablus, 1167); p. 979 (Jerusalem, 1177); p. 1026 (Jerusalem, 1182); p. 1063 (Acre, 1184); 'Documents relatifs à la successibilité au trône et à la régence', in *RHC Lois*, II, p. 415 (Acre, 1268); 'L'Estoire d'Eracles Empereur et la conqueste de la terre d'outremer', I, p. 474 (Acre, 1276).

Christians, nobles and non-nobles alike.'[42] Burgesses, it should be added, gave formal agreement to important exemptions and donations. As earlier mentioned, in 1120, Baldwin II exempted those entering the gates of Jerusalem from taxes on certain cereals and vegetables, and a number of burgesses counter-signed the royal charter of approval.[43] When the king introduced a law in Acre concerning where in the *fonde*, the marketplace, indigenous Christians could trade and the amount of sales tax they were obliged to pay, he did so with the agreement of his vassals, the merchant communes and the burgesses.[44] The Latin rural settlement of Bethgibelin was given to the order of St John with the agreement of the burgesses of Jerusalem;[45] one may compare this gift with Raymond of Tripoli's donation to the Hospitallers of Crac des Chevaliers (1142) which was done 'nutu et consilio burgensium'.[46] As a further example, Walter Brisebarre, lord of Beirut's eleemosynary donation to the order of St Lazarus (1164) was witnessed by 'all the knights and burgesses of the city of Beirut'.[47]

The purpose and function of a *parlement* were demonstrated at one of the earliest assemblies convened in Nablus in 1120. The twenty-five canons of this assembly reveal that it dealt principally with ecclesiastical affairs and was unlike the councils of Jerusalem and Acre which were attended by laymen and dealt exclusively with temporal affairs. It was chiefly a gathering of Church leaders also attended by lay people. This description, notwithstanding, the Council of Nablus may be considered a precursor and a model for later general assemblies. Kedar pointed out that in the early twelfth century the term *concilium* was used in Europe and the Latin East to designate general assemblies irrespective of whether they were convened to discuss ecclesiastical or temporal affairs,[48] and in Mayer's opinion, the assembly at Nablus should be classed as both a *parlement* and a synod.[49] The assembly, significantly, was convened by the king and some of the twenty-five canons drawn up were concerned with temporal issues. It was, in the words of William of Tyre, a 'curia generalis', a term he used to describe later assemblies which were convened to discuss temporal matters but were attended by churchmen.[50]

---

42 William of Tyre, p. 1044.

43 Bresc-Bautier, no. 27, p. 89.

44 Kausler, p. 282 (cf. Beugnot, 'Livre des assises', p. 178).

45 Delaville Le Roulx, *Cartulaire général*, no. 116, p. 98.

46 Delaville Le Roulx, *Cartulaire général*, no. 144, pp. 117–18; Riley-Smith, *The Knights of St John in Jerusalem and Cyprus, c.1050–1310* (London, 1967), p. 464, note 1; J. Richard, *Le Comté de Tripoli sous la dynastie toulousaine, 1102–1187* (Paris, 1945), p. 81.

47 A. de Marsy (ed.), 'Fragment d'un cartulaire de l'Ordre de Saint-Lazare, en Terre Sainte', in *AOL* II (1884), no. 21, p. 139.

48 Kedar, 'On the Origins of the Earliest Laws of Frankish Jerusalem', pp. 326–7.

49 Mayer, 'The Concordat of Nablus', pp. 531–3. See also Kedar, 'On the Origins of the Earliest Laws of Frankish Jerusalem', pp. 326–7.

50 William of Tyre, pp. 757, 760, 786. An assembly of laymen and churchmen, for instance, held in Nablus in 1167, and which agreed that a tax of 10 per cent should be levied

At Nablus King Baldwin II, the patriarch of Jerusalem, Warmundus, and leading members of the Church and laity dispensed twenty-five canons dealing with issues of adultery, sodomy, marriage, theft and miscegenation. The assembly set out punishments for particular crimes and decreed whether a case should be heard in a secular or ecclesiastical court.[51] It has been suggested by Kedar that there were marked similarities between some of these canons and Byzantine legal writings of the eighth century, in particular the *Ecloga*.[52] The new laws were written down and copies deposited in the archives of many churches in the kingdom. William of Tyre, for instance, (writing in the 1170s–1180s) had available to him a copy of the text.[53] But were such laws subsequently enforced by *seigneurs justiciers* in their lordships? The twenty-third canon, for example, prescribed severe punishment for those accused of theft; a thief judged to have stolen possessions valued at more than one besant would have a hand or foot amputated or an eye cut out.[54] However, in 1168 in the Latin community of Bethgibelin which was under the jurisdiction of the order of St John, a law established by the Hospitallers to deal with thieves instructed merely that they should be placed under the authority of the master.[55] I have discussed the subject of secular legislation by ecclesiastical institutions in more detail elsewhere.[56] Suffice to say at this point, that legal discrepancy between Nablus and Bethgibelin suggests laws agreed at general assemblies were not necessarily enforced uniformly in the kingdom of Jerusalem.[57]

If the Council of Nablus was mainly concerned with ecclesiastical affairs, the *parlement* held in Jerusalem in 1183 was summoned to deal with the issue of a general tax. William of Tyre relates how a written account of the assembly had been made and it was included verbatim in his chronicle,[58] providing yet more evidence that in the twelfth century written records were used to promulgate the decisions of *parlements*, and that these records were probably kept in the church

---

from all land belonging to the Church in order to pay for King Amalric's campaign to Egypt, was described by William as a 'curia generalis'; William of Tyre, p. 882.

51 The canons of Nablus have been re-edited by Kedar in 'On the Origins of the Earliest Laws of Frankish Jerusalem', 'appendix', pp. 331–4. The surviving text is derived from the copy made for the church at Sidon. See Edbury, 'Law and Custom in the Latin East', p. 74.

52 Kedar,'On the Origins of the Earliest Laws of Frankish Jerusalem', pp. 313–20.

53 William of Tyre, pp. 563–4.

54 Kedar, 'On the Origins of the Earliest Laws of Frankish Jerusalem', 'appendix', p. 334.

55 Delaville Le Roulx, *Cartulaire général*, no. 399, p. 273.

56 See below, pp. 182–95.

57 Kedar comes to a different conclusion and views Bethgibelin as an exception to the rule of the uniform enforcement of the canons of Nablus in the kingdom of Jerusalem; 'On the Origins of the Earliest Laws of Frankish Jerusalem', pp. 310–11.

58 William of Tyre, pp. 1044–5. See B.Z. Kedar, 'The General Tax of 1183 in the Crusading Kingdom of Jerusalem: Innovation or Adaption?' *EHR*, 89 (1979): 339–45.

archives of certain cities. After much deliberation, we are informed, the *principes regni* agreed that a poll tax should be levied for the common benefit of the whole kingdom. To facilitate the collection of tax, the kingdom of Jerusalem was divided into two administrative regions. The tax collected from cities and villages situated between Haifa and Beirut had to be sent to Acre where it would be kept in a box with three locks. One key was entrusted to the archbishop of Tyre, another to Joscelin of Courtenay, the royal seneschal, and another to the appointed tax collectors of Acre. The tax, on the other hand, collected from cities and villages situated between Haifa and Jerusalem had to be sent to Jerusalem and kept in a similar box. The only persons with access to this box were the patriarch, the prior of the church of the Holy Sepulchre, the castellan of the Tower of David and the tax collectors appointed for Jerusalem. It was decided that in every city burgesses, indigenous Christians, Muslims and Jews, who were worth more than one hundred besants, should pay a tax of 1 per cent of the value of their movable goods – including anything which they had given as a loan – and 2 per cent of their income. Those, however, who were worth less than one hundred besants had to pay *pro foco* (hearth-money) one besant. Each city had to appoint four trustworthy tax collectors described by William of Tyre as *cives*, or city inhabitants, suggesting they were burgesses. It is reasonable to assume that the appointed men were of non-noble status considering burgesses fulfilled a similar tax collecting role as financial officers of the crown in Cyprus in the mid-fourteenth century, and from the account of Leontios Makhairas, it may be conjectured that the island's poll tax (*testagium*), introduced at the end of the thirteenth century, was administered by burgesses.[59]

William of Tyre's account of the council of Jerusalem illustrates how in times of need, royal government with typically the agreement of fief-holders, alongside members of the High Court, churchmen, burgesses and jurors of the *Cour des Bourgeois*, centralised administration and legislation, and formulated general policy, in this case taxation. Accounts detailing the decisions of such meetings were written and copies made for promulgation. Regardless of the fact that there probably existed no general code of law in the kingdom, *parlements* were summoned to propose laws of common interest pertaining to secular and ecclesiastical jurisdiction. That said, *seigneurs justiciers* attended the general meetings as legislators in their own right. There is no question that they willingly participated in the Jerusalem assembly conscious of the need to shore up the defences of a kingdom with inherent military weaknesses. They accepted city inhabitants including burgesses should carry the burden of taxation, and rather than each lord keeping hold of the money collected from his domain, acknowledged that a centralised treasury could fund more sensibly the defences of the kingdom. But I return to the earlier point, whether *seigneurs justiciers* could be compelled to

---

59 Leontios Makhairas, *Chronicle*, ed. and trans. R.M. Dawkins (2 vols, Oxford, 1932), vol. 2, p. 197. See also P.W. Edbury, *The Kingdom of Cyprus and the Crusades, 1191–1374* (Cambridge, 1991), p. 195.

enforce laws of property and person in their lordships as agreed by assembly is debatable.

The *parlement* remained an essential forum for coordination in the thirteenth century. The surviving account of the *parlement* at Acre in 1251 is further testimony of the process of general legislation in the kingdom. It is a description, quintessentially, of the structure of debate, the method of argumentation and compromise which prefaced the introduction of new laws. The meeting was held at the house of the lord of Beirut and was attended by John, lord of Arsuf and constable of the kingdom, members of the High Court and the royal *Cour des Bourgeois* of Acre. It is quite possible the well informed author of the 'Livre contrefais' had before him an account of the Acre *parlement* of 1251 when composing his law book. An existing written account would have been in keeping with twelfth-century practice of recording the decisions of assemblies. Of interest to the Nicosian author were the rather arcane tenets of court procedure discussed at the Acre assembly. According to his source, in the presence of the city High Court and court of burgesses, John of Arsuf spoke of the need to write down everything which was said and done in the courts of secular justice.[60] This was the main focus of the *parlement* whose members agreed new procedure was necessary, but Philip of Montfort, lord of Tyre and Toron fearing 'recort de cort' would be diminished, argued that the memory of the court should have precedence over written records.[61] In other words, registers should be consulted only as a last resort. This resolute insistence is difficult to understand especially if the source of concern was the authenticity and trustworthiness of written records; the court registers were, after all, to be kept by a public authority. But objectors who viewed written evidence with an element of distrust and favoured memory as the definitive method of establishing truth were not uncommon in the Middle Ages.[62] Philip of Montfort, it seems, convinced the lord of Arsuf and others present of the validity of his argument, but it was decided only in appropriate cases could memory have precedence over written record.[63] In fact, the importance of memory in judgement-making survived in the *Cour des Bourgeois* of Nicosia well into the fourteenth century: the 'Livre contrefais' refers on several occasions to decisions being made according to 'les escrit ou le recort de la court'.[64]

The *parlement* of Acre had the authority to propose new legislation but ultimately it required royal approval. At the time of the *parlement*, Henry I of Cyprus was regent of the kingdom of Jerusalem, but since the arrival of Saint Louis in Palestine (1250), the authority of the regent had been usurped. Louis was de facto ruler of the kingdom and the *parlement* was required to seek his approval

---

60 'Livre contrefais', pp. 247–8.

61 'Livre contrefais', p. 248.

62 M.T. Clanchy, *From Memory to Written Record. England 1066–1307* (London, 1979), pp. 232–6.

63 'Livre contrefais', p. 249.

64 'Livre contrefais', pp. 296, 299, 302, 309.

for its new proposals, but as he was absent from Acre fortifying the city of Caesarea, it was determined that agreement on the introduction of written records should be postponed until his return. If, indeed, Louis gave his approval in person, then this could not have taken place until Lent 1254; according to John of Joinville, he had up to then been fortifying the cities of Jaffa and Sidon, and returned to Acre for only a few weeks in preparation for his journey back to France.[65] Eventually, however, the *parlement* reconvened to ordain the new law as well as the amendment proposed by Philip of Montfort, and 'par generau conseill et le assent et l'aveement des sages, fut ordené escrivain et livres en la basse court'.[66] Interestingly, the law established an *escrivein* and registers only in the *Cour des Bourgeois* and it was not until several decades later that the High Court underwent similar changes. When this was done Henry II was king of Jerusalem and Cyprus,[67] suggesting the court began keeping written records sometime after 1285. It seems that deep-seated distrust of the written word persisted among certain elements of the nobility for several years after the innovation of record keeping in the *Cour des Bourgeois*.

Law-Making in the Thirteenth Century – The Livre de la Cour des Bourgeois

The advent of registers in the *Cour des Bourgeois* takes us up to the mid-thirteenth century, a period which for legal historians was chiefly characterised by the institutional and jurisdictional developments taking place in Acre. The existence of the laws of this city has, undeniably, heavily influenced our understanding of the burgess class. Consequently, developments in the other cities where *Cours des Bourgeois* similarly existed, written records of court judgements were kept – as agreed at the *parlement* of 1251 – *assises* legislated and customs practised from the twelfth century onwards have been largely ignored. What is more, although Prawer believed the 'Livre de la Cour des Bourgeois' dealt inclusively with the 'whole stratum of burgesses of the kingdom' because 'there were no local urban customs',[68] it was not a general burgess law book of the kingdom of Jerusalem. So we cannot use it to generalise about burgess laws and court procedures. There were other burgess laws and even law books which have not survived but which were alluded to by the Cypriot author of the 'Livre contrefais'. It is quite evident the Cypriot author was not intimating the existence simply of individual acts of legislation, but acknowledging the composition of other *livres*. The argument that cities like Tyre and Caesarea had their own law books is not inconceivable. Indeed, judging from the kinds of laws the author of the 'Livre contrefais' extracted from

---

65 John of Joinville, *Histoire de Saint Louis*, ed. M. Natalis de Wailly (Paris, 1868), p. 220.

66 'Livre contrefais', p. 249.

67 'Livre contrefais', p. 249.

68 Prawer, *Crusader Institutions*, p. 372.

these *livres*, they covered various aspects of burgess jurisdiction, ranging from issues on the alienation of *heritages*, inheritance and escheat, to legal procedure and high justice. It also seems apparent that the author of the 'Livre de la Cour des Bourgeois' had knowledge of procedure in not only the *Cour des Bourgeois* in Acre, but also Jerusalem, Jaffa, Bethlehem and Ibelin.

Of course, Acre in the thirteenth century was secure defensively and well off commercially, and we would naturally expect a well established burgess community to flourish in these favourable conditions. It had enjoyed several decades of stability and continuity, unlike Jerusalem which after its loss in 1187 was in Latin hands for a final time in 1229, following a peace treaty between Emperor Frederick II and the Ayyubid Sultan al-Kamil. The history of burgess Acre and its laws should be considered within this context of rapidly changing fortunes for the Latin kingdom. The city's surviving law book is a unique source, undeniably, both as an insight into the life of its inhabitants, and as a work which, if read correctly, provides insight into the workings of Latin jurisdiction. From its pages we are able to construct a picture more complete than anywhere else in the kingdom, of a society steadfast in its belief that law promoted higher cultural and religious values, and resolutely safeguarded the rules defining the status of person and property. What we read in the 'Livre des assises de la Cour des Bourgeois' is reliably a reflection of society in Acre in the first half of the thirteenth century, and perhaps beyond. It was not, as some may argue, a private treatise with little or no contemporary relevance, but, as its name implies, a book of the court of burgesses of the city, a public work – of which at this time there may have been more than one copy – preserved by this legal burgess body and consulted by its jurors. It was not, essentially, a snapshot of legislation in any particular period, but compiled over a broad length of time perhaps by more than one author.

The original manuscript (or manuscripts) of the 'Livre des assises de la Cour des Bourgeois', also known as the 'Liber de justitia et jure',[69] has not survived, although there are seven known versions written in French, Italian and Greek and dating from the fourteenth, fifteenth and sixteenth centuries.[70] A copy of the Venice French manuscript was written in 1436 by Perrin Hémy and served as a model for an Italian translation of 1531 carried out on the orders of the Republic of Venice.[71] The other French manuscript of Munich was believed by Grandclaude to have been written between 1315 and 1317 by an official of the *Cour des Bourgeois*

---

69 This is the title given in the rubric of the first chapter of the law book – 'Incipit liber de justicia et jure'; Kausler, p. 43 (cf. Beugnot. 'Livre des assises', p. 19).

70 The Italian and Greek versions are incomplete and are therefore of less importance than the French manuscripts in Venice and Munich. Manuscript Fr.19026 contains only the first 78 chapters of the law book.

71 A sixteenth-century copy of this official Italian translation is contained in Ms Italian 29, published by P. Canciani, *Barbarorum Leges Antiquae*, vol. 2 (Venice, 1783).

in Nicosia.[72] Grandclaude cleverly demonstrated that of the two versions the Munich manuscript was closer to the original. He convincingly argued, for instance, the 'Livre de la Cour des Bourgeois' had originally been written in chapters and that these divisions had been more accurately reproduced by the copyist of the Munich manuscript.[73] Moreover, the twenty Latin chapters which appear in the Munich but not in the Venice manuscript were contained in the original law book.[74] He maintained that the 'Livre de la Cour des Bourgeois' had been written in French by a single author because, in his opinion, there can be distinguished a unique style of writing throughout the law book.[75] Furthermore, he suggested the law book had been composed in the 1240s.[76] But it is important to stress Grandclaude was principally concerned with demonstrating the superiority of the Munich manuscript and his treatment of the actual text was only superficial. A closer inspection of the 'Livre de la Cour des Bourgeois' does uncover evidence of a single author probably responsible for writing the bulk of the text, but, importantly, the law book describes certain developments in the royal *Cour des Bourgeois* in Acre which could not have come into effect until after 1251, and includes certain laws which could not have been legislated until the 1260s. For this reason, it may be argued that either the author of the 'Livre de la Cour des Bourgeois' was writing sometime after 1251 or there were later compilers of the law book.

In his introduction to the 'Livre de la Cour des Bourgeois', Beugnot suggested the law book had been written during the first half of the reign of Baldwin IV, between the years 1173 and 1180.[77] He established the *dies ad quem* as 1187 because certain chapters in the law book indicated Jerusalem was still in the hands of the Christians and had not yet fallen to Saladin. In a counter argument Grandclaude pointed out Jerusalem also belonged to the Christians between 1229 and 1244, and that it was more likely the laws were written during this period. With greater precision he narrowed down the date to between 1243 and 1244; in chapter 267 appears the phrase 'la dame de la ville' – this, he conjectured, referred to Alice who was proclaimed regent of the kingdom on 5 June 1243.[78] In further

---

72 Grandclaude, *Etude critique sur les livres des assises de Jérusalem*, pp. 33, 35. Kausler's edition of the 'Livre de la Cour des Bourgeois' (1839) was based on the Munich manuscript, while Beugnot's edition in the *Recueil des Historiens des Croisades, Lois* (1843), was based on the Venice manuscript. The latter was also used by Victor Foucher in his edition, 'Assises du Royaume de Jérusalem', part 1, 'Assises des bourgeois' (Rennes, 1840).

73 Grandclaude, *Etude critique sur les livres des assises de Jérusalem*, pp. 55–6.

74 Grandclaude, *Etude critique sur les livres des assises de Jérusalem*, pp. 60–61. Beugnot beleived these Latin chapters to be interpolations.

75 Grandclaude, *Etude critique sur les livres des assises de Jérusalem*, pp. 63, 64.

76 Grandclaude, *Etude critique sur les livres des assises de Jérusalem*, p. 70.

77 A.A. Beugnot, Introduction to *RHC Lois*, II, p. xxxvii.

78 Kausler, p. 324 (cf. Beugnot, 'Livre des assises', p. 207). There has been expressed a note of caution about extrapolating from this single chapter a date of composition for the

support of his theory, he cited a chapter which mentioned the 'livre dou conquest', otherwise known as the *Estoire d'Eracles Empereur*, a translation of the first twenty-two books of William of Tyre's *Historia Hierosolymitana*, written at the beginning of the thirteenth century.[79] While generally agreeing with Grandclaude that the 'Livre de la Cour des Bourgeois' was being written in the 1240s, I do, however, disagree with some of the arguments which led to this conclusion. For instance, while it is generally accepted Acre had become capital of the kingdom in the thirteenth century, his assertion that this fact may be derived from the law book is not convincing.[80] He cited chapter 140 as evidence that whereas Acre is revealed as having a viscount presiding over its *Cour des Bourgeois*, Jerusalem, contrastingly, has only a *bailli*, an official of lesser standing.[81] But Grandclaude failed to notice in chapter 4 viscount and *bailli* are used interchangeably suggesting the two officers were of equal standing.[82] In fact, the 'Livre contrefais' mentions a 'bailly de Famagouste',[83] whereas a charter of 1300 refers to a 'vicecomes Famaguste'.[84] Evidence that the title of the two officers were used interchangeably may also be found in the rubric of a chapter concerning law in this coastal city: 'Ce sont les chozes et l'ordenement que le bailly de Famagouste doit oyr par court, et le visconte aussi'.[85]

Grandclaude also drew attention to a law on marriage and consanguinity which could have only come into effect after the Lateran Council of 1215. According to this chapter a third degree was a minimum requirement for marrying blood relatives,[86] but he failed to explain why a preceding chapter contains the pre-1215 law of consanguinity which extends to the seventh degree marriage between blood relatives.[87] The fact two conflicting laws were included is puzzling, and it is difficult to understand why an author working on the 'Livre de la Cour des Bourgeois' after 1215 would write down a law no longer in force. We can make sense of this apparent contradiction if we accept the 'Livre de la Cour des

---

whole law book; see G. Recoura, 'Les Assises de Jérusalem. A propos d'un livre récent', p. 158.

79 Grandclaude, *Etude critique sur les livres des assises de Jérusalem*, pp. 67–8.

80 Grandclaude, *Etude critique sur les livres des assises de Jérusalem*, pp. 66–7.

81 Kausler, p. 159 (cf. Beugnot, 'Livre des assises', p. 98); Grandclaude, *Etude critique sur les livres des assises de Jérusalem*, p. 67.

82 Kausler, pp. 46–7 (cf. Beugnot, 'Livre des assises', p. 21). On the possibility that the titles *bailli* and viscount were used interchangeably in the principality of Antioch see Cahen, *La Syrie du nord*, p. 461.

83 'Livre contrefais', p. 323.

84 C. Desimoni (ed.),'Actes passés à Famagouste de 1299–1301 par devant le notaire génois Lamberto di Sambuceto', in *AOL*, II (1884), pp. 63–4. For evidence of the post of *bailli* in Limassol in the 1290s, see M. Michelet (ed.), *Procès des Templiers*, ed. M. Michelet (2 vols, Paris, 1841–51), vol. 1, p. 223.

85 'Livre contrefais', p. 323.

86 Kausler, p. 177 (cf. Beugnot, 'Livre des assises', p. 109).

87 Kausler, p. 175 (cf. Beugnot, 'Livre des assises', p. 108).

Bourgeois' was a compilation, written possibly by more than one author, in which perhaps was preserved a law written before 1215. This theory could also explain why the law book contained at least one other example where two corresponding laws were written down even though one had been superseded by the other. In one chapter outlining the procedure of sale, a law compelled the vendor to pay the court one mark of silver and the buyer three besants.[88] Elsewhere, however, it was stated the buyer was obliged to pay only one besant and one *rabouin*.[89] The figure of three besants corresponds to the amount mentioned in the charter of 1269 when Pelerin Coquerel sold a *borgesie* to Hugh Revel, the master of the Hospitallers. The court received three besants 'por la raison dou dit acha'.[90] The law concerning sales tax may have been revised sometime in the 1260s.

Viewed as a compilation there is further reason to believe the 'Livre de la Cour des Bourgeois' was being written after 1244. Chapters 161 and 283 which refer to an 'escrivein de la cort',[91] must have been incorporated sometime after 1251 when it was proposed at a *parlement* in Acre that the *Cour des Bourgeois* should have an *escrivein*.[92] Indeed, the first surviving charter to mention this official – 'Renier nostre escrivein' – was drawn up in Acre in 1269.[93] Additionally, in one of the chapters describing the duties of an *escrivein*, a discussion on the validity of charters alludes to written registers which the Acre *parlement* of 1251 also proposed should be kept by the court. It may be inferred from a previous chapter that only charters bearing the seal of a *seigneur justicier* were legally binding. Now when, for example, a sale was authorised in the royal *Cour des Bourgeois* and a record of it made in its register, this was deemed sufficient proof of the transaction, and, therefore, any charter which was drawn up by the court subsequently did not require the seal of the king to be valid.[94] Beugnot interpreted the passage as meaning written records were kept in the *Cour des Bourgeois*, but failed to relate this to the question of dating the law book.[95] He did, however, draw attention to the charter of 1269 which seems to corroborate his reading of the passage. According to the document, the order of St John had purchased from Pelerin Coquerel a house situated in Acre and the transaction recorded in the register of the *Cour des Bourgeois*. Following a request from the Hospitallers, the viscount, Hue de Hadestel, drew up this charter as a legally-binding warranty of the sale, and in

88 Kausler, p. 66 (cf. Beugnot, 'Livre des assises', p. 36).

89 Kausler, p. 350 (cf. Beugnot, 'Livre des assises', p. 224).

90 Delaville Le Roulx, *Cartulaire général*, no. 3334, p. 196.

91 Kausler, pp. 160, 343 (cf. Beugnot, 'Livre des assises', pp. 99, 219). A distinction is made in the law book between an *escrivein* of the *Cour des Bourgeois*, a notary (*notaire*), and the 'escrivein sarasinois ou fransois' who were employed as scribes and interpreters in the ports of the 'fonde' and the 'chaine' (Kausler, pp. 160, 344–5, cf. Beugnot, 'Livre des assises', pp. 99, 220).

92 'Livre contrefais', p. 246.

93 Delaville Le Roulx, *Cartulaire général*, no. 3334, p. 196.

94 Kausler, p. 159 (cf. Beugnot, 'Livre des assises', p. 98).

95 Beugnot II, 'Livre des assises', p. 99, note a.

conformity with the rules laid down in the 'Livre de la Cour des Bourgeois', the valid document did not carry the seal of the king but only that of the court.[96] In conclusion, the chapters concerning written registers and charters were included in the law book sometime after 1251.

But is it possible to give a date as to when the principal author, and subsequent authors, of the 'Livre de la Cour des Bourgeois' were writing? Although the evidence so far presented suggests the law book had begun to be compiled before 1215, and that quite possibly the principal author was writing in the latter decades of the twelfth century, I am still inclined to believe the main author of the work was compiling laws between 1229 and 1244 when Jerusalem was in Christian hands. A third hand, however, may be detected in those laws which originated in the second half of the thirteenth century, possibly in the 1250s. Indeed, it is possible that new compilations of the law book were being made in Acre after this date. John of Ibelin writing in the 1260s, made reference in his treatise to the 'livre des assises de la Court de la Borgesie', but his statement that it contained the oath of office sworn by jurors of the burgess court cannot be corroborated.[97] To my knowledge the oath is not in the law book, and appears only in the 'Livre contrefais' of Nicosia.[98] It may be John had a copy of the 'Livre de la Cour des Bourgeois' which contained it.

The 'Livre de la Cour des Bourgeois' is a detailed account of the composition and procedure of the *Cour des Bourgeois*, in particular the duties of the presiding head of the court, the viscount and of the burgess jurors. The law book differentiates between who could and could not plead in cases of litigation, and includes a section on the rights natives had to sue in court. It also sets out the ways in which the *Cour des Bourgeois* dealt with misdemeanours, whether by imposing fines, sentences of imprisonment or physical punishments. Within this judicial framework, the legal standing of the native population is defined in reference to manumission and the status of freed slaves. A number of chapters, moreover, deal with the rules governing the sale, purchase and lease of *borgesies*; with the rent owed by tenants of *borgesies* annually; and with the lending of money and the pledging of property. The possession of movable and immovable property as vifgage, and the legal rights and responsibilities of a lender and borrower are treated at length. The law book also deals with marriage and the legal rights of a husband, wife, children and relatives in issues of inheritance, dowry, illegitimacy, the making of wills and intestacy. And information is included about two other courts dealing primarily with commercial cases in Acre, the *Cour de la Fonde* and the *Cour de la Chaine*. All in all, it is a law book of impressive scope and discourse. It builds up a picture of city life, and, in its construct, bears out the opinion that in the thirteenth century the system of burgess justice in this city was as well formed as any urban system in contemporary Europe. Its chapters delineate

96 Delaville Le Roulx, *Cartulaire général*, no. 3334, p. 196.

97 John of Ibelin, p. 52.

98 'Livre contrefais', pp. 237–8.

the correct procedures of jurisdiction, set out the rights of burgesses in Acre, and, above all else, mark out the circumstances under which men and women had recourse to the *Cour des Bourgeois*. Hence, in many ways it served as a kind of handbook of instruction for any person who was interested in the finer points of law. The evidence consistently suggests the 'Livre de la Cour des Bourgeois' was not merely a private treatise or work of jurisprudence, but a law book compiled for legal use in the period it was composed. The argument, let us not forget, that there was more than one compiler of the 'Livre de la Cour des Bourgeois', could imply the law book was generally well known in Acre. One of its authors, who had perhaps been a member of the *Cour des Bourgeois*, was careful to stress that his work was an accurate description of the established laws of the time, and emphasised the immediate relevance of the law book to anyone wishing to understand fully what legislation should be practised in the burgess court. He was not merely engaged in legal theory in order to impress on readers his knowledge. Inherently, the laws contained in this book had practical application. In the thirteenth century, the laws of the royal burgess court of Acre corresponded to those set out in the 'Livre de la Cour des Bourgeois'. If proof be needed that legal writers and court officials worked in tandem, a brief survey of the charters of Acre reveals a congruity between law book and actual practice, whether this was in respect to the sale, exchange and donation of *borgesies*, the rights of wives, children and nearest relatives in matters of tenancy, or issues of inheritance and debt. Unquestionably, the one reflected the other, and this fact extended to court procedure, as, for example, the role of officials, witnesses and the use of symbolic objects to signify conveyance of seisin. The law books, moreover, give the impression of a rigid legal system prevailing in Acre and Nicosia, and to a certain extent the charters bear this out. Thus, for instance, the formulaic jargon of the 'Livre de la Cour des Bourgeois' and the 'Livre contrefais' concerning who could and could not possess *borgesies* was repeated in the charters drawn up by the courts. However, of the two types of documentation the charters are more illustrative of certain flexibility in the legal system. Though we learn from the law books viscounts presided over a *Cour des Bourgeois*, the charters reveal castellans of the Tower of David, seneschals and even burgess judges carried out similar responsibilities. In truth, the law books marked out the contours of a basic legal system. Their authors articulated the scope of burgess jurisdiction, whilst the courts dealt with unprecedented cases requiring the reinterpretation or amendment of existing rules.

But if it is accepted that the laws of the 'Livre de la Cour des Bourgeois' were practised in a royal *Cour des Bourgeois*, in which royal city was this court situated? There is not a general consensus: Richard[99] and Mayer[100] were of the opinion this was the law book of Jerusalem, while Grandclaude maintained that it was a collection of the laws prevailing in Acre. He cited chapters 236 and 237 on

99 Richard, *The Latin Kingdom of Jerusalem*, p. 410.
100 Mayer, *The Crusades*, p. 176.

the *Cour de la Fonde* and customs duty in support of his theory, as well as what could be inferred from chapter 267, to support his view the law book must have been composed by an inhabitant of Acre during the regency of Alice.[101] Certainly, there were other laws in it relevant to Acre, most notably chapter 43 (the *Cour de la Chaine*[102]) and chapter 144 (the merchant communes).[103] However, in chapter 221, one of the authors describes the legal process of summoning defendants in the *Cour des Bourgeois* in Jaffa,[104] while in chapter 140 he discusses the admissibility of charter evidence in Jaffa and Jerusalem.[105] Elsewhere, he deals with an issue of court procedure concerning the *Cour des Bourgeois* in Jerusalem.[106] The *Cours des Bourgeois* in Bethlehem and the *ville neuve* of Ibelin are also the subject of chapter 224.[107] Terminological inconsistency is further apparent. In some chapters the author describes legislation as 'assise de Jerusalem'[108] or 'assise de la terre de Jerusalem',[109] but in other instances he is prone to generalising, employing the phrases 'assise dou reaume de Jerusalem',[110] and 'assise de la terre dou roiaume de Jerusalem'.[111] On at least two occasions he describes laws as having application 'en tot le reaume de Jerusalem'.[112]

Given its date, however, the law book must have been compiled in Acre. The laws contained in it may be divided into three categories. First, there were the laws which from as early as the twelfth century originated in the royal city. Secondly, the laws established in Jerusalem and adopted – as was customary practice – by the *Cour des Bourgeois* in Acre. And thirdly, the laws in Acre which were in use throughout the kingdom of Jerusalem, including legislation arising from the decisions of general assemblies such as the one held in Acre in 1251. But the 'Livre de la Cour des Bourgeois' is a substantial work containing laws whose origin cannot be easily accounted for. One may speculate that these were of European derivation, a theory which was of special interest to Prawer whose study of the 'Livre de la Cour des Bourgeois' led him to conclude that the author used as his template an anonymous source of Provençal origin called *Lo Codi* written in

---

[101] Kausler, pp. 270–82, 324 (cf. Beugnot, 'Livre des assises', pp. 171–8, 207); Grandclaude, *Etude critique sur les livres des assises de Jérusalem*, p. 69.

[102] Kausler, p. 75 (cf. Beugnot, 'Livre des assises', pp. 42–3).

[103] Kausler, p. 162 (cf. Beugnot, 'Livre des assises', pp.100–101).

[104] Kausler, p. 147 (cf. Beugnot, 'Livre des assises', p. 156).

[105] Kausler, p. 159 (cf. Beugnot, 'Livre des assises', p. 98).

[106] This chapter describing court procedure in Jerusalem is not found in the Kausler edition; see Beugnot, 'Livre des assises', p.155.

[107] Beugnot, 'Livre des assises', p.155.

[108] Kausler, pp. 98, 109, 121, 144, 344 (cf. Beugnot, 'Livre des assises', pp. 59, 66, 74, 88, 219).

[109] Kausler, p. 70 (cf. Beugnot, 'Livre des assises', p. 39).

[110] Kausler, pp. 69, 71 (cf. Beugnot, 'Livre des assises', pp. 38, 39).

[111] Kausler, pp. 78 (cf. Beugnot, 'Livre des assises', p. 44).

[112] Kausler, p. 327 (cf. Beugnot, 'Livre des assises', p. 209. See also p. 47).

Arles in c.1149.[113] This link could be verified he argued because some laws of the 'Livre de la Cour des Bourgeois' were a direct translation of passages contained in *Lo Codi*. In his opinion, of the 297 chapters of the 'Livre de la Cour des Bourgeois' 63 were translated from this Provençal treatise. The choice of *Lo Codi* as a model, he suggested, was due to the fact that it described legal practices identical to those existing in the kingdom of Jerusalem.[114] Nonetheless, Prawer viewed the 'Livre de la Cour des Bourgeois' as being more than a private treatise, believing its laws corresponded to the 'judicial realities of the kingdom'.[115]

An examination of *Lo Codi* does reveal basic similarities between this law book and the 'Livre de la Cour des Bourgeois'. There are similar rules, for instance, regarding marriage and the right of a wife to inherit the possessions of her husband if he died without an heir;[116] the inheritance rights of illegitimate children;[117] the disinheritance of children;[118] and the obligations inheritors had, for example, to repay the debts of the deceased.[119] Other basic similarities include issues of leasehold,[120] pledge[121] and the property rights of freed slaves.[122] In terms of court procedure, both law books echo the right of a plaintiff, the *actor*, and the defendant, the *reus*, to legal representation by a professional advocate;[123] the admissibility of charter evidence in certain legal cases;[124] and circumstances under

---

[113] H. Fitting and H. Suchier (eds), *Lo Codi. Eine Summa Codicis in Provenzalischer Sprache aus der Mitte des XII Jahrhunderts* (Halle, 1906). Prawer, *Crusader Institutions*, pp. 362–79.

[114] Prawer, *Crusader Institutions*, p. 378. R. Caillemer, 'Lo Codi et le droit provençal au XIIe siècle', *Annales du Midi*, 18 (1906): pp. 494–507; E. Bonduard, 'Lo Codi, ancien livre de droit provençal', *Revue du Midi* 13 (1899): 458–66; J. Tardif, 'Une Version provençal d'une somme du code', *Annales du Midi*, 5 (1893): 34–70

[115] Prawer, *Crusader Institutions*, p. 377.

[116] Kausler, pp. 202–203 (cf. Beugnot, 'Livre des assises', p. 125), cf. Fitting and Suchier, vi, 25, pp. 193–4.

[117] Kausler, pp. 193–4 (cf. Beugnot, 'Livre des assises', pp. 119–20), cf. Fitting and Suchier, v, 20, pp. 172–3.

[118] Kausler, pp. 266–8 (cf. Beugnot, 'Livre des assises', pp. 169–70), cf. Fitting and Suchier, iii, 17, pp. 49–50.

[119] Kausler, pp. 208–209 (cf. Beugnot, 'Livre des assises', p. 130), cf. Fitting and Suchier, vi, 48, pp. 210–11.

[120] Kausler, p. 122 (cf. Beugnot, 'Livre des assises', p. 75), cf. Fitting and Suchier, iv, 69, p. 142.

[121] Kausler, p. 101 (cf. Beugnot, 'Livre des assises', p. 62), cf. Fitting and Suchier, viii, 24, p. 298.

[122] Kausler, pp. 222–3 (cf. Beugnot, 'Livre des assises', p. 138), cf. Fitting and Suchier, vi, 20, p. 192.

[123] Kausler, p. 51 (cf. Beugnot, 'Livre des assises', p. 26), cf. Fitting and Suchier, ii, 5, p. 13.

[124] Kausler, p. 159 (cf. Beugnot, 'Livre des assises', p. 98), cf. Fitting and Suchier, iv, 33, p. 95.

which a trial could be adjourned.[125] It is important to remember, however, that the 'Livre de la Cour des Bourgeois' was not a word for word translation of *Lo Codi*, and although the similarities between the two law books suggest that a copy of the Provençal codex had been available to Latin jurists in the kingdom of Jerusalem, there were many laws contained in one law book but not in the other. It should also be noted that the author of the 'Livre de la Cour des Bourgeois' organised his subject matter in an entirely different manner to the author of *Lo Codi*. The strong suggestion is the 'Livre de la Cour des Bourgeois' was not a private treatise; the law book was not simply a thirteenth-century translation of parts of *Lo Codi*, but an invaluable contemporary legal source. If the author had a copy of *Lo Codi* then he used it selectively to reflect laws which were current at the time, whilst relying otherwise on his knowledge of burgess laws formulated in the kingdom.

Law-making in the Kingdom of Cyprus

The pages of the 'Livre de la Cour des Bourgeois' incorporated several decades of law-making activity. And of such value was this law book that it may have remained a source of reference to lawmakers and law practitioners right up to the fall of Acre in 1291. It was of importance precisely because it formed a vital bridge between legislation on the mainland and the island of Cyprus. The 'Livre de la Cour des Bourgeois', as well as other burgess law books of the kingdom of Jerusalem, were well known to Latin jurists of Cyprus. According to Grandclaude, the Munich manuscript was a copy of the 'Livre de la Cour des Bourgeois' made in c.1317 by André an *escrivein* of the court in Nicosia.[126] To his copy the *escrivein* attached the most important royal ordinances (up to 1317) kept with the registers in the house of the viscount.[127] It was not a unique practice, however, for the jurors of the *Cour des Bourgeois* in Nicosia to consult a law book of the kingdom of Jerusalem when making judgements. The law book of John of Ibelin, which in the second half of the thirteenth century was kept in a box in the cathedral of Nicosia, had a similar influence on the workings of the High Court. Whenever there was difficulty resolving a dispute, the law book was carried to the court 'pour esclercir ledit cas, selon ce qui estoit use au royaume de Jerusalem'. It was decreed the royal ordinance authorising this practice 'doit joindre au Livre des Assises', that is the law book of John of Ibelin.[128]

It may be argued with some conviction that the 'Livre de la Cour des

---

125 Kausler, pp. 146–7 (cf. Beugnot, 'Livre des assises', p. 90), cf. Fitting and Suchier, iii, 11, p. 44.

126 Grandclaude, *Etude critique sur les livres des assises de Jérusalem*, pp. 35–7.

127 'Bans et ordonnances', p. 366. According to the rubric of the ordinance dated 1301, Viscount Hue Pistiau 'l'on fist atachier a ce livre aucuns autres ordenemens que la cort a fait et que l'on a trove as livres de la cort'.

128 'Bans et ordonnances', pp. 378–9.

Bourgeois' was well known outside Acre by Latin jurists. Either the original law book or a copy must have been transferred to the royal *Cour des Bourgeois* of Nicosia sometime in the second half of the thirteenth century, before a further copy was made in c.1317. It is worth remembering that in the following years, Nicosia did not have its own law book, which could mean the 'Livre de la Cour des Bourgeois' remained having an influence on the legislation of this royal city and the development of its *Cour des Bourgeois*. In actual fact, the laws of Nicosia were finally collected in a law book of the first half of the fourteenth century. The anonymous author describes his law book as 'le Livre contrefais au livre des Assises; et pour ce que celui qui l'a fait et dité, l'a fait escrire par grant dezir, et non pas par seurté de son sens'.[129] The 'livre des Assises' he refers to was probably the 'Livre de la Cour des Bourgeois' of Acre.

Unlike the 'Livre de la Cour des Bourgeois' the 'Livre contrefais' seems to have been written by only one author. Not only is this person unknown, but it is also difficult to establish when he was writing. He mentions that in 1325 King Hugh IV (1324–1359?) ordered to be built a house in which should be kept the box and the written registers of the High Court.[130] This means the author was writing sometime after 1325, probably during the reign of Hugh. He does, however, provide some important autobiographical details. He was over seventy years of age when he composed his law book, and of the forty years he was employed by the royal *Cour des Bourgeois* in Nicosia, eleven years were spent as a juror, another eleven years as an *escrivein* and eighteen years as an *avantparlier*.[131] Writing in the first person he sometimes states that he was an eyewitness to what took place in the *Cour des Bourgeois* in Nicosia, suggesting he may have drawn from his own experiences as a member of this court.[132] His long association with the court explains his understanding of the duties of its officials, as well as the procedures which were to be followed in civil and criminal cases. In his opinion, an *avantparlier* should be well informed of 'assises et usages et bones costumes',[133] and he clearly had an extensive knowledge of the burgess laws of the kingdoms of

[129] 'Livre contrefais', p. 235. The text of the 'Livre contrefais' is contained solely in the Venice manuscript (fr. 12206) which was chosen by the Venetians in 1531 for their translation of only folios 279 to 315 (Grandclaude, *Etude critique sur les livres des assises de Jérusalem*, p. 30. A copy of this is preserved in the Ms Italian 29. See *Barbarorum Leges Antiquae*, vol. 2).This first part of the book the Venetians entitled 'volume d'assise pladeante de la corte del viscantado del regno de Cypro' ('Livre contrefais', p. 235, note 1), and in the last chapter of the first part the author announces that the subsequent discussion of court procedure would focus on 'la maniere dou plaidoyer'. It is for these reasons that the law book of Nicosia, divided into two parts, was also known as the 'livres du pledeant et du plaidoyer' ('Livre contrefais', p. 292).

[130] 'Livre contrefais', pp. 250–51.

[131] 'Livre contrefais', p. 319.

[132] 'Livre contrefais', pp. 306, 308.

[133] 'Livre contrefais', p. 245.

Jerusalem and Cyprus as he cites regularly the works of Latin jurists.[134] He also mentions Raymond and Nicholas Anteaume as having been prominent lawyers – the Anteaumes were a wealthy and influential burgess family of Acre and Cyprus.[135] It may also be ascertained he had access to a manuscript of the 'Livre de la Cour des Bourgeois', because chapters 15 and 16 of the law book are reproduced word for word in the 'Livre contrefais'.[136] As was explained earlier, the court in Nicosia was in possession of the 'Livre de la Cour des Bourgeois' from the second half of the thirteenth century, and the author of the 'Livre contrefais' may have had before him this version of the law book, or the copy made by the *escrivein* of the court in 1317.[137]

The evidence strongly suggests that as a member of the *Cour des Bourgeois* the author of the 'Livre contrefais' knew a number of Latin law books. He had access to a relatively extensive legal library and was very well informed. In a chapter on the transference of *borgesies* he writes: 'Encores une autre choze, que elle a esté dite et trovée en aucuns des livres'.[138] In a further two chapters on property rental he mentions, 'je ais leu en aucuns livres',[139] and 'je ai trouvé en escrit en aucuns livres des Assizes'.[140] When discussing city *heritages* he alludes to 'aucuns livres' where there was described the law of a year and a day.[141] In reference to inheritance and escheat he hints at the existence of another law book,[142] and when discussing the crime of murder he commends 'aucuns bons livres' from which he

---

[134] 'Livre contrefais', pp. 268, 303, 306–307, 310–11, 313 (John of Ibelin); pp. 305, 310–311, 317–18 (Philip of Novara).

[135] 'Livre contrefais', pp. 339–40.

[136] Kausler, pp. 55–6 (cf. Beugnot, 'Livre des assises', pp. 28–9), and cf. 'Livre contrefais', pp. 316–17.

[137] The ordering of folios in the Venice manuscript makes it difficult to establish where the 'Livre contrefais' finishes. Foucher's edition of the law book ends with the chapter concerning the dispute in 1300 between Henry II and the jurors of the *Cour des Bourgeois* in Nicosia (folio 339) (*Assises du Royaume de Jérusalem*, part 2, 'Le Plédéant et le Plaidoyer', Rennes, 1840). Beugnot, however, goes up to folio 357 of the Venice manuscript and includes text relating to judicial duel – Venice Ms, folios 197–200 ('Livre contrefais', pp. 327–35) as well as extracts from the Latin jurists (see, for example, 'Livre contrefais', xxvi, pp. 336–7; xxvii, pp. 337–9; xxix, pp. 341–4. It is possible, though unlikely, that these extracts did not belong to the original 'Livre contrefais', but were added by the copyist. See Grandclaude, *Etude critique sur les livres des assises de Jérusalem*, p. 92). Interestingly, the same text on judicial duel is found in the Munich manuscript, which does not include the 'Livre contrefais'. This suggests that the text on the jurisdictional competence of the *Cour des Bourgeois* in matters of duelling was incorporated into the 'Livre contrefais' either by the author or a copyist.

[138] 'Livre contrefais', p. 271. See also p. 305.

[139] 'Livre contrefais', p. 288.

[140] 'Livre contrefais', p. 290.

[141] 'Livre contrefais', p. 311.

[142] 'Livre contrefais', p. 311:'Et je ais oy dire a aucuns des sages et leu en aucun livre'.

acquired his information.[143] When stating who had right to plead in court he writes, 'je trové en escrit que il y a une maniere de gent qui ne pevent plaidoier pour autrui'.[144] And the rule prohibiting freed slaves from pleading was also found in 'aucuns livres'.[145] When describing the procedure for summoning defendants to court he attributes his knowledge of legal protocol to what he had read 'à tous les plus des livres'.[146] Moreover, in chapter twenty-five he mentions having consulted a law book on the issue of murder: 'Moult sercha et enquist celui qui ce livre a fait ... et trova en aucun livre ce qui ici est escrit'. This law book, he adds, was written by 'grans seignors et sages sur le fait et la matiere dou murtre'. One of these wise men, we are told, was John of Ibelin, lord of Arsuf, who was knowledgeable of cases of judicial duel in the High Court and the *Cour des Bourgeois*.[147] As the author of the 'Livre contrefais' was discussing *borgesies* then it is quite probable that some of these 'livres des Assizes' were the burgess law books of the kingdoms of Jerusalem and Cyprus which had coexisted with the 'Livre de la Cour des Bourgeois'.

Possibly these *livres*, and certainly the legal documents and written registers of the *Cour des Bourgeois* in Nicosia, were preserved in the *huche*.[148] The box was kept in the house of the viscount and it was the duty of the *escrivein* to bring it to the court when instructed.[149] It was the Acre *parlement* of 1251 which had agreed a *huche* should be made accessible only to the viscount and two other 'homes liges' elected by the jurors.[150] This was to be the procedure in Acre and possibly other places in the kingdom with a *Cour des Bourgeois* – the lords of Tyre and Caesarea were, among others, present at this *parlement*.[151] At Acre, it was further decided that whatever was said in court should be written down; a particular criticism being that usually when court reconvened after an adjournment – which could last for more than a year[152] – the testimony of claimants and defendants were remembered only vaguely.[153] It will be seen how deferment and adjournment were integral legal procedure necessitating the keeping of registers which not only recorded what was said and done, but also specified the days when claimants or defendants had to appear in court should cases be delayed. Apart from adjournments, the registers kept a record of sales, donations, exchanges and pledges of *borgesies*; the lease of property on a temporary or short-term basis; the rent owed by lessees; and the

[143] 'Livre contrefais', p. 319.
[144] 'Livre contrefais', p. 317.
[145] 'Livre contrefais', p. 317.
[146] 'Livre contrefais', p. 296.
[147] 'Livre contrefais', p. 326.
[148] 'Livre contrefais', p. 243.
[149] 'Livre contrefais', p. 243.
[150] 'Livre contrefais', p. 248.
[151] 'Livre contrefais', p. 246.
[152] Kausler, p. 147 (cf. Beugnot, 'Livre des assises', p. 90).
[153] 'Livre contrefais', p. 247.

sentences passed by jurors, whether fines, or corporal or capital punishments.[154] Royal ordinances were also attached to the registers. When in 1318 Henry II ordained a particular oath should be sworn by any person purchasing a *borgesie* in Nicosia,[155] the viscount, we are told, 'le fera atacher au livre de la cort'.[156] The author of the 'Livre contrefais' informs us that it was a duty of the *escrivein* to keep a record of the 'drois et des raizons dou roy'.[157] Moreover, the oath of office sworn by the viscount and his jurors was attached to the court register.[158] A royal ordinance informing the court of the oath of office was preserved, as was a later ordinance (1300) modifying the words of this oath.[159]

Although composed in the first half of the fourteenth century, the 'Livre contrefais' is of equal importance as a source of the thirteenth century. It incorporates many of the laws constituted in the kingdom of Cyprus up to the time the author was writing. He is historically aware and traces the provenance of certain legislation. There are references, for instance, to the laws of King Henry I (1232–1253) and King Henry II (1286–1306) on such matters as the alienation of *borgesies* and the functions of the *Cour des Bourgeois*.[160] But, significantly, the 'Livre contrefais' differs from the 'Livre de la Cour des Bourgeois' in that it focuses more closely on the powers of the burgess court. Its author demonstrates greater interest in the interpretation of law by court jurors, and the legal procedures accompanying judgement-making. In the first twelve chapters of the first book he describes the official duties of those employed in the royal *Cour des Bourgeois* in Nicosia. The number of jurors who in court assisted a viscount or his deputy is also known from the law book, whereas for the kingdom of Jerusalem we have to rely on the witness lists of charters for this information. The next seven chapters of the 'Livre contrefais' are a historical account of how the judgements of the *Cour des Bourgeois* in Acre in the mid-thirteenth century came to be based on written registers rather than collective memory. Several of the remaining chapters in the first book outline the various ways property could be alienated. The pledging of *borgesies* is treated at length, in particular the legal contract prefacing the loan of money in return for immovable collateral. A loan usually took the form of a vifgage and the author sets out the onerous responsibilities of the debtor – the 'seignor de la gagier' – to repay the money he had been advanced. Failure to comply with the rules of pledge could mean the lender was free to sell the property – by public auction if he so wished – in order to recover the loan. The author also

---

154 'Livre contrefais', pp. 243, 249.

155 'Livre contrefais', p. 253.

156 'Bans et ordonnances', p. 373.

157 'Livre contrefais', p. 243.

158 The rubric to the royal ordinance reads: 'Ce est la maniere dou sairement que le vesconte doit faire quant il entre en l'ofice dou visconte, selonc se que maistre Andre l'escrivain le porta dou livre de la cort'.

159 'Bans et ordonnances', pp. 370–71.

160 'Livre contrefais', pp. 249, 253, 264, 295, 315, 320, 321, 322.

discourses on permanent alienation and the basic rights direct heirs or nearest relatives had to challenge sale or donation.

The second book of the 'Livre contrefais' deals primarily with litigation and court procedure in criminal matters. The author describes in detail the procedures of high justice and the powers of the court to arraign and punish criminals.[161] Interestingly, however, the 'Livre contrefais' is silent on certain legal issues relating to non-feudatories not under the jurisdictional competence of the *Cour des Bourgeois*. Charter evidence reveals that in Famagusta commercial matters were heard in the *Commerchium*, the customs court – which was presided over by a *bailli* and kept a register of mercantile contracts[162] – in the same way that in Acre they were heard in the *Cour de la Chaine*.[163] Further evidence suggesting the legal powers of the *Cour des Bourgeois* in Nicosia were devolved to other tribunals is found in a charter of 1324, in which was recorded a petition made to the king by the Venetian commune on behalf of one of its citizens, Marco Contarini. The terms of this dispute are not clear except the case was to be heard in both the *Cour des Bourgeois* and the chancery, a significant development in the Nicosian legal system which seems to have had no counterpart in the kingdom of Jerusalem.[164] Besides revelation the chancery was vested with a degree of jurisdictional authority, it is surprising the royal *Cour des Bourgeois* could not have dealt completely with the dispute. One can only surmise certain elements of this case were outside its competence. There is no indication in the 'Livre contrefais', however, that the royal chancery in Nicosia had any powers of burgess jurisdiction.

The author of the 'Livre contrefais' had eleven years experience as *escrivein*, and this would have given him extensive access to the court registers and the royal ordinances kept with them. As such, he incorporates in his law book a number of edicts on various matters including rules of eleemosynary donation (1305),[165] court procedure surrounding the alienation of *borgesie* and the oath sworn by property buyers (1318).[166] An ordinance on the jurisdictional competence of the *Cour des Bourgeois* in Famagusta is also reproduced.[167] There is, nevertheless, little known about royal legislation in the kingdom of Cyprus, except that when a king issued an edict he presented it in written form to the jurors of the court through his representative the viscount. It was a responsibility of the *escrivein* to proclaim this as law to the city burgesses. The existing royal ordinances of Cyprus highlight this

---

161 'Livre contrefais', pp. 293–52.

162 A. Evans (ed.), *Francesco Balduci Pegolotti: La pratica della mercatura* (Cambridge, Mass., 1936), pp. 88–9.

163 Müller, *Documenti sulle relazioni delle città toscane*, pp. 123–4.

164 G.M. Thomas and R. Predelli (eds), *Diplomatarium Veneto-Levantium*, (2 vols, Venice, 1880–99), vol. I, p. 199: 'Il sunt plusours erremens soluen que le Roy a entendu, e deuent estre alla cansellarie et alla cort dou uisconte et autre part'.

165 'Livre contrefais', p. 269; 'Bans et ordonnances', p. 366.

166 'Livre contrefais', p. 253; 'Bans et ordonnances', p. 373.

167 'Livre contrefais', pp. 323–4; 'Bans et ordonnances', p. 365.

procedure. In 1305 Viscount Johan de Bay 'aporta cest escrit desous devisé, de par le roi, et comanda de faire crier'.[168] In the same year the viscount presented the court with two further royal edicts.[169] But what measure of influence did burgesses have in the making of these laws? In 1300 the issue of legislation was a source of disagreement involving the king and the jurors of the *Cour des Bourgeois* in Nicosia. King Henry II issued an ordinance on the arraigning of criminals, and as was customary presented the written legislation to the viscount for him to pass on to the *Cour des Bourgeois* in order that it may be enforced. On this occasion, however, the jurors of the court demurred, arguing that in substance the ordinance contravened other laws which they had sworn to safeguard. The viscount, Hugh Piteau, agreed, and when subsequently a pertinent case came before the court the new legislation was not applied. This apparently caused further discord among the jurors some of whom, whilst agreeing in principle the ordinance was unjust, did not think it right for the court to disobey a royal edict. These particular jurors, Pagan Visconte, William le Rous and Thibaut de l'Arcevesque, were described as *hommes du roi* although their special relationship to Henry is not entirely clear.[170] Comparison, though, can be made with the kingdom of Jerusalem where jurors of the royal *Cour des Bourgeois* who possibly belonged to the king's household or held properties directly from him, were described in the witness lists of charters as 'burgenses regis'.[171] Henry's decisive response was to remove the jurors from their office for three days. In so doing he stamped his authority on the court and its jurisdiction. When finally allowed back into court the jurors were presented in writing a new oath of office obliging them to respect the 'spessiau coumandement' of the king.

This contretemps seems to suggest that in the twelfth century in royal domain some laws at least were made without the advice of burgesses or jurors of the *Cour des Bourgeois*. Whilst in the mid-thirteenth century the king and his court agreed he should receive the *conseill* of his burgesses when issuing laws directly affecting them, in Nicosia at the beginning of the fourteenth century, the disagreement between the king and the burgess jurors exemplified how the king could still legislate without the consent or advice of the *Cour des Bourgeois*. The insistence of the *hommes du roi* in Nicosia that it was wrong to disobey a royal edict was reminiscent of the *Cour des Bourgeois* in Acre which did not attempt to overturn the ordinance on street cleaning issued by King Baldwin. The resulting actions of the king demonstrated ultimately the powerlessness of jurors, like their counterparts in Acre, to do anything about royal legislation.

It was mentioned previously how royal legislation in certain cases required

---

168 'Bans et ordonnances', p. 366.

169 'Bans et ordonnances', p. 367: 'Visconte sire Johan de Bai dona l'escrit de se banc desous devisé, de par le roi, qui comanda de faire le crier'. And p. 367: 'Douna le visconte le banc desous escrit à faire le crier'.

170 'Livre contrefais', pp. 321–2.

171 See below, p. 140.

reinterpretation and amendment by the court of burgesses. This represented another facet of law-making – the setting of precedent. Although in 1300 King Henry II consolidated his powers as a legislator, he did concede there were certain cases heard in the *Cour des Bourgeois* which were not covered by existing legislation. The new oath he ordered the jurors of Nicosia to swear reaffirmed their authority to set precedent,[172] in the same way, interestingly, the jurors of the Venetian quarter in Tyre in the thirteenth century had been conceded the right to hear cases of dispute and make judgement as they saw fit.[173] The jurors of the court in Nicosia were to make judgements 'celonc lor conoissance' in those cases not covered by any law. Their decisions were written down in the court registers, but whether these were automatically ordained law is not known – it has been suggested, however, that laws in the kingdom of Jerusalem were the result of precedents rather than 'previously undertaken legislative work'.[174]

Jurors could set precedent but were also within their rights to modify certain aspects of a law if in its present form it could not be applied in a particular case. In Nicosia, for example, the law of entail prohibited some families from selling their *borgesies* even if they were unable to subsist from farming their land. The law did not even countenance the temporary transfer of *borgesies*, thus prohibiting any form of pledge. But as the author of the 'Livre contrefais' admits, 'necessité n'a point de loi'.[175] The court had the capacity to make special dispensation to a burgess who was compelled by hardship to sell his *borgesie*. The court could also make an exception if a burgess in captivity had to sell his *borgesie* in order to raise ransom money for his release.[176] In these exceptional cases jurors were not contravening but rather amending the law in order to accommodate the particular needs of burgesses.

The Laws of the Kingdom of Jerusalem and Antioch

It is appropriate in a discussion of the dissemination of law to consider the interrelatedness between law books of the eastern Mediterranean. It is relevant to

---

172 'Livre contrefais', pp. 237–8.

173 Berggötz, p. 141.

174 Richard, *The Latin Kingdom of Jerusalem*, p. 69; Edbury, *The Kingdom of Cyprus and the Crusades*, pp. 186–7. For Antioch see Cahen, *Syrie du nord*, p. 31. It is possible that ultimately the decisions of the *Cours des Bourgeois* became law in the same way that the High Court in Cyprus is known to have had legislative powers to pass *assises*. In 1312, for example, the High Court passed an *assise* dealing with such issues as the ownership of strayed falcons, see C. Perat, 'Un Diplomate gascon au XIVe siècle: Raymond de Piis, nonce de Clément V en Orient', *MAHEFR*, xliv (1927): 82–3; See also, L. de Mas Latrie (ed.), *Histoire de l'île de Chypre sous le règne des princes de la maison de Lusignan* (3 vols, Paris, 1852–55), vol. 2, p. 423; 'Bans et ordonnances', pp. 368–70, 373–7.

175 'Livre contrefais', p. 270.

176 'Livre contrefais', p. 271.

compare the laws prevailing in the kingdoms of Jerusalem and Cyprus with those which existed in the principality of Antioch. The *assises* of Antioch were codified in the early thirteenth century but have survived only in an Armenian version. The *Assises d'Antioche* is the oldest surviving collection of burgess laws in the Latin East, and is useful because apart from the 'Livre de la Cour des Bourgeois' it is the only other Levantine source on laws of burgess marriage, inheritance, debt and lease. The original *Assises d'Antioche* were compiled by one or more authors during the reign of Prince Bohemond IV (1201–1233), although the date of composition has been narrowed down to before 1219.[177] The translation of the text was made by the constable Sempad (b. 1206), brother of King Hethoum I (1226–1269) of Cilician Armenia, sometime after 1254 but before 1265.[178] Sempad had received the laws from Simon, constable of Antioch.[179] The adoption of Antioch's legislation should be considered within the wider context of Frankish influence on the kingdom's commercial, political and religious restructuring, following the union of the Armenian Church with Rome in 1198 and continuing with the westernising reforms of Leo II (1198–1219).[180] Although the *Assises d'Antioche* was rendered into Armenian several French words were preserved, most significantly *bourgeois*.[181] Evidently, in Lesser Armenia in the thirteenth century there existed a class of native Latin Christians whose status, like other burgesses, was defined by their freedom to buy, sell, lease and engage property, and who were subject in civil and criminal matters to a court of justice based on the *Cour des Bourgeois* in Antioch.

Judging from the slender length of the text – fifteen chapters appertaining to burgess law – it may be safe to assume that the *Assises d'Antioche* was only an abridged version of a more complete legal code, which makes any comparison between the laws of the principality and the kingdom of Jerusalem difficult, and hinders any assessment of the influence, if any, that one had on the legislation of the other. However, certain laws of the *Assises d'Antioche* were basically similar to those of the 'Livre de la Cour des Bourgeois': for instance, with regard to dowry rights of women;[182] inheritance rights of children and of nearest relatives;[183] the making of wills;[184] the loan of money and the engagement of property;[185]

---

177 Alishan, p. xx; Cahen, *La Syrie du nord*, p. 31. With regard to Sempad's knowledge of Frankish historians, see S. der Nersessian, 'The Armenian Chronicle of the Constable Sempad', *DOP*, xiii (1959): pp. 143–68.

178 Alishan, p. xix; Cahen, *La Syrie du nord* , p. 29.

179 T.S.R. Boase, 'The History of the Kingdom', in *The Cilician Kingdom of Armenia*, ed. T.S.R. Boase (Edinburgh, 1978), pp. 27–8.

180 S. der Nersessian, 'The Kingdom of Cilician Armenia,' in R.L. Wolff and H.W. Hazard (eds), *History of the Crusades: The Later Crusades, 1189–1311* (Wisconsin: The University of Wisconsin Press, 1969), vol. II, pp. 650–51; Boase, p. 22.

181 Cahen, *La Syrie du nord* , p. 29.

182 Alishan, pp. 44–6.

183 Alishan, pp. 44–50.

184 Alishan, p. 48.

legislation regulating the use of weights and measures in trade;[186] and high justice and judicial duel.[187] In other respects, the Antioch text adds little to our knowledge of the legal standing of indigenous peoples in the principality or of the procedures which took place in the court. Furthermore, it may be seen that certain elements were peculiar to the *Cour des Bourgeois* in Antioch. First, the officers who presided over the court were the viscount and the *duc*, the latter of whom had no counterpart in the kingdom of Jerusalem.[188] This was perhaps revealing of Byzantine influences, as the office of *duc* may have been based on the Greek duke who exercised administrative functions in the eleventh century.[189] Secondly, the viscounts of the court in Antioch were not necessarily feudatories – as was the case in Acre and other cities in the kingdom of Jerusalem – but could belong to the burgess class. One example was the burgess Godefridus Raembaldus who in the 1130s officiated as viscount of the court.[190] Burgesses, moreover, were elevated to the position of *duc*.[191] These basic differences caution against generalising about similarities between the status of burgesses in the principality of Antioch and the kingdom of Jerusalem.

The Laws of the Kingdom of Jerusalem and the Frankish Principality of Achaia

It is a matter of debate as to whether the laws of the kingdom of Jerusalem were adopted by the rulers of the principality of Achaia in the Peloponnese in the thirteenth century. The laws of this principality, the *Liber de consuetudinibus Imperii Romanie*, otherwise known as the *Assises de Romanie*, were codified by an anonymous author in the early decades of the fourteenth century.[192] A version of the text, written sometime between 1333 and 1346,[193] has survived, and in the prologue the author included passages borrowed from the legal treatise of John of Ibelin.[194] These passages recount how the laws and courts of justice were established by the first Latin settlers in the kingdom of Jerusalem. The second part of the prologue elaborates further on this story, tying in the development of

185 Alishan, pp. 70–72.

186 Alishan, p. 78; cf. Kausler, p. 350 (cf. Beugnot, 'Livre des assises', p. 224).

187 Alishan, pp. 62–3.

188 Cahen, *La Syrie du nord*, pp. 457–8.

189 T.S. Asbridge, *The Creation of the Principality of Antioch, 1098–1130* (Woodbridge, 2000), pp. 193–4.

190 Bresc-Bautier, nos 73–4, 76–7.

191 Cahen, *La Syrie du nord*, p. 457.

192 G. Recoura (ed.), *Les Assises de Romanie* (Paris, 1930), pp. 44–6.

193 For evidence of this date, see D. Jacoby, *La Féodalité en Grèce médievale. La 'Assises de Romanie': Sources, application et diffusion* (Paris, 1971), pp. 75–82.

194 Recoura, *Les Assises de Romanie*, pp. 146–8. For the corresponding passages, see John of Ibelin, pp. 51–4.

legislation in the empire of Constantinople with that of the kingdom of Jerusalem. It relates how, following the Fourth Crusade and the conquest of Constantinople in 1204, the Emperor Baldwin I sent to Jerusalem for written laws which were received and read before his barons who swore to maintain and preserve them in their domains.[195] Although the veracity of this account may be called into question, it has been argued the story is plausible if it is accepted that in the kingdom of Jerusalem there was formulated a collection of written legislation in the twelfth century – the *Letres dou Sepulcre* – and that these laws were taken to Constantinople by Syrian jurists such as Ralph of Tiberias.[196] There are reasons to believe, nevertheless, the account given in the *Assises de Romanie* was a myth concocted in the fourteenth century. First, I have presented my reasons questioning the existence of the *Letres dou Sepulcre*, meaning the prologue of the *Assises de Romanie* was based on a false account of the thirteenth century. Secondly, while the author of the *Assises de Romanie* states that the written legislation of Jerusalem had been transferred to Constantinople after 1204, even in the Syrian jurists' accounts it is stated the *Letres dou Sepulcre* had been lost in 1187 when Jerusalem fell to Saladin.[197] It may be the author was alluding to a body of written laws other than the *Letres dou Sepulcre*, perhaps the *Livre au Roi*, which was probably written between 1197 and 1205.[198] This, however, seems unlikely, as the author in composing the *Assises de Romanie* intended to make a direct link between original twelfth-century laws and the laws of Achaia.

The author of the *Assises de Romanie* was doubtless influenced by the Syrian jurists. But there is little evidence the legislation of Achaia in the thirteenth century had originated in the kingdom of Jerusalem. There is little to go on when comparing burgess jurisdiction in the kingdom of Jerusalem with that in the principality of Achaia. The laws contained in the *Assises de Romanie* are concerned mainly with feudal justice and the legal relationship between lord and fief-holder. A considerable number of laws also apply to Greek villeins and the legal standing of non-Latin Christians. But laws appertaining to burgesses, *borgesie* tenancy, or for that matter city dwelling, are very few.[199] Other than definition of the basic freedom of Latin Christians, there are no references to the existing burgess system of justice in the principality, and the only mention to the

---

195 Recoura, *Les Assises de Romanie*, p. 150.

196 La Monte, 'Three Questions Concerning the Assises de Jerusalem', pp. 208–209; cf. P. Topping, 'The Formation of the Assizes of Romania', *Byzantion*, XVII (1944–45), pp. 304–14. On the visit of Ralph of Tiberias to Constantinople, Villehardouin, *La Conquête de Constantinople*, ed. E. Faral (2 vols, Paris, 1961), vol 2, p. 124; J. Longnon, *L'Empire latin de Constantinople et la principauté de Morée* (Paris, 1949), pp. 67–8.

197 Philip of Novara, 'Le Livre de forme de plait', p. 522.

198 On the date of composition, Grandclaude, *Etude critique sur les livres des assises de Jérusalem*, pp. 46–7; M. Greilsammer, 'Structure and Aims of the Livre au Roi', in B.Z. Kedar, H.E. Mayer and R.C. Smail (eds), *Outremer. Studies in the History of the Crusading Kingdom of Jerusalem Presented to Joshua Prawer* (Jerusalem, 1982), pp. 218–26.

199 Recoura, *Les Assises de Romanie*, chapters 23, 37, 38, 118, 143, 152, 193.

involvement of burgesses in commerce is a law exempting them, as well as feudatories, from custom and sales duty (*comerchio*).[200] In theory, at least, they were, like burgesses in Acre in the thirteenth century, to be consulted by the prince when making legislation which directly affected them, in particular whenever a general tax such as *tallea* was to be levied.[201] And in the matter of *borgesie* tenancy, the legal rights of a widow to inherit the property of a deceased husband were relatively similar to those of her counterpart in the kingdom of Jerusalem.[202] Certainly, however, there exists no evidence of influence which the 'Livre de la Cour des Bourgeois' may have had on the legislation of the principality in the late thirteenth century. In truth, there were marked differences between the two societies. In Achaia there was no legal restriction against feudatories possessing *borgesies*, as was generally the case in the kingdom of Jerusalem; the *Assises de Romanie* treats *borgesie* as the property of all freemen (*franchi homini*). There is even suggestion in one of the chapters certain burgess cases could be heard in a seigneurial court.[203] It is important to stress furtherthat whereas in the kingdom of Jerusalem all Latin Christians, whether feudatories or burgesses, enjoyed a social and legal status above that of non-Latin Christians, in the principality of Achaia the integration of *archontes* within the ranks of feudatories from the middle of the thirteenth century meant some Greek Orthodox Christians attained a social standing higher than Latin Christian burgesses.[204] The laws of the 'Livre de la Cour des Bourgeois', therefore, many of which discriminated against indigenous people on grounds of religion, and emphasised the legal rights of burgesses above all non-Latin Christians, would have been of no relevance in the principality of Achaia.

---

[200] Recoura, *Les Assises de Romanie*, p. 255. See D. Jacoby, 'From Byzantium to Latin Romania: Continuity and Change', in B. Arbel, B. Hamilton and D. Jacoby (eds), *Latins and Greeks in the Eastern Mediterranean after 1204* (London, 1989), pp. 14–15.

[201] Recoura, *Les Assises de Romanie*, p. 172: 'Lo Principo non puo meter a li suo feudatarii over a li franchi homini, ni a li villani de quelli, taie, ni colte per alguna condition, ni per che nome se sia, ni alguna cossa, senza conseio et consentimento cossi de li legii e feudadi, come etiamdio de li altri franchi'.

[202] Recoura, *Les Assises de Romanie*, p. 186.

[203] Recoura, *Les Assises de Romanie*, p. 279: 'Quando alguna a quistion contra homo lezio de caxon de feo, et vuol produr testemonii contra quello, lo signor non puo cometer la examination de li testemonii se no a lezio ... *Et se la quistion non sera feudal, o civil, over burgesiaticha ... la examination de li testemonii se cometera a chi plaxera, purch'el sia libero*'.

[204] On the assimilation of Greeks within the social, political and administrative elite of Achaia, see D. Jacoby, 'The Encounter of Two Societies: Western Conquerors and Byzantines in the Peloponnesus after the Fourth Crusade', *The American Historical Review*, 78 (1973): 892–9; D. Jacoby, 'Les Archontes Grecs et la Féodalité en Morée Franque', *Traveaux et Mémoires du Centre de Recherche d'Histoire et Civilisation Byzantines*, 2 (1967): 470–71; Jacoby, 'From Byzantium to Latin Romania', pp. 1–7.

Conclusion

Examination of the sources points to the strong probability that there was no general law book of the kingdom of Jerusalem. However, there is much evidence in the twelfth century of legislative activity – including the formulation of certain laws of general application – in the cities and rural villages. We have seen that legislative assemblies were attended by burgesses and feudatories from all over the kingdom, and at these meetings laws were recommended, debated and amendments suggested. Issues concerning the kingdom as a whole, for example taxation, were important enough to warrant such meetings. Besides general assemblies some laws were enforced 'par tout le reaume de Jerusalem'. In addition, *seigneurs justiciers* legislated in their lordships, and there is evidence to believe cities other than Acre and Nicosia had their own burgess law books. Furthermore, it seems ecclesiastical institutions like the order of St John had the authority to make legislation; charters reveal that some customs were peculiar to certain Latin settlements, which suggests the existence of local differences in laws. But in spite of these differences, there was uniformity in particular aspects of burgess jurisdiction. A reason for this may be because cities and *villes neuves* adopted each other's customs. In terms of the process of law–making it has been argued the king did not require consent from burgesses when making laws and it was his choice whether to seek their advice. This is not to say, however, that the role of burgesses in legislation was insignificant. Court precedent was a notable tool of legislation, and it may be safely assumed the royal *Cours des Bourgeois* dealt with many unique issues. Even if not all precedents were ordained law, they were still written down in registers which could be consulted whenever similar cases arose. Despite, therefore, the relatively ineffectual powers of jurors when faced with legislation they did not agree with, their ability to set precedents, to amend existing laws, and to keep records of judgements and make them available for consultation, added to the prestige of the *Cour des Bourgeois* as a legal body possessed of the powers to define or redefine certain rules within its community.

Chapter 3

Borgesies

The formation of a free middle class following Latin settlement of Syria and Palestine in the early twelfth century differed in certain aspects to what was taking place in contemporary Europe. In the latter case, one may discern in the sources demographic and topographical changes, namely urban growth, agrarian expansion and long-distance migration. Distinguishable, moreover, were efforts on the part of secular and ecclesiastical overlords to ease the pressures of urbanisation, to accommodate the overspill of rural population in particular areas by constructing villages ex nihilo, and to improve agricultural production in the new settlements. But these social changes together with a growing economy were over a period of time both natural and inevitable. In an altogether different context, the rulers of the kingdom of Jerusalem engineered social change. There were different elements at play. In the beginning the pressure was to reserve property for the sole use of Latin Christians, and to hold on to a small European population the core of which was made up of crusaders. There was, additionally, no significant migration to replenish this minority of people. But, as it has been observed, the characteristics of Latin settlement within the boundaries of the kingdom of Jerusalem 'resembled, in many aspects, the settlement types which existed in southern Europe during the same period'.[1] In fact, similarities were not simply confined to the layout and demography of rural Latin communities, and the basic principles and terminology used to describe tenancy in Latin Eastern cities and *villes neuves* originated in Europe. The term *burgensis*, designating a freeman of a *burgus* (a city or rural bourg), generally appears in French charters from the turn of the eleventh century, and in Normandy around three decades later.[2] Furthermore, the term *burgagium*, designating a type of tenure commonly held by freemen, was first adopted in Norman charters of the early decades of the twelfth century.[3] In England, the free inhabitants of the Anglo-Saxon *burgh* had certain tenurial rights equivalent to those of their counterparts in Normandy, and in the twelfth century the word

---

1 Ellenblum, *Frankish Rural Settlement*, p. 36.

2 Musset, 'Peuplement en bourgage et bourgs ruraux en Normandie du Xe au XIIIe siècle', pp. 180–81.

3 Musset, 'Peuplement en bourgage et bourgs ruraux en Normandie', p. 181. See also Yver, 'Le Droit privé des villes de l'ouest de la France, spécialement des villes normandes', p. 137.

burgagium began appearing in English charters.[4] Perhaps, therefore, we should also look to Normandy and England for the origin of the terms *burgensis* and *burgesia* which were first used to describe person and property in charters of the kingdom of Jerusalem dating from 1110[5] and 1179 respectively.[6] The French word *borgesie*, finally, attained common usage in the law books of the thirteenth century. But would it be accurate to suggest further that the characteristics defining *borgesie* tenure were of Anglo-Norman origin? Certainly, there were fundamental similarities which are highlighted below, but in many other respects *borgesie* tenure in the Latin East developed independently. After all, in Normandy burgage did not become a fully defined and distinct type of tenure until probably the mid-thirteenth century.[7]

As there are no surviving collections of burgess laws other than those of Acre and Nicosia, we have to rely on the evidence of charters. There are relevant charters drawn up in the courts of Acre and Jerusalem – including the patriarch's lordship – Tyre, Caesarea and Haifa. The characteristics of the *borgesie* as well as the procedures of alienation and the duties of court officers and jurors who witnessed transactions, are demonstrated in documents mostly contained in the cartularies of the Church of the Holy Sepulchre[8] and the military order of St John, recording the lease, sale, exchange and eleemosynary donation of property to Church institutions *inter vivos* and *post obit*. The charters of the Teutonic Order and the order of St Lazarus have also been made use of.[9] There is a paucity of charters regarding burgesses and *borgesies* in thirteenth-century Cyprus, but what I have discovered bear out significantly the evidence of Nicosian legislation contained in the 'Livre contrefais'.

The evidence for rural *borgesies* is found mostly in charters of the twelfth century recording Latin settlements in districts of Syria and Palestine. It is possible to ascertain from these documents the rules of tenancy established in some villages and the services and taxes owed by settlers. Other facets of rural life, including the

---

4 Musset, 'Peuplement en bourgage et bourgs ruraux en Normandie', p. 201. On burgage tenure in England in the eleventh and twelfth centuries, see Morley de Wolf Hemmeon, *Burgage Tenure in Mediaeval* England (Cambridge, Mass., 1914); J. Tait, *The Medieval English Borough. Studies on its Origins and Constitutional History* (Manchester, 1936); R.R. Darlington, 'The Early History of English Towns', *History*, 23 (1939): 141–50; Génestal, *La Tenure en bourgage*, pp. 160–66.

5 *R.R.H.*, no. 59, p.13.

6 The term *burgesia* appears in *R.R.H.*, no. 576 (1179), no. 858 (1212) and no. 1242 (1255).

7 E.Z. Tabuteau, *Transfers of Property in Eleventh-Century Norman Law* (North Carolina, 1988), p. 308 (note 168); Yver,'Le Droit Privé des villes de l'ouest de la France, spécialement des villes normandes', p. 137; Musset, 'Peuplement en bourgage et bourgs ruraux en Normandie', p. 200.

8 Bresc-Bautier, no.1–185, including appendices.

9 Marsy, pp. 121–57.

type of work carried out by burgesses, particularly in viticulture and sugar and oil production, have been the subject of a number of archaeological studies.[10]

Those of non-noble status who remained in the Holy Land received shares of property known as *borgesies* first in the conquered cities and then in the newly created rural settlements. As the population of cities gradually expanded in the twelfth century, boundaries were redrawn and adjunct settlements created on the outskirts known as *burgi*. Property in these places was further divided into *borgesies*. The history of the *burgus* of Montmusard, in Acre, is fairly well known, although as populations expanded elsewhere, and the need for space became more urgent, other fringe communities were formed notably in Tyre, Nablus and Tripoli.[11] It is of interest that the Latin Eastern *burgus* developed along similar lines to its European model both as a suburb of a city or a rural settlement. These new villages were centres of agriculture, but some, like Bethgibelin and Castellum Regis in western Galilee, were fortified and heavily defended because of their isolation and vulnerability to attack. One thing they had in common though was their inhabitants were tenants of *borgesies*. The laws and customs of the kingdom recognised properties in the possession of Latin Christians as *borgesies*, in the same way that this generic term of European origin had in the preceding century evolved in meaning to denote not just property of *burgi* but of all settlement types.

The Division of Borgesie Properties

It seems to have been the case that Latin settlers brought with them the fundamental rules of *borgesie* tenancy, which in Europe in the latter half of the eleventh century had become more defined and distinct from other types of property, and typically associated with the class of freemen. Throughout the twelfth century the principles of property possession were imported from Europe, and as in Acre, either *Lo Codi* or some other influential sources were adopted by the legislators of this city. In several respects, whether alienation – the lease, sale, bequest, pledge and donation 'in alms' of *borgesies* – or the symbolic acts of transfer accompanying legal procedures in the *Cours des Bourgeois*, comparisons

---

10 Ellenblum's field study of more than 200 Frankish rural sites has revealed the structure and size of rural buildings, the organisation of houses in villages and the division of farming land; Ellenblum, *Frankish Rural Settlement*, pp. 86–158; Boas, 63–8; D. Pringle, 'Magna Mahumeria (al-Bira): The Archaeology of a Frankish New Town in Palestine', in P.W. Edbury (ed.), *Crusade and Settlement. Papers Read at the First Conference of the Society for the Study of the Crusades and the Latin East and Presented to R.C. Smail* (Cardiff, 1985), pp.147–68.

11 Kohler, p. 178; Marsy, p. 156; D. Puncuh (ed.), *I Libri iurium della Repubblica di Genova* (4 vols, Rome, 1992–98), 1/2, no. 331 (*burgus* of Tyre); Bresc-Bautier, no. 146, p. 285 (*burgus* of Nablus); Strehlke, no. 44 p. 35 (*burgus* of Tripoli), no. 104, pp. 82–4; Ellenblum, *Frankish Rural Settlement*, pp. 43, 53.

can be drawn with practices in European courts. There were similarities not least between duties performed by confirmers and witnesses in public acts of transfer, and the role of courts in preventing or resolving the claims of disputants. The rules of vifgage and mortgage, relating to borrowers' pledge of movable or immovable property to lenders, also warrant attention as they closely corresponded to French and English laws of property. It should be stressed, however, that this legal similitude arising from the adoption of European practices either by the first Latin settlers or their descendants, does not detract from the argument that several important aspects of *borgesies* tenure developed in a unique way, and reflected the process of Latin settlement in the eastern cities and the *villes neuves*. I have already touched upon burgess laws discriminating against indigenous peoples on grounds of religion. This discrimination was reflected in the rules of *borgesies* possession.

From the beginning, all tenants, both under the control of the king and his tenants-in-chief, were accounted for and subject to courts of jurisdiction. The king was ultimate proprietor and beneath him were tenants some of whom enjoyed rights of jurisdiction over territory they had been enffeofed or granted 'in alms'. In royal and seigneurial domains *borgesies* leaseholders were not owners of their properties, but as the author of the 'Livre contrefais' acknowledges, the freedom of tenancy meant they could sub-lease either the whole or part of their holdings under terms of *encensive*.[12] As the law of property developed and the legal language used to describe tenancy evolved, *borgesies* located in a city became known as *heritages*.[13] City houses, which were usually two, three or four storeys high, could be especially rewarding if leased out to more than one tenant.[14] To take a theoretical example, a tenant leasing a two-storey house from the king was permitted to lease the upper storey to a sub-tenant who was conveyed seisin of the property in the *Cour des Bourgeois*. The tenant, thereafter, owed the king *cens* on the whole property while he himself received *cens* from the sub-tenant.[15] In an actual example of 1184, the Hospitallers, tenants of the king and prominent leaseholders in Acre, leased a *borgesie* in the city to a sub-tenant, Bisanson, *ad censum* for twenty-nine besants a year.[16] The rental due was, as in this latter case, money, although alternative or additional services could be performed by a tenant of a *borgesie* to his lord or superior tenant. The terms of tenancy were defined by the lease of a property whether permanent or temporary. There was a distinction made between a *borgesie* held under terms of *encensive*, a property in other words leased in perpetuity and owing dues indefinitely or until such time as when the

---

12 'Livre contrefais', p. 273.

13 'Livre contrefais', p. 287.

14 Bresc-Bautier, no. 68, p. 165; Boas, p. 30.

15 In summary, the king was *seigneur justicier* and *seigneur de l'encensive* in relation to the tenant; the tenant was *seigneur de l'eritage* in relation to the king and the *seigneur de l'encensive* in relation to the sub-tenant; and the sub-tenant was *seigneur de l'eritage* as regards his share of the property.

16 Delaville Le Roulx, *Cartulaire général*, no. 663, pp. 445–6.

tenancy was terminated, and *borgesie* leased for a limited period of time including life.[17] *Borgesies* could be grouped into two further categories: first, property which in the hands of a leaseholder was unburdened by the superior tenant from the payment of rent or the rendering of services, such exemption being conditional and normally ceasing to exist once the tenant sold his tenement; and secondly, property which was originally conceived by a *seigneur justicier* as a *franc borgesie*; this retained its status of exemption from dues whether it was alienated to a new tenant or passed from one generation to the next.

In the law books *encensive* described the permanent transfer of seisin to a tenant with full rights of alienation and inheritance, rights which remained as long as the tenant or his successor paid *cens* yearly. By contrast, *rente* was temporary leasehold the characteristics of which were distinguishable as early as 1136 when the canons of the Holy Sepulchre gave Andrew and his wife Hosana permission to build a house on land belonging to the church in Jerusalem. The land was a *borgesie* held from the king by the canons. The terms of the leasehold were approved and witnessed by the royal *Cour des Bourgeois* which agreed the couple could hold the tenancy for life, paying the church two besants a year, and if Andrew predeceased his wife or vice versa, the remaining spouse could remain living in the house as long as the rent was paid annually. When both died, the house would once again revert to the canons who assumed sole possession because the lessees did not possess seisin of the property in perpetuity, neither being vested with rights of inheritance or alienation.[18] For many poorer burgess families, the offer of land presented an opportunity to build a home, and although religious orders usually profited financially from the lease of *borgesies*, they were also prepared, as in this case, to make charitable exceptions by charging only peppercorn rents. They of course benefited from the construction of new houses they would eventually possess.

Andrew and Hosana's temporary leasehold was to last for a lifetime, although this was a generous concession on the part of the canons of the Holy Sepulchre. It was more typical for *rente* to last between three months and a year, accommodating visiting merchants and pilgrims in the coastal cities. Short-term tenancy held obvious advantages to lessors as they were freer to modify the terms of tenure without conceding seisin and right of alienation.[19] There was also the financial benefit to be had from short-term lease, so it was necessary to have laws

---

17 In the 'Livre contrefais', a *borgesie* leased for a defined period of time was described as a *rente* property. The royal *Cour des Bourgeois* in Nicosia was responsible for the management of city *borgesies*, including 'houses, gardens, lands and other things similar and of the *rente* and *encensive* of these *borgesies*'; 'Livre contrefais', p. 251.

18 Bresc-Bautier, no. 103, pp. 222–3.

19 In Antioch, the short-term lease of a *borgesie* on a monthly or yearly basis compelled a lessee to pay the lessor the whole amount of rent he owed him if he was not able to fulfil the terms of his lease. He could be excused this payment if he was leaving for Europe or Cyprus, but not if he wished to go to other cities like Tyre or Acre; Alishan, p. 70.

which would disincline merchants and pilgrims from entering into contracts of leasehold when they had neither the intention nor the means of honouring them. A measure of the popularity of temporary leasehold is found in the inventories of Italian possessions in Acre and Tyre, where, according to the Genoese inventory of the *consules* William di Bulgaro and Simone Malocello, *borgesies* were rented *ad passagium* – when the fleets were in. These properties were specially set aside for lease by visiting merchants who rented houses and shops for a period of some months[20] or for a year, *ad annum*.[21] In the Venetian quarters in Acre and Tyre *borgesies* were similarly administered. Marsiglio Zorzi's inventory for Tyre listed two shops which were rented monthly,[22] and another house *ad annum*.[23] The church of St Mark's was also in possession of several *borgesies* within the Venetian quarter. Near the square it had two shops which it leased yearly for nine besants and twelve besants,[24] and a further two small shops it leased monthly.[25] In the Venetian quarter in Acre, the inventory records that some *borgesies* were leased *ad censum*, whilst other properties were rented monthly and 'cum uenit caravana'.[26] For the Italian communities the arrival of the *passagium*, and the increased traffic of merchants, pilgrims and other visitors, was undoubtedly a boon to the local economy. There was a conscious effort on the part of the commune to take advantage of this seasonal swell in the number of visitors, by reserving premises for short-term rental even though the rest of the year they may have remained vacant. But it was, reciprocally, beneficial to those who wished to stay in Acre or Tyre for a few months to trade. Some visitors even received preferential treatment, thus the Venetian quarter made sure that properties were set aside for rent specifically by merchants arriving from Venice.[27]

Short-term leasehold may be associated with the needs of a growing economy, but on the whole, burgess settlement in eastern cities and villages was built upon *encensive* tenure. A tenant who held his property under terms of *encensive* was obliged to pay his lord *cens* (a fixed rent) annually on a feast day – a saint's day

---

20 C. Desimoni (ed.), 'Quatre titres des propriétés à Acre et à Tyr', in *AOL*, II (1884), p. 216: 'Fuit summa de eo quod apautatae fuerunt ad passagium'.

21 Desimoni,'Quatre titres des propriétés à Acre et à Tyr', p. 216: 'Incipiunt hic apautus ad annum et fuerunt apautus ad annum'. And p. 219 for similar terms of leasehold in Nicosia and Famagusta.

22 Berggötz, p.145:'Habet duas stationes.cum locantur, recipitur pro una quoque mense xxiiii Biz'.

23 Berggötz, p.148:'Habetur de ea, cum potest locari, Biz. unus in anno'. There were of course *borgesies* which were held under terms of *encensive* in the Venetian quarter in Tyre. A shop, for example, was leased to Thomas Dulce for two besants (Berggötz, p.148). This was similarly the case in the Genoese quarter; Desimoni, 'Quatre titres des propriétés à Acre et à Tyr', p. 219: 'Incipiuntur census qui annuatim redduntur et solvuntur comuni'.

24 Berggötz, p. 143.

25 Berggötz, p. 145.

26 Berggötz, p. 176.

27 Berggötz, p. 173:'que non locatur nisi mercatoribus, qui venerunt de Venecia'.

usually served as a reminder to a lessee of when rent was due. The rent collected by the lord from the properties he leased out was one source of revenue, but it should be distinguished from additional tax levied on his *borgesies*. The collection of *tallea* was generally speaking a seigneurial right.[28] The tenant (or *seigneur de l'eritage*) paid *cens* in money or in kind proportionate to the size of the property concerned, because payment was not merely a token gesture. Rather the payment of *cens* could be a heavy burden reflecting the size or location of the property, and certainly in the village settlements there were occasional rental exemptions with the aim possibly of drawing new settlers.[29] This was common practice in contemporary Europe where lords of *burgi* offered generous terms of settlement in order to attract new migrants. It is also known that in thirteenth-century Normandy, lords who wished burgesses to settle in their cities demanded only a nominal payment of *cens* from their tenants.[30]

The collection of *cens* was an important source of income for the city lords, the Italian communities and the military orders. In the inventories of rent collected by the Church of the Holy Sepulchre in Jerusalem (c.1160–c.1187) and the Venetians (compiled between 1242 and 1244) and Genoese (1249) in Acre and Tyre,[31] the amount of *cens* collected varied from city to city and from house to house, suggesting the amount paid was proportionate to the value of the property. Of course over several decades property prices in the kingdom reflected inflationary changes, and as such it is difficult to make a comparison of like with like. A rough estimate as to the value of one besant may be derived from the calculation that a knight's fief between 1165 and 1265 could be worth about 300 besants.[32] However, the inventories do provide a snapshot of rents paid by tenants at any one time and at any one place. A case in point is the inventory of Genoese possessions in Acre where rents *ad censum* in 1249 ranged from between one besant and thirty besants. A notable difference, but one which is understandable from a commercial point of view, is that rents *ad annum* – leaseholds with a terminal date – were generally much higher than rents ad *censum*. Rents *ad annum* were a very lucrative source of revenue with rents ranging from between ten and 300 besants a property.[33] By and large, lessors could obtain the highest monthly rents from commercial premises, in particular shops. Certain shops in the Venetian quarter in Tyre were according to Marsiglio Zorzi leased out for twenty-four besants a month, or the sum of 288

---

28 See, for example, Guy of Lusignan's confirmation of Pisan privileges in Acre (1189), including the right to collect *tallea* from nationals living in houses situated outside their quarter; Müller, no. 32, p. 38.

29 Bresc-Bautier, no. 126, pp. 252–3.

30 Génestal, pp. 90–93.

31 Bresc-Bautier, no. 168, pp. 321–2, Berggötz, pp. 142–45; Desimoni, 'Quatre titres des propriétés à Acre et à Tyr', pp. 215–21.

32 Riley-Smith, *The Feudal Nobility and the Kingdom of Jerusalem*, p. 10.

33 Desimoni, 'Quatre titres des propriétés à Acre et à Tyr', no. 2, pp. 216–21.

besants a year.[34] High rental is implicative of the profitability of these sought after business outlets. But such a commercial undertaking was not without risk. Although rent was temporary, lessees were obliged to enter into a contract of leasehold extending over several months. The rules of tenancy in Antioch where lessees bound by the terms of a contract were not permitted to terminate prematurely their leasehold excepting in certain cases, also suggests they were committed to paying a considerable amount of rent, perhaps in advance, whether successful in their commercial venture or not.[35]

The Alienation of Borgesies

The tenant of a *borgesie* could sell, exchange, donate, or pledge his property to Latins and native Christians. He could also lease it for a period of time to Latins, native Christians and, possibly, non-Christians. The characteristic alienability of burgess property was the basis of its popularity, and, it may even be suggested, partly the reason why Latin settlement in Syria and Palestine was successful. Latin society was strengthened and stabilised by a property hierarchy – stretching from the lord of the domain down to the lowest leaseholders – and bound together by a system of jurisdiction which rigidly enforced the rules of tenure. Foremost, the permanent alienation of a *borgesie* could not be carried out privately, and for a transaction involving property in lay hands to be accepted in law it had to have taken place in no court other than the *Cour des Bourgeois*.[36] Throughout the histories of the kingdoms of Jerusalem and Cyprus there was no digression from this legal principle. Private alienation would have weakened the basis of Latin settlement because this meant *seigneurs justiciers* exercised less control over who was in possession of property. Other requirements were stringently applied. A charter detailing the transfer of a property was judged invalid if drawn up by a notary outside the court, and its authenticity had to be guaranteed by the seal of the viscount or his deputy. Written evidence had also to be signed by witnesses who, if a transaction was contested, could be called upon for their testimony in deciding a case.[37] Before the advent of registers in the *Cour des Bourgeois*, charters were an essential means of proving possession of property.

The status of a *borgesie* meant the tenant had rights we would normally associate with a freeholder. But a fundamental difference existed. Although a *borgesie* under terms of *encensive* was granted in perpetuity, the rights of the tenant were conditional from the time he first acquired his property. His leasehold was based on obligations he had as a permanent resident responsible for the upkeep

---

34 Berggötz, p. 145.

35 Alishan, p. 70.

36 Kausler, p. 249 (cf. Beugnot, 'Livre des assises', p. 158): 'Por ce que vente ne se peut faire de borgesie sans cort'.

37 Kausler, pp. 160–61 (cf. Beugnot, 'Livre des assises', pp. 98–100).

of his house or the cultivation of his land. Therefore, a *seigneur justicier* was within his right to expropriate property and a superior tenant (the *seigneur de l'encensive*) could sequester a *borgesie* if the lessee defaulted on the payment of rent or failed to carry out other services required of him.[38] It was also the case that a *seigneur de l'eritage* who failed to pay rent without acquiring consent to defer payment, could forfeit his *borgesie* a year and a day after the money was due. The *seigneur de l'encensive* could seize his tenant's property and in his hands it became a gage for the payment of rent in arrears.[39] This underlines the fact that although a burgess leased *borgesies* under terms of *encensive* in perpetuity, his status as a tenant was based on obligations he had to fulfil a service from one year to the next. By the fourteenth century, however, the law in Cyprus seems to have adopted a more conciliatory approach. It was decreed that default on payment should not mean automatic loss of property, and so if a tenant was unable to pay *cens* and the *seigneur de l'encensive* accepted the reason for non-payment, the tenant could be permitted to abandon (*guerpir*) his *borgesie* until such time as he was able to pay. The tenant or his descendants had the right to reclaim the property by paying the arrears of rent, provided the *seigneur de l'encensive* had not leased the *borgesie* to someone else.[40]

A superior tenant of a *borgesie* could sell his right to collect *cens* from his sub-tenant. The *vente des encensives* is further evidence *cens* was not merely a nominal payment, but a valuable and saleable source of yearly income for a lessor. The buyer, in such a sale, constituted a third party, and purchased not the *borgesie* but the right to collect *cens* from the property. It is difficult to form a clear picture of this type of alienation in Nicosia as the 'Livre contrefais' only briefly mentions that a *seigneur de l'encensive* could sell the rent he received from a sub-tenant.[41] Probably, the procedure to authorise this type of sale in court – which again was mandatory – was no different to that accompanying permanent alienation of immovable property. One common factor in Nicosia was sales tax; the person who purchased the right to collect rent was obliged to pay three besants and two *solidi* to the *Cour des Bourgeois* for seisin.[42] The brief treatment of *vente des encensives* in the 'Livre contrefais' does leave some questions unanswered. Why would a tenant choose this type of sale, and what enduring rights of tenure did he have after disposing of the yearly income he received from rent, bearing in mind he retained seisin of the *borgesie*?

Most probably, *vente des encensives* was done out of pressing financial need,

---

38 Kausler, pp. 123–4 (cf. Beugnot, 'Livre des assises', p. 76).

39 Kausler, p. 124 (cf. Beugnot, 'Livre des assises', p.76); 'Livre contrefais', pp. 274–6.

40 'Livre contrefais', p. 274.

41 'Livre contrefais', p. 259: 'Chascun peut aussi vendre l'encensive que il a sur aucun heritage, et de ceste vente doit ausi desaizine en saizine et paier la saizine III bezans et II sos'.

42 'Livre contrefais', p. 259.

an immediate solution perhaps to a burden of debt. But as in any form of permanent transaction, a tenant had to weigh up the short-term financial advantage of a sale, against the long-term disadvantage of giving away his right and the right of his heirs to a rent which could eventually amount to a sum much greater than what he was selling it for. But what advantages did the tenant gain from retaining seisin of the property? Besides preserving his status as a burgess – property, as it has been argued, defined status – it may be he benefited from other non-monetary services attached to the lease. Presumably, he remained free to sell, donate or bequeath the *borgesie* to his heirs. Equally, the purchaser of the *cens* was free to resell, donate or bequeath the yearly collection of rent, but his successors had no rights over seisin of the property. The sale of *cens* was total and forever binding; it is not known whether the conveyance of rent could be done for a temporary period of time. Whether indeed the law permitted a man to sell only a part of the *cens* he received from a *borgesie* while retaining the other part – a practice admissible under Norman law in the twelfth century[43] – is also a matter of conjecture.

Though there is no reference to *vente des encensives* in the 'Livre de la Cour des Bourgeois', there are extant two charters dating from the late twelfth and thirteenth centuries which are of relevance. The first, originating in Jerusalem in 1179, bears some resemblance to this type of sale, though, unfortunately, the text is ambiguously worded. Nicholas Manzur was *seigneur de l'encensive* of a house and some land situated in the vicinity of Jerusalem near a cistern of his. This property was sub-leased from him by Helen Parmentier who owed rent of ten besants a year for the house and twenty besants for the land. Helen had given the land to the Hospitallers on the condition they carried on paying Nicholas Manzur the *cens* including the ten besants she had paid yearly for her house. Subsequently, Nicholas Manzur sold to the Hospitallers the perpetual *cens* they owed him for 300 besants – 'tam predictam terram quam supranominatos bisantios xxx libere et quiete habeant' – and, thereafter, the order was exempted from the yearly payment of rent, a right which it was to enjoy in perpetuity. As this kind of service-exemption constituted a sale, the agreement was overseen by the royal *Cour des Bourgeois*. The author of the charter, acknowledging the legal challenges which this agreement may invite – in particular on account of the perpetual nature of the transaction – recorded the consent and legitimacy conferred by the court, and the promise made by Nicholas Manzur and his wife to guarantee the permanency of the deal. Although the king was present – which may testify to the importance of this sale – Rohard, castellan of the Tower of David, acted as head of the court of seven burgess jurors. Sales tax of two besants and two *solidi* was paid to the court.[44]

Evidence of *vente des encensives* in Acre is found in a charter of 1273. A Thomas de Bailleu sold to Conrad of Nevel, Grand Commander of the order of

43 A discussion of sale of rent in twelfth-century Normandy is found in R. Génestal, *Le Rôle des monastères comme établissement de crédit: Etudié en Normandie du XIe à la fin du XIIIe siècle* (Paris, 1901), p. 87ff.

44 Delaville Le Roulx, *Cartulaire général*, no. 554, p. 376.

Teutonic Knights, the right to collect 175 besants and 22 corroubles in rent from certain houses he possessed in the city. The vendor and the buyer appeared before the *Cour des Bourgeois* – which was made up of the viscount and twelve jurors – and in a typical procedure the viscount disseised Thomas de Bailleu of the right to collect *cens*, then, symbolically, vested himself with seisin before transferring right to Conrad of Nevel. Conrad purchased the rent as well as a *heritage* also belonging to Thomas for a total sum of 6720 besants, and paid three besants to the court in sales tax. An important provision of the document, and one which we shall see repeated frequently in charters of sale, is that the lord of the domain, in this case the king, has the basic right to pre-empt the sale.[45]

Rental Payment and Franc Borgesie

Cens or *rente*, payments in money, were the dominant forms of dues imposed on *borgesies*, but they were not necessarily the only forms. Although not mentioned specifically in the charters, additional and obligatory services are alluded to. There is mention, occasionally, of the *servicium* owing on a particular *borgesie*.[46] Certainly in contemporary Europe city property could be burdened by extra services the lord of the property wished to enforce.[47] The extent, however, to which services and other forms of rental dues over and above money-rent were entrenched in *borgesies* tenancy is difficult to evaluate. The reduction of labour rent and rent services in contemporary Europe has been well documented by historians,[48] and if the importance of a money economy in the kingdom of Jerusalem and Cyprus is to be accepted, this may have had a similar effect on tenancy in the East.

Bearing in mind the various forms of payment levied on *borgesies*, it is possible to consider what was meant by a rental-exempt property and a *franc borgesie*. A rental-exempt *borgesie* was a property that previously burdened by *cens* and other services, was granted to a tenant free of these exactions totally or partially. In c. 1126 Ralph de Fontaines conceded to Godfrey de Arcu, a loyal servant of his, a vineyard in Jerusalem situated near the patriarch's lordship, which he was to possess 'with hereditary right and with the freedom even to sell or to give it to whomever he wished, and this (he would hold) without any exactions and

---

45 The text of this document was edited by Marie-Luise Favreau-Lilie in 'The Teutonic Knights in Acre after the Fall of Montfort (1271): Some Reflections', in B.Z. Kedar, H.E. Mayer and R.C. Smail (eds), *Outremer. Studies in the History of the Crusading Kingdom of Jerusalem* (Jerusalem, 1982), 'appendix', pp. 283–4.

46 Delaville Le Roulx, *Cartulaire général*, no, 399, pp. 273.

47 Génestal, p. 118.

48 P. Spufford, *Money and its Use in Medieval Europe* (Cambridge, 1988), p. 240ff., R. Fossier, *La Terre et les hommes en Picardie jusqu'à la fin du XIIIe siècle* (Paris, 1968), pp. 93–9.

any services owed'.[49] The charter makes no specific reference to *cens*, but the clause 'sine omni conditione et omnis servitii debito', alludes to exemption from various ancillary services associated with the tenancy of the *borgesie*. Ralph of Fontaines was perfectly entitled as a possessor of a *borgesie* to make these exemptions in favour of his long-time servant, provided he received permission to do so from the royal *Cour des Bourgeois*. Yet, he himself as tenant of the king was not necessarily immune from the payment of *cens* and services he owed the crown for the same property. In this case there is no evidence the property in question was definable as a *franc borgesie*. We should recognise instead that a *franc borgesie* 'returned no *cens* to the king or to any other person'.[50] It was the initial choice of the *seigneur justicier* to grant a 'free *borgesie*' and to exempt the recipient from the *cens*. The 'Livre de la Cour des Bourgeois' states exemption only from yearly *cens* but does not elaborate on whether other forms of obligatory services prevailed. What is certain, however, is that a *franc borgesie* remained invariably subject to the jurisdiction of the *Cour des Bourgeois*, and any subsequent alienation of the property by the recipient had to take place in the court and in the presence of the king's representative. In Acre, at least, the seller of a *franc borgesie* paid the court no sales tax, whereas the buyer was obliged to pay three besants.[51]

The *franc borgesie* was the creation of the *seigneur justicier*, but it is important to determine whether such a property was considered as such from the beginning, or whether in fact its status resulted from the lord exempting a tenant from the payment of *cens*. The theory that the act of freeing, of redefining the terms of a tenancy through exemption, was one way of creating a *franc borgesie*, is supported by two charters of the twelfth century. In 1137, William, patriarch of Jerusalem, granted Walter de Lucia permission to sell a house he had built in the patriarchal lordship to Robert Medicus for eighty besants. The transfer of seisin was witnessed and authorised by the court of the patriarch. The conveyed leasehold was an *encensive* committing Robert to payment of one besant a year in return for rights of inheritance and alienation. Three decades later (1167) Robert sold the same house to the Hospitallers who as new tenants continued paying the patriarch the *cens* of one besant a year.[52] There was nothing unusual about this process of alienating a conventional *borgesie*, but in another charter of 1167, Patriarch Amalric, having received a number of houses from the order, conceded in return a plot of land and exempted the Hospitallers from the payment of *cens* owing on the house they had purchased from Robert Medicus. In this instance, the *franc borgesie* was created by freeing a property permanently from *cens* it had previously been burdened with. Its status was redefined indefinitely in rental terms and in legal terms.

A *franc borgesie* could be given for various reasons. In 1161, Queen Theodora

49 Bresc-Bautier, no. 96, pp. 214–15.

50 Kausler, p. 66 (cf. Beugnot, 'Livre des assises', p. 36).

51 Kausler, p. 66 (cf. Beugnot, 'Livre des assises', p. 36).

52 J. Delaville Le Roulx (ed.), *Les Archives, la bibliothèque et le trésor de l'Ordre de Saint-Jean de Jérusalem à Malte* (Paris, 1883), no. 25, pp. 107–108.

gave Richard Anglicus, a servant in her household, a house in Jerusalem free in perpetuity.[53] The concession was done in gratitude for his loyal service, in the same way that in 1189, Conrad of Montferrat granted Martin Rocia, a Genoese, a *franc borgesie* in Tyre 'pro bono servicio et maxima fidelitate'.[54] The freeing of property from rent could even be offered as incentive to resolve a disagreement. In Jerusalem in 1153, Patriarch Fulcher gave to Benscelinus and his wife Goda a *franc borgesie* after they had ended a dispute with the church over certain properties in Bethany.[55] Release from the payment of *cens* once certain conditions had been met could also be written into a charter of leasehold. In 1239, the Church of Mount Zion leased in perpetuity a plot of land *pro censum* in the vicinity of Acre to the Teutonic Knights for twenty besants a year. It was agreed that if in future the Teutonic Order wished to give the church another plot of land 'free in perpetuity', it would be exempted from the payment of *cens* owing on its property in Acre.[56] This provision seems to have been written into the leasehold agreement by the Teutonic Knights as an incentive to the church to fix the rent at a reasonable rate for the foreseeable future.

There are charters which confirm the existence of *franc borgesie* tenancy in the kingdom of Cyprus, as well as hinting at other idiosyncrasies of this property type. In 1247, John of Ibelin, count of Jaffa, sold to Eustorgius, archbishop of Nicosia, four gardens in the city, for the considerable sum of 2500 besants. The properties were to be enjoyed by the archbishop 'francement et quitement'. A particularly striking provision of this document is the grant to the buyer of unconditional freedom of alienation, stating that Eustogius could sell, donate and engage the properties 'à qui qu'il vous plaira, soit eglise ou maison de religion, ou à gens lais'.[57] In the light of what we know about *borgesie* possession, this was a significant condition given that in the kingdoms of Jerusalem and Cyprus there was general legislation prohibiting the sale of city property to churchmen and members of the military orders.[58] This may have been an exceptional agreement between John and Archbishop Eustogius, but an alternative explanation is that rules governing the alienation of *francs borgesies* may have been less stringent than those governing conventional *borgesies*, meaning the possessor of a *franc borgesie* had greater freedom when deciding to sell, donate or pledge his property.

In the past, *francs borgesies* have been associated with allods, the logic of the argument being that some of the first crusaders who acquired property through the arbitrary seizure of land, that is the 'law of conquest', owned their possessions as freeholds and were vested with absolute control of their possessions.[59] It is true

53 Marsy, no. 20, p. 138.
54 Strehlke, no. 24, p. 21.
55 Bresc-Bautier, no. 114, p. 234; see also no. 102, pp. 220–22, and no. 65, pp. 160–61.
56 Strehlke, no. 86, p. 68.
57 Mas-Latrie, *Histoire de l'île de Chypre*, pp. 647–8.
58 For Nicosia, see 'Livre contrefais', pp. 255, 265.
59 Prawer, *Crusader Institutions*, pp. 240–62.

commentators like Fulcher of Chartres, Albert of Aachen and Raymond of Aguilers, gave accounts of how the victorious Latins conquered cities and arbitrarily laid claim to Muslim houses they entered.[60] The picture they painted was one of overwhelming victory, the Muslims in the cities swept away, their possessions seized and their properties confiscated. Displacement was total, but a closer reading of the text reveals a more prosaic process of occupation. The crusade leaders anticipated the disorder which would follow victory, and accepted men had to be rewarded for their efforts and housed immediately. However, in their eyes, the 'law of conquest' and the division of property should be a more ordered state of affairs. Indeed, such a process of occupation seems to have been a common way of rewarding men who had taken part in a siege, and was not confined to the early years of the kingdom's formation. In the second half of the twelfth century, Usamah ibn-Munqdh related how Latins on entering Apamea placed a sign of the cross on whatever house they claimed as their possession.[61] Interestingly, Usamah also referred to Baldwin I's march on Damascus in 1113 and how the knights, anticipating victory, had sold in advance the houses in the city to the burgesses with them (*burjasi*).[62] The accuracy of this statement though is questionable, as Usamah's intention in making it was to suggest the over-confidence of the Latins before their subsequent defeat by the Muslims.

But the 'law of conquest' evolved in the twelfth century. The right of a man to lay claim to a house in Muslim hands after entering a city, no longer applied if the property had previously been abandoned by a Latin Christian. This new legal dimension was inevitable given that city burgesses were frequently displaced by occupying armies or forced to abandon their properties because of the threat of invasion. When Acre fell to the armies of King Philip of France and King Richard of England in 1191, the burgesses – soldiers presumably who had fought to win back their city as well as previous inhabitants – came and requested Philip to return the *borgesies* they had been forced to abandon in 1187, and which were now in the hands of the knights who had re-conquered the city. The burgesses claimed right of possession because they had not sold their tenements. Their core argument was that they were tenants in perpetuity and their rights as possessors of *borgesies* had been interrupted by enforced abandonment but not negated. The king, with the counsel of his barons, agreed and instructed those who proved possession could reclaim their property.[63]

However city properties were acquired, the point remains that there is no strong evidence of *allodia* in the kingdom of Jerusalem. There is after all no mention of this type of holding in the law books. Surely freeholders were as much

---

60 Fulcher of Chartres, p. 304; Albert of Aachen, p. 479; Raymond of Aguilers, p.150ff.

61 Usamah Ibn Munqidh, *Kitab al-i'tibar*, ed. P.K. Hitti (Princeton, 1930), p. 148.

62 Usamah Ibn Munqidh, *Kitab al-i'tibar*, p. 115.

63 *Ernoul, Chronique d'Ernoul et de Bernard la Trésorier*, ed. L. de Mas-Latrie (Paris, 1871), pp. 274–6.

in need of the protection of the law as ordinary leaseholders, and would, if they truly existed, have warranted mention as well as the special exemptions they enjoyed. It is only conceivable that for a very short period after the occupation of a city, Latin Christians held property as freeholders. But this was only a temporary status which was not recognised by the law or the lord to whom new inhabitants had to make known themselves and their possessions. In the cities there were strict rules as to who could acquire property, and so too in the Latin rural villages where settlement seems to have been planned and the controlling authority alone had the right to create and lease properties. There is, therefore, little or no evidence *francs borgesies*, or for that matter *francs fiés*, were, in the truest sense of the word, synonymous with *allodia*. Rather, a *franc borgesie* was property owing no *cens* to the lord of the domain, in the same way the possessor of a *franc fié*, as defined by John of Ibelin, owed no money-rent service or homage to a lord.[64] Yet, immunity from certain exactions did not necessarily confer absolute freedom on the possessor or total detachment from the lord of the domain in whose jurisdiction the property was located. In the case of a *franc fié*, the lord retained certain inalienable rights beyond that of homage and service, and in a discussion of the French *franc fié*, Hubert Richardot argued that although the holder of this fief – otherwise known as a *feudum francum* or *feudum honoratum* – was exempted from the performance of services and the swearing of homage, he was still obliged to render *fides*, faithfulness, and security to his lord.[65] So there had been partial exemption and not absolute freedom. In the case of a *franc borgesie* the argument for partial exemption is even more compelling. The 'Livre de la Cour des Bourgeois' mentions only immunity from the payment of *cens* for those who possessed *francs borgesies*, a statement which cannot be readily taken as meaning total exemption from all services. The alienation of a *franc borgesie* remained under the lord's jurisdiction, so unlike *allodia*, its transfer required the permission of his court. The *seigneur justicier* had the right, therefore, to authorise or to oppose the alienation of his property and to make record of its sale in the court register. Evidence which proves possession of a *franc borgesie* did not constitute absolute ownership, and that the *seigneur justicier* retained jurisdiction over the permanent transfer of such a property, can be found in one of the French continuations of the History of William of Tyre. In 1276, King Hugh departed from Acre in anger, one reason being the indignation he felt toward the Templars for having purchased the *casale* of Fauconerie from a certain knight, Thomas of St Bertin, without his permission. The knights, informs the continuation, 'tenoit le dit casal de *borjoysie*, dont il ne devoit homage ne service'. They had purchased the *casale* 'sanz congie dou roy'. Apart from the interesting reference to the homage which may have been paid by tenants of a conventional *borgesie*, the fact that though Thomas of St Bertin had been exempted from all service, the king demanded right of jurisdiction over the

---

64 John of Ibelin, p. 309.

65 H. Richardot, 'Francs-fiefs. Essai sur l'exemption totale ou partielle des services de fief', *Revue Historique de Droit Français et Etranger*, 27 (1949): p. 229ff.

sale of this *franc borgesie*.[66] Perhaps the king had for some reason previously objected to the alienation of this village, or the Templars had participated in this private alienation in order to challenge the authority of the royal *Cour des Bourgeois* in Acre. Whatever the case, King Hugh had judged their actions as an undermining of his powers of consent as he recognised no freehold tenure in his domain. Such an abuse of the laws of tenancy was not unique however. Illegal property alienations in the thirteenth century may have accounted for a significant but undetectable number of transactions. Indeed, in Cyprus private and unlawful transfers seem to have got out of hand, so much so that in Henry II's ban of 1298 all members of the Church and Italian merchants were to surrender their properties except those 'who can prove they held their *borgesies* by the concession and consent of the seigneur'.[67]

The episode involving King Hugh and the Templars is important in highlighting how in the latter part of the thirteenth century no type of burgess tenancy – at least in royal domain – had evolved into absolute ownership. *Franc borgesie* should not be interpreted as meaning free and private possession, and we should not automatically assume a holder exempted from *cens* was not subject to some other monetary payment. The charters do in fact mention payment *pro recognoscimento*. In the inventory of Genoese possessions in Acre a distinction was made between tenants of *borgesies* who paid the commune yearly dues *ad censum* and those who paid *pro recognoscimento*. The inventory gives two examples, one of which reads, 'Domus Iacobi de Levanto, pro recognoscimento annuatim ... bisancii iv'.[68] The inhabitants of the two *borgesies* were not burdened by *cens* but made a token payment yearly to the Genoese commune who then recognised the special status of their holdings. As this was a nominal due the sum they paid did not reflect the true value of the properties leased. The inference is that these houses in the Genoese quarter were *francs borgesies*, an explanation all the more plausible if it is accepted their occupants who returned rent *pro recognoscimento*, could remain burdened by monetary exactions other than cens, in the same way in contemporary Europe the holders of some *francs fiés* remained paying their lords a recognative rent in perpetuity.[69] In the kingdom of Cyprus, correspondingly, there were different types of monetary exaction depending on the nature of the tenancy. The 'Livre contrefais' makes a distinction between types of *borgesies* and rents: 'encensive', 'redevance' and 'autre reconoissance'.[70] It seems in Nicosia some tenants returned rent *pro recognoscimento* in lieu of *cens*.

As we have seen, all quarters of a Latin Christian eastern city, apart from those parts inhabited by indigenous peoples, were made up of *borgesies* as well as *francs*

66 'L'Estoire de Eracles Empereur et la conqueste de la terre d'outremer', I, p. 474.

67 'Bans et ordonnances', p. 361.

68 Desimoni, 'Quatre titres des propriétés à Acre et à Tyr', p. 221.

69 Richardot, 'Francs-fiefs. Essai sur l'exemption totale ou partielle des services de fief', p. 268.

70 'Livre contrefais', p. 276.

borgesies holdings. Some were places of habitation, whilst others served as premises from which burgesses could ply their trade. On the whole, all leaseholders paid rent commensurate to the market value of their property, apart from those who, as highlighted above, had special exemption to pay only a nominal rent. The holders of *borgesies* were a privileged class of people and especially those who were in possession of so-called 'free' burgage tenure. There was, however, a class of city dwellers, all be it a very small one, who though living in *borgesies* were not entitled to the same privileges as their neighbours. In Nicosia these people, who were described as 'serfs du roi', were probably servants of the royal household whose *borgesies* were tied properties.[71] Servants retained their *borgesies* whilst in the service of the king, but were not permitted to lease, sell, donate or pledge their properties. They did not have the burgess right of unconditional freedom of alienation, and as the *borgesies* were tied properties it is unlikely their children had right of inheritance.[72] Therefore, a buyer seeking to purchase the *borgesie* of a 'serf du roi' was in contravention of the law: the property would not escheat to the buyer and he would lose any money he had paid for it. Equally, a lender who held the property of a 'serf' as security against a loan was contravening the law.[73]

The Heritage de Fié

The alienation of *borgesies*, as it has been consistently argued, was subject to a burgess court, but there was, significantly, a type of hybrid property in the cities which stands out as an exception to this rule. In cases where a city tenement had been joined in some formal manner to a fief, the legal standing of the *borgesie* was modified. The author of the 'Livre contrefais' sets out the terms of this tenancy-type in rather esoteric terms, stating that the *Cour des Bourgeois* 'se uze et se doit uzer de toutes manieres de bourgesies sauve d'aucunes qui sont esté faites par la Haute Court, *si com sont pluzors maisons et jardins et chans qui sont joins as fiés*'.[74] What was this type of property which was described elsewhere in the law book as *heritage de fié*? Was it a *borgesie* which in some way formed part of a fief? The author of the *Livre au Roi* wrote that the fief of a deceased feudatory should escheat to his eldest child, but that 'borgesies qui au dit fié n'apartienent, si com sont maisons et terres et jardins et vignes', should be equally divided among

---

71 'Livre contrefais', p. 259: 'Sachés que il y a une autre maniere de ventes des heritages, qui sont des sers dou roy, et par le coumandement qui a esté fait en la court, que nul serf ne serve dou roi ne puisse vendre ne doner ne engager son heritage ne aliene'. Henry II's ban of 1298 exempted his servants from the ruling that churchmen and Italian merchants had to hand over their illegally held *borgesies*; 'Bans et ordonnances', p. 361.

72 'Livre contrefais', p. 259.

73 'Bans et ordonnances', p. 371.

74 'Livre contrefais', p. 251.

the other children.[75] That is to say, if the *borgesie* had been part of a fief it would have escheated to the eldest child. A different set of inheritance laws thus prevailed.

Heritage de fié tenancy was common in the thirteenth century, and the distinctiveness of this property-type, a *borgesie* or part of a *borgesie* incorporated in a fief, is confirmed by the 'Livre contrefais'.[76] A further description indicating the uniqueness of *heritage de fié* can be found in the *Assises de Romanie* of the principality of Achaia where it is written, 'Et si lo Principo far puo borgesia de feo, over parte de feo'.[77] The appeal of *heritage de fié* to feudatories was threefold. First, they could hold *borgesies* which otherwise they would not have been permitted to because of the law of the land. Secondly, they could enjoy the alienation and inheritance rights of this type of property. And, thirdly, they could not be subject in any way to the lesser *Cour des Bourgeois*, because the jurisdiction of such property was entrusted to the High Court or a seigneurial court. But it is not wholly clear how *heritages des fiés* were created. Was it the case that fief-holders joined the *heritages* of which they were tenants to their fiefs? Did this require the permission of the *Cour des Bourgeois* once the jurisdictional authority which it had over *heritages* was transferred to the High Court or a seigneurial court?

The rear-vassal who possessed a *heritage de fié* owed service both for the fief and the *borgesie* either directly to the king or to his lord. If he wished to lease the *borgesie* only he could do so in a seigneurial court. In theory, his fief could not be alienated separately from the *borgesie* and vice versa, but it was not unprecedented for the property to be divided. The legal complications this created were many, but there were it seems occasions when fief-holders alienated their *heritages* in the royal *Cour des Bourgeois* without informing the court that the properties they were selling were *heritages des fiés*.[78] But of what benefit was this to the knights? We may suppose that by contravening the rules of *heritage de fié* they were able to alienate only the *borgesie* and not the whole of their fief. In other words, they could manipulate the legal system to their own ends, either subjecting their tenancy to the High Court, or, when it suited their finances, reverting to the burgess court. By all accounts, this was a common practice and one which was done discreetly with not much danger of detection. As, on the whole, city properties were *borgesies*, there was a difficulty in distinguishing property attached to fiefs.

---

75 M. Greilsammer (ed.), *Le Livre au Roi* (Paris, 1995), pp. 241, 263–6.

76 'Livre contrefais', p. 315: 'Il avint que le bon Henri ... vost et coumanda que tous les heritage qui estoient de fiés fussent especefiés et par previleges et par Segrete et par toute autre maniere, et furent mis par escrit. Lesqués se troverent pluisours desdis heritages, *que tout l'eritage estoit dou fié; et autre, que la moité estoit dou fié et l'autre moité de la bourgesie. Et fu doné à la court, à ce que la court ce deust prendre bien garde de non souffrir que teil heritage de fié ce puisse aliener que en la Haute Court*'.

77 Recoura, *Les Assises de Romanie*, no. 142, p. 249.

78 'Livre contrefais', p. 313.

Recognising the need for a register of all *heritages de fiés*, in 1297 Henry I of Cyprus instructed the royal *secrete* to keep a record of *borgesies* appertaining to the fiefs of his feudatories. It was discovered that many were in possession of this hybrid property in Nicosia,[79] and there was an obvious need to distinguish *borgesies* subject to the High Court from those under the jurisdiction of the *Cour des Bourgeois*. The *secrete* acted as a central office which could be consulted by officials if there was any doubt about the legally defined status of a particular property.

By the time a land register was established in Nicosia, *heritage de fié* tenancies had existed in the cities of the kingdoms of Jerusalem and Cyprus for many decades. The documented evidence of *borgesies* pertaining to feudal holdings can be dated back to the twelfth century. In 1186, Guy of Lusignan, king of Jerusalem, conceded to his seneschal, Joscelin of Courtney, 'a certain house in Acre which pertains to the fief of Chabor'.[80] And in his inventory, Marsiglio Zorzi listed the names of Venetian noble families who were granted fiefs and houses by the Venetian commune. William Jordan received a fief and a house in the Venetian quarter in Tyre as did Roland Contarinus.[81] To my knowledge there were no fiefs – apart from money-fiefs – in the cities, and if it is argued that all urban properties were *borgesies*, then it may be that these were examples of *heritage de fiés*.

Further legal documentation from the early thirteenth century is illustrative not only of the jurisdictional authority of the High Court over *heritage de* fié, but also of the particular circumstances which necessitated the separation of a *borgesie* from a fief. The court case which took place in Acre in 1206 was also confirmation of the legal principle which asserted the indivisible nature of the *heritage de fié* according to the 'assises of the kingdom of Jerusalem and Cyprus'.[82] John le Tor appeared before the High Court and John of Ibelin regent for Maria of Jerusalem requesting permission to sell his house in the city.

> Johannes Tortus in presenciam meam [John of Ibelin] et regalem curiam veniens a me et ab hominibus domine Marie [Maria of Jerusalem] ... poposcit licenciam vendendi domum suam Accon pro debitis suis solvendis ... cum ipse Johannes Tortus vidisset, quod non potuisset habere licentiam vendendi domum suam, dixit, quod eum oportebat vendere feodum suum vel domum pro debitis suis solvendis.[83]

Applying rigidly the tenets of the law, and in keeping with the terms of *heritage de fié* as set out later in the 'Livre contrefais', the High Court initially rejected John le Tor's request and denied him permission to sell separately his house in order to pay

79 'Livre contrefais', p. 315.

80 Strehlke, no. 22, p. 20.

81 Berggötz, pp. 158–61.

82 'Livre contrefais', p. 313.

83 Strehlke, no. 41, p. 33. In a charter of 1212, John le Tor appears as viscount of Acre; H.F. Delaborde (ed.), *Chartes de la Terre Sainte provenant de l'abbaye de Notre-Dame de Josaphat* (Paris, 1880), no. 46, p. 96.

off his debt. It was this kind of legal inflexibility and determination to act to the letter of the law, which, it would seem, obliged some knights to sell their *borgesies* separately from their fiefs without first seeking legal consent. Fortunately for John le Tor, the High Court in Acre was more understanding, and reversed its decision so that he was not compelled to sell his whole fief in order to resolve his financial difficulties.[84] There was compromise on this occasion even though the court was ceding jurisdictional authority over property to the *Cour des Bourgeois*. But if King Hugh's concerns in Nicosia are anything to go by, this kind of legal flexibility could not have been common practice even in the kingdom of Jerusalem in the early thirteenth century, and left knights seeking other ways of dividing their property.

The court case, however, involving John Le Tor, is unique in the sources, so can we be fully certain that his was an example of a *borgesie* joined to a fief or was it simply held by him as a fief-holder? If the latter were true, John would still have been obliged to go to the royal *Cour des Bourgeois* to sell his *borgesie*. Instead, this was a *heritage de fié* under the jurisdiction of the High Court. The court's initial unwillingness to authorise the sale of a *heritage de fié* gave way to an acknowledgement of the impracticality of the law in this instance. John le Tor was permitted to sell his house to the knights of the Teutonic Order for 2700 besants, and as payment for her consent Maria of Jerusalem received 200 besants.

The indivisible nature of the *heritage de fié* was a bone of contention in the thirteenth century because fief-holders regarded this special property as being exempted from certain *assises* governing other *borgesies*. For instance, some fief-holders believed *heritages des fiés* to be immune from the *assise de la teneure d'an et de jour*. This law, introduced in the earliest years of the kingdom, determined that a person could rightfully possess the *borgesie* of a tenant who had neglected his property for more than a year and a day. There had been concern that many people were abandoning their properties in the East only to return to them when there was greater guarantee of security.[85] But in order to emphasise that *heritages des fiés* were not exempted from the law of a year and a day, the author of the 'Livre contrefais' gave the example of a fief-holder who sold his *heritage* in the *Cour des Bourgeois* without informing the court that this was a *heritage de fié*. After the buyer had held the property for a year and a day without challenge, the descendants of the fief-holder claimed the sale was illegal because such a property should not be alienated in any court other than the High Court. They also claimed that because of its indivisibility, a tenant should not be permitted to sell a *heritage* as it belonged to a fief which was subject to its own terms and conditions. In defence, the buyer argued that the *heritage*, irrespective of its former status, was

---

84 Strehlke, no. 41, p. 33: 'Cum vidissent, quod oportebat predictum Johannen Tortum ex necessitate vendere feudum suum vel domum pro debitis suis solvendis, mihi dederunt in consilium, ut ei darem licenciam vendendi domum suam ob feudum retinendum'.

85 William of Tyre, p. 446.

acquired by him legally, and, crucially, it was held for over a year and a day without any challenge to his tenancy. As the period of time within which a claim could be legally brought by a plaintiff had been exceeded, and as the transaction in the *Cour des Bourgeois* was legally binding, the buyer was permitted to keep his *heritage*. From then on, any matters concerning the property would be heard in the *Cour des Bourgeois*.[86] If, therefore, in the early twelfth century the purpose of the *assise* of a year and a day had been to discourage men from neglecting the properties they possessed in the cities of the kingdom, in the thirteenth century it was being used to realise three objectives: first, to limit cases of litigation; secondly, to protect those who acquired their *borgesies* legitimately and had rights of tenancy in perpetuity which could not be removed from them after a certain period of time; and thirdly, to prohibit discrimination between the rights of fief-holders and burgesses, as both *heritages des fiés* and *borgesies* were subject to the rules of the *assise de la teneure d'an et de jour*. If, for that matter, the 'Livre contrefais' is to be believed, some *heritages des fiés* were created because fief-holders, under the impression that *borgesies* which formed part of fiefs were exempted from the *assise de la teneur*, had joined their city properties to their fiefs believing this would make them immune from such a law.[87] They hoped the exemption of the *assise de la teneure* would extend to their fiefs. But in Nicosia the *assise de la teneure* was applicable to all who possessed *heritages des fiés*, including fief-holders, churchmen, members of the military orders and the merchant communities and burgesses.[88]

Borgesies in the Latin Villes Neuves

I have so far described properties in the cities, but rules of *borgesie* tenancy in the Latin villages were no less distinctive. One difference, however, between urban and rural life was that whilst in the urban centres there was no limit, it would seem, on the number and size of *borgesies* which burgesses could possess, in the villages, which were carefully planned and regulated by their secular or ecclesiastical overlords in much the same mould as European *villes neuves*, there were strict rules governing what proportion of land settlers could receive – at least initially – for cultivation and the building of a house.[89] Land was divided according to a unit known as a *carruca* which has been estimated as measuring between three or four

86 'Livre contrefais', p. 311; Prawer, *Crusader Institutions*, pp. 343–57.

87 'Livre contrefais', p. 314: 'Que ce l'eritage qui fuce dou fié fuce esté excepté au fait de l'assize de la teneure, *pluizour, pour avoir l'avantage de non perdre leur heritage, heussent volentiers joint lor heritage aveuc leur fiés*; ... puisque ... n'a esté faite ne ordenée, ains a esté faite et ordenée l'assize de l'an et dou jour'.

88 'Livre contrefais', p. 311.

89 Bresc-Bautier, no. 125, pp. 251–2, and no. 127, pp. 253–4.

ha – equivalent to the European *carruca* – and thirty-five ha (86.45 acres).[90] It is not clear from the sources, however, what system was used to decide how much each settler should receive, but in some cases land, when granted originally, was divided equally among settlers, and as *borgesies* could be freely bought and sold, some burgesses acquired over time a greater share of landed property than others. In the original grant in Bethgibelin there was equal division and each tenant received two *carrucae*.[91] However, according to a charter of Nova Villa, a village also under the jurisdiction of the Church of the Holy Sepulchre, two settlers were allocated one *carruca* of land and a third two *carrucae*.[92] The grant of a large share of land was, nevertheless, not always to the benefit of a burgess, considering the rigorous rules of cultivation laid down by the Holy Sepulchre and the fines imposed on farmers who neglected their properties. These were pressing concerns for those impoverished and unable even to subsist from farming. In Magna Mahumeria the church gave permission to Ainard Cavallom to sell his vineyard to Martin Carpenter for 26 besants because of his straitened circumstances,[93] and a plot of land in the village was abandoned by Robert Ungarus and his wife because they were unable to cultivate it 'secundum statutum morem'.[94] Crop failure meant tenants could not always pay their rents, and the Church, though benevolent in granting property to new settlers, was a much more ruthless overlord when its own interests were being harmed. Land tax was burdensome and burgesses were no more advantaged than natives in villages belonging to the Holy Sepulchre. One can imagine that many burgess farmers survived on a subsistence level, whilst others more fortunate, possessed farms which returned greater crop yields, and prospered by selling their foodstuffs locally or in neighbouring towns and cities. It is known that two farmers of Magna Mahumeria, Hugo de Tarsus and Raoul of Paris – first generation farmers as their names suggest – were wealthy winegrowers and tenants of sizeable vineyards in the village.[95] In their lifetime they had become wealthy by managing to create large holdings from the purchase of smaller ones, and had farmed the land to the satisfaction of the canons. But the clustering of *borgesies* had also its downside. As smaller tenants and their families sold or abandoned their properties, the village's overall population diminished. The Church was well aware of this decline and the detrimental effect it had on the local economy. But either

---

90 Ellenblum, *Frankish Rural Settlement*, pp. 98–9 and note 15. Riley-Smith believes there were three types of *carrucae* which varied in size from place to place in the kingdom of Jerusalem. The Frankish *carruca*, he suggests, was equivalent to 25–26 acres; the Saracen *carruca* was the amount of land that could be ploughed in a single day by a pair of draught animals; and a third type was measured by the amount of grain that could be sown; Riley-Smith, *The Feudal Nobility and the Kingdom of Jerusalem*, pp. 41–2.

91 Delaville Le Roulx, *Cartulaire général*, no. 399, p. 273.

92 Bresc-Bautier, no. 126, p. 253.

93 Bresc-Bautier, no. 121, pp. 245–6.

94 Bresc-Bautier, no. 121, p. 247.

95 Bresc-Bautier, no. 123, pp. 249–50.

because of a bequest or eleemosynary donation, the canons re-acquired the two large vineyards once belonging to Hugo de Tarsus and Raoul of Paris, and in c.1158 they again divided this fertile and more profitable outlying area of the village among the farmers of Magna Mahumeria and new settlers. On receiving their share tenants were conceded rights of inheritance and alienation, and were free to leave the village if they chose. They were required to pay tithe to the Holy Sepulchre as well as *terragium*, a land tax equal to half their agricultural produce.[96]

Like its city counterpart, the rural *borgesie* was alienable and hereditary, and its tenant required the approval of the village court in order to transact his property. But the freedom of alienation which a tenant enjoyed was qualified. In the case of Magna Mahumeria he was prohibited from selling to Hospitallers, Templars or other members of the Church or the fief-holding class.[97] Again it seems there were no free holdings and private transactions were unlawful. The court carefully managed who could hold property, and through the procedure of alienation, and written documentation, it confirmed the services owed by burgess farmers. This included the payment of tithe to the Church and *terragium*, an annual rent in kind amounting to between a quarter and a half of crop production. It is also very likely that men of a certain age, even in ecclesiastical settlements, would have been expected to carry out some form of military duty. Above all else, there was a need to cultivate a sense of self-sufficiency in all areas of life. The community in Magna Mahumeria was self-sufficient in the truest sense, both in agricultural as well as legal terms, and the only contact the inhabitants had with the *Cour des Bourgeois* of nearby Jerusalem was perhaps in cases of criminal justice outside the jurisdictional scope of the court of the Holy Sepulchre. Otherwise they lived by the customs of the village. The primary occupation of village inhabitants, who were described as *habitatores* or *burgenses*,[98] was olive growing and viticulture, although settlers in Magna Mahumeria were also involved in building, carpentry and metalwork.[99] Agricultural industries like wine and oil production were not only commercially profitable to the canons, but also to the individual farmers.[100] The *dispensator*, an officer of the Church, oversaw the work carried out by the settlers, had the authority to fine those who cultivated their land poorly[101] and collected payments they owed in the *curia Sancti Sepulcri*. The farmers were privileged holders of *borgesies*, but even more so than city inhabitants, there were strict conditions of settlement which they had to abide by.

Rural inhabitants swore loyalty to their lord. A charter of Magna Mahumeria (1156) including the names of 142 men and no women, suggests that only the male

---

96 Bresc-Bautier, no. 123, pp. 249–50.

97 Bresc-Bautier, no. 123, pp. 249–50.

98 Bresc-Bautier, no. 121, p. 245, no. 125, p. 251, no. 127, p. 254.

99 Ellenblum, *Frankish Rural Settlement*, p. 82.

100 Ellenblum, *Frankish Rural Settlement*, pp. 90–91.

101 Bresc-Bautier, no. 123, p. 249.

head of each household was expected to take the oath.[102] This pledging of loyalty may have been obligatory in other Latin villages, especially those under the control of the Holy Sepulchre. The charter of Magna Mahumeria is also useful in tracing the origins of settlers. From the list of names forty-four are known to have come from the West.[103] These men had probably recently arrived in the kingdom – as opposed to the thirty names of second generation settlers coming from places in the Latin East – and would not have been familiar with any laws of tenancy in the kingdom of Jerusalem other than those of the Church of the Holy Sepulchre. Some of the settlers in the *castrum* of Bethgibelin were also recent arrivals from Europe, and of the thirty-one settlers named in the charter of 1168 a number had come from the regions of Auvergne, Gascony, Flanders, Lombardy and Catalonia.[104] Generally, the largest number of European settlers in Magna Mahumeria and Bethgibelin were from the central, southern and western parts of France, and a few also from northern Spain and regions in Italy. In Bethgibelin the other settlers were from nearby Latin villages including one burgess from Hebron, two from Ramla and one from as far away as Edessa.[105] But we must question why these men and women chose to live in Bethgibelin and Magna Mahumeria over city-life, say in Jerusalem. Although I have argued against overestimating the degree of continuous European migration and its role in the formation of the kingdom, I certainly agree that internally the movement of Latin Christians, either as a result of enforced displacement, or relocation to places with more favourable farming conditions, was a factor in the development of Levantine villages. Lower rental dues, reduced taxes and farming opportunities would have been important incentives.

The basic rules of tenancy in a Latin village did not differ from those in the cities. A tenant could lease a house in perpetuity with right of alienation and pay *cens* owing on the *borgesie*. When in 1160 the Holy Sepulchre leased a house in Magna Mahumeria to Suard and his family, Suard was obliged to pay the Church eight besants a year in rent and in return was free to sell his house to other burgesses. The rent was inalienable and whoever bought the house remained burdened by the *cens*.[106] In the same year the canons conceded a house to Stephen Pasnaie with rights of inheritance and alienation. Stephen owed yearly rent of five besants, and the Church reserved the right of pre-emption should he wish to sell his house.[107] Pre-emption was requisite because the Church retained the option of re-acquiring the property outright by offering to purchase it for a price that was typically – in both the cities and villages of the kingdom – less than its market value and at times markedly so. In this legal respect, the rights of village families are not specifically mentioned in the charters of Magna Mahumeria, but the

102 Bresc-Bautier, no. 117, pp. 237–40.

103 Bresc-Bautier, no. 117, pp. 237–39; Ellenblum, *Frankish Rural Settlement*, p. 75.

104 Delaville Le Roulx, *Cartulaire général*, no. 399, p. 273.

105 Delaville Le Roulx, *Cartulaire général*, no. 399, p. 273.

106 Bresc-Bautier, no. 125, pp. 251–2.

107 Bresc-Bautier, no. 127, pp. 253–4.

hereditary nature of *borgesies* meant that their position as successors could not be ignored in any process of alienation. The role of the court in Magna Mahumeria would have been to hear cases of disputed transactions, but although the development of laws in the royal domain in the twelfth and thirteenth centuries enabled nearest relatives to pre-empt, to challenge or to repurchase alienated property, it can not be certain what legal options were available to villagers.

Besides sale, a tenant of a rural village could also exchange his property (*commutationes*). When in c. 1158 a large vineyard was divided for cultivation by the settlers, the canons of the Holy Sepulchre gave Guibert Papais and his wife Usanne a share of this tract of land in exchange for another they possessed in the village. Similarly, Galterius Carpenter received a share in exchange for a vineyard he had been cultivating. These burgesses owed the Church tithe but interestingly not *terragium* – as they did not pay land tax for their original properties, this right was transferred to their new properties which they were to hold 'free and exempt'. It is interesting how this tax exemption was carried from one *borgesie* to the next, a privilege which a tenant would have been anxious to safeguard. It was a right comparable to exemption from yearly *cens*, and like the special terms of *franc borgesie*, the tenant may have been exempted from land tax, but remained subject to another money-rent service in this case *terragium*. Exemption was, therefore, only partial, not absolute freedom from the Church of the Holy Sepulchre in whose domain and jurisdiction the property was located.

As far as we can tell, the basic rights and duties of settlers were uniform. The same rules of tenancy were repeated in Latin villages, as was the practice of removing the payment of *cens* on certain houses in order to draw new settlers. In Nova Villa in the second half of the twelfth century, measures to enlarge the village included giving settlers enough land to cultivate and build a house on, and according to a charter of 1160, Guido Camelarius, Gerard Caprellus and Hugo of Jaffa were permitted to build houses which were to be exempted from the burden of *cens*. The *borgesie* consisted of the farm land, including the house, and each tenant was obliged to pay one quarter of the annual production of grain and vegetables, and one fifth of fruits and olives. This was a condition of tenancy and if a tenant defaulted on payment the Church of the Holy Sepulchre could appropriate the whole property. But taken on their own, presumably, these houses were held by the burgesses as *francs borgesies* because they paid no rent, and if they chose to sell their houses this rent-exempt status would have passed on to the new tenants.

As was customary elsewhere, property in Nova Villa was alienable and hereditary, and the Church reserved the right of pre-emption. These rules, it was stated, were introduced 'according to the custom of Magna Mahumeria'.[108] Similarly, in Casale Imbert burgesses received houses in perpetuity free and exempt from all exactions, but were obliged to pay *terragium* on their crops,

---

108 Bresc-Bautier, no. 126, p. 253.

vineyards and orchards.[109] According to the original terms of the *charte de peuplement* of Bethgibelin, furthermore, each tenant received a plot of land upon which to build a house, and in a fertile area stretching from Bethgibelin to the valley of Tamarin, a place less than a mile north-west of the town, each settler received two *carrucae* of land where he could grow fruits, cereals and vegetables. The burgess tenant was obliged to pay the Hospitallers the yearly *terragium*, the tenth on his crops and fruits, except olives, and certain other customary payments, whilst the confirmation of the *charte de peuplement* in 1168 added to the original terms. It is made clear that the objective of the Hospitallers was to populate Bethgibelin with more settlers ('ut terra melius populetur'), and to do this the Hospitallers relinquished primarily the right of pre-emption. A steady influx of migrant settlers could not be guaranteed, but how could the order sustain the population growth of its settlement by removing the right to pre-empt a sale? For the Hospitallers pre-emption was a means of monitoring property transfer in their fortified village, but this legal right to interfere in the alienation of *borgesies*, in effect the authority to impede, somehow discouraged the creation of new tenancies. The objective was to make the process of alienation more favourable to the needs of the burgess tenants. By relinquishing the power of pre-emption, villagers would be encouraged to farm new land and build new houses more easily saleable and more attractive to new settlers. The tenants, moreover, could sell their properties to whomsoever they wished except to fief-holders and clergy.[110]

Villages as Borgesies

The size of a *borgesie* could vary from a plot of land in a *ville neuve* – enough for a burgess family to subsist from – or a multi-storey house in a city comprising of a number of smaller lease holdings, to tenements of quite considerable size. There was, indeed, a type of *borgesie* which the law books of Acre and Nicosia do not mention: the whole village as a single *borgesie*. The native rural village, the *casale*, which consisted of *rustici*, their dwellings, vineyards, olive groves and pasturages, was normally granted to the class of feudatories, but appears occasionally in the charters as a *borgesie*. Presumably, the possessor of a village *borgesie* enjoyed the revenues accruing from proportional rents imposed on villeins and their crops, while he as a tenant owed *cens* to the lord in whose domain this property was situated, and was subject to the *Cour des Bourgeois* which had jurisdiction over his village. As we saw earlier, a feudatory, Thomas of St Bertin, sold the *casale* of Fauconerie to the Templars, a village he possessed as a *borgesie* and for which he owed no tenurial service.[111]

---

109 Strehlke, no. 1, p. 1: 'Balduwinus. domos dedit, ipsis etiam et eorum heredibus quiete, libere et sine omni calumpnia vel impedimento habendas et iure perpetuo possidendas'.

110 Delaville Le Roulx, *Cartulaire général*, no. 399, p. 273.

111 'L'Estoire d'Eracles Empereur et la conqueste de la terre d'outremer', I, p. 474.

I have found further evidence of burgesses in possession of village *borgesies* in a document of 1141, which gives the names of Huldre, Anschetinus, Porcel, Bacheler, Gerard Bocher and Gaufridus Agulle as tenants of *casalia*.[112] The possibility arises that these persons concerned, who are known to have been burgesses, may have been elevated to the class of feudatories, although there is no evidence that this was the case. Porcel, Bacheler and Gerard Bocher appear in c. 1125 as jurors of the *Cour des Bourgeois* of Jerusalem,[113] whilst in 1120, Porcel, Bacheler and Godfrey de Arcu appear in the witness list of a charter of Baldwin II, in which he exempts agricultural merchants entering Jerusalem from all taxes.[114] Porcel and Godfrey de Arcu also appear as burgesses in a royal confirmation of 1136.[115] In the 1120s, Godfrey de Arcu was a servant of Ralph of Fontaines from whom he received a *borgesie*,[116] and by 1144 Godfrey was being referred to in a charter as a 'baron'.[117] This did not mean he was necessarily a feudatory, bearing in mind that in the twelfth century the word 'baron' had a broader meaning and was used additionally to describe a person called upon to give counsel to his lord.[118] Burgess tenants of village *borgesies* were undoubtedly individuals of standing, men of notable achievement who had risen to a position of authority or influence. Some perhaps were royal advisers or court officials, as, for example, Huldre who may be identified with Holdredus, a juror and a judge of the *Cour des Bourgeois* of Jerusalem.[119] Theirs was a unique position because not only were they in possession of extensive tenements, and grew wealthy from the revenues collected from native villagers, they were also, like feudatories, heads of their villages.

Invaluable evidence of *borgesies* villages is found outside the kingdom of Jerusalem. A charter of the principality of Antioch is particularly revealing. It records that in 1163 the abbey of St Abraham conceded to a *confrater* of the order of St John, Peter Jay, the village of Naharia and two houses in the city of Antioch.[120] When later selling his village to the Hospitallers, Peter Jay was described by Prince Bohemond of Antioch as 'my burgess'.[121] Peter was obviously a wealthy man of notable standing who was considered by Bohemond as a trusted subject. St Abraham conceded the property in perpetuity to Peter Jay except for the rights of the sitting tenant, the wife of William Hostiar, who was leasing the village

---

112 Delaville Le Roulx, *Cartulaire général*, no. 140, pp. 115: 'casale Huldre et de Porcel, et de Gaufrido Agulle, et de Anschitino, et de Bacheler, et de Girardo Bocher'.

113 Bresc-Bautier, no. 96, p. 214.

114 Bresc-Bautier, no. 27, p. 89.

115 *RRH*, no. 64, pp. 40–41.

116 Bresc-Bautier, no. 96, p. 214.

117 Bresc-Bautier, no. 38, p. 109.

118 Riley-Smith, The *Feudal Nobility and the Kingdom of Jerusalem*, p. 18.

119 Bresc-Bautier, no. 34, p. 100, no. 97, p. 215, no. 99, p. 218, no. 102, p. 222, no.103, p. 223; Ellenblum, *Frankish Rural Settlement*, p. 111.

120 Delaville Le Roulx, *Les Archives*, no. 19, pp. 97–9.

121 Delaville Le Roulx, *Les Archives*, no. 24, pp. 104–105.

and two houses in Antioch from the abbey *ad censum*. Under the terms of the agreement, on acquiring the *borgesie* Peter Jay would become the superior tenant of this woman who would carry on paying him the *cens* as previously. He in turn became tenant of the abbey to whom he owed sixteen besants a year. The abbey reserved for itself the right of pre-emption and received from Peter Jay 150 besants for the sale of the *borgesie*. There were other transferences of rights. In particular, Peter Jay acquired the same powers ('potestatem et dominium') which the abbey had in dealing with non-payment of *cens*, meaning that he could confiscate the *borgesie* if William Hostiar's wife failed to pay him rent.[122]

Examples of burgess tenants of village *borgesies* are few as usually it was ecclesiastical institutions and feudatories who were in possession of this type of property. In 1171, the Church of the Ascension of the Mount of Olives exchanged with the Hospitallers the *casale* of Cafran in return for houses in Jerusalem being sub-leased by twelve tenants owing a total of 130 besants in rent a year. Interestingly, the exchange took place in Acre and was overseen by the *Cour des Bourgeois* of Jerusalem, perhaps in the city for a *parlement*.[123] The straight exchange of properties in the court suggests Cafran was a *borgesie*, and as a measure of its significant worth, the Church received in return several city properties owing a considerable amount of rent. Other documentation provides a clearer idea of the value of this property-type. In c. 1155, a feudatory, Gibelin, sold his village *borgesie* of Saphoria to the Church of the Holy Sepulchre for 180 besants and some furs. The transaction took place in the *Cour des Bourgeois* of Jerusalem, and although the viscount or castellan of Jerusalem was not named, the list of witnesses included the *dapifer regis*.[124] The sale of the village 'with all its lands and appurtenances' was approved by the king, and in order to assure the permanency of the transfer Gibelin's sons-in-law Hugo and William acted as *fidejussores*. These men and their successors were committed to defending the validity of the sale against any future claimants. Gibelin's wife Agnes gave her approval and his son Anselin received from the canons five besants and a sword. Most probably on this occasion, the material countergift served as an evidentiary role, a reminder to Anselin that he had no right of inheritance to the property.[125]

Sale, Exchange, Pledge and Bequest of Borgesies

Although a person leasing a *borgesie* under terms of *encensive* had right as tenant to sell his property, it was a general custom in the cities and *villes neuves* to include a ban against the sale of property to non-Christians. In an earlier chapter,

[122] Delaville Le Roulx, *Les Archives*, no. 19, pp. 97–9.

[123] Delaville Le Roulx, *Cartulaire général*, no. 422, p. 291.

[124] The standing of the seneschal as presiding head of the royal *Cour des Bourgeois* in Jerusalem is discussed below, pp. 143–4.

[125] Bresc-Bautier, no. 130, pp. 256–7.

the formulation of this discriminatory rule of tenancy was traced to the very first years of the kingdom's existence. It was meant to favour Europeans over natives, and considering the ban was extended to include knights and churchmen, its purpose was to support especially the settlement of Latin non-feudatories. To take an example, in Jerusalem Benscelinus and his wife Ahoys could not sell a house which they leased from the Church of the Holy Sepulchre to Templars or Hospitallers (1153).[126] The same restriction was placed on those selling their properties in Magna Mahumeria (c.1158)[127] and Parva Palmarea (1180).[128] In thirteenth-century Acre, Guy de Ronay leasing a house from the Hospitallers, was forbidden to sell his *borgesie* to members of the Church including the other military orders unless he received the permission of the order of St John (1219).[129] And in Acre, in 1255, tenants of the Hospitallers were not permitted to alienate their houses to churchmen, feudatories, members of the merchant communities and peasants.[130] This same prohibition applied in Tyre.[131] It is, nevertheless, interesting to note, that though qualified alienation was from the beginning an essential rule, over time, and perhaps reflecting changing ideas regarding the possession of property, proscription against certain members of society holding *borgesies* was not strictly enforced. We see often specified formulaically in the deeds of sale that the *borgesie* could not be alienated to churchmen or knights, although, significantly, the prohibition was ultimately at the discretion of the court. The charters are unequivocal proof that feudatories as well as native Christians commonly purchased *borgesies*, and it is yet further evidence of the powers of the court of burgesses to interpret the law as it saw fit. But of course, it did all this with the full approval of the lord of the domain. In Cyprus, in 1298, Henry II issued a ban ordering all members of the Church and of the merchant communities who possessed *borgesies* in Nicosia to hand them over to the crown within six months, except those who could prove they had royal approval when acquiring their property.[132] But despite the restrictions which were in place, one possible means for feudatories to acquire *borgesies* was through marriage into the burgess class. This would explain why a royal ordinance of Nicosia (1296) declared it unlawful for a burgess to marry his sister, daughter, or any relative to a knight or to his son.[133]

Burgesses would have been aware of the basic property laws of their community, and even if there was anything about which they were not certain, the

---

126 Bresc-Bautier, no. 114, p. 235.

127 Bresc-Bautier, no. 123, p. 249.

128 Delaville Le Roulx, *Cartulaire général*, no. 19, p. 909.

129 Delaville Le Roulx, *Cartulaire général*, no. 1656, p. 261.

130 J. Delaville Le Roulx (ed.), 'Titres de l'hopital des Bretons d'Acre', in *AOL*, I (1881), no. 1, p. 426.

131 Strehlke, no. 56, p. 46.

132 'Bans et ordonnances', p. 361. See also p. 263.

133 'Bans et ordonnances', p. 359.

seemingly drawn out process of alienation in the court of burgesses ensured that all conditions of property transference were met. The actual procedure of sale in the *Cours des Bourgeois* of Acre and Nicosia is given full treatment in the law books, although our understanding of procedure in other cities and *villes neuves* is based to a great extent on the charters. In a typical sale a property changed hands between a vendor and a buyer with the approval of the lord of the domain. A buyer obtained perpetual tenancy of a property and promised to pay the annual rent owed by the previous tenant. According to law, the alienation of *borgesies* had to be authorised by the *Cour des Bourgeois* in whose jurisdiction a particular property was located.[134] It was the responsibility of the vendor to appear in court whereupon he would inform the viscount that he wished to sell his *borgesie*. He would then describe the property to be sold, give precise details of its size and location, provide the name of the buyer, who should also be present, and make known the price agreed for the property. The role of the court was to publicise the sale, to legalise the transaction and to transfer seisin from the vendor to the buyer. Whilst the duty of the jurors, in any case before the advent of written records, was to store in their memory whatever terms of alienation were agreed, and to act as future reference should the sale be challenged. In court, in Nicosia at least, a buyer was legally required to swear on oath that he was purchasing the *borgesie* for himself, as it was unlawful to act on behalf of another person. This sworn declaration was not introduced in Nicosia until the fourteenth century and seems to have had no equivalent in the kingdom of Jerusalem, although in Acre it was customary for the vendor to swear a particular oath. When in 1273 Set Lehoue sold a *borgesie* in the city to *dame* Ysabiau he swore 'le sairement' of the *Cour des Bourgeois*.[135]

In court the vendor would offer a *verge*, a wooden staff, to the viscount, signifying the conveyance of seisin. The viscount would then offer the staff to the buyer in a symbolic gesture demonstrating that seisin of the property now belonged to him.[136] The ceremonial conveyance of seisin had its roots in European practices where symbols such as cups, rings, sacred books, knives and even charters, were vestiges of pre-literate ritualistic procedures of sale. In fact, the advent in western Europe of written documentation in the conveyance of seisin had not superseded but rather complemented the use of symbolic objects.[137] In Nicosia, the *verge* was used even when a *borgesie* was exchanged,[138] or inheritance divided among family members,[139] and it is a reasonable assumption that some kind of symbolic

---

[134] Kausler, p. 148 (cf. Beugnot, 'Livre des assises', p. 156): 'Nus hom ne deit plaidier en autre Cort de Borgesie, se non en cele meysme vile où les maisons, ou la terre, ou les vignes sont'.

[135] Favreau-Lilie, 'The Teutonic Knights in Acre after the Fall of Montfort (1271): Some Reflections', p. 282.

[136] 'Livre contrefais', p. 253.

[137] M.T. Clanchy, *From Memory to Written Record* (London, 1979), pp. 127, 205.

[138] 'Livre contrefais', p. 272.

[139] 'Livre contrefais', p. 277.

procedure was adopted in all the burgess courts of the kingdom of Jerusalem as well as certain times in the High Court. A charter of 1269, written about the same period the 'Livre de la Cour des Bourgeois' was being compiled, illustrates how the president of the court, the *bailli* (also known as the viscount), administered the sale of a *borgesie* in Acre by receiving seisin of the property from the vendor, Pelerin Coquerel, and then offering it to the treasurer of the order of St John.[140] In the same court, in 1273, the viscount, Pierre d'Amineis, received seisin of a *heritage* belonging to the vendor Set Lehoue, before transferring it to the buyer *dame* Ysabiau.[141] The use of objects to symbolise the transaction of seisin was a popular practice similarly adopted in ecclesiastical courts whose development in certain aspects, especially the transfer of property, mirrored that of the secular courts of burgesses. A charter originating in the court of the bishop of Acre is illustrative of this symbolic practice. In 1273, Richard Anglicus, a wealthy citizen of Acre (*cives Acconensis*), sold his houses in the 'ruga taneriae' to the order of St John for 1700 besants. One of the houses owed one besant *ad censum* to Godfrey bishop of Hebron, who oversaw this sale and accepted symbolically the *baculus*, the staff, from Richard, who was from this point on disseised of this and the other houses. The Hospitallers received the staff and so too seisin. The parallels in procedure between secular and ecclesiastical jurisdictions are apparent.[142]

Since the validity of sales and donations of *borgesies* could be challenged in court, buyers or recipients needed to be assured of the permanency of a transaction and, if required, to vindicate their claims to a particular property.[143] The actual process of alienation, incorporating, for example, a vendor or a donor's promise to defend the legality of a transaction, and the consent of his nearest family and relatives as witnesses and guarantors of a sale or a grant 'in alms', were regarded as important elements in legitimising the transfer of burgess property. It was particularly important the family of a tenant agreed to a sale, and it was in the interests of the buyer that the consent of those with inheritance rights be sought so they could be discouraged from disputing in future the legitimacy of the alienation. This was necessary because a *borgesie*, at least under laws of Acre, escheated to those most closely related to a tenant, irrespective of whether he had died intestate (*desconfès*) or not.[144] One may even argue that uncontested alienation was so important that developments in the court of burgesses – for instance, the establishment of registers – arose because of a need to facilitate the transference of property, enabling the buyer, his spouse and children to assume confidently right of

140 Delaville Le Roulx, *Cartulaire général*, no. 3334, p. 196.

141 Favreau-Lilie in 'The Teutonic Knights in Acre after the Fall of Montfort (1271): Some Reflections', p. 282.

142 *RRH*, 1389, p. 362.

143 On disputes and arbitrations in the court of burgesses, see Strehlke, no. 45, pp. 36–7; Müller, pp. 439–40.

144 Kausler, p. 205 (cf. Beugnot, 'Livre des assises', p. 127).

inheritance over his newly purchased property.[145]

The court of burgesses slowly evolved basic procedures of alienation. The names of the vendor and the buyer appearing in court would be recorded by a notary in a charter, as well as the price of the *borgesie* being sold; the amount of *cens* which was owed and the location of the property; the amount of sales tax paid to the court; the names of the witnesses and of the vendor's family who had consented to the sale; the rights of the tenant and the rights of his lord. Documentation was written proof of the validity of the sale and of the unwavering commitment of those involved to permanent alienation. Peter de Caors, selling his *borgesie* in Jerusalem, promised to defend the legitimacy of the sale against any future claimants.[146] When John Marrain alienated his property to the Hospitallers in Acre, he promised that neither he nor anyone acting on his behalf would renounce the transfer of the *borgesie*.[147] In a sale of 1179, Stephanie, wife of Nicholas Manzur, acted as guarantor of the transaction that was made between her husband and the order of St John, and on the back of the charter she autographed her consent.[148] In 1235, Nicholas Anteaume promised to 'defend and to guarantee' the transaction he had made with the Hospitallers.[149] In Acre, in 1260, John Grifus promised the Hospitallers he would be guarantor for a year and a day after the transfer of his *borgesie* to them, and would be unswerving in his efforts to renounce the claims of all challengers in court and outside of court.[150] In an earlier charter of 1232, John, lord of Beirut, and John, lord of Caesarea, acted as guarantors of a sale involving a close relative, John, count of Jaffa, son of the deceased Philip of Ibelin, and the order of St John. They appeared in court and pledged to defend the alienation of the house against the challenges of Alice of Montbéliard, widow of Philip and her daughter Maria, who were contesting the sale. They promised to defend the legitimacy of the transaction for the period of a year and a day.[151]

So far, I have described transactions which involved two parties: the buyer and seller. However, not all alienations were so straightforward. Evidence of *borgesies* leased jointly either by co-purchasers, co-recipients of a donation, or co-inheritors of a property, is rare, but the fact that shared tenancy was discussed in the 'Livre

---

145 Kausler, p. 65 (cf. Beugnot, 'Livre des assises', p. 35); 'Livre contrefais', pp. 260–61. In Acre and Nicosia relatives of a tenant had power of pre-emption when a *borgesie* was being sold, and the right within a period of seven days to buy back a property sold outside the family. The new tenant was obliged by law to sell the *borgesie* to them for the price he had originally paid.

146 *Les Archives*, no. 34, pp. 120.

147 Delaville Le Roulx, *Cartulaire général*, no. 2714, p. 773.

148 Delaville Le Roulx, *Cartulaire général*, no. 554, p. 376.

149 Delaville Le Roulx, *Cartulaire général*, no. 2126, p. 493.

150 Delaville Le Roulx, *Cartulaire général*, no. 2949, p. 887.

151 Delaville Le Roulx, *Cartulaire général*, no. 2015, pp. 434–5.

contrefais' suggests it was not uncommon.[152] According to the law book, if a *borgesie* of a deceased man escheated jointly to his children, or if they purchased a property together, they the *partizons* were each entitled to a share of the property. The *partizons*, who had all to be in agreement, could divide the *borgesie* among themselves under the supervision of the *Cour des Bourgeois*. The law placed much emphasis on collective action so that all decisions were reached equitably and with the full knowledge of all parties involved. They were to be present in the court where each, starting with the eldest, was offered the *verge* to symbolise his share of seisin, before he was obliged to pay five besants to the viscount. Presumably, the payment of *cens* and any services owing to the lord of the *borgesie* were divided equally,[153] and the duties of each tenant were legally recognised so there could be no confusion over individual rights of alienation and inheritance.[154] But division did not simply mean revenues or crop yields were shared equally among the co-tenants. It meant actual partition of the land so each person knew precisely the borders of his share, and could, if he so wished, sell it separately. Thus, for instance, public and legal recognition was conferred on a sale in 1175 when Peter de Caors received the consent of his brothers Rainald and Hugo to sell his share of their inheritance, a house, to a Clarembald for fifty besants.[155] Clarembald received seisin of his share of the property, and as a tenant of the king acquired the right to alienate it 'as was customary' in Jerusalem. The court approved the sale and on behalf of the king received sales tax of two besants and two *solidi*.[156] Interesting in this context is a document of 1273 concerning a *heritage* in Acre in the joint possession of the churches of St Antoine and St Sarguis. Evidently, the churches had leased jointly the property to Set Lehoue who was now selling it to a *dame* Ysabiau. As new tenant Ysabiau was obliged to pay yearly rent of five besants to St Antoine and three besants to St Sarguis.[157] It would appear St Antoine possessed a greater share of the *heritage*, but it may be conjectured that previously both churches had received or purchased the property jointly.

Though we rely to a great extent on the 'Livre contrefais' for our knowledge of sale in Cyprus, there are some charters which are revealing of *borgesies* alienation on the island. A document of 1292 informs us that a court was convened to authorise the sale of a *borgesie* in Nicosia, and included Andrea of Nablus, viscount of the city, and Johanne de Bitunes and Baldwin Eltardo, 'juratis curie dicti vicecomitis'. From my understanding of this ambiguously worded text,

---

[152] Tabuteau, *Transfers of Property*, offers a brief analysis of joint tenancy, joint alienation and joint donation in eleventh-century Normandy.

[153] In the 'Livre contrefais', one chapter is also entitled: 'Ici parlera sur le fait des partizons des encensives'; 'Livre contrefais', p. 277.

[154] 'Livre contrefais', p. 277.

[155] Delaville Le Roulx, *Les Archives*, no. 46, pp. 135.

[156] Delaville Le Roulx, *Les Archives*, no. 46, p. 136.

[157] Favreau-Lilie, 'The Teutonic Knights in Acre after the Fall of Montfort (1271): Some Reflections', p. 282.

Gerald of Antioch, a canon, sold his house to John, archbishop of Nicosia, for 2800 besants. The archbishop agreed to use money he had received from the sale of a separate house to the order (of Minores?) for 4000 besants, so that he could pay Gerald the money he owed him. Typically, the archbishop was conveyed the freedom to buy, sell and bequeath his property, and as a requisite of sale, it was incumbent on Gerald, as vendor, to guarantee and to endorse thereafter the terms under which this transaction had been concluded 'in judico et extra judicium'.[158] It was earlier mentioned how this proviso was commonly included in charters originating in *Cours des Bouregois* on the mainland. I also touched upon the issue of litigation and the vulnerability of buyers to the challenge of claimants. The threat of legal challenge after the sale of a *borgesie* in Nicosia is confirmed in this charter.

We know from the 'Livre contrefais' that a vendor was under legal obligation to endorse the legitimacy of the transaction for a year and a day. There were cases, however, where the vendor was required to commit himself and his heirs in perpetuity to defending and validating the tenurial rights of the buyer and his heirs.[159] A commitment for all time is indication that alienation of a *borgesie* was always open to challenge. Because of Nicosian legislation, which afforded descendants legal opportunities to dispute past transactions, there was a strong probability that in the near or distant future a legal claim would be made by a *chalenjour* (disputant) as to the validity of a sale. In the charter recording John of Ibelin's sale of gardens in Nicosia to archbishop Eustorgius in 1247, John and his heirs were committed to defending and guaranteeing the legitimacy of the transaction. As long as, therefore, the property was not resold, there existed a special bond between the vendor, the buyer and their descendants. The guarantee of sale obviously encouraged Eustorgius to purchase the gardens for the large sum of 2500 besants, and as further incentive it was promised that if for some legal reason the archbishop lost possession of the gardens, John would endeavour 'de restorer le à vous, ou à ceux qui l'auront ou tenront pour vous'.[160]

Apart from the regulatory powers of the courts, the burgess laws of the kingdoms of Jerusalem and Cyprus further reinforced in perpetuity the control which the lord had over the alienation of property in his domain. He was entitled to the intrinsic right of pre-emption on *borgesies* being sold by his tenants. Pre-emption, however, which was a feature of alienation in the cities and *villes neuves*, was not an exclusive right of the *seigneur justicier*, but rather a basic right of the *seigneur de l'encensive*.[161] A sub-tenant wishing to sell a property had first to settle a price with a buyer, and it was at this point that the superior tenant could intervene to buy the *borgesie* for an agreed amount less than the price offered by the

158 Mas-Latrie, *Histoire de l'île de Chypre*, pp. 675–7.

159 'Livre contrefais', p. 253.

160 Mas-Latrie, *Histoire de l'île de Chypre*, p. 648.

161 Delaville Le Roulx, *Cartulaire général*, no. 399, p. 273, gives an example of pre-emption in Bethgibelin.

buyer.[162] In this regard, a sub-tenant who wished to alienate his property required permission not only from the *seigneur justicier*, but also from his superior tenant or his successors who retained the right of pre-emption indefinitely. In Jerusalem in 1178, the order of St John approved the sale by John Fulco of two houses in the city to William of Blanchgarde for ninety-seven besants. The order was *seigneur de l'encensive* which meant that if William of Blanchgarde chose to sell his *borgesie* he had first to offer the property to the Hospitallers for one besant less than the price to be paid by other prospective buyers.[163] When in 1184, in Acre, Bisanson bought a *borgesie* for 223 besants from the wife of the deceased Peter Bertasia, the order, which was superior tenant and *seigneur de l'encensive*, had right of pre-emption amounting to one mark of silver.[164] I should further add at this point, that besides the right of pre-emption, the lord of the domain or superior tenant had, for a certain period of time after the procedure of sale had been completed in court, legal permission to repurchase a *borgesie*. It again reinforced the hold which he retained over his property. Revealing of this practice is a document of Acre recording Thomas de Bailleu's sale of a *heritage* to the Teutonic Knights in 1273. The king had one year in which to repurchase the property by paying the order money it had previously paid Thomas – the special price which he was entitled to under terms of pre-emption no longer applied. But an interesting condition of this sale, and an example of the complicated nature of *borgesie* alienation, was that Thomas could remain living in the house for the year while paying the order a nominal rent of one dernier.[165] It may be inferred from this type of sale that a buyer had only conditional possession of a *borgesie* after the procedure of alienation had been concluded in the *Cour des Bourgeois*. I think, however, that the right of the lord of the domain or a superior tenant to repurchase a *borgesie* was not automatic but optional, a legal proviso, which if the buyer and seller of the property concerned agreed, could be written into a contract of sale. This seems to have been the case in Nicosia. Recognising that those who were penurious may out of necessity sell their *borgesies*, legislators in Nicosia decreed that a vendor and a buyer could reach an agreement whereby the buyer granted (*fait grace*) the vendor and his descendants a period of time, usually a year, within which to recover their property. If they were able to do this, they had first to repay the vendor the cost of the *borgesie* plus the three besants and two *solidi* which the

---

162 In Nicosia pre-emption was fixed at one mark of silver (or twenty-five besants) less than the price offered by the buyer; 'Livre contrefais', p. 258.

163 Delaville Le Roulx, *Les Archives*, no. 47, p. 136.

164 *Cartulaire général*, no. 663, p. 445. In 1155, in a *post obit* gift to the Hospitallers in Acre, the order of St John promised to pay the donor either eighty besants a year or ten marks of silver, which suggests that in this period one mark of silver was worth eight besants (*RRH*, no. 311, p. 80).

165 Favreau-Lilie, 'The Teutonic Knights in Acre after the Fall of Montfort (1271): Some Reflections', p. 284. The nominal payment of one dernier was paid, similarly, by the possessor of a vifgage, whilst living in the property; see below, p. 109.

latter had paid the court in sales tax. The buyer did not acquire seisin of the property until the end of this period of grace, and as such could not alienate it.[166]

Before proceeding to examine other types of *borgesie* transference, it should be considered the taxation which was levied from alienation. In Acre in the thirteenth century, sales tax was paid to the king by tenants who sold *borgesies* in a royal domain, except *francs borgesies*.[167] Generally-speaking, in the kingdom of Jerusalem the payment 'pour cele vente' was made by both vendor and buyer and the amount owed varied in the cities and *villes neuves*. The law of Acre compelled the vendor to pay the court one mark of silver and the buyer three besants.[168] This money, it would seem, was both intended for the royal coffers and administrative costs. In Nicosia, sales tax was paid 'for seisin', and the viscount on behalf of the king received from the buyer three besants, and the scribe and the sergeant of the court one *solidus* each.[169] Again, a condition of alienation in the secular courts of burgesses was replicated in the Church courts where a sales tax was applied to property under ecclesiastical jurisdiction. In 1239, the abbey of St Mary of the Latins granted Giot and John, sons of Michael of Jerusalem, permission to sell a vineyard located in the vicinity of Jerusalem to the Teutonic Order. It was stipulated that if the Teutonic Order were to sell the property the abbey would be entitled to three besants 'pro venditione'.[170] The sales tax, it should be added, was a flat rate and did not take into account the market value of the *borgesie* being sold, nor the amount of *cens* owing on the property each year. This is an interesting observation because proportional taxation was introduced in the *villes neuves*. In Bethgibelin in 1168, the Hospitallers received one besant for the sale of every *carruca* of land, and if the property sold was more or less than a *carruca* the order received a part of a besant proportionate to the size of the land. In addition, a farmer was obliged to pay one *rabouin* when selling a house or a vineyard.[171] In Magna Mahumeria, sales tax was high, the Church of the Holy Sepulchre receiving

166 'Livre contrefais', pp. 257–8.

167 Kausler, p. 66 (cf. Beugnot, 'Livre des Assises', p. 36). It seems that sales tax was also on some occasions paid to the immediate possessor of a *borgesie* and not necessarily to the lord of the domain. Before 1178, John Fulk sold his houses in Jerusalem to William Baptisatus for ninety-seven besants, and the Hospitallers, who were entitled to *cens* of one besant a year as well as right of pre-emption, received for the sale two besants and two *solidi*. They confirmed the alienation and the name of four brothers are given as witnesses to the transfer of seisin between the two tenants. The order was clearly only a superior tenant as the sale was approved by the royal *Cour des Bourgeois* in the presence of Balian, castellan of the Tower of David and eight jurors. It is possible that the court also received sales tax although it is not recorded in this charter; Delaville Le Roulx, *Les Archives*, no. 46, pp. 135–6, and no. 47, pp. 136–7.

168 Kausler, p. 66 (cf. Beugnot, 'Livre des assises', p. 36).

169 'Livre contrefais', pp. 253, 260.

170 Strehlke, no. 88, p. 70.

171 Delaville Le Roulx, *Cartulaire général*, no. 399, p. 273.

half the cost of a sale.[172] It may be that high taxation reflected the attempts of landowners to benefit from increased demand among Latins for settlement in rural villages. This explanation would be difficult to reconcile with the previously held assumption that Frankish society was predominantly an urban society.[173] For Ellenblum, on the other hand, the kingdom's internal security in the twelfth century was greater than has been thought previously, and Latin settlement in the rural territories was more widespread and indicative of economic growth.[174] He suggested that Magna Mahumeria was viewed by contemporaries as a particularly suitable place to settle, and possibly for this reason the Church of the Holy Sepulchre could make more demands from Latin farmers without disinclining them from settling.[175] This may account for the high tax imposed on the sale of *borgesie* as well as on crop yields. But the theory that the kingdom enjoyed greater internal security in the twelfth century does not convince completely. When and for how long did this state of security exist? There were of course periods of relative stability but this would have been accompanied by uncertainty. Magna Mahumeria and Bethgibelin were undoubtedly successful settlements, and this was perhaps the reason why they could collect more tax from their residents. But it can not be extrapolated that this was characteristic of the time, or that necessarily other settlements were in an equally privileged position to raise sales tax.

We must consider that sale was not the only option available to a tenant. Exchange was the permanent alienation of property not for money but for property of similar value. There survive few charters of exchange and of those discussed below, two originated in Acre and four in Jerusalem. Queen Melisende exchanged houses she possessed in Acre for baths belonging to the order of St John (1149),[176] and the Hospitallers exchanged a house in the city for another belonging to Nicholas Anteaume (1235).[177] In Jerusalem, Bernard, abbot of the Church of the Ascension of the Mount of Olives, gave the Hospitallers the *casale* of Cafran and received from them a number of houses and shops (1171);[178] Patriarch William exchanged a garden in the city for two shops which belonged to the Hospitallers (1141);[179] Roger Clericus exchanged some houses located in St. Stephen's Street for a house belonging to Gaufridus de Karitate in Malquisinat Street (1157);[180] and the canons of the Holy Sepulchre exchanged a shop in Malquisinat Street for

---

172 Bresc-Bautier, no. 123, p. 249: 'Et si aliquis vineam suam vendere voluerit, cum nostro consilio vendat et mediam partem precii nobis persolvet'.

173 Smail, *Crusading Warfare*, pp. 57–63; Prawer, *Crusader Institutions*, pp. 102–103; Benvenisti, p. 219.

174 Ellenblum, *Frankish Rural Settlement*, pp. 19, 32–3, 72, 80.

175 Ellenblum, *Frankish Rural Settlement*, p. 72.

176 Delaville Le Roulx, *Cartulaire général*, no. 180, pp. 140–41.

177 Delaville Le Roulx, *Cartulaire général*, no. 2126, pp. 493–4.

178 Delaville Le Roulx, *Cartulaire général*, no. 422, pp. 291–2.

179 Delaville Le Roulx, *Les Archives*, no. 6, pp. 74–5.

180 Delaville Le Roulx, *Les Archives*, no. 16, pp. 93–4.

derelict land belonging to the Hospitallers in the city (1175).[181] The general law prohibiting the sale of *borgesies* to fief-holders and members of the Church was reiterated in charters of transfer, and extended the prohibition to exchange.[182] *Eschange de Heritage*, as it was referred to in the law books, had its own procedure in court. After permission for the exchange had been granted, a formal and symbolic court ceremony, as in the act of sale, signified the mutual transfer of *borgesies*, making public what was initially a private agreement between two tenants. In Nicosia, the tenants concerned were expected to appear before the *Cour des Bourgeois* where the viscount acknowledged their standing as both donor and recipient of each other's *borgesie*. Each in turn proceeded to offer the *verge* to the viscount to signify that he had been disseised of his property. The viscount then seised either tenant with the tenement of the other and the concomitant duties, services and *cens* they were expected to fulfil. Each was obliged to pay the court five *solidi* for expenses.[183]

Unlike a conventional sale where a charge against a buyer of non-payment would have been difficult to disprove without the testimony of witnesses, in the act of exchange the property was tangible and indubitable evidence of the legitimacy of a transaction. Even so, there were legally enforced measures aimed at assuring the permanency of an exchange. When in 1171 the church of the Ascension exchanged the village *borgesie* of Cafran in return for houses belonging to the Hospitallers in Jerusalem, its abbot, Bernard, promised: 'We (the brothers of the Ascension) ought to free them (the Hospitallers) from all claims Christian men make for this village, and they similarly ought to free us from those claiming our shops and houses'.[184] A common form of assurance was to promise, as did Guerin, master of the Hospitallers, when exchanging houses with Nicholas Anteaume, to guarantee his concession of the *borgesie* 'libere et quiete, sine revocatione aut contrarietate'.[185]

In the types of alienation so far described, the tenant chooses to dispose of a *borgesie* completely either for money or property of equal value. But a *borgesie* could benefit its possessor in another way: it could serve as collateral.[186] In the eyes of the law, a property could be given as a gage, and as the many laws of pledge contained in the 'Livre de la Cour des Bourgeois' and the 'Livre contrefais' attest, immovable collateral was very important in the money-economies of Acre and Nicosia. For a propertied burgess borrowing against a *borgesie* was a popular means of raising money, but also a highly risky one. Even though his property was transferred to a lender only temporarily, he would have requested legal assurances specifying in formal language the terms and conditions of his agreement. In court a

---

181 Delaville Le Roulx, *Cartulaire général*, no. 483, p. 333.

182 Delaville Le Roulx, *Cartulaire général*, no. 2033, p. 412.

183 'Livre contrefais', p. 272.

184 Delaville Le Roulx, *Cartulaire général*, no. 422, p. 291.

185 Delaville Le Roulx, *Cartulaire général*, no. 2126, p. 493.

186 Kausler, p. 227 (cf. Beugnot, 'Livre des assises', p. 141).

gage was given either 'for a term' or 'without a term'. If engaged for a specific term – in Acre this was known as a *terme noumé*, and in Nicosia a *terme moti*[187] – there existed a fixed period for repayment, after which time the lender could confiscate the gage if the debt had not been settled.[188] Conversely, property or possessions pledged without a term signified that a gage was terminated whenever the money was repaid. It was an open-ended agreement which may have appealed more to a lender because whilst in his possession there existed greater opportunity to profit from the collateral. When a *borgesie* was engaged the court recognised that seisin of the property was held by the lender until the debt was paid off.[189] This type of temporary possession known as a vifgage was very common in contemporary Europe.[190] For the duration of time a lender was in possession of a vifgage he had certain legal rights. In Acre, for instance, he could reside in the house he held as a gage for a nominal payment to the borrower of one dernier until settlement of the debt.[191] Like the Norman vifgage, the lender could also collect profits accruing from the collateral – if, for example, he leased the property – though this would have to be deducted from the amount of the loan.[192] Contrastingly, a mortgage transaction allowed a borrower to retain possession of his property, and in some cases permitted profits from the collateral collected by the lender to serve as interest on the loan.[193]

Concerned that the terms of vifgage may favour lenders disproportionately, the lawmakers introduced legislation reinforcing the rights of borrowers to sue in court for the return of property held illegally. The law envisaged dispute arising between lender and borrower as to the true value of a gage, and whether a debt had been repaid fully or partially. Ultimately, it was the decision of the jurors as to the collateral value of the gage.[194] The rules of court procedure if a borrower wished to sue were set out in the 'Livre de la Cour des Bourgeois'; as in other legal cases, a dispute would be heard in the *Cour des Bourgeois* with jurisdiction over the property concerned. There were, in addition, legal provisions made in case a borrower – who wished to emigrate or was in failing health – did not want to abandon his *borgesie* to the lender. An option was to donate his property instructing the beneficiary that when he eventually sold the gage in order to settle

---

187 See, for example, Kausler, p. 103 (Beugnot, 'Livre des assises', p. 63), and 'Livre contrefais', p. 268.

188 Kausler, pp. 86–7 (cf. Beugnot, 'Livre des assises', p. 51).

189 Kausler, p. 87 (cf. Beugnot, 'Livre des assises', p. 52).

190 Tabuteau, *Transfers of Property*, pp. 80–81; Génestal, *Le Rôle des monastères*, pp. 1–3.

191 Kausler, p. 66 (cf. Beugnot, 'Livre des assises', p. 37).

192 Kausler, p. 66 (cf. Beugnot, 'Livre des assises', p. 37).

193 For a discussion of mortgage transactions in western Europe, see Tabuteau, *Transfers of Property*, p. 81; Génestal, *Le Rôle des monastères*, pp. 3–16; and L.V. Delisle, *Etudes sur la condition de la classe agricole et l'état de l'agriculture en Normandie au Moyen Age* (Evreux, 1851), pp. 208–10.

194 Kausler, p. 87 (cf. Beugnot, 'Livre des assises', p. 52).

the debt, he could keep any remaining money.[195] The process whereby a borrower repaid a loan and recovered his gage was known as *desgagier*.[196]

In Nicosia, pledge like all property deals required the consent of the *Cour des Bourgeois*, but unlike the sale of *borgesies*, which since the time of King Henry I had required the presence in court of at least five jurors, the pledging of property was witnessed by a viscount and only two jurors.[197] In Acre, similarly, a viscount and at least two jurors were required for a court to be quorate.[198] In their presence a tenant gave his *borgesie* as collateral to a lender, specifying the amount of money he had borrowed, and the period of time he had to pay back the loan. He then offered the *verge* to the viscount symbolising the transfer of seisin from himself to the president of the court, who in turn conveyed seisin to the lender. This was obviously a temporary arrangement as the lender had no right over the *borgesie* other than custody of the gage. If the money had not been paid after the specified period of time the lender could sue the borrower for repayment. The terms of the agreement were written down in the register of the court and consulted in case of dispute.[199] I have come across one charter recording a vifegage agreement in the royal *Cour des Bourgeois* in Acre. The document was written in 1274 so we can be more or less certain that the basic laws of property and tenancy practised by this court were those contained in the 'Livre de la Cour des Bourgeois'. Marguerite, widow of Nicole de la Monee, formerly a juror of the court,[200] was heavily in debt to the Teutonic Knights, and transferred all the houses she possessed in Acre to the order, instructing the brothers to collect the *cens* owing on the properties, except sixty besants a year for her to live on. This was agreed in the *Cour des Bourgeois* in the presence of Guillaume de Flori and twelve jurors. The order was to hold the houses as vifgage since it could collect profit which accrued from the collateral and gradually deduct it from the money it was owed. In court Marguerite permitted only possession of the rent to be conveyed to the order; Johan Sas, treasurer of the order, was to collect the rent 'por ses dettes paier'. She reserved the right to collect a share of the rent from the properties, and, presumably, when the debt was paid off, she resumed tenancy of the *borgesies*.[201] But in what way did the Teutonic Knights benefit from this loan? A possible explanation is that underlying the terms of this repayment was the avoidance of usury. The order may have accrued profit from the houses it held in vifgage over and above the amount of money it had originally lent Marguerite.

---

195 'Livre contrefais', p. 268.

196 'Livre contrefais', p. 268.

197 'Livre contrefais', p. 279.

198 Kausler, p. 66 (cf. Beugnot, 'Livre des assises', p. 37).

199 'Livre contrefais', p. 279.

200 Nicole de la Monee appears in the 'Livre contrefais' as a member of the *Cour des Bourgeois* that attended the *parlement* of Acre in 1250; 'Livre contrefais', p. 246.

201 Favreau-Lilie, 'The Teutonic Knights in Acre after the Fall of Montfort (1271): Some Reflections', 'appendix', p. 284.

There was an obvious risk entrusting seisin of a *borgesie* to a lender who, if the borrower defaulted on payment, could sell the property in order to recover his money. But he was able to do this only with permission from the *Cour des Bourgeois*, otherwise it was illegal to alienate the property or, as the law in Acre stipulated, to donate it to the Church 'in alms'.[202] To compound matters further for the borrower, he had no control over the sale of his *borgesie*, and under the terms of law, the lender was given the option of auctioning off the property to the highest bidder. This type of sale was known as *vente au criage dou seigneur* and existed in Acre and Nicosia. A gage which was confiscated to be sold was legally defined as a *gage abandon*.[203] The process of alienation was expeditious taking only a few days to complete under guidelines laid down by the *Cours des Bourgeois*. Hence, when a buyer was found, the court followed the typical procedure authorising sale. According to the 'Livre contrefais', seisin, symbolised by the *verge*, was transferred from the lender to the viscount and then to the buyer who paid the money for the property plus sales tax.[204] Similarly, in Acre the *Cour des Bourgeois* publicised sale of a confiscated gage for only three days then sold it to the highest bidder. If the money raised was insufficient to cover the loan, the borrower was still liable for the remainder of the debt. However, bearing in mind the gage in some cases may have been of a much greater value than the loan, the borrower was entitled to any additional money once the debt had been paid.[205]

That a burgess could offer to engage his *borgesie* would not necessarily persuade a lender to part with his money. The nomination, however, of one or more persons to act as guarantors underwriting a loan, would have seemed to a lender a more financially sound proposition. In England a gage was guaranteed by a person 'who makes himself responsible for another person's payment of a debt or performance or an undertaking'.[206] This onerous responsibility was reiterated in the 'Livre de la Cour des Bourgeois' when describing a guarantor as a 'segont detor'.[207] That is to say, a guarantor (the *plege*) undertook to settle a loan if after a certain period the borrower, for reasons deemed legitimate, was unable to repay the money.[208] The law in Acre aimed to ensure that a guarantor fulfilled his legal obligations, whilst at the same time safeguarded his rights as 'segont detor'. His obligations were toward the borrower and if necessary his heirs; the death of a borrower meant that his wife or children inherited his financial burdens, though under terms of law, the guarantor had to continue securing the loan for the whole of the period which had been agreed. Only at the end of this period was the

202 'Livre contrefais', pp. 279–80; Kausler, pp. 210–11 (cf. Beugnot, 'Livre des assises', p. 131).

203 Kausler, p. 217 (cf. Beugnot, 'Livre des assises', p. 135).

204 'Livre contrefais', p. 256.

205 Kausler, p. 67 (cf. Beugnot, 'Livre des assises', p. 37).

206 F. Pollock and F.W. Maitland, *The History of English Law* (Cambridge, 1968), p. 185.

207 Kausler, pp. 93–4 (cf. Beugnot, 'Livre des assises', p. 57).

208 Kausler, p. 94 (cf. Beugnot, 'Livre des assises', p. 57).

guarantor exempted of his responsibilities, irrespective of whether the borrower or his heirs successfully obtained from the lender an extension on the loan.[209] The 'Livre de la Cour des Bourgeois' makes it known that rules of guarantee were very strict, and without good reason a guarantor could not renege on his promises.[210] This was especially true in agreements involving more than one guarantor, where responsibility for the payment of debt was shared equally and where the release from obligation of any of the persons concerned not permitted.[211] By the same token, the rules governing borrowers were strict. From my understanding of the law, if a borrower offered his *borgesie* to a lender as security, he had permission to retain possession of his property, and his guarantor received certain privileges over this collateral. It is noteworthy that unlike vifgage, where the lender enjoyed temporary seisin of a *borgesie*, in this agreement the guarantor alone could sell the property, repay the lender, and release himself of his financial responsibilities. It is stated that any attempt by the guarantor to transfer the *borgesie* to the lender for him to sell was an infraction of the law. [212] These rules seem to be more in keeping with a mortgage agreement.

To summarise, in Acre and Nicosia in the thirteenth century, the practice of money-lending and of borrowing against collateral was very common among the class of burgesses. Vifgage seems to have been the most popular type although possibly *borgesies* were also mortgaged. Property was engaged for a term or without a term; in the former case the gage was terminated after a specified period and in the latter case whenever the loan was paid. The law books only discuss final payment in lump-sum, although in the loan agreement between Marguerite and the Teutonic Knights, the order collected the rent from the vifgage and recovered the money it was owed in instalments. A borrower's nomination, furthermore, of a guarantor was done as a token of his word that a loan would be repaid, although in the event he defaulted the guarantor had to assume the burden of debt. In any engagement it was the role of the *Cour des Bourgeois* to witness and approve the terms of collateral, and to adjudicate in matters of dispute. The court was the focal point of an uninterrupted legal agreement, meaning that changes in circumstances, whether a guarantor took on the debt, or the heirs of a deceased borrower inherited a debt, did not alter its continued responsibility of ensuring vifgage or mortgage agreements were honoured by all parties involved.

The description of *borgesie* alienation has revealed several aspects of burgess law and property, and not least the rather complicated legal process of sale, exchange and pledge, which brought together all parties, namely the buyer and seller, borrower and lender, and other concerned individuals including wives,

---

[209] Kausler, p. 103 (cf. Beugnot, 'Livre des assises', p. 63).

[210] See, for example, Kausler, p. 105 (cf. Beugnot, 'Livre des assises', p. 64).

[211] Kausler, p. 97 (cf. Beugnot, 'Livre des assises', p. 59). It was, however, expedient for a borrower to nominate additional guarantors in case one died or neglected his responsibilities. See Kausler, p. 102 (cf. Beugnot, 'Livre des assises', p. 62).

[212] Kausler, pp. 107–108 (cf. Beugnot, 'Livre des assises', p. 66).

children, near relatives and witnesses, before the court where the ritualistic procedure of transfer of seisin was observed, the conditions of tenancy defined and tax, when a transaction had taken place, collected by the lord of the domain and his officials. The charters are confirmation of this legal ritual and regulation, and even if it is claimed there did exist allodial properties which were alienated in private and thus did not warrant documentation, the law books are unambiguous proof that all persons who wished to sell, exchange or pledge city property were expected to go before a court of burgesses. All things considered, the sale and acquisition of property was, on the part of the vendor and buyer, a decision not taken lightly. For the vendor, the money which could be had from the sale of a *borgesie* may have been a motivational factor, but the potentially legal repercussions and challenges of disposing of property remained a disincentive. Exchange was no less a complicated and potentially troublesome process, whilst the pledging of property was always a risky venture.

However, looked at in a more positive light, the intrinsic value and alienability of a *borgesie* was a source of wealth and security to its tenant. If, in any case, he was not enticed by profit or compelled by necessity, an alternative option for a tenant was to hold on to his *borgesie* in perpetuity. Let us consider this right which was an integral characteristic of *encensive* tenure. In Cyprus there developed a type of *borgesie* which was inalienable, purely hereditary. A tenant had the right to bequeath a *borgesie* to a successor, requesting that under the terms of his legacy the property may not be alienated but to entail from one heir to the next.[213] Although a burgess could be more generous in his bequest to one of his children, right of primogeniture does not seem to have prevailed in the burgess laws of the kingdoms of Jerusalem and Cyprus.[214] Bequests came in two forms: testamentary and verbal. A written will was the ideal but a burgess was allowed to give a verbal bequest, a *testamentum nuncupativum*. Reminiscent of the thirteenth-century debate among lawmakers over the appositeness of memory in the decision-making process of the court of burgesses, the spoken word remained as vital as the written word in the drawing up of wills. In 1264, the burgess Saliba's bequest to the Hospitallers of a house in Acre and to the rest of his family individual sums of money, was a good example of a *testamentum nuncupativum*, and the charter which was drawn up, including the names of those who witnessed his gift, guaranteed the Hospitallers' right of inheritance.[215]

Bearing in mind that the validity of a will depended on the memory of individuals, there were strict guidelines as to who could act as witness. In Acre there were chosen at least three trustworthy men – women, minors, slaves and those who had lost their right of *respons de cort* were excluded – who committed themselves for a period of time to endorse the legitimacy of a verbal bequest

213 'Livre contrefais', pp. 269–70.

214 Kausler, p. 208 (cf. Beugnot, 'Livre des assises', p. 129). See also Beugnot, 'Introduction', p. xlvii.

215 Delaville Le Roulx, *Cartulaire général*, no. 2105, pp. 191–2.

against any challenges which may arise.[216] As always, the court made sure the transfer of property was done legitimately and disqualified certain persons from acting as beneficiaries. A minor, for example, was entrusted to a guardian – either a close relative or a person specially chosen to safeguard his interests – who could use the bequest to bring up the child until he or she was of legal age to inherit.[217] Unmarried women, furthermore, could not inherit. Though burgess law by and large protected the right of a wife to a share of property acquired jointly with her husband, outside of marriage it remained inequitable.[218] But the objective of the law was not so much to punish unmarried women as to endorse the sanctity of marriage. Therefore, in Acre the children of an invalid marriage forfeited their right of inheritance, and only members of a collateral branch of the family could reclaim the property within a year and a day of its confiscation.[219] What we understand by this is that the testator was in violation of the law – as claimed by those who challenged the bequest – because he had no rightful heir, either wife or children, which meant the property automatically reverted back to the lord of the domain and his court. It is yet further testimony of the enduring power of repossession which a lord of the domain, or at least a *seigneur de l'encensive*, had over a *borgesie*. It re-emphasises the character of a *borgesie* as property which though held by a tenant in perpetuity under inviolable terms, ceased to be his should the rules of tenancy be broken, or certain conditions remain unfulfilled. But in dealing with such contentious issues, the role of the court was to arbitrate fairly and to enforce the law consistently, taking possession of a property if it could be proved beyond doubt that the lease of a tenant and his successors should come to an end. A *seigneur de l'encensive* in Acre could, in this respect, claim possession of the property of a tenant who had died intestate and with no relatives.[220] And similar rules of intestacy existed, for instance, in the Venetian quarter in Tyre where the commune was able to acquire the houses of Balmene, a Turcopole, and a certain Johannes Garabellus, who had died intestate and without heirs.[221]

Only within a legitimate marriage could the rights of a woman be guaranteed, but in terms of inheritance did a wife take precedence over children or vice versa? In Acre the law dictated that if a man died intestate his property and movable possessions should escheat to his wife who had priority over other relatives.[222]

---

216 Kausler, pp. 213, 219–20 (cf. Beugnot, 'Livre des assises', pp. 132, 136).

217 'Livre contrefais', p. 281.

218 'Livre contrefais', pp. 254: 'Sachés que tous homes et femes frans et sans aucun servage pevent vendre et acheter bourgesies, persoune qui soit en son droit aage; *car l'aage de l'ome est quant it a compli quinze ans, et l'aage de la femme quant elle est mariée ou veve, ou que elle ait voué chasteté*'.

219 Kausler, p. 178 (cf. Beugnot, 'Livre des assises', p. 110). On the inheritance rights of illegitimate children, see Kausler, p. 193 (cf. Beugnot, 'Livre des assises', p. 119).

220 Kausler, p. 205 (cf. Beugnot, 'Livre des assises', p. 127).

221 Berggötz, pp. 148, 149.

222 Kausler, pp. 202–203 (cf. Beugnot, 'Livre des assises', p. 125).

Similarly, in the principality of Achaia in the thirteenth century, the right of a wife to inherit her husband's property if he died intestate took precedence over the right of his children.[223] This, nevertheless, does not seem to have been the case in Nicosia where according to legislation the property of a husband who died intestate escheated automatically to his children who had precedence over his wife.[224] Indeed, the proviso that only legitimate children enjoyed principal right of inheritance was written into an agreement of 1297, when Pisanello de Richobaldo of Famagusta recognised the right of his future wife to inherit certain possessions, assuming they had no legitimate child heir. It was a principle which seemed to have general application on the island as according to the document it was a 'custom of the kingdom of Cyprus'.[225] In fact, Levantine law usually favoured children. The inheritance rights of offspring were repeated in the legislation of thirteenth-century Antioch where the property of a deceased escheated automatically to his wife, provided he did not have children.

A tenant, as earlier explained, was free to bequeath the whole or part of his *borgesie*,[226] and as long as a legally valid testament or verbal bequest existed, the gift of the testator escheated automatically to his heir without further need for court procedure, provided the basic requirements of inheritance were met. However, in Nicosia, the *Cour des Bourgeois* took a different position when a donor made a gift *inter vivos* – a legal term which meant that the gift had been made during the lifetime of the donor – even to one of his children. Any kind of private donation was not permissible in the eyes of the law, because all forms of property transfer were subject to court jurisdiction. According to legal convention, the *Cour des Bourgeois* oversaw the donation of any *borgesie* and recognised the terms of an agreement. In court the donor would offer the *verge* to the viscount acknowledging symbolically he was disseised of his property. In turn, the viscount conveyed the *verge* to the donee – or if absent a representative – to signify his right of possession.[227] A donor could, however, attach certain requisites when making a donation *inter vivos*. Thus, for instance, a *borgesie* could be given on the condition that the donee would not alienate or engage the property until he reached a certain age. A donor, furthermore, had the option of donating his *borgesie* temporarily whilst reserving the right to recover it from the donee when he chose. One can only imagine that this was a charitable act because though the donor granted the donee permission to enjoy usufruct and, to all intents and purposes, assume the freedoms of a tenant to sub-lease the *borgesie* for a short term and collect rent, he was,

---

223 Recoura, *Les Assises de Romanie*, no. 38, p. 186: 'Se lo homo muor intestado, la moier sociede in li beni mobeli et inmobeli burgesiastichi; ma se ello non avera moier lo fiol sociede, et se lo sera fioli, o fie, tuti sociede ingualmentre'.

224 'Livre contrefais', p. 281.

225 M. Balard (ed.), *Notai genovesi in oltremare: atti rogati a Cipro da Lamberto di Sambuceto (11 Ottobre 1296–23 Giugno 1299)* (Genoa, 1983), p. 37.

226 'Livre contrefais', p. 268.

227 'Livre contrefais', pp. 265–6.

nevertheless, granted possession of the property only temporarily and did not have right of alienation or inheritance. The death of a donor did not even diminish the right of his children or nearest relatives to recover the *borgesie*.[228]

Eleemosynary Donation

The permanent or temporary alienation of *borgesies* by donation, sale or exchange to other laymen, did not affect in any way the jurisdictional authority of the *Cour des Bourgeois*. The court was the focal point of all procedures of transference. There was though an exception to this rule and one which warrants further investigation because it was of such significance. The eleemosynary donation of a *borgesie* to the Church, or a charitable donation 'in alms', resulted in the conveyance of jurisdiction over the property concerned from a *Cour des Bourgeois* to an ecclesiastical court. Essentially, this common act of charity[229] modified the legal standing of a *borgesie* by removing it from royal or seigneurial jurisdiction, a legal immunity which required principally the permission of a donor's lord. The ecclesiastical institution could bequeath the property, further donate it 'in alms', or lease it to a sub-tenant in perpetuity. It also had jurisdictional control over the *borgesie* and was 'free and exempted' from service, or 'absolved from customary payments', which usually meant it was not obliged to pay *cens*. Importantly, the act of charity and the legal definition of the property as tenure 'in alms', did not eliminate but rather suspend the service and the jurisdiction which had hitherto existed. As the evidence shall show, in the possession of the Church a *borgesie* retained its intrinsic alienability, so that if the ecclesiastical institution which received the property sold it to a layman it automatically reverted to the *Cour des Bourgeois* of the secular lord in whose domain it was located. It should be pointed out that a *borgesie* rendered *in elemosinam* did not require any secular service from the recipient apart from prayers for the benefactor and his family. But in some cases a monetary countergift did change hands. This practice has led some historians to argue that a material countergift was nothing more than a disguised sale because the Church was not permitted to purchase *borgesies*.[230] As there exists no evidence to support this contention or proof that countergifts reflected the true market value of the property being donated, I have included this type of transaction under the general discussion of eleemosynary grants. Indeed, rather than being a disguised sale, it is more likely that a countergift was the compensation which the Church paid the donor in order to deter the person, his relatives or others from challenging the donation in future.

---

228 'Livre contrefais', pp. 266–7.

229 On eleemosynary donations to the order of St John, see Riley-Smith, *The Knights of St John*, pp. 457–8.

230 Prawer, *Crusader Institutions*, p. 293.

Like the significant gestures accompanying the sale of a *borgesie*, there were also procedures symbolising the making of a gift. A charter of 1163 recounts how Eustace and Adam Niger granted land in Jerusalem to the Hospitallers, and the donor invested the recipient with the *borgesie* by placing his hands symbolically on a church altar to signify the spiritual nature of the donation.'[231] The placement of hands or other symbolic object on an altar reflected similar practices in contemporary Europe.[232] In a donation of 1255, a knight, John Marrain, conceded to the Hospitallers land he possessed outside Acre. After the donation had been concluded in the *Cour des Bourgeois* 'de manu in manum', the donor, recipient, witness and court notary went on the same day to the donated land, and John Marrain took some earth and placed it in the hand of Hugo Revel, master of the order of St John.[233] The public ceremony was a constant reminder to witnesses of the permanency and legitimacy of the donation.[234]

Typically, a donor would grant property to the Church *in puram et perpetuam elemosinam*, 'in pure and perpetual alms', 'irrevocably', 'without impediment' or 'diminution', stressing at times that a *borgesie* had been given *inter vivos*, as opposed to *mortis causa*, when the property was transferred only after his or her death. In 1253, Nicholas de Arcu conceded to the Hospitallers a house 'in elemosinam ... inter vivos';[235] in 1255, John Aleman, lord of Caesarea, granted to the Hospitallers various *borgesies* 'in puram, liberam et perpetuam elemosinam ... inter vivos';[236] and in 1260, John Grifus, a fief-holder of Acre, conceded to the Hospitallers property in Acre 'inter vivos et irrevocabiliter'.[237] The Church or religious order which received the *borgesie* was usually requested to pray for the eternal salvation of the donor, his wife and children, his mother and father and all his close relatives.[238] The formal transfer of property took place in the local *Cour des Bourgeois* because a private agreement between the donor and the recipient would have rendered a donation which lacked public and legal conferment invalid. When in 1235 Stephanie granted to the Hospitallers the houses of her deceased father, she stated 'in order that the donation remains fixed and unchanged in perpetuity, the (gift) is made in the (burgess) court of Jerusalem'.[239] In the royal domain the conveyance of *borgesies* into ecclesiastical hands was sanctioned by the king. In fact, it was not unknown for the king to approve eleemosynary grants

231 Delaville Le Roulx, *Cartulaire général*, no. 312, p. 226.

232 Tabuteau, *Transfers of Property*, pp. 120–22; Génestal, *Rôle des monastères*, p. 28.

233 Delaville Le Roulx, *Cartulaire général*, no. 2714, p. 773.

234 Tabuteau, *Transfers of Property*, p. 119; S.E. Thorne, 'Livery of Seisin', *Law Quarterly Review* 52 (1936): 348–52; J. Yver, *Les Contrats dans très ancien droit normand (XIe–XIIIe siécles)* (Domfront, 1926), pp. 34–8; Clanchy, *From Memory to Written Record*, pp. 206–207.

235 Delaville Le Roulx, *Cartulaire général*, no. 2662, p. 750.

236 Delaville Le Roulx, *Cartulaire général*, no. 2732, p. 779.

237 Delaville Le Roulx, *Cartulaire général*, no. 2949, p. 887.

238 Delaville Le Roulx, *Cartulaire général*, no. 312, p. 226.

239 Delaville Le Roulx, *Cartulaire général*, no. 2127, p. 494.

of *borgesies* in return for the proffering of spiritual service to him. In 1173, King Amalric approved the donation of a *borgesie* to the Hospitallers, and in recognition of royal consent, the brothers prayed for the eternal salvation of his soul and the souls of his children.[240]

There is further evidence of eleemosynary donations in the Italian quarters. In the Venetian quarter in Tyre, grants 'in alms' were made by Maria Cauco and Michael Lunizo, who gave a house to the church of St Mark's 'for the redemption of his soul'.[241] Such property came under the jurisdiction of the ecclesiastical court of the quarter. In Tyre the Venetians claimed that in their third part of the city the church of St Mark's was exempt from the jurisdiction of the diocesan court of the archbishop, an exemption confirmed by the papacy in 1200 and 1247.[242] As a consequence, in the thirteenth century, Venetian burgesses were no longer subject in ecclesiastical matters to the archbishop of Tyre, but were instead subject to the jurisdiction of the Church court in Venice.

As in all forms of permanent transfer, donation 'in alms' was not immune from the challenge of claimants who objected to the gift of property, particularly as it had been given to the Church freely. It may be argued that a countergift was a sum of money which the Church paid to a donor as a form of compensation and an inducement to consent. But in instances where an ecclesiastical institution was neither willing nor able to offer a financial gift to discourage litigation, it was eager to ensure in the drafting of a charter of donation that as many members of the donor's close family gave their written and formal approval to the donation. When Audiarde, widow of Otto of Verdun donated a *borgesie*, a courtyard, in Jerusalem to the Hospitallers (1173), she did so in the royal *Cour des Bourgeois* in the presence of her sons Guy and Henry, her daughters Isabella, wife of John Aschetin, Benedicta wife of Joffrid, son of Simon Judicus, and Jasze wife of Henry Balistar. Her daughters, their husbands and children gave their consent and promised to defend the legitimacy of the donation.[243] But to what extent could a donor commit subsequent generations, heirs and potential heirs to a donation? Any formal agreement given by a donor's relative was no guarantee that in future this same person would not challenge the grant of property made to the Church. Indeed, there were disputes left to the *Cour des Bourgeois* to resolve, and as *borgesie* was property defined by its hereditary character, the right of patrimony could always be claimed by those challenging an alienation.

It is difficult to argue unreservedly that a countergift was a concealed sale, primarily because it is impossible to infer from the charters whether a sum of

---

240 Delaville Le Roulx, *Cartulaire général*, no. 444, p. 309: 'Factum est hoc in curia domini regis Amalrici in Jerusalem, qui hoc donum laudavit, consensit, et pro salute anime sue et totius generis sui confirmavit'.

241 Berggötz, p. 143.

242 B. Hamilton, *The Latin Church in the Crusader States: The Secular Church* (London, 1980), p. 291.

243 Delaville Le Roulx, *Cartulaire général*, no. 444, pp. 308–309.

money paid by the Church to a donor reflected the true value of the property. In addition, the theory that material countergifts were disguised sales does not account for the basic fact that the secular lord of the property always retained the jurisdictional right to prohibit an eleemosynary donation if he suspected an ulterior motive at play. Emily Tabuteau has argued in her study of eleemosynary grants in eleventh-century Normandy, that the practice of giving a material countergift served both as an evidentiary role, in other words a public reminder of the transfer of property to the Church, and significantly, as a preventative role, discouraging donors, confirmers and their heirs, who received something in return for their donation, from challenging a gift. To support her argument Tabuteau cited charters recording material countergifts as having been given 'in witness', or 'in memory', or 'in recognition', a terminology reminiscent of that used to describe countergifts in the kingdom of Jerusalem.[244] On receiving a *borgesie* from Audiarde, the Hospitallers made a countergift of 760 besants to the widow 'for recognition and confirmation of her gift'.[245] The formula was repeated in Eustace and Adam Niger's donation to the Hospitallers which the order rewarded with 500 besants for the purpose of 'agreement and confirmation'.[246] I am, however, not convinced that Tabuteau's theory can be applied wholly to the kingdom of Jerusalem bearing in mind the huge sums of money which were being paid by the Church. Nevertheless, it is difficult to argue in support of the opposing theory of a concealed sale when the actual transaction had to be overseen by the *Cour des Bourgeois*. Arguing, therefore, from the premise that eleemosynary donations and countergifts required the legitimacy of the court, it may have been the case – as has been pointed out in relation to other donations 'in alms' to the order[247] – that this was sometimes a method of approved sale which secured for the recipient the benefits of an eleemosynary grant. The order was given a donation 'in alms' and in exchange the benefactor received a countergift. Subsequently, this method of sale would be confirmed by the lord *in elemosinam*.

In principle, a *borgesie* granted 'in alms' became subject to Church jurisdiction. For this reason a royal confirmation of 1138 in which King Fulk conceded houses to the Holy Sepulchre seems at first sight to be contradictory. It is written:

> Has itaque domos liberas et quietas ego rex Fulco concedo et confirmo habendas et possidendas jure perpetuo predicte ecclesie et ejusdem canonicis, et ab omni consuetudine solutas, *salva justicia regali quam rex debet habere*, in elemosinam quam ipse dat sancte Ecclesie.[248]

In a similar vein, King Baldwin III conceded to the canons in 1155 houses in Jerusalem 'in elemosinam ... ab omni exactione liberas et quietas, *salvo tamen*

244 Tabuteau, *Transfers of Property*, pp. 116–18.
245 Delaville Le Roulx, *Cartulaire général*, no. 444, p. 309.
246 Delaville Le Roulx, *Cartulaire général*, no. 312, p. 226.
247 Riley-Smith, *Knights of St John*, p. 424.
248 Bresc-Bautier, no. 33, p. 97.

regio jure'.[249] If the fundamental principle of European canon law exempted property granted to the Church from secular jurisdiction, why, therefore, were the kings of Jerusalem claiming for themselves *justicia regalis*?[250] Was this a departure from traditional rules governing eleemosynary donations? It is unlikely in such cases the judicial rights of the Church were being encroached upon, and a more plausible explanation is that some form of compromise between secular and ecclesiastical jurisdiction was taking place. A distinction was drawn in the kingdom of Jerusalem between the legal status of the *borgesie* and that of the tenant. For instance, a *borgesie* in the possession of a knight of Jerusalem was subject to the royal *Cour des Bourgeois* of that city, but in all other legal matters not relating to the tenement, the knight, if a fief-holder, was answerable to the jurisdiction of the High Court. Thus jurisdiction was divided between the two courts. A similar distinction may have existed between the legal status of the tenant and of the tenement with regard to royal claims of jurisdiction over *borgesies* granted 'in alms'. The properties in Jerusalem which were conceded to the Church of the Holy Sepulchre by Fulk and Baldwin III, meant that the tenements passed under ecclesiastical jurisdiction, whereas the tenants of the *borgesies* remained legally bound to the royal *Cour des Bourgeois* of the city.

F. Pollock and F.W. Maitland observed in their study of eleemosynary tenure in thirteenth-century England, that a mere gift did not automatically acquit the ecclesiastical recipient from secular exactions.[251] The terminology of exemption determined whether immunity was total or partial, a determination based on several factors, not least royal or seigneurial confirmation of the gift. Only a king or a lord could accord total exemption when making a donation *in elemosinam*, as the unburdened property passed directly from the hands of the *seigneur justicier* into the hands of the recipient to be enjoyed 'free and absolved from all services'.[252] In 1160, Hugh, lord of Caesarea, conceded to the order of St Lazarus a house and a garden in Jerusalem which it was to hold from him 'liber et absolutus ab omni servitio'; free from the payment of *cens*, and absolved entirely from the performance of services.[253] Notably, Hugh granted St Lazarus a further house belonging to Arnald Gala, a brother of the order. The terms of the donation are of particular interest.

---

249 Bresc-Bautier, no. 42, p. 118.

250 On the principles of eleemosynary donation as laid down in European canon law, see A.W. Douglas, 'Tenure *in Elemosinam*: Origins and Establishment in Twelfth-Century England', *The American Journal of Legal History*, 24 (1980): 95–132. Consider also E.G. Kimball, 'Tenure in Frank Almoign and Secular Services', *EHR*, 43 (1928): 341–53.

251 Pollock and Maitland, *English Law*, p. 245: 'If the donee wished to get rid of the service altogether, he had to go to the donor's superior lords and ultimately to the king for charters of release'.

252 The notion that only a lord could make an eleemosynary donation that was completely exempt, was expressed by the author of the mid-thirteenth-century Norman *Summa de legisbus*. See E.J. Tardif (ed.) *Coutumiers de Normandie*, v. 2: *La Summa de legibus Normannie in curia laicali* (Rouen and Paris, 1896), p. 100.

253 Marsy, no. 18, p. 137.

> Quicumque in ea preter aliquem fratrem Sancti Lazari habitaverit servitutem domino Cesariensi sicut alii burgenses reddiderit. Quamdiu in ea aliquis fratrum illorum manebit, libere et quiete eam possidebunt.

Lord Hugh did not commit himself to the promise of unconditional immunity, but rather suspended service on the condition that terms of tenancy were met. Crucially, the service-exempt status of the *borgesie* was determined by the status of the tenant, meaning that if the brothers of St Lazarus were to sub-lease the house to anyone other than members of the order, the legal right of immunity from secular exaction would cease to take effect, and the lay tenant of the *borgesie* would be subject to service *sicut alii burgenses*. With regard to the conditional suspension of secular services, a charter of 1160 in which Baldwin III confirmed the gift of a *borgesie* to the Church of the Holy Sepulchre was cast in similar terms.

> De cetero domum Achon fundatam quam Lambertus Als uxorque sua Agnes, concessu regis Fulconis patris mei, ecclesie Sancti Sepulcri, hac vidilect conditione, libere et quiete possidendam concessit, ne venditione vel commutatione sive quolibet alio modo a se eidem liceat et, si fecerint, regia majestas ex ea servicium habeat, sepedictis canonicis hac predicta ratione confirmo.[254]

The proviso the king attached to this donation did differ slightly to that of the lord of Caesarea inasmuch as it made specific reference to permanent alienation which again would have rendered the *borgesie* subject to secular jurisdiction. In essence, however, the conditions written into the royal confirmation were no different; the performance of secular services was suspended provided that the property was not transferred back into secular hands. If this were to happen, the new tenant would owe service to the king his immediate lord.

Two documents of the twelfth and thirteenth centuries trace the history of a *borgesie* in Jerusalem from 1169, when Ancelin of Brie confirmed the leasehold on certain houses in the city granted by his mother Gille to John, a rope-maker, to 1235, when Stephanie daughter of John gave the houses 'in alms' to the order of St John, and their lease cost twenty-seven besants a year.[255] Presumably, sometime in the intervening decades, and perhaps before 1187, Stephanie had inherited the properties from her father, and taking into account the fact that from 1187 to 1229 Jerusalem was in Muslim hands, it may be suggested the right of inheritance or uninterrupted right of possession prevailed. The gift 'in alms' which took place in the *Cour des Bourgois* in Jerusalem, transferred the houses out of John's familial line of descent and into ecclesiastical jurisdiction. The donation required the approval of the king and Stephanie's superior tenant who in the original charter of lease appeared as Ancelin of Brie. But what happened to the *cens* owed to Ancelin

254 Bresc-Bautier, no. 45, p. 125.

255 Delaville Le Roulx, *Cartulaire général*, no. 2127, p. 494.

and his descendants? There are two possible explanations. Either the beneficiary (the Hospitallers) got rid of this exaction altogether by going to the donor's (Stephanie) superior tenant (the descendants of Ancelin of Brie) and ultimately to the king for charters of release, or Stephanie took upon herself the burden of secular debt, because as sub-tenant she was not in a position to induce the descendants of Ancelin to waive the *cens*. She may have promised, therefore, to carry on paying them rent annually. I have not, however, been able to find evidence in any of the charters and law books of the kingdoms of Jerusalem and Cyprus to support this latter explanation, although the existence of this type of tenure 'in alms' in contemporary Europe is easily verifiable.[256]

We have seen that only the *seigneur justicier* could grant *borgesies* 'in alms' with total immunity from the payment of rent and the performance of secular services. One option for him was to suspend exactions on the condition that the property did not pass into secular hands. A tenant of a *seigneur justicier* could grant a *borgesie* 'in alms', if he received permission to do so from his lord, and as the gift of Lambert of Als demonstrated, the free and perpetual character of the property in the hands of the Church of the Holy Sepulchre was defined by the royal charter of release. The Church had received a house from Lambert, but in order to be rid of the secular service pertaining to the property altogether, it required from the king a charter of confirmation and conferment of immunity from the royal *Cour des Bourgeois*. It may have been the case, however, that a lord's confirmation exempted the recipient from *cens* on a particular property as long as the donor assumed the burden of secular service.

In evaluating the charters of donations 'in alms' it is evident that in the possession of the Church the *borgesie* retained its basic features, in particular its alienability. Certainly, an eleemosynary grant modified the jurisdictional standing of a *borgesie* by subjecting it to a Church court as well as exempting the ecclesiastical recipient from secular exactions, even if in some cases this was conditional. There is, however, no suggestion that donation modified those other characteristics which commonly defined a *borgesie*. On the contrary, the freedom of the recipient to alienate property was unimpeded. The Hospitallers, for example, received from Nicholas de Arcu a house in Acre 'which they shall have, hold, possess, and thereafter do whatever is pleasing to them concerning matters of property'.[257] Similar terms of freedom were extended to the Hospitallers on receiving a house from John Grifus,[258] whilst in the confirmation of Baldwin III the right of alienation was expressly stated.[259] One further condition does seem though to have prevailed in the principality of Antioch. In 1186, Bohemond of Antioch confirmed the donations 'in alms' of *borgesies* to the Hospitallers, and gave them permission to sell their properties provided they

---

256 Tabuteau, *Transfers of Property*, p. 38.

257 Delaville Le Roulx, *Cartulaire général*, no. 2662, p. 750.

258 Delaville Le Roulx, *Cartulaire général*, no. 2949, p. 887.

259 Bresc-Bautier, no. 45, p. 125.

had held them for at least a year and a day.[260]

The basic rules governing the tenancy and transfer of *borgesies* whether administered by an ecclesiastical court or a *Cour des Bourgeois* were to be found everywhere, and, significantly, the alienation of *borgesies* previously granted to the Church 'in alms' did not require the permission of the king or secular lord, being overseen by an ecclesiastical court. When in 1153 Baldwin, the bishop of Beirut, made a *post obit* gift of his house in Jerusalem to the Hospitallers – a house which had been previously given to him 'in alms' – the donation was witnessed by an ecclesiastical court.[261] In 1160, when Bernard Bursarius sold his house to Richard Jaferinus, the canons of the Church of the Holy Sepulchre witnessed and confirmed the transfer of seisin. Although these cases concerned Church courts, the customary rules found elsewhere in the kingdom prevailed. Richard Jaferinus received rights of alienation and inheritance; he owed the canons fourteen besants *ad censum*, and they received right of pre-emption.[262] The same fundamentals of tenure were part of the terms of the donation made by John Grifus to the Hospitallers in Acre (1260). The gift included a house which Isabella had leased from John for sixteen besants *ad censum*. The conveyance of the tenement to the order meant not only would Isabella become a tenant of the Hospitallers, but also that she would be answerable to ecclesiastical jurisdiction in matters of occupancy.[263] Also in Acre, in Montmusard, the Templars, who possessed property in the south-western corner of this suburb, leased an area of land, which they had been previously given 'in alms', to the order of St Lazarus (1240). This was an *encensive* tenancy and the order was obliged to pay the Templars rent of fifteen besants a year in perpetuity. St Lazarus was free to develop the land and was, it seems, planning to build on this site a property to house some of Montmusard's leper colony. The Templars promised to build them a road linking the properties of St Lazarus to a cistern it possessed in the suburb. St Lazarus, like any sub-tenant of a *borgesie*, had freedom of alienation, and the Templars, like any secular lord, had the right to pre-empt any future sale. In fact, according to the agreement, the Templars could delay alienation for a period of ten days, and if they chose to buy back the property they would acquire it for a price which was, symbolically, one mark of silver less than that offered to other buyers. St Lazarus could not alienate to churchmen, secular fief-holders, or members of the merchant communities.[264] A document of 1143 yields further evidence of the uniformity of *borgesie* tenure in Jerusalem. When the canons of the Holy Sepulchre leased a house and a shop in the city to Bernard, they instructed, as was the custom, that if Bernard wished to alienate his property he could do so only to burgesses. Additional clauses of tenancy confirmed explicitly the right of the church to repossess the *borgesie* if

---

260 Delaville Le Roulx, *Cartulaire général*, no. 783, p. 495.

261 Delaville Le Roulx, *Cartulaire général*, no. 100, p. 88.

262 Bresc-Bautier, no. 124, pp. 250–51.

263 Delaville Le Roulx, *Cartulaire général*, no. 2949, pp. 887–8.

264 Marsy, no. 39, pp. 155–7.

Bernard failed to pay the *cens* owing on the property.[265]

In Cyprus, similarly, ecclesiastical institutions had rights to sub-lease *borgesies* to tenants in perpetuity under terms of *encensive* with full rights of inheritance and alienation. Church courts, moreover, had authority to exercise jurisdiction over tenants in matters pertaining to their properties. In a charter of 1245, for instance, the archbishop of Nicosia, Eustorgius, leased *pro censu* certain houses in the city to Andronicus Teupetomeno and his brothers and sister. The tenants were to pay rent in kind yearly.[266] From the evidence of this document we may safely assume that in Nicosia the essential characteristics of a *borgesie* in Church hands were not modified, in the same way that on the mainland a *borgesie* in the possession of an ecclesiastical institution retained its essential features, including its alienability.

Post Obit or Deferred Donation

An eleemosynary gift to the Church was intended to take effect immediately, transferring seisin of the donated property to the ecclesiastical institution once the consent of the *Cour des Bourgeois* had been received. A *post obit* or deferred donation, *mortis causa* as opposed to *inter vivos*, delayed the transfer of the *borgesie* until after the death of a donor who in his lifetime retained possession of a property. This was also somewhat different to a death-bed gift, inasmuch as the person making the donation was not expected to die imminently. If joined by his wife in the making of a gift, the donor could request the transfer take effect only after both their deaths; in some cases deferment could be extended until after the death of children.[267] Like any donation 'in alms', a *post obit* required the permission of the secular lord in whose domain the *borgesie* was located. In his will the donor set out the terms and conditions under which the *borgesie* was to be transferred, and as with all gifts 'in alms', the donor received spiritual privileges from the ecclesiastical recipient, usually prayers *pro redemptione*, for the salvation of his soul and the souls of his wife, children and nearest relatives. A woman called Mabilia made a *post obit* gift to the Church of the Holy Sepulchre 'pro redemptione anime mariti et filii mei et anime mee' (1132).[268] Martin Mazuc gave some properties in Acre to the Hospitallers 'pro salute anime mee' (1201).[269] Bernard of Béziers and his wife Ahoys made a *post obit* donation to the Holy Sepulchre 'pro salute nostra et parentum nostrorum' (c.1130).[270] In the Venetian quarter in Tyre, Lady Raymunda, a widow, possessed a house which after her death would automatically escheat to the commune. She promised neither to

pri-f

---

265 Bresc-Bautier, no. 68, p. 165.
266 Mas-Latrie, *Histoire de l'île de Chypre*, p. 646.
267 Tabuteau, *Transfers of Property*, p. 24.
268 Bresc-Bautier, no. 97, p. 214.
269 Delaville Le Roulx, *Cartulaire général*, no. 1145, p. 8.
270 Bresc-Bautier, no. 98, p. 216.

alienate it nor bequeath it.[271] In some of the cases the bequest was accompanied by the acceptance of the donor as a *confrater*, *consoror* or *cliens* of the ecclesiastical institution receiving the gift. Members of a confraternity received a countergift from the Church concerned, whereby in return for the donation of their *borgesies* each in his or her lifetime could turn to the Church for some form of sustenance. A great number of laymen in the twelfth century were supported as brothers and sisters in the confraternity of the Hospitallers.[272] *Post obit* gifts were also made for material gain, as when in 1155, Agnes, wife of the knight Galius, made a deferred donation of houses in Acre to the Hospitallers, who promised to pay her an annuity of eighty besants a year, 'quamdiu vivat', and to give to her daughter a piece of samite.[273]

The assistance provided by the Church might motivate a donor to bequeath a *borgesie*. The wife of Peter de Yspania, a *consoror* of the Holy Sepulchre, left to the canons her house in Jerusalem in St Anastasia Street.[274] Bernard Bedewin, a *confrater*, left his house to the canons, also situated in St Anastasia Street near the house of Albert Lombard.[275] Sustenance could be offered in the form of food or clothing: Mabilia received bread and wine daily and meat on Sunday;[276] Bernard of Béziers and his wife received food and clothing;[277] whilst the Hospitallers were instructed 'to serve' Marin Mazuc.[278] Donors, however, were not always impecunious. Marin Mazuc donated four shops in Acre to the Hospitallers; he would have usufruct while he was alive and the order one silver mark a year. Mabilia bequeathed her house and received from the Holy Sepulchre 170 besants in recompense. Bernard of Béziers and Ahoys became *confratres* in c.1130, but far from being poor, they sold in 1135 a *borgesie* in Jerusalem to the Holy Sepulchre for 200 besants.[279] And in 1264, the *testamentum nuncupativum* of Saliba, a *confrater* of the order of St John in Acre, was testimony to the wealth he had accumulated in his lifetime. He left the Hospitallers a house in Acre which he had bought for 475 besants and to the rest of his family individual sums of money.[280]

The donor of a *post obit* gift made the ecclesiastical recipient heir to his property. In his bequest Marin Mazuc stated, 'ipsam domum (Hospitalis) heredem meam facio'.[281] Accordingly, the *borgesie* could not escheat to the donor's wife or offspring unless it was specifically stated that the transfer of the property to the

---

271 Berggötz, p. 168.
272 Riley-Smith, *Knights of St John*, pp. 242–6.
273 *RRH*, no. 311, p. 80.
274 Bresc-Bautier, no. 168, p. 322.
275 Bresc-Bautier, no. 168, p. 322.
276 Bresc-Bautier, no. 97, p. 215.
277 Bresc-Bautier, no. 98, p. 216.
278 Delaville Le Roulx, *Cartulaire général*, no. 1145, p. 7.
279 Bresc-Bautier, no. 70, p. 167.
280 Delaville Le Roulx, *Cartulaire général*, no. 2105, pp. 191–2.
281 Delaville Le Roulx, *Cartulaire général*, no. 1145, p. 8.

Church should not take effect until after the death of a spouse or a child. In 1151, Martin Caroana confirmed a *post obit* gift which he and his wife Teiza (now deceased) had made to the Holy Sepulchre. With the agreement of his son, Bonnet, he stipulated that if he and his second wife were to have children they would have no right of inheritance, and guaranteeing further the terms of the donation, he promised that he would not sell these possessions which he retained during his lifetime.[282] The need for such confirmation says much about the concerns the Church might have had in vindicating its rights to eleemosynary grants in general and *post obit* gifts in particular. In the latter case, because the transfer of a gift might take place several years after the initial grant – in which time the donor remained in possession of his property – there was a greater likelihood of the donation being contested by relatives.[283] Confirmation and countergifts served to pre-empt such challenges. It is relevant to add, however, that not all challenges were made by a donor's immediate family or relatives. In Acre the law recognised that a lender had the right to dispute a borrower's bequest 'in alms'. Under the terms of law, the charitable gift was deemed invalid, and, accordingly, the *Cour des Bourgeois* on behalf of the lender could seize all the property and possessions of the deceased man, sell them and recover the debt. Subsequent to the sale, any remaining money would be passed on to the ecclesiastical beneficiary.[284]

Conclusion

The law codes of Acre and Nicosia as well as the charters of the twelfth and thirteenth centuries, reveal how the process of alienation was generally uniform in the cities and rural settlements of the kingdoms of Jerusalem and Cyprus however different local customs may have been. All tenants, sub-tenants and their descendants had a right to alienate their *borgesies*. Sale was the transfer of a *borgesie* from a vendor to a buyer, the conveyance of seisin in a secular or Church court with jurisdictional competence over such property. The court conferred public recognition on the sale in measures aimed at assuring the permanency of the transaction: the symbolic disseising of a vendor and the investing of the purchaser with seisin of the property. The drafting of a charter, moreover, was a record of consent binding the vendor to the terms of the sale and the buyer to the conditions of his tenancy. As far as the alienation of *borgesies* was concerned, a tenant of Acre would not have been unaccustomed to the tenancy laws of Jerusalem, Tyre or Nicosia. What is more, it has been argued that the basic features of *borgesie* tenure were of west European origin, in particular Norman and English. Comparison has shown that in the twelfth and thirteenth centuries Latin Christian settlers in Syria,

---

[282] Bresc-Bautier, no. 113, p. 233.

[283] Tabuteau, *Transfer of Property*, p. 26; Yver, *Les Contrats dans très ancien droit normand*, pp. 34–8.

[284] Kausler, pp. 210–11 (cf. Beugnot, 'Livre des assises', p. 131).

Palestine and Cyprus continued to adopt European customs and traditions, whether to define property tenancy or to devise procedures of alienation in the *Cour des Bourgeois*. I believe, however, that in other ways development was not parallel. By contrast, the evidence of charters confirms the view that the essential features of *borgesie* tenure in the kingdom of Jerusalem were clearly recognisable from the first decades of the twelfth century. An explanation for this should perhaps be sought in the unique diversity of religions in the kingdom and of the legal practices which discriminated against non-Christians. From the outset secular and ecclesiastical courts ensured that only Christians could buy and sell *borgesies*, and in order for such a rule to be enforced effectively this type of tenure had to be defined by law concisely. The discussion has also highlighted the alienability of *borgesies* which were sold, exchanged, donated, or pledged. It is evident *borgesies* were in the hands of the king in his domain and the lords in theirs; of the merchant communities, particularly the Venetians, Pisans and Genoese; and of ecclesiastical institutions such as the Church of the Holy Sepulchre, the orders of St John and St Lazarus and the Teutonic Knights. *Borgesies* existed in the cities, rural *villes neuves*, merchants' quarters and the patriarch's lordship in Jerusalem. The many basic rules of *borgesie* tenancy were consistent throughout the kingdoms of Jerusalem and Cyprus, and probably in Antioch as well.

Chapter 4

Courts of Burgess Jurisdiction

A significant achievement of the first crusaders was the transition they were able to make from mere occupiers of the mainly coastal fringes of Palestine and Syria, to permanent settlers and rulers of a large kingdom the centre of which was the holy city of Jerusalem. This success was based in part on a uniform system of justice which aimed to strengthen the status of European immigrants vis-à-vis the indigenous population, and to meet the needs of burgess communities in all parts of this eastern colony. In the aftermath of conquest it was agreed by the crusaders that the laws of settlement should be built upon the premise that the king was technically proprietor of all land in the kingdom of Jerusalem. He was proprietor of royal domain, the cities of Jerusalem and Acre, for instance, as well as of lordships held-in-chief of him.[1] The king held the kingdom, as John of Ibelin stated, from no one but God,[2] and as proprietor of all fiefs and *borgesies*, he owed no man or woman homage or service.[3] In the hierarchy of jurisdiction he exercised a dual role of authority. On the one hand, he was *seigneur justicier* in royal domain exercising jurisdiction over burgesses through his *Cours des Bourgeois*, whilst on the other, he was, as jurists described him, *chef seignor*, suzerain over all subjects even those living outside the boundaries of royal domain.[4] This was the core structure of the kingdom built upon the stable foundation of a nobility composed of his tenants-in-chief, which in the beginning respected the position of the king as ultimate proprietor of all *borgesies* in the lordships and ruler over all burgesses. The relationship of the king to burgesses in the whole kingdom was manifest in the *Assise sur ligece* established by Amalric (1163–1174), which stated that not only all rear-vassals were to swear liege-homage to the king for their fiefs,[5] but also the king could demand fealty from burgesses in fiefs held in-chief of him, in other

---

1 Philip of Novara, 'Le Livre de forme de plait', p. 541; Riley-Smith, *The Feudal Nobility and the Kingdom of Jerusalem*, p. 139.

2 John of Ibelin, p. 309.

3 John of Ibelin, p. 309; 'L'Estoire d'Eracles Empereur et la conqueste de la terre d'outremer', I, p. 475.

4 John of Ibelin, pp. 603–606.

5 John of Ibelin, pp. 307–308; Philip of Novara, 'Le Livre de forme de plait', p. 527; James of Ibelin, 'Livre', in *RHC*, *Lois*, I, p. 457; Riley-Smith, *The Feudal Nobility and the Kingdom of Jerusalem*, p.145ff.; Riley-Smith, 'The Assise sur Ligece and the Commune of Acre', *Traditio*, XXVII (1971): 179–204; Prawer, *Crusader Institutions*, pp. 36–44.

words burgesses living outside the royal domain.[6] Though this principle was enshrined in law in the second half of the twelfth century, it was almost certainly of earlier provenance. A similar oath of fealty sworn by burgesses before the *Assise sur ligece* was issued, may be found in the *charte de peuplement* of Magna Mahumeria, a village under the jurisdiction of the Church of the Holy Sepulchre. In c.1155, each burgess tenant was obliged to swear fealty to the Holy Sepulchre 'except for the fealty [which they owed] the king of Jerusalem'.[7] The date of the *charte de peuplement* preceded the issuing of the *Assise sur ligece*, suggesting the *assise* was based on an existing practice which, at least in the royal domain, bound all free subjects to the king.

In his treatise of the mid-1260s, John of Ibelin provided a useful sketch of the prevailing system of *cours et coins et justise*, the right to courts, seal and jurisdiction, and described the kingdom's creation from knowledge or assumptions he had about the early years of the crusader states.[8] He also included a list, based on a text of the latter years of the twelfth century, of seigneurial courts and *Cours des Bourgeois* which subsequently came into existence. John knew of thirty-seven *Cours des Bourgeois* in cities, towns and villages, and of these four were royal courts – Jerusalem, Acre, Nablus and Darum – and thirty-three others were established in the twenty-two lordships. John related the courts in the kingdom to settlements of burgesses when he wrote that these had been established by the kings and their tenants-in-chief who had appointed a viscount in every city and in every place where a substantial number of Latins resided. Peter Edbury, however, sounded a note of caution when he cast doubt on the reliability of this list as an accurate or comprehensive guide, and placed question marks over its completeness, the date of its composition and the period in time – either in the twelfth or thirteenth century – which it represented.[9] John himself admitted that there may have been courts in the kingdom of which he was not aware[10] – his list was, after all, a simplified picture, merely a snapshot of the prevailing system of justice – and there is no reason to doubt him or to think he was trying to mislead. At any rate, the overriding impression is that the thirteenth-century jurists cannot be relied upon to fully articulate the complexities of burgess jurisdiction existing both in secular and ecclesiastical domains, whether this was in the shape of the *Cours des*

6 John of Ibelin wrote: Et que se le rei voleit aveir la feauté des gens (burgesses) qui estoient manant ès cités, et ès chastiaus, et ès bors, que ces homes (vassals) tenoient de lui, que il li juracent toz feauté, et que il li fucent tenus par cette feauté de ce que les homes de ces homes li sont tenus par la ligece faite par l'assises au chief seignor'; John of Ibelin, pp. 307–308.

7 Bresc-Bautier, no. 117, pp. 237–8.

8 John of Ibelin, pp. 603–606, contains the final chapters of John's treatise including the list of towns and cities with *Cours des Bourgeois*.

9 P.W. Edbury, *John of Ibelin and the Kingdom of Jerusalem* (Woodbridge, 1997), pp. 157–162.

10 John of Ibelin, p. 606.

Bourgeois, the courts of the merchant quarters, the courts of bishops – including that of the patriarch in his lordship in Jerusalem – or the secular courts of ecclesiastical institutions found in rural villages under ecclesiastical jurisdiction.

John anachronistically described the early courts as *Cours des Bourgeois*, but the intention of the list was to convey the idea that an effective system of justice existed throughout the kingdom upholding the rights of Latin Christians. In each of the twenty-two lordships was established *cours et coins et justise*. It followed that the great lords of seigneuries such as Caesarea, Beirut and Sidon were in their domains *seigneurs justiciers*, tenants-in-chief of the king, and fief-holders subject to the jurisdiction of the High Court in Jerusalem. Consequently, there existed in every seigneury two levels of jurisdiction. On one level, a lord was a tenant of the king and a subject of his court. On a second level, he was overall possessor, though not proprietor, of property in his domain and *seigneur justicier* vis-à-vis tenants of fiefs and of *borgesies*. His *Cour des Bourgeois* was composed of jurors and presided over by an officer, usually a viscount, who approved all transfers of property and judged criminal and civil cases on his behalf.

There were other Latin settlements unbeknown to John with populations large enough to justify the establishment of their own burgess courts. He was after all principally concerned with seigneurial jurisdiction and as such had lesser interest in *Cours des Bourgeois* which apart from his list were mentioned only twice in the treatise.[11] The list of secular courts is only a partial representation of burgess jurisdiction as a whole. Richard believed there were at least four Latin settlements – Legio (al-Lajjun), Caco (Qaqun), Calansue (Qalansuwa) and Mirabel – which in the twelfth century had viscounts and thus presumably *Cours des Bourgeois*.[12] This is a logical explanation, admittedly, if we discount the possibility that in these places a viscount, as official representative of his lord or king, fulfilled a role other than a purely legal one. Ellenblum, nevertheless, drew similar conclusions to Richard about several other Frankish village-settlements in Palestine and Syria. Recently, he uncovered evidence proving the existence of Latin settlements not accounted for by John and the probable establishment in these places of *Cours des Bourgeois*, including the fief of the camerarius regis – and its three villages of Latin settlers – Casale Imbert and Castellum Emmaus, all of which were situated in royal domain.[13] But it cannot be said with certainty these villages had *Cours des Bourgeois*, bearing in mind that the burgesses of rear-fiefs with no right of jurisdiction were subject to the burgess court of the lord in whose domain they were located. Casale Sancti Egidii (Sinjil), for instance, was held by Robert, a rear-vassal of the viscount of Jerusalem, who was obliged to provide three knights to the army of the king.[14] Robert did not have right of *cours et coins et justise* in

11 Edbury, *John of Ibelin and the Kingdom of Jerusalem*, p. 162.

12 Richard, *The Latin Kingdom of Jerusalem*, p. 127 (p. 160, note 2).

13 Ellenblum, *Frankish Rural Settlement*, pp. 41–53, 175–8.

14 Edbury, *John of Ibelin and the Kingdom of Jerusalem*, p. 120; Ellenblum, *Frankish Rural Settlement*, pp. 103–105.

Casale Sancti Egidii, and as such all property transactions were subject to the royal *Cour des Bourgeois* in Jerusalem. As he was, however, superior tenant, all transactions required his approval. When in 1175 the Church of the Holy Sepulchre sought his permission to buy houses and land in the village from Benedictine monks, the purchase took place in the presence of the royal *Cour des Bourgeois*.[15]

Besides the establishment of Church courts – which are the subject of the following chapter – alternative forms of burgess justice were evident in the kingdom. The patriarchal lordship in Jerusalem is of particular interest. The patriarch was neither subject to the High Court nor rendered temporal services to the king for his quarter of the city. Located in the north-western part of Jerusalem, the patriarch's lordship possessed its own system of courts, officials and jurors. The patriarch was *seigneur justicier* and assisted by his household.[16] A question to consider is whether the patriarch possessed the full authority of jurisdiction enjoyed by the secular lords. How were secular cases, including those which touched on matters of high justice, judged? The jurisdictional structure of the patriarchate should perhaps be compared to the ecclesiastical lordships mentioned in John's list. The archbishop of Nazareth and bishop of Lydda-Ramla, who were lords of Nazareth and Lydda, owed knight-service, were subject to the jurisdiction of the High Court,[17] and in each of their lordships was a *Cour des Bourgeois*. Lydda is particularly interesting as it was the first settlement to be established in the kingdom, when in 1099 it was given, along with neighbouring Ramla, to Robert of Rouen who was installed as bishop and granted right of jurisdiction over the new settlement. Once Jerusalem was conquered the bishop held his landed property as a fief of the newly elected ruler Godfrey of Bouillon. By 1102, however, the bishop was no longer in possession of Ramla, and instead it was a royal castellany which by 1120 had passed into the possession of the count of Jaffa as a fief of the county of Jaffa.[18] John of Ibelin listed Ramla as a possession of the lordship of Jaffa with its own *Cour des Bourgeois*.[19] There was as a consequence two *Cours des Bourgeois*, one in Ramla and one in Lydda, and although both places were within the diocese of the bishop of Lydda, only one was within his lordship.

Neither is it possible from John's list to gauge the rate of development of courts

---

15 Bresc-Bautier, no. 160, p. 312. See also Delaville Le Roulx, *Cartulaire général*, no.192, pp. 149–50 (1150).

16 Mayer, *The Crusades*, p. 171; S. Reynolds, *Fiefs and Vassals: The Medieval Evidence Reinterpreted* (Oxford, 1994), pp. 210–14.

17 Edbury, *John of Ibelin and the Kingdom of Jerusalem*, p. 116; Hamilton, *The Latin Church*, pp. 131, 137. The bishop of Lydda owed the service of ten knights and the archbishop of Nazareth six knights; John of Ibelin, p. 608.

18 H.E. Mayer, 'The Origins of the Lordships of Ramla and Lydda in the Latin Kingdom of Jerusalem', in *Kings and Lords in the Latin Kingdom of Jerusalem* (Aldershot, 1994), pp. 538–40, 542–6; Prawer, *Crusader Institutions*, pp. 112–16.

19 John of Ibelin, p. 603.

of burgesses in the various regions of the kingdom. Further investigation is required. The lordship of Jaffa-Ascalon, a double county created by Baldwin III in 1154, possessed a *Cour des Bourgeois* in each of its towns.[20] Ibelin (Yibna) too had a court and belonged to the lordship of the family of the same name.[21] This fortified town was constructed by the Latins, along with Blanchegarde (Tall al-Safi) and Bethgibelin in the 1130s and 1140s to encircle Fatimid Ascalon, and was granted to Barisan the Old in 1141.[22] Ibelin is one of only two rural Latin settlements mentioned in John of Ibelin's list of places with a *Cour des Bourgeois* – the other is Bethgibelin – for which there is additional evidence concerning the function of its court. This evidence is an overlooked passage in the 'Livre de la Cour des Bourgeois'. The law book makes an indirect reference to the *Cour des Bourgeois* in Ibelin when discussing the authority of a court over property situated within the boundaries of its jurisdiction. The case concerns a plaintiff who in the royal *Cour des Bourgeois* in Jerusalem claimed rightful inheritance of a *borgesie* in this Latin village. The man was not, however, permitted to plead 'ce non en ville (Ibelin) où l'eritage est de bourgessie'.[23] In other words, he could only plead in his court in Ibelin. The law book is evidence of the existence of this court before 1187.

The principality of Galilee was further listed by John as having courts of burgesses in Tiberias and Safad.[24] There were also *Cours des Bourgeois* in Sidon and Beaufort and in Caesarea.[25] The lord of Bethsan had a court of burgesses as did the lord of Kerak and Montreal in Transjordan – the courts in Montreal (Shobak) and Kerak date from after 1115 and 1142, respectively.[26] The towns of Gaza, Merle and Chastel Pelerin all had *Cours des Bourgeois*, although the fact that these places were in the thirteenth century under the control of the Templars is not mentioned by John. He lists Gaza as pertaining to the lord of Blanchegarde, but as Edbury has pointed out, this was probably a scribal error, and that in the original text the lords of Blanchgarde and Gaza each had a *Cour des Bourgeois*. It was

20 Mayer, *The Crusades*, p. 112; Mayer, 'The Double County of Jaffa and Ascalon: One Fief or Two?', in P.W. Edbury (ed.), *Crusade and Settlement* (Cardiff, 1985), pp. 181–90; Edbury, John of Ibelin, p. 603.

21 William of Tyre, pp. 434, 572, 706–707; J. Prawer, *The Latin Kingdom of Jerusalem. European Colonialism in the Middle Ages* (London, 1972), p. 133; Edbury, *John of Ibelin and the Kingdom of Jerusalem*, pp. 4–5; Prawer, *Crusader Institutions*, pp. 105, 106.

22 Mayer, *The Crusades*, p. 88; Benvenisti, p. 207; Ellenblum, *Frankish Rural Settlement*, pp. 16–17, note 10.

23 Beugnot, 'Livre des assises', p. 155.

24 Safad was transferred to the Templars in 1168; Ellenblum, *Frankish Rural Settlement*, p. 214 and note 2; Edbury, *John of Ibelin and the Kingdom of Jerusalem*, p. 160.

25 For an example of the workings of the burgess court in Caesarea, see Delaville Le Roulx, *Les Archives*, no. 27, pp. 110–11.

26 Edbury, *John of Ibelin and the Kingdom of Jerusalem*, pp. 135–6; Mayer, *The Crusades*, pp. 71, 88; Prawer, *Crusader Institutions*, pp. 109–110; Ellenblum, *Frankish Rural Settlement*, p. 141.

similarly the case with Merle and Chastel Pelerin whose courts are listed as belonging to the lord of Arsuf, but which probably belonged to the lord of Caesarea.[27] John further omits to mention the jurisdictional authority of the order of St John over the settlement of Bethgibelin. Edbury has proposed various reasons for these omissions although he does not think it likely that the kings of Jerusalem prevented the orders from acquiring authority over the *Cours des Bourgeois* in their towns.[28] I have drawn my own conclusions below when discussing the settlement of Bethgibelin which may have had a burgess court or, more precisely, an ecclesiastical court, from as early as the 1130s.[29]

The Kingdom of Cyprus after 1192

These examples of towns, cities and rural villages build up a picture of the growth of burgess society and the development of burgess jurisdiction in the twelfth century. Apart from the courts of royal domain, the most important being Jerusalem and Acre, there were also the courts of burgess settlements in lordships under secular or ecclesiastical authority which constituted further Frankish expansion. In addition, there were the rural *burgi* and *castra* scattered throughout the kingdom, including the ecclesiastical village-settlements with Church courts which replicated in several respects the juridical competence of a *Cour des Bourgeois*. The process of settlement, or colonisation, if we may call it that, was representative of the expansion of burgess justice in all its forms. I should like at this point to extend the description of eastern Latin justice to include the kingdom of Cyprus. Cyprus was acquired by Guy of Lusignan in the spring of 1192 and, according to a contemporary account, he encouraged feudatories and burgesses to migrate to the island with promises he would generously endow them with city property. Enticed by this benevolence and the relative safety of the island, many Latins, we are led to believe, took Guy of Lusignan at his word and migrated to Cyprus. Guy was doubtless aware that to subjugate the native population as an occupying force with limited manpower and resources at his disposal, would have ended in ruin. He learnt the lesson of his predecessors. The Templars, rulers of the island before him, had attempted to govern with an iron hand and had failed miserably. Even King Richard I of England who had seized power in Cyprus in 1191 before selling his rights in the island to the Templars, had no overall policy of long-term settlement. Indeed, comparisons with the first crusaders and the difficulties they initially encountered in their occupation of Palestine and Syria are apt.

But what had prompted this exodus of people? War was a critical factor. Devastating defeat at Hattin in the summer of 1187 and annihilation of the Latin

27 Edbury, *John of Ibelin and the Kingdom of Jerusalem*, p. 159.

28 Edbury, *John of Ibelin and the Kingdom of Jerusalem*, p. 160.

29 See below, pp. 189–91.

army, left the cities on the mainland still in Latin hands vulnerable. Acre quickly fell to Saladin on 10 July of that year, Ascalon on 4 September and Jerusalem on 2 October. In echoes of 1099, there were few fighting men to defend the kingdom, and, according to one source, there were in 1187 scarcely fourteen knights in Jerusalem.[30] *L'Estoire d'Eracles Empereur et la Conqueste de la Terre d'Outremer* has lengthy passages on the fears and uncertainties of residents in Ascalon and Jerusalem faced with the threat of Saladin's advancing army. This most interesting account further describes the surrender of Acre, Haifa, Arsuf, Cesarea, Jaffa, Beirut and Sidon. Tyre had managed to survive, and its ruler, Conrad of Montferrat, anxiously sought the loyalty and support of not only the city nobles, but also the burgess community in his political ambitions against King Guy. Decisions affecting the whole city were increasingly reached 'with the counsel' of burgesses who owed their growing influence partly to their commercial success.[31] But of course in economic terms there existed a gulf between wealthy burgesses and the largely impoverished majority who were often dependant on the charity of others. We read in *L'Estoire d'Eracles* about the efforts made by the whole community in Jerusalem to organize charitable donations to help the needy.[32] In such times of hardship, many burgesses were worse off even than their indigenous counterparts. Other contemporary historians describe everyday life, and like the invaluable history of William of Tyre which takes us up to around 1184, draw more on the experiences of the burgess class. The translators and continuators of William are of no less value, especially the chapters of the French continuation, *L'Estoire d'Eracles*, which describe the years between 1184 and 1187. The decision of the author to condense certain passages of an ecclesiastical nature,[33] while in his continuation to emphasize more social aspects, would have appealed in their familiarity to a wider lay audience in France where this translation was made sometime in the early 1220s. Writing in the vernacular, the *borjois,* as they are described, are a focal point of interest, and from 1187, the large populations of city rich and poor are portrayed as living in increasing isolation and fearing Muslim attack.

Immigrants to Cyprus came from all parts of the kingdom of Jerusalem, particularly, observed one fourteenth-century commentator, Acre, Tripoli, Antioch and Cilician Armenia.[34] And as a result of this movement of people, 'Einssi

30 M. Salloch (ed.), *Die Lateinische Fortsetzung Wilhelms von Tyrus* (Leipzig, 1934), p. 75.

31 Müller, no. 23, p. 26.

32 'L'Estoire d'Eracles Empereur et la conqueste de la terre d'outremer', p. 13.

33 P.W. Edbury and and J.G. Rowe, *William of Tyre: Historian of the Latin East* (Cambridge, 1988), pp. 4–5.

34 L Legrand (ed.), 'Relation du pèlerinage à Jérusalem de Nicolas de Martoni, notaire italien (1394–1395)', in *ROL*, III (1895), p. 631.

peuploia li rois Guiz l'ille de Chypre'.[35] The scale and impact of migration on the island in the late twelfth century is, however, open to debate. According to narrative traditions, Guy sent messengers to communities of burgesses on the mainland offering them a new life on the island.[36] This migration may have been gradual, a steady stream of men and women drawn to the island as word spread of favourable living conditions. Alternatively, burgesses displaced by Muslims from their homes may have migrated to the island en masse, especially as from the 1190s Latin Christians were increasingly confined to the coastal strip stretching from Tyre in the north to Jaffa in the south and not including Jerusalem. In any case, burgesses had put up an ultimately doomed defence of their cities. Many had been killed fighting whilst others unable to pay the ransom demanded by Saladin had been sold into slavery. Survivors were scattered far and wide. Ibn al-Athir recounts how 'Franks', including a slave girl of his from Haifa, were living in Aleppo.[37] But of those who escaped the fighting, a large number considered their exile to be only temporary. When in 1191 Acre was recovered, the city's burgesses returned to reclaim their properties as rightful possessors.

Increased migration to Cyprus was more discernible in the early thirteenth century, and reflected the growing importance of the island as a hub of eastern Mediterranean commerce. The culturally-diverse cities of Nicosia, Limassol, Famagusta and Paphos benefited most from the influx of migrants from the mainland, and as it has been claimed, from every region of western Europe.[38] It is of note that Latin immigrants apparently lived solely in urban agglomerations, because there is no evidence of *villes neuves* in the kingdom of Cyprus.[39] Apart from the rural Greek indigenous population, Latin society on the island was urban in character, and of those burgesses who did come to settle, many were drawn by the commercial incentives on offer in the cities.

Another wave of migration seems to have taken place in the 1240s. In a letter of Innocent IV to the archbishop of Nicosia and the bishop of Limassol, he commends the efforts the Church is making to alleviate the suffering of impoverished Syrian refugees, and entreats that no person interfere with the work

---

35 M.R. Morgan (ed.), *La Continuation de Guillaume de Tyr (1184–1197)* (Paris, 1982), p. 139.

36 Morgan, *La Continuation de. Guillaume de Tyr*, p. 139.

37 Ibn al-Athir, *al-Kamil fi'il tarikh*, ed. C. J. Tornberg (12 vols, Beirut, 1966–67), vol. 11, p. 541.

38 The cultural diversity of Latin cities in Cyprus has been likened to contemporary heterogeneity in the kingdom of Jerusalem: J. Richard, 'Le Peuplement latin et syrien en Chypre au XIIIe siècle', *BF*, 7 (1979), p. 161; P.W. Edbury, *The Kingdom of Cyprus and the Crusades, 1191–1374* (Cambridge, 1991), p. 22; Ellenblum, *Frankish Rural Settlement*, p. 78.

39 P.W. Edbury, 'The Franco-Cypriot Landowning Class and its Exploitation of the Agrarian Resources of the Island of Cyprus', in *Kingdoms of the Crusaders: From Jerusalem to Cyprus* (Aldershot, 1999), p. 5.

being carried out.[40] From the mid-thirteenth century, the process of Christian resettlement was on a scale of growing significance, and so seemingly great was the demand for property, that after the cataclysmic events of 1291 the growing influx of mainland refugees contributed to a housing shortage on the island.[41] By this date, there is of course less reason to believe contemporary accounts of Christian dispossession and exodus to Cyprus were exaggerated, and yet tantalizingly, the sources provide only few clues as to how burgesses were actually resettled. The narrative sources are generally silent on this matter, and the few surviving charters reveal simply who were in possession of *borgesies*. As with early Latin settlement in Palestine and Syria, we may only conjecture how *borgesies* in royal domain were distributed. It is a safe assumption, however, that some Greek Christians lost their properties in the cities after the conquest of 1192 in order to make way for Latin immigrants.[42] It is also certain that the thirteenth century saw the emigration not only of Latins but also of indigenous Syrian Christians and Muslims to Cyprus.[43] The laws of Nicosia did not discriminate against Syrian Christian immigrants and even native Greek Christians who wished to purchase *borgesies*. Naturally, this freedom to buy property, and the wide-ranging commercial opportunities which existed, meant that some Latin and non-Latin Christians came to Cyprus in the thirteenth century more out of choice than necessity. It goes without saying that the Pisans, Genoese, Venetians and other merchant communities played a significant role in the island's development. The privileges they were granted, their commercial activities, as well as the houses, shops and other properties they received in Limassol and Famagsusta, have been well documented.[44] In terms of the involvement of burgesses in the island's commercial trade, substantial material is found in the acts of the Genoese notaries, in particular Lamberto di Sambuceto (documents dating from 1296 to 1307).[45]

---

40 J.L. La Monte (ed.), 'A Register of the Cartulary of the Cathedral of Santa Sophia of Nicosia', *Byzantion*, V (1930): 467.

41 G. Raynaud (ed.), *Les Gestes de Chiprois* (Geneva, 1887), p. 516.

42 P.W. Edbury, 'The Lusignan Regime in Cyprus and the Indigenous Population', in *Kingdoms of the Crusaders: From Jerusalem to Cyprus* (Aldershot, 1999), p. 6.

43 For reference to Muslims living in Cyprus, see 'Livre contrefais', p. 254.

44 See, in particular, D. Jacoby, 'The Rise of a New Emporium in the Eastern Mediterranean: Famagusta in the Late Thirteenth Century', *Meletai kai Ipomnimata*, I (1984): 145–79; Edbury, *The Kingdom of Cyprus and the Crusades*, pp. 103, 110–11; M. Balard, 'L'Activité commerciale en Chypre dans les années 1300', in P.W. Edbury (ed.), *Crusade and Settlement* (Cardiff, 1985), pp. 251–63. For evidence of the involvement of European and native merchants in Cypriot trade from the end of the thirteenth century, see Balard, *Notai genovesi in oltremare: atti rogati a Cipro da Lamberto di Sambuceto (11 Ottobre 1296–23 Giugno 1299)*.

45 Balard, *Notai genovesi in oltremare: atti rogati a Cipro da Lamberto di Sambuceto (11 Ottobre 1296–23 Giugno 1299)*; and Balard (ed.), *Notai genovesi in oltremare: atti rogati a Cipro. Lamberto di Sambuceto e Giovanni de Rocha (3 Agosto 1308–14 Marzo 1310)* (Genoa, 1984).

Apart from matters of commerce, the notarial evidence affords some perspective on burgess marriage, testamentary disposition and manumission.

In their governance of Cyprus, successive Latin kings adapted the legal and administrative institutions which were a legacy of Byzantium, in much the same way that they preserved aspects of Muslim administration in the kingdom of Jerusalem.[46] They also transplanted into the island many of the laws and institutions established in the royal and seigneurial domains of Palestine and Syria. The status of the class of burgesses was by this time more legally defined, and the court of burgesses more fully developed. Burgesses who arrived in Cyprus had even greater expectations. They had become accustomed to the principle of judgement by peers and dual legislative process – the practice of advising the king in matters which directly affected their community. Among the Cypriot population, burgesses considered themselves to be in a more privileged position. If justice in the kingdom of Jerusalem discriminated between Latins and non-Latins, and between courts of burgesses and courts of native Christians, Muslims and Jews, so too in Cyprus disparate groups were accommodated within the prevailing legal system and burgesses distinguished from the indigenous Greek Orthodox population. On the whole, the Greek Orthodox remained living in the countryside,[47] although the number who resided in the cities was not insignificant. In fact, by the mid-fourteenth century, the Greek community and the influence of the Orthodox Church in Nicosia were not diminishing but rather strengthening, and the fear that this was damaging the authority of the Latin Church was expressed by Pope Urban V in a letter he wrote to Peter of Lusignan, king of Cyprus (1368), admonishing the many feudatories and burgesses living in Nicosia and other cities in the island, who were permitted to marry and baptise their children in their homes and who regularly attended churches of the Greek Orthodox faith.[48] If, therefore, this blurring of religious lines was viewed by the papacy as undermining social order, it was believed a more rigid system of justice and legislation would reinforce the basic differences between Latins and non-Latins. Notably, further ingredients in this religious mix were the Muslims and native Christians who had migrated from Palestine and Syria. In Cyprus, and in particular in Nicosia and Famagusta – the cities for which we have most evidence – they encountered relatively the same laws they had been subject to in the kingdom of Jerusalem.

The Development of the Cour des Bourgeois

The full legal powers of the *Cour des Bourgeois* were not realised until the middle of the thirteenth century. In the eyes of John of Ibelin, the court had been formed

46 Edbury, *The Kingdom of Cyprus and the Crusades*, p. 20.

47 Edbury, *The Kingdom of Cyprus and the Crusades*, p. 14. On the Greek rural *paroikoi*, see Edbury, 'The Franco-Cypriot Landowning Class and its Exploitation of the Agrarian Resources of the Island of Cyprus', pp. 3–4.

48 Mas-Latrie, *Histoire de l'île de Chypre*, vol. 3, pp. 757–8.

during the rule of Godfrey of Bouillon (1099–1100), and established 'en totes les cités et en tos les autres leus dou reiaume'.[49] He also believed that in the first years of the twelfth century, there was already in existence a class of jurors drawn from the ranks of Latin Christians who served in the court of burgesses and were bound by a common oath of office.[50] John's propensity to exaggerate legislative work undertaken in the first two years of the kingdom's existence, cautions against ready acceptance of this account of the formation of the courts of burgesses. However, despite condensing to a few years developments in the *Cour des Bourgeois* which, it may be discerned from the charters and law books, were achieved gradually over the following decades, his premise that from an initial stage courts of burgesses were established in the cities of the kingdom should not be doubted. And although his assertion that an oath was sworn by jurors from early on is questionable, there is, nevertheless, indisputable evidence that from the beginning there existed a distinct group of burgesses who attended court regularly to witness and legitimize legal proceedings.

In Acre and Nicosia in the thirteenth century, the court of burgesses was known as the *Cour des Bourgeois*, the *Basse Cour* – the Low Court as opposed to the High Court of fief-holders – and the *Cour de la Visconte*, the court of the viscount.[51] In Jerusalem it was referred to as the 'royal court'.[52] It was also, according to the author of the 'Livre contrefais', known as the *Cour des Bourgesies* owing to its authority over all types of burgess properties.[53] In its earliest manifestation, in the charters dating from the first decades of the twelfth century, the court was composed simply of a viscount and burgess *testes*. It was a public assembly, a meeting place attended by burgesses who appear collectively in the charters as witnesses.[54] Their presence signified the openness and legitimacy of the court to deal with matters concerning the local burgess community. The principle of justice by peers and the fundamental right of freemen to participate in the process of decision-making were concepts current in many parts of contemporary western Europe.[55] It is not inconceivable that such an assembly fulfilled a political and legislative role, because, as earlier highlighted, it was customary for the burgess community in Acre to give *conseill* whenever the king wished to pass a law which concerned them.[56]

---

49 John of Ibelin, p. 53.

50 John of Ibelin, p. 52.

51 'Livre contrefais', pp. 249, 296.

52 Bresc-Bautier, no. 110, p. 231.

53 'Livre contrefais', p. 251.

54 Bresc-Bautier, no. 96, p. 214.

55 Reynolds, *Fiefs and Vassals*, pp. 51–2, 103–104.

56 Kausler, pp. 350–51 (cf. Beugnot, 'Livre des assises', p. 225). On the wider political and administrative role of the courts in western Europe, S. Reynolds, *Kingdoms and Communities in Western Europe, 900–1300* (Oxford, 1984), p. 24.

A charter of 1120 is one of the earliest examples of a royal decree being witnessed by a viscount with the assistance of his burgesses.[57] A charter of c.1125 is the earliest surviving evidence for a viscount authorising the sale of a *borgesie* in Jerusalem,[58] and a royal confirmation of 1129 is the earliest surviving evidence for a viscount's approval of donations of *borgesies* to the order of St John 'in alms'.[59] For the first time also, in a charter of c. 1130, the viscount of Jerusalem, Anschetinus, appears in the court of the patriarch giving royal approval to a *post obit* gift of a house made to the canons of the Holy Sepulchre.[60] The 'royal court' of burgesses in Jerusalem first appears in a charter of 1149 authorising the lease of a house; at that time the court was composed of a viscount and eight burgess witnesses,[61] whilst in 1175 there is a reference to a 'full court', a *plena curia* composed of fourteen jurors.[62] In the twelfth century burgess members of the royal court were variously described as *viri Hierosolymitani*, *burgenses regis*, *regie majestatis jurati* or *jurati civitatis*.[63] They were the king's men, foremost, who qualified as court jurors partly because of their status as permanent residents of Jerusalem. Selected to enforce the non-feudal laws of their city, they constituted as a whole the most authoritative body to represent the interests of their community.

In Acre, the person appointed to the office of *bailli de la ville* fulfilled the same legal, administrative and financial role as the viscount. There seems to have been no apparent distinction between the official duties of both, and the titles *bailli* and viscount were used interchangeably in the law books. The viscount of Acre was chosen by the king from the class of fief-holders on the advice not of his burgesses but 'with the counsel of his fief-holders'. He was to 'love God, be faithful and loyal, and dispense justice to those who came before him to make a claim'.[64] He was the 'leutenant de seignor', his representative in the *Cour des Bourgeois* in the same way the seneschal was the king's representative in the High Court.[65] His authority as president of the court and his powers of enforcing judgements were greater on account of his high-ranking status and his being chosen directly by the king. This was a particular strength of the system of justice in the kingdom, because in some parts of western Europe, in the absence of a recognised authority, the practice of allowing parties to choose an arbitrator over their case lessened the power of the assembly to enforce judgements effectively.[66] There could be no

---

57 Bresc-Bautier, no. 27, pp. 88–9.

58 Bresc-Bautier, no. 95, pp. 212–13.

59 *RRH*, no. 130, p. 32.

60 Bresc-Bautier, no. 98, pp. 215–16.

61 Bresc-Bautier, no. 110, p. 231.

62 Delaville Le Roulx, *Les Archives*, no. 34, p. 121.

63 *RRH*, no. 516, p. 137; Bresc-Bautier, no. 47, p. 131, no. 116, p. 237; Delaville Le Roulx, *Les Archives*, no. 34, p. 121.

64 Kausler, p. 46 (cf. Beugnot, 'Livre des assises', p. 21).

65 'Livre contrefais', p. 347.

66 Reynolds, *Kingdoms and Communities*, pp. 26–7.

dispute as to who presided over the court, but wary of the dangers of investing too many powers in an individual and of possible breach of trust, the lawmakers of the kingdom reserved the right of the king to remove from his position a viscount who abused his authority.[67]

In the *Cour des Bourgeois* of Nicosia, the viscount, who possessed his own seal, was similarly 'a knight and especially a liegeman of the king'.[68] Another viscount (also described as *baili*) was the king's representative in the *Cour des Bourgeois* in Famagusta.[69] A royal decree of 1355 mentions three other viscounts (described as *baillis*) in Limassol, Paphos and Cape Andreas.[70] The viscount was the 'governor and justiciar' of the *Cour des Bourgeois* and convened the court three times a week in a place designated by the king. Meeting so regularly to hear cases defined the position of this legal assembly at the heart of the burgess community. On the days when the court was convened, the viscount was assisted by his sergeants, at least two jurors and an *escrivein* who kept a written record of the court's proceedings.[71] The practice of writing down in French all transactions of *borgesies* – sale, gift, gage and exchange – as well as all dispute – claim and response, *pozemens*, *esgars*, *counoissances* and *conseills* – had been transplanted into the island sometime after 1251 when at a *parlement* in Acre the nobles, many of whom were holders of *borgesies*, had accepted the proposal put forward by John of Arsuf constable of Jerusalem, to keep written records in the court.[72] Hitherto, the *recort de cort*, the court's collective memory of its judgements, was the established custom.[73] The *escrivein*, who accompanied the viscount when in court, was in possession of the chests (*huches*), containing the written registers, and drew up the charters of property transactions.[74] It would appear that though some members of the 1251 assembly had advocated continued reliance on memory as admissible evidence in a case, by this period the process of judgement-making, based solely on the written records of the court, had more or less taken over. Even earlier there was greater acceptance of this practice. The scribe in the court in Acre kept registers and drew up charters of resolutions, *pais de contrast* (dispute) *ou de*

---

67 If it was discovered the viscount was not a liegeman of the king he could be expelled from the city; Kausler, p. 48 (Beugnot, 'Livre des assises', p. 23); Riley-Smith, *The Feudal Nobility and the Kingdom of Jerusalem*, p. 36.

68 'Livre contrefais,' pp. 236, 243. See also p. 250.

69 A charter of 28 April 1300 makes reference to a 'vicecomes Famaguste et juratorum curie domini regis Famaguste'; Desimoni, 'Actes passés à Famagouste de 1299–1301 par devant le notaire génois Lamberto di Sambuceto', p. 63.

70 'Bans et ordonnances', p. 377.

71 'Livre contrefais', p. 239.

72 'Livre contrefais', pp. 246–9.

73 The establishment of the office of *escrivein* was also proposed at the *parlement* of 1250; 'Livre contrefais', p. 247.

74 For each charter – sealed with the seal of the viscount – the *escrivein* received one besant; 'Livre contrefais', p. 243.

murtre, which could be consulted and used as evidence in any future disagreements.[75]

In court the viscount directed proceedings, heard claims by plaintiffs and instructed his sergeants to summon defendants before the court.[76] The jurors in Nicosia were supposed to reach their decisions impartially, unanimously and independently of the viscount,[77] in the same way that in thirteenth-century Acre, jurors were expected to hear 'la clamor et le respons' and to make fair and independent judgements.[78] These were high ideals indeed, preserving the principle of judgement by peers, whilst at the same time curbing the overall powers of the president of the court whose role it was to direct and to advise on points of law, but not to impose his own decisions on the sitting jurors. Although it is not possible to know from how early on this form of decision-making was introduced in the *Cour des Bourgeois*,[79] the principle of judgement by peers, or at least the conviction that the court should be composed of burgess witnesses or jurors, was in existence from the earliest years of the twelfth century.

As his full title suggested, a viscount was community chief over and above his role as presiding head of the court of burgesses. The viscount of Nicosia took it upon himself to policy the streets with twelve of his sergeants.[80] In a similar capacity, the lord of Tyre's viscount upheld law and order, patrolling the streets day and night accompanied by *placierii*, his sergeants and other servants. He was given permission, most notably, to enter the Genoese quarter to arrest malefactors whom he believed to be subject to the jurisdiction of the lord's *Cour des Bourgeois*.[81] A further officer under the authority of the viscount of Nicosia was the *mathesep* (Arab. *muhtasib*) whose duty it was to police the community, rooting out fraud among traders in the city markets.[82] A reference to a *mathesep*, found in the inventory of Marsiglio Zorzi, mentions that such an officer, also known as a *iusticarius*, was established in Tyre by King John (1210–1225).[83] The viscount of Nicosia could arrest any person caught breaking the law, whether a burgess, churchman or non-Latin, and if the offence committed was outside the scope of his jurisdiction he would hand over the prisoner to the relevant ecclesiastical court or the *Cour des Syriens*.[84] Besides these duties the viscount was responsible for

---

75 Kausler, p. 160 (cf. Beugnot, 'Livre des assises', pp. 98–9).

76 'Livre contrefais', p. 239.

77 'Livre contrefais', p. 242.

78 Kausler, p. 47 (cf. Beugnot, 'Livre des assises', p. 21).

79 It was similarly employed in the High Court where neither the king nor his representative, the seneschal, could interfere in the judgements of the sitting feudatories.

80 'Livre contrefais', pp. 240, 244.

81 Desimoni, 'Quatre titres des propriétés des Génois à Acre et Tyr', no. 4, p. 227.

82 'Livre contrefais', pp. 243–4.

83 Berggötz, p. 140.

84 Each month the viscount provided the king with a list of all prison detainees, as well as informed him of any judicial duel which was to take place; 'Bans et ordonnances', pp. 328, 372.

collecting the rent owed the king from the lease of his *borgesies*. The rent was paid into the court where it was safeguarded, and accounts of the revenues were made which every three months were submitted to the *bailli* of the *Grant Secrete* by the court *escrivein*.[85] Evidently, a *Cour des Bourgeois* functioned both as a court and as a financial office. This fact gives greater weight to the argument that in the twelfth century the *Cour des Bourgeois* evolved as the legal, financial and administrative arm of the *seigneur justicier* in the burgess community. It can be seen that in some rural Latin settlements, like Magna Mahumeria, the *curia* also combined both legal and financial functions.[86]

The viscount of Nicosia was responsible for ensuring that a court was in session on Mondays, Wednesdays and Fridays, and swore an oath of office promising to make judgements and deliver fair sentences to all men and women, especially widows, minors and the impoverished.[87] By the laws of Cyprus, if a court could not be convened in the port city of Famagusta on any of the aforementioned days because the requisite number of jurors could not be assembled, the viscount of the town could transfer the case to his counterpart in Nicosia so the *Cour des Bourgeois* of that place could make judgement.[88] This demonstrates the legal dependence of Famagusta on Nicosia. It also proves that at any one time there was in Famagusta only a small number of jurors regularly participating in its court and able to meet the legal needs of the community. This conveyance of jurisdiction was in contradiction of the legal principle prevailing in the kingdom of Jerusalem that a burgess should always plead in his local *Cour des Bourgeois*.[89] In such cases the ideal gave way to practical considerations.

The law books, though informative, are not always revealing of the variations in legal practices. From the charters of the twelfth and thirteenth centuries, we can see that the viscount was not alone in presiding over the *Cour des Bourgeois*. The number of people both feudatories and non-feudatories who qualified as heads of court was larger than originally thought. And, significantly, their position was not necessarily to deputise for the viscount in his absence, but to share in the presidency of the court. The *dapifer regis*, the royal seneschal, was one such person. He represented the king in court and was of such standing and influence that he has been described as the 'alter ego of the king'.[90] He was his lord's deputy 'in the courts of his kingdom', and apart from his duty to administer the leasing of crown lands,[91] he presided over the High Court and supervised the *Grant Secrete* which kept records of fiefs and the services owed for them, as well as the accounts

85 'Livre contrefais', p. 241.

86 Bresc-Bautier, nos 121–5, pp. 244–52.

87 'Livre contrefais', pp. 238, 239.

88 'Livre contrefais', p. 324.

89 Beugnot, 'Livre des assises', p. 155.

90 La Monte, *Feudal Monarchy*, pp. 116–18. Riley-Smith, *The Feudal Nobility and the Kingdom of Jerusalem*, p. 59.

91 John of Ibelin, pp. 578–9.

of the *Cour des Bourgeois*. All scribes, whether employed in the court of burgesses, the *Cour de la Chaine* or the *Cour de la Fonde*, were answerable to the seneschal, and the accounts of revenues of all three courts were rendered to the royal office.[92] John, seneschal of Baldwin III, presided over the *jurati Jerusalem* when a knight Gibelin sold the village *borgesie* of Saphoria to the Church of the Holy Sepulchre (c.1155).[93] In the seigneuries of the kingdom the seneschal also officiated in the *Cour des Bourgeois*. In Caesarea, Hugo, the lord's seneschal, presided over 'the court of city jurors' – eight burgesses – when in 1167 Isabella sold her shop to John a priest. It is later explained that in Jerusalem a seneschal was also present in the patriarch's household, and presided over the patriarchal court in cases concerning burgesses living in the ecclesiastical lordship.[94]

A further two persons took the place of the viscount as head of the royal *Cour des Bourgeois*: in Jerusalem the castellan of the Tower of David and the *judex*. It is known that the castellan Rohard (1165–1179) was president of the court on at least six occasions relating to the sale and exchange of *borgesies*,[95] and another castellan, Baldwin de Pinquini, authorised in court the donation 'in alms' of a house in the city to the order of St John.[96] The appearance of the castellan in the charters is, however, uncommon, and it may be that he was only expected to deputise for the viscount in his absence. He does not seem to have been as involved as the royal seneschal in the general affairs and administration of the burgess community. Relatively little is also known about the *judex* who assumed a similar position as head of the court. What is certain is the office dates back to the eleventh century. In parts of Italy at that time, the *judex*, a man well learned in law, acted both as president and judge of the court.[97] In the kingdom of Jerusalem Adalardus, *judex* of the Genoese quarter in Tyre, is mentioned in the Genoese inventory of 1250.[98] In 1135, the purchase of a house in Jerusalem by the Hospitallers was authorised by the burgess jurors as well as Seibertus, the judge.[99] When in 1136 the canons of the Holy Sepulchre leased land in the 'royal part' of the city to Andrew and his wife Hosanna they were given permission to do so by the jurors of

92 Kausler, pp. 344–5 (cf. Beugnot, 'Livre des assises', p. 220).

93 Bresc-Bautier, no. 130, p. 257.

94 See below, pp. 180–81.

95 Delaville Le Roulx, *Cartulaire général*, no. 312, pp. 225–6, (1163), no. 554, p. 376 (1179); *RRH*, no. 492, pp. 129–30 (1171); Delaville Le Roulx, *Les Archives*, no. 34, pp. 119–20 (1175), no. 47, pp. 136–7 (1178), no. 46, pp. 135–6 (1178). In 1175, Rohard granted permission to the Holy Sepulchre to purchase houses and vineyards in Casale Sancti Egidii; the village was within royal domain, and, therefore, transactions of *borgesies* required the authorisation of the royal *Cour des Bourgeois*; Bresc-Bautier, no. 160, pp. 311–12; Ellenblum, *Frankish Rural Settlement*, p. 104.

96 Delaville Le Roulx, *Cartulaire général*, no. 2127, p. 494.

97 Reynolds, *Kingdoms and Communities*, p. 32.

98 Desimoni, 'Quatre titres des propriétés des Génois à Acre et à Tyr', no. 4, p. 224.

99 Bresc-Bautier, no. 70, p. 168.

Jerusalem and Holdredus, the judge.[100] In Jerusalem in 1175, when Gila sold her house to the Hospitallers, no viscount, castellan or seneschal was present in the court, and approval was given by Simon the judge and five jurors.[101] What is most interesting about the *judices*, however, was their status. They were burgesses. Holdredus was undoubtedly the burgess whose name appears in a list of witnesses to an agreement in 1135 between Maria of Bethany and the canons of the Holy Sepulchre.[102] I have found Seibertus included in a list of burgesses of Jerusalem in a deed of c.1124, when he was witness to the transaction of a house belonging to George the rays and authorised by viscount Anschetinus.[103] And as for Simon, he was a juror of the royal court in Jerusalem in 1171 and witness to a sale in 1173.[104] We may assume that burgesses who were promoted to the post of *judex* were the most respected in the community for their legal knowledge. In Cyprus in the fourteenth century, the *judices* were legal specialists employed by the chancery – which had attained in this period a judicial function – and served as members of the royal entourage, sought after by the king for their understanding of the law. A number of these men are known to have studied in the West.[105]

In the service of the court and under the authority of the viscount or other presiding heads were the *jurati*. These men, who were inclined to serve their community in a juridical capacity, worked as jurors in the *Cour des Bourgeois* – either involved directly in the procedures of the court, or employed to carry out its instructions – and the *Cour de la Fonde*, the court in Acre which judged inter-communal cases involving Muslims, Jews and native Christians. They were the regular attendants of the court – distinguished from the many others who appeared as witnesses to legal proceedings – and were chosen, probably by the viscount, for their probity and elevated status in the community. They were the equivalent of the European *scabini*, the lawmen, judgement-makers and representatives of lesser freemen in their locality.[106] Not much is known about the early witnesses and to what extent their duties and their standing in the judicial system resembled that of

---

100 Bresc-Bautier, no. 103, p. 223.

101 Delaville Le Roulx, *Les Archives*, no. 33, p. 119.

102 Bresc-Bautier, no. 102, p. 222. See also no. 97, p. 215.

103 Bresc-Bautier, no. 95, p. 213.

104 Delaville Le Roulx, *Cartulaire général*, no. 422, p. 292; Delaville Le Roulx, *Les Archives*, no. 30, p. 115.

105 Edbury, *The Kingdom of Cyprus and the Crusades*, pp. 190–91. The careers of Bartholomew of Conches and Philip Chappe were typical of those who studied in the West before entering the king's employ. For Bartholemew of Conches, see L. de Mas-Latrie (ed.), *Nouvelles preuves de l'histoire de Chypre sous le règne des princes de la maison de Lusignan*, (Paris, 1873–74), p. 64; and for Philip Chappe, see John XXII, *Lettres communes*, ed. G. Mollat (Paris, 1904), vol. 1, no. 9950.

106 B. Althoffer, *Les Scabins* (Nancy, 1938); R. Byl, *Jurisdictions scabinales* (Brussels, 1965), pp. 1–13; Reynolds, *Fiefs and Vassals*, pp. 411, 423; Edbury, *John of Ibelin and the Kingdom of Jerusalem*, p. 164.

the later *jurati*. However, like the Carolingian *scabini*, they constituted a permanent body knowledgeable of local laws and customs. There were certain individuals who appeared regularly alongside the city viscount in the charters of the early twelfth century, and carried on serving in the court in the next few decades. Gaufridus Acus was one such person, as was Bacheler and Porcel; all of whom appear as witnesses with viscount Anschetinus in a royal charter of 1120.[107] Bacheler and Porcel were also present in the court in c.1124,[108] and Gaufridus Acus in 1132.[109] Holdredus was another who regularly attended the court from the early 1130s before being promoted to *judex*.[110] All of this evidence points to the formation of a body of experienced burgesses serving in the royal court in the first third of the twelfth century. It is, however, doubtful the *jurati* were of a professional standing. There is no mention in the 'Livre contrefais' of the *jurati* receiving incomes, although officials like the *escrivein*, *mathesep* and the sergeant did.[111] In the earliest witness lists the professions of burgesses were occasionally recorded. For example, when in 1135 a man called Bernard sold his house in Jerusalem to the church of the Holy Sepulchre, five of the *testes* were 'all goldsmiths'.[112] In a document of 1171, the juror Alderbertus was described as a butler of the patriarch,[113] and in another document the juror Lambertus was a money-changer.[114] In all likelihood, service in the court was a civic duty, but one which carried great honour for the person chosen.

Jurors were to be of good character, law-worthy men of the class of burgesses.[115] The viscount and jurors of Nicosia swore to make judgements according to the 'good usages and good customs of the kingdom of Jerusalem and Cyprus'.[116] Those who qualified for jury service were 'bourgois et Frans, de la loi de Roume'.[117] Jurors were the 'loyal men' and the 'wise and good men' of their community and their standing, it seems, elevated them above other burgesses.[118] In Jerusalem some were privileged enough to be part of the royal[119] or patriarchal[120]

---

107 Bresc-Bautier, no. 27, p. 89.

108 Bresc-Bautier, no. 96, p. 214.

109 Bresc-Bautier, no. 97, p. 215.

110 Bresc-Bautier, no. 97, p. 215.

111 'Livre contrefais', pp. 241–4.

112 Bresc-Bautier, no. 70, p. 168.

113 Delaville Le Roulx, *Cartulaire général*, no. 422, p. 292.

114 Delaville Le Roulx, *Cartulaire général*, no. 312, p. 226.

115 'Livre contrefais', p. 236; Kausler, pp. 48–9 (cf. Beugnot, 'Livre des assises', p. 23); D. Hayek, *Le Droit franc en Syrie pendant les croisades: Institutions judicaires* (Paris, 1925), pp. 93–105.

116 'Livre contrefais', p. 238.

117 'Livre contrefais', p. 236.

118 Kausler, pp. 48–9 (cf. Beugnot, 'Livre des assises', p. 23); 'Livre contrefais', p. 321.

119 Bresc-Bautier, no. 47, p. 131, no. 51, p. 138.

120 Bresc-Bautier, no. 162, p. 315.

households. In Acre in 1251, the jurors qualified as *domini*,[121] as did the jurors in a charter of Jerusalem in 1186.[122] And according to the 'Livre de la Cour des Bourgeois', the eyewitness of two jurors to a murder was of value equal to that of two liegemen.[123] Jurors, furthermore, were Latins of both European and native Syrian origin. I have found evidence of one native juror of the royal *Cour des Bourgeois* of Jerusalem, perhaps a Christian convert. Rainald Sicherius (or Segghir; Arab. Zaghir) appears in the charters as juror of the court from 1149 to 1163.[124] In Famagusta, moreover, a juror by the name of Abraymus (Ibrahim?) *bancherius*, was a member of the *Cour des Bourgeois* of the city in 1300. He, along with Pellegrinus de Castello and Liacius Imperatoris are *iurati curie domini regis Famaguste*.[125] Jurors, additionally, had to be laymen; a royal edict of Cyprus prohibited clergymen from becoming jurors.[126] In Nicosia a juror had to swear the same oath as the viscount, promising to make *esgarts*, *conoissances* and *conseill*, according to the 'good customs of the kingdom of Jerusalem and Cyprus'.[127]

Neither the 'Livre de la Cour des Bourgeois' nor the 'Livre contrefais' mention how jurors were chosen, and there is no suggestion they were elected by the burgess community. It was, ultimately, the decision of the *seigneur justicier* to choose or to dismiss them. When in 1300 the viscount Hugh Piteau and the jurors of the *Cour des Bourgeois* in Nicosia refused to accept a royal edict modifying the procedure for arraigning criminals in the court, King Henry II dismissed them all. Although he initially instructed he no longer wished these men to be jurors, he reconvened the court after three days with the same members but a different viscount.[128] The implication is that the king could choose the jurors who he believed best served his interests. On this occasion their service was retained because, first, the viscount was replaced with someone presumably more sympathetic to royal demands, and, secondly, it was acknowledged that a number of the jurors who were closely allied to the king had initially objected to the stance of their fellow members. The split it would seem was between men who had been chosen to serve in the court from the wider burgess community, and those who belonged to the royal household and repaid the king with loyalty. At any rate, the principled stance by a majority of jurors whilst revealing of their self-confidence in voicing objection and questioning the process of legislation, was, in its failure, ultimate proof that their role was merely to enforce the law. And like the royal

121 'Livre contrefais', pp. 246–7.

122 Delaville Le Roulx, *Catulaire général*, no. 803, p. 503.

123 Kausler, p. 314 (cf. Beugnot, 'Livre des assises', p. 200).

124 *RRH*, p. 64 (no. 225), p. 69 (no. 273), p. 71 (no. 80), p. 75 (no. 295), p. 103 (no. 391).

125 Desimoni, 'Actes passés à Famagouste de 1299–1301 par devant le notaire génois Lamberto di Sambuceto', pp. 63–4; Richard, 'Le pleuplement latin et syriens', p. 171.

126 'Bans et ordonnances', p. 361.

127 'Livre contrefais', p. 238.

128 'Livre contrefais', pp. 320–22.

burgess courts of the kingdom of Jerusalem in the preceding two centuries, they had no authority to negate royal ordinance.

Turning to the subject of composition, we see that in Jerusalem in the second half of the twelfth century, a *plena curia*, a full court, was made up of fourteen *jurati*.[129] But the charters are proof that the number which assembled was usually less. In an eleemosynary donation of land in Jerusalem to the Hospitallers (1163) the *Cour des Bourgeois* was composed of nine jurors,[130] whilst in a sale of 1173 there were eight jurors.[131] In another eleemosynary donation to the Hospitallers in 1235 there were only four jurors.[132] Perhaps the size of the jury reflected the seriousness of a case or the significance of an alienation or a donation. In Acre we see similar variations. In the thirteenth century, a full court must also have been fourteen persons as this was the number of all jurors of the royal *Cour des Bourgeois* who in 1251 attended the *parlement* in that city.[133] This number did vary. In an eleemosynary donation to the Hospitallers (1260) six jurors were present.[134] The same number was present in court according to an earlier charter of 1232.[135] In Nicosia the viscount was assisted 'by twelve persons or more', and the number changed depending on the procedure being carried out.[136] A viscount and at least two jurors were required if a *borgesie* was being pledged, and if a property was being sold five jurors were enough for a court to be quorate.[137]

After hearing the case of a plaintiff, the jurors determined what had to be proved by a defendant and the method of proof – this could take the form of an oath, judicial duel or more commonly the corroborating evidence of witnesses (*garens*). The jurors of the *Cour des Bourgeois* were also witnesses to the legitimacy and permanency of a transaction. In Nicosia a vendor had to appear before the jurors in whose presence he would be disseised by the viscount and the seisin of his property transferred to the buyer. But in order to legitimise a sale in this city was it necessary for a viscount to be present? Although the author of the 'Livre contrefais' defined the *Cour des Bourgeois* as a judicial body composed of a viscount and at least two jurors,[138] there were exceptions to this rule. It was court procedure in Nicosia that whenever a person claimed the property of a deceased

---

[129] Delaville Le Roulx, *Cartulaire général*, no. 34, p. 121.

[130] Delaville Le Roulx, *Cartulaire général*, no. 312, p. 226.

[131] Delaville Le Roulx, *Les Archives*, no. 47, p. 137. See also, Delaville Le Roulx, *Cartulaire général*, no. 803, p. 503.

[132] Delaville Le Roulx, *Cartulaire général*, no. 2127, p. 494.

[133] 'Livre contrefais', pp. 246–7: 'Et furent auci tous les jurés d'Acre de la Cour des Bourgeois', followed by fourteen names.

[134] Delaville Le Roulx, *Cartulaire général*, no. 2949, p. 888.

[135] Delaville Le Roulx, *Cartulaire général*, no. 2015, p. 435.

[136] 'Livre contrefais', p. 236.

[137] 'Livre contrefais', p. 279. In Famagusta the viscount was assisted by at least two jurors when the court met on Monday and Wednesday, and by a full court ('la court plenerie') on Friday; 'Livre contrefais', p. 324.

[138] 'Livre contrefais', p. 237.

and intestate relative, the viscount was required to appoint in his place a juror to hear this case.[139] And if a viscount was for whatever reason unable to attend court, he was within his right to elevate a juror to a position of seniority over the others in order that that person might deputise on his behalf. The deputy presided over all legal matters relating to a dispute, ensured the procedures of the court were written down in the registers and, like the viscount, went to the houses of plaintiffs who were unable to attend.[140] Indeed, the absence of a viscount in certain legal procedure is elsewhere evident. In Jerusalem in 1155, Alois and her husband Gerard sold two shops to the canons of the Holy Sepulchre for 170 besants. There to witness the transfer of seisin was Peter Salomon and Gibertus Papais, 'jurors of the king', and four other burgesses.[141] As no officer of the crown was present it would seem that the presence of the jurors sufficed to legitimise the transaction. In a similar case in 1186, the Hospitallers leased a house in Jerusalem to John Poterius solely in the presence of the nine jurors of the court.[142] As in all these cases, the court proved flexible enough to adapt to its needs and circumstances, whether promoting a member of the jury to deputise on behalf of a viscount in absentia, or endowing itself with the requisite powers to carry out legal affairs without the presence of a presiding head.

The requirement that all jurors of the *Cour des Bourgeois* were to be burgesses of the Law of Rome presented a problem, it seems, to Latin communities in Cyprus. If a sufficient number of jurors in Famagusta could not be assembled in court on Monday or Wednesday, then the court was postponed until Friday. Failing this, liegemen of the crown were even permitted to sit in court in place of jurors to make judgments.[143] But a case of this kind clearly contravened the abiding principle that burgesses were to be judged by their peers. What may be inferred from this judicial arrangement is that in Famagusta there was an assembly of burgesses and feudatories who were knowledgeable of the law, knew the workings of the court and from whose ranks the viscount drew his jurors. In comparison with the indigenous Greek population, the Latin community in Famagusta was relatively small and the choice of burgesses who could qualify as jurors limited, which may explain the dependency, as noted earlier, of the city on the *Cour des Bourgeois* of Nicosia. Nevertheless, if judgement by peers was a cornerstone of jurisdiction in the burgess courts of the kingdom of Jerusalem, in Cyprus it had become a mere ideal which under certain circumstances proved impracticable.

---

139 'Livre contrefais', p. 346.

140 'Livre contrefais', p. 241.

141 Bresc-Bautier, no. 116, p. 237.

142 Delaville Le Roulx, *Cartulaire général*, no. 803, p. 503.

143 'Livre contrefais', p. 324.

The Competence and Procedures of the *Cour des Bourgeois*

The *Cour des Bourgeois* had jurisdiction over burgesses and over all the tenants of *borgesies* whether they were feudatories, churchmen – provided the property was not held 'in alms' – or native Christians. The royal *Cours des Bourgeois* in Jerusalem and Acre, as well as the lords of the kingdom who had powers of *cours et coins et justise*, administered in their *Cours des Bourgeois* high justice or justice of blood. The evidence relating to the maritime communities is, however, not so clear-cut because the right to establish a burgess court in these quarters did not mean automatic right of high justice. The authority to pass sentence of death or mutilation could, for example, be reserved by the overlord to his own court. It all depended upon how much he was willing to cede judicial power without undermining his authority and that of his court. The powers of the *Cour des Bourgeois* were wide-ranging. It had the authority to judge the most serious offences carrying the heaviest sentences, including damage against person (*cop aparent*) and property (*brizeure*), murder, larceny, treason and perjury.[144] It punished offenders with death or the amputation of limb, and in Acre and Nicosia permitted judicial duel to prove innocence or guilt in criminal cases, or in cases in which goods worth more than one mark of silver were in dispute.[145] The *Cours des Bourgeois* in Nicosia and Famagusta had competence over larceny, *cop aparent* and *brizeure*, as well as *murtre* – which was murder without witnesses – and *homesside* – a killing done in self-defence but before witnesses.[146] The 'Livre contrefais' gives a further list of legal business carried out in the court in Nicosia. Apart from criminal cases, it oversaw the sale, donation and exchange of *borgesies* located within its boundaries – as private transactions were expressly forbidden; the leasing of property in perpetuity under terms of *encensive*; the inheritance and division of property among relatives of a deceased; and *chalonges* arising from dispute over rights of possession. It was also responsible for enforcing royal *bans*, manumission and jurisdiction over some aspects of marriage.[147]

As we have seen, most burgess properties were subject to the *Cour des Bourgeois*, including *franc borgesie*, and *heritages des fiés* – *borgesies* joined to fiefs – were subject to the jurisdiction of the High Court or a seigneurial court. The burgess court, furthermore, had jurisdiction over *borgesies* leased by feudatories under terms of *encensive*, although in all other civil and criminal matters a feudatory was subject to the High Court or a seigneurial court. A churchman who

144 Kausler, pp. 59–60 (cf. Beugnot, 'Livre des assises', p. 32).

145 Kausler, pp. 85, 326 (cf. Beugnot, 'Livre des assises', pp. 50, 208); 'Livre contrefais', pp. 326–35, 343; In Antioch duelling was also prohibited in cases worth less than one mark of silver; Alishan, *Assises d'Antioche*, p. 58.

146 'Livre contrefais', pp. 252, 323–4, 342. The distinction between *murtre* and *homesside* was also made by John of Ibelin, p. 88. In Nicosia sentence of corporal or capital punishment was recorded by the notary in the court register; 'Livre contrefais', p. 243.

147 'Livre contrefais', pp. 251–3.

purchased a *borgesie* was equally subject to the *Cour des Bourgeois* in matters of tenancy, although all other aspects of jurisdiction over him belonged to the local Church court. A further exception were *borgesies* sub-leased in Nicosia for short-term – usually for a year and without the conveyance of seisin – to sub-tenants who did not have right of alienation. Such sub-lets had to be authorised in the High Court in the presence of the *bailli* of the *Secrete*.[148] The duties of the *secrete* varied, but as a financial office it kept records of revenues collected by the king's viscounts, *baillis* and scribes. Its registration of *borgesie* leaseholds may be seen as an extension of its duties as a financial office, and, most probably, in all the lordships of the kingdom of Jerusalem the *secretes* fulfilled similar administrative functions.[149] The rule of short-term leasehold applied to all '*borgesies* whether houses, gardens, fields and vineyards and those properties called *heritages* because they are inside the city'.[150] But it seems peculiar that the High Court should have authority over this type of lease. It is possible only feudatories leasing *borgesies* were under the jurisdiction of the High Court of Nicosia, although it is difficult to infer this from the 'Livre contrefais' which discusses various aspects of short-term lease irrespective of whether the primary leaseholder was a feudatory or a burgess.[151] This practice, however, seems to have been a Cypriot innovation because there is no indication in the 'Livre de la Cour des Bourgeois' that temporary lease in Acre was under the jurisdiction of the High Court.

The affairs of the *Cour des Bourgeois* were carried out according to basic procedure. The jurors of the court were expected to have extensive knowledge of the law because they were formally obliged to provide *conseill*, legal advice, should a plaintiff or defendant request it.[152] In Nicosia any person appearing in court was permitted *conseill* in confidence from two jurors, one of whom had to be chosen by the viscount. It was a formal procedure of the court that if the chosen jurors were absent on the day of the trial, the plaintiff or defendant could request a delay of up to seven days in order for them to seek new advice.[153] A relevant comparison can be made with the High Court in Jerusalem where it was common practice for vassals to be appointed to aid others with *conseill*. These counsellors, importantly, who advised their clients on procedure, and how to respond to charges brought against them, were not professional advocates. And in the same way that

[148] 'Livre contrefais', p. 287: 'Mais quant as apaus, il ne ce doient faire en ceste court (the *Cour des Bourgeois*), ains ce doit faire et ce font plusiours fois en la presence dou roi et de la Haute Court, et par devant le bailli de la Segrete et des segretains'.

[149] 'Livre contrefais', p. 241; 'Bans et ordonnances', p. 372; Riley-Smith, *The Feudal Nobility and the Kingdom of Jerusalem*, pp. 58–60.

[150] 'Livre contrefais', p. 287.

[151] 'Livre contrefais', pp. 287–92.

[152] Kausler, p. 334 (cf. Beugnot, 'Livre des assises', p. 213). In the court in Antioch it was general practice that orphaned children under the age of fifteen (age of majority) could receive advice from any one of the jurors; Alishan, *Assises d'Antioche*, p. 50.

[153] 'Livre contrefais', p. 304.

vassals, who also served as judges, emerged as informed and experienced practitioners of the court,[154] jurors of the *Cour des Bourgeois* acquired expertise in legal aspects of civil and criminal justice. As was mentioned, in the kingdom of Jerusalem in the thirteenth century, jurors of the *Cour des Bourgeois*, well-versed in law and judicial procedure, were appointed *judices* to preside over the court.

The role of the juror as counsellor should be distinguished from the role of the *avantparlier* who not only dispensed judicial recommendation but also argued a case on behalf of a plaintiff or a defendant.[155] The professional class of *avantparliers* was made up of well-learned men familiar with legal procedure and the workings of the law, knowledgeable of precedents which had been set, and privy to the written records of the court. They would have studied the law books to which they had access, like all officials of the court including the author of the 'livre contrefais', who informs us that jurors with a thorough grasp of the law could fulfil the functions of advocacy. What though was the precise role of the *avantparlier*? Having agreed to take on a case he would, on behalf of the *clamant*, that is the plaintiff, inform the court of the claim being made and request the *respondant*, the defendant, be summoned to the court to answer charges levelled against him. The claim was concluded with a common legal expression: 'Et de ce se met en l'esgart de la court, sauf son retenaill'.[156] The procedure of *mettre retenail* permitted a man to present new evidence in a plea should the initial judgement go against him.[157] The plea was considered and the court made *esgart* – or *conoissance*[158] – that is a judgement as to the merits of the claim. The burgess law books placed much emphasis on the importance of respecting the procedure of litigation, as well as employing the appropriate legal expressions whenever mounting a challenge or defence. The same was true in the High Court where the complexities of procedure were carefully pointed out by the feudal jurists.[159] If it was decided to proceed with the case, the viscount would instruct the sergeant to find the defendant, and summon him to appear before the court within fifteen days. The claim, the *esgart* and the number of days the defendants had to answer accusations were all written down in the court register.

Procedure in the *Cour des Bourgeois* had to be well-organized and equitable. The court recognised those circumstances when it was not always convenient for a burgess to answer a summons immediately. A burgess may have possessed a *borgesie* which was being claimed by another person in a city where he did not reside. But according to legal custom a dispute had to be heard in the court under whose jurisdictional competence the property concerned was located, meaning a

---

154 Riley-Smith, *The Feudal Nobility and the Kingdom of Jerusalem*, pp. 132–3.

155 'Livre contrefais', p. 245.

156 'Livre contrefais', p. 294.

157 Riley-Smith, *The Feudal Nobility and the Kingdom of Jerusalem*, p. 132.

158 'Livre contrefais', p. 294: 'La court fera son esgart, voles sa conoissance'.

159 John of Ibelin, pp. 108, 109, 114–15; Philip of Novara, 'Le Livre de forme de plait, p. 540.

defendant might have been obliged to appear before a *Cour des Bourgeois* that was some distance from where he lived.[160] For this reason, the fairest procedure was for the jurors of the court to defer judgement as many times as was legally acceptable, in order to allow for the defendant to make his case and thus lessen the probability of the plaintiff winning by default. In Nicosia a person could be summoned up to three times in total, and the final summons was made by the viscount in person at the house of the defendant accompanied by at least two jurors – as this was the number required if the court was to be quorate – the *escrivein* and the plaintiff. This summons was done 'celonc l'esgart de la court', meaning legal procedure had been strictly observed by the jurors and the legal process carried out impartially – there could be no excuse for a defendant to be absent from the trial.[161] In Acre, it was common procedure for a person to be summoned up to three times and if contumacious the court could seize the *borgesie* being contested.[162] But judging from the efforts the court made to resolve dispute, expropriation was a final resort if all else failed. All available options were exhausted before more punitive actions were taken. The *Cour des Bourgeois* in Nicosia when making *esgarts* had various means of compelling a person to appear before it. In a case concerning a dispute over a *borgesie*, for instance, it could judge that the plaintiff should have seisin of the property until the defendant responded to the claim being made. The plaintiff held the *borgesie* as a kind of gage, a security against the failure of the defendant to appear in court, although he had no right of alienation and could not keep any rent accruing from the *borgesie* whilst in his possession. The property had to be returned to the defendant if the court found in the latter's favour. If, however, after a year and a day the defendant had not appeared nor had any family member challenged the case, the property reverted permanently to the plaintiff with full rights of alienation and inheritance.[163]

Once the case proceeded in court, the legal process allowed for a number of adjournments. Again, the rules of adjournment depended upon whether the plaintiff or defendant resided inside or outside the jurisdictional boundaries of the court in which he was being judged.[164] In Acre, a person who did not appear on the day he had agreed with the disputant and the viscount, could be fined seven and a half *solidi* and his case even revoked[165] If, however, he was indisposed and required a further adjournment, he could exercise his right of *contremande*. In order to do this he had to have a witness to swear on oath that he was absent with reason and to request a delay.[166] In the same way a debtor could nominate a guarantor to

[160] Beugnot, 'Livre des assises', p. 155. See also Kausler, pp. 147–8 (cf. Beugnot, 'Livre des assises', p. 156).

[161] 'Livre contrefais', p. 295.

[162] Kausler, pp. 247–8 (cf. Beugnot, 'Livre des assises', p. 156).

[163] 'Livre contrefais', pp. 298–9.

[164] Kausler, p. 138 (cf. Beugnot, 'Livre des assises', pp. 84–5).

[165] Kausler, p. 137 (cf. Beugnot, 'Livre des assises', p. 84).

[166] Kausler, p. 139 (cf. Beugnot, 'Livre des assises', p. 85).

underwrite a loan, a defendant could nominate a person to guarantee that he would appear in court on the day which had been agreed. Should the defendant be absent, the guarantor was liable to any claim being made by the plaintiff.[167]

Legal disputes between burgesses from different cities which did not involve immovable property were always heard in the court of the defendant.[168] To reiterate, in cases where the possession of property was being contested, claims had to be made in the court in whose jurisdictional boundaries the *borgesies* were located. So competence was determined by the location of the property and not the person. The 'Livre de la Cour des Bourgois' gives the example of a plaintiff claiming possession of a *borgesie* located in the rural settlement of Ibelin. The plaintiff wished to sue the defendant in the court of Jerusalem where the man was staying, but was unable to because any legal action had to take place in the court which had authority over the *borgesie* concerned.[169] There were further legal guidelines in what may be described as mixed cases. Disputes, for instance, between burgesses and churchmen went before an ecclesiastical court and were attended by the viscount and burgess jurors of the city.[170] The *Cour des Bourgeois* whilst deferring judgement to the Church, was, nevertheless, represented by its officials who could guarantee the legal rights of the burgess were respected. Criminal cases, moreover, which involved both burgesses and feudatories were judged in the High Court or, if in a lordship, in a seigneurial court. It was also inevitable disputes would arise between burgesses and *Suriani*, and those which were punishable by the loss of life or member were heard in the *Cour des Bourgeois*.[171]

A considerable time of the court was taken up dealing with disputes over money. Apart from pledge, which directly concerned the conveyance of burgess property as collateral, the lending of money did not require court consent, and, understandably, arrears arising from private loans were the basis of much litigation. Several *assises* of Acre dealt specifically with debt and the powers of the *Cour des Bourgeois* over *borgesies* of burgesses who owed money. The court was to protect the rights of creditors, even those deceased, and of their families.[172] In like manner, its responsibility was to ensure a burgess was not wrongly accused of owing money, but if actually in debt that he paid what he owed without impinging the rights of his wife and children.[173] Even so, the law stressed upon the responsibilities of descendants as rightful heirs to carry the burden of debt, or risk the loss of their property which the court had authority to confiscate. These legal principles of the thirteenth century are particularly relevant because it can be

167 Kausler, pp. 143–4 (cf. Beugnot, 'Livre des assises', pp. 87–8).
168 Kausler, p. 138 (cf. Beugnot, 'Livre des assises', pp. 84–5).
169 Beugnot, 'Livre des assises', p. 155.
170 Kausler, p. 54 (cf. Beugnot, 'Livre des assises', pp. 27–8).
171 John of Ibelin, p. 55.
172 Kausler, p.164 (cf. Beugnot, 'Livre des assises', p. 102).
173 Kausler, pp. 85–6, 209–10 (cf. Beugnot, 'Livre des assises', pp. 50–51, 130–31).

proven they originated in the previous century. The *Cour des Bourgeois* of Acre dealt with the issue of debt in a case of 1184. The deceased Peter Bertasia had pledged his house to Bisancon against a loan and Peter's widow agreed to repay the money. This exemplified the duty of the wife to carry the debt of her husband as outlined in the *assises* of Acre. According to the agreement, Bisancon recompensed himself by buying the house for 223 besants, the amount of money he was owed, and the *Cour des Bourgeois* approved of the way the loan was repaid. Bisancon also received the consent of the Hospitallers from whom Peter Bertasia had previously leased the house. As new tenant Bisancon owed the Hospitallers *cens* of twenty-eight besants a year.[174]

I have not come across any other charter illustrating how the *Cour des Bourgeois* dealt with cases of debt, although a document originating in Antioch in 1166 may demonstrate the court's power to enforce repayment. The deceased burgess Peter Jay had borrowed an amount of money from creditors which he had not been able to pay back. The creditors appealed to the court of burgesses in Antioch to recover the money and the court recognised the debt. The phrase 'debitum in curia cognitum fuit ac propalatam' is significant and needs explaining. *Recognoscere* in medieval Europe signified recognition of debt in a court of law. In England *recognizance* was either a judgement obtained by a creditor from a court before advancing money to a debtor, or a confession by a debtor that he owed money which he was liable to repay through sale of his property. The court in Antioch had recognised the debt and the right of creditors to demand the debt be paid off through the sale of movable goods belonging to Peter Jay, whether perishable goods or livestock ('mobilis et supellectilis'). As this was not sufficient to repay the loan, they requested from the court that any property belonging to Peter Jay be sold. This was approved as the property was purchased by a Hospitaller, Bartholomeus Moissac, and the creditors received the 3200 besants which they were owed. Although no mention is made of Peter Jay's descendants, presumably any inheritance rights which they may have claimed were forfeited because of the need to repay the debt. Bartholemeus Moissac, therefore, acquired all rights of tenancy and inheritance.[175]

The issue of debt and how it was dealt with in the *Cour des Bourgeois* touches upon the rights and responsibilities of husbands, wives and near relatives. The lending and borrowing of money was, notwithstanding, only one aspect of matrimony over which the court of burgesses had power. The first relevant point to make is that the institution of marriage was regulated by both the Church and secular courts, although the law book of Acre draws an essential distinction between matters under ecclesiastical authority and matters subject to the jurisdictional competence of the *Cour des Bourgeois*.[176] Thus, the Church determined on which days in the Christian calendar a man and a woman could

174 Delaville Le Roulx, *Cartulaire général*, no. 663, pp. 445–6.

175 Delaville Le Roulx, *Les Archives*, no. 24, p. 105.

176 Kausler, pp. 196–7 (cf. Beugnot, 'Livre des assises', p. 121).

marry and invalidated any union which it believed was in violation of this rule.[177] The Church also saw as its duty the preservation of marriage as a purely Christian union: the 'Livre de la Cour des Bourgeois' repeats the decree issued at the Council of Nablus of 1120, that opposing faith was a diriment impediment to marriage. Yet, interestingly, interfaith marriage as perceived in the law book was not condoned simply on grounds of religion, but because in the eyes of legislators it was incompatible with the prevailing system of community property which stipulated that a Christian wife was entitled to half the movable possessions and immovable property she acquired jointly with her husband.[178] Significantly, such a law implies the existence of interfaith marriage. In fact, it has been remarked that the 'Livre de la Cour des Bourgeois' disapproved of such a union because it was not licit (*iuste*) but not necessarily because it was invalid.[179] The concern of objectors was whether marriage validated the right of a non-Christian spouse, for example, to a share of the property acquired jointly with her husband, and whether the offspring of such a marriage were legitimate. Indeed, the toleration of interfaith marriage may explain why the draconian laws of the Nablus Council punishing such relationships were absent from the law book of Acre in the thirteenth century.[180]

Laws of matrimony in the kingdom of Jerusalem probably reflected accurately those of the western Church[181] – we have seen in an earlier chapter how the authors of the 'Livre de la Cour des Bourgeois' took care to update the law on consanguinity and to incorporate the amendments introduced at the Fourth Lateran Council in 1215.[182] It was equally true that some laws of marriage practised in the *Cour des Bourgeois* were fundamentally rooted in western tradition. The laws defining the status of a woman in particular were imported from Europe and reintroduced in the *assises* of Acre and Nicosia.[183] Let us consider that more than

---

177 Kausler, pp. 194–5 (cf. Beugnot, 'Livre des assises', p. 120).

178 Kausler, pp. 196–7 (cf. Beugnot, 'Livre des assises', p. 121).

179 J.A. Brundage, 'Marriage Law in the Latin Kingdom of Jerusalem', in B.Z. Kedar, H.E. Mayer and R.C. Smail (eds), *Outremer. Studies in the History of the Crusading Kingdom of Jerusalem Presented to Joshua Prawer* (Jerusalem, 1982), p. 260; A. Esmein, *Le Mariage en droit canonique* (Paris, 1891), pp. 216–19.

180 Kedar has proposed that the absence of references to 'illicit sexual relations between Franks and Muslims may be taken as evidence that the relevant Nablus canons had been activated' after 1120, although this does not explain why the canons were not repeated in the law book, particularly as he has argued that these did become 'law of the Frankish Kingdom of Jerusalem'; Kedar, 'On the Origins of the Earliest Laws of Frankish Jerusalem', pp. 330–31.

181 Brundage, 'Marriage Law in the Latin Kingdom of Jerusalem', p. 263. For a general view of marriage customs and Church jurisdiction in the eleventh and twelfth centuries, see C.N.L. Brooke, *The Medieval Idea of Marriage* (Oxford, 1989), p. 56ff.

182 See above, p. 51.

183 J. Richard, 'Le Statut de la femme dans l'orient latin', *Recueils de la Société Jean Bodin*, XII, *La Femme*, 2e partie (1962): 381.

anything the status of a woman burgess in Acre was defined by the legal principles of marital possession. The law in this context differentiated between what was bestowed by a man to a woman prior to marriage; what was brought into a marriage by either spouse, such as a bridal gift; and what was acquired jointly by a husband and wife. With regard to betrothal, if a man gave property to his betrothed he could ask for its return should the marriage not take place.[184] However, when property was brought into a marriage by either spouse, a wife retained certain inalienable rights over her dowry. Her bridal gift took the form of money, clothing, a house, or even a slave, and was made on the condition that her future husband did not act in any way detrimental to her wealth or well-being. Thus, by citing her husband's profligacy as proof of his irresponsible nature she was within her right to request its immediate return.[185] There is evidence that in Cyprus a premarital agreement could be drawn up setting out the contributions a man and woman wished to make to their marriage, and their individual rights of possession and bequest if they had children or if one spouse predeceased the other. In an agreement from Famagusta (1297), a Pisanello de Richobaldo received from Benedicta, 'future sponse et uxori mee', a dowry worth 2100 besants. In return he gave to her a bridal gift of 2400 besants. He agreed that if his wife-to-be predeceased him and they had no legitimate children, she had permission to bequeath an amount of money that was of similar value to her dowry. She was free to make separate donations to the Church 'in alms' and to her closest relatives. Whether these terms of marriage and dowry in Famagusta were similar to those in Nicosia is difficult to determine especially as the 'Livre contrefais' has little to say about bridal gifts. The document does state, however, that the agreement was in keeping with the 'custom of the kingdom of Cyprus'.[186]

But obviously not everything was brought into a marriage. *Borgesies* and other possessions were also acquired jointly by husbands and wives, and parallels may be drawn between laws in Acre regarding this and contemporary France, where the well-established system of community property dealt specifically with marriage and tenancy, with the subdivision of jointly acquired property (*acquêts* or *conquêts*) between spouses, and with the subjection of each half of an estate to either spouse's testamentary disposition.[187] Under similar terms in Acre, a wife was adjudged to have joint tenancy of a *borgesie* only if she had acquired it with her husband.[188] There are some charters which do indeed record the joint acquisition of

184 Kausler, pp. 181–2 (cf. Beugnot, 'Livre des assises', p. 112).

185 Kausler, p. 188 (cf. Beugnot, 'Livre des assises', p. 116).

186 Balard, *Notai genovesi in oltremare: atti rogati a Cipro da Lamberto di Sambuceto (11 Ottobre 1296–23 Giugno 1299)*, no. 27, p. 37. See also no. 128, p. 153.

187 C. Donahue, 'What Causes Fundamental Legal Ideas? Marital Property in England and France in the Thirteenth Century', *Michigan Law Review*, 78 (1979): 66–7.

188 Kausler, p. 198 (cf. Beugnot, 'Livre des assises', p. 122): 'S'il avient que un home et sa feme ont encemble conquis vignes ou terres ou maisons ou jardins, le dreit dit que la feme doit aver la moitié de tout, par dreit et par l'assise dou reaume de Jerusalem'.

borgesies by married couples. In 1178, William Baptizatus and his wife Johanne bought two houses situated in Jerusalem for ninety-seven besants.[189] In 1186, John Poterius and his wife also bought a house in Jerusalem for 200 besants.[190] In a sale of 1235, John Grifus, a knight and his wife Mary were joint tenants of a plot of land situated outside Acre owing five besants a year to the Church of St Mary of the Latins; they sold it to the Teutonic Knights.[191] But what was meant by joint tenancy and how were acquests divided? Certainly, the law of community property entitled each spouse to half a property (*moitié de tout*). This division was not merely theoretical and for legal reasons it was essential either spouse knew precisely what his or her share constituted. The 'Livre de la Cour des Bourgeois' mentions that lands, vineyards, orchards and houses were acquired jointly, but says nothing about how it was decided who was entitled to what.[192] Perhaps at the time a husband and wife purchased a *borgesie*, the *Cour des Bourgeois* formally recognised which parts of the property each was designated. We have also to conjecture whether the law permitted a joint *borgesie* to be divided into two separate properties. If, say, a husband bequeathed his share of a house to someone either related or not related to him, did this person become joint tenant with the widow of the deceased man, or did he become a possessor of a separate property with individual rights of tenancy? The same question may be applied to the wife who predeceasing her husband was permitted to leave her share of a *borgesie* to her children even if the husband chose to retain possession of his share.[193] Whatever the case may have been, it is manifest that the characteristic features of community property, and the intrinsic right of either spouse to donate his or her share of a *borgesie*, made disagreement among family members more probable. It should not be assumed, however, that the concept of material equality between married couples was totally unconditional. In the eyes of Acre law the particular rights a wife possessed over her share of a property remained subordinate to those of her husband.[194] A wife was not free to alienate her share of a property until after the death of her husband.[195] In other words, while both spouses were alive, a wife required her husband's consent to sell, donate or pledge her share.

The Cases Concerning Native Peoples

In so many ways the *Cour des Bourgeois* was the focal point of burgess community life. And with few exceptions – those cases involving feudatories,

---

189 Delaville Le Roulx, *Les Archive*, nos 46–7, pp. 135–7.
190 Delaville Le Roulx, *Cartulaire général*, no. 803, p. 503.
191 Strehlke, no. 80, p. 63.
192 Kausler, p. 198 (cf. Beugnot, 'Livre des assises', p. 122).
193 Kausler, pp.199, 203–204 (cf. Beugnot, 'Livre des assises', pp. 122, 126).
194 Kausler, pp. 244–5 (cf. Beugnot 'Livre des assises', p. 153).
195 Kausler, p. 199 (cf. Beugnot, 'Livre des assises', p. 122).

churchmen or native people – the court dealt with burgess inhabitants within its locality. But we should remember that Latins constituted only a part – perhaps a minority – of the overall population of an eastern city. There were additionally minor courts dealing with small claims of Syrian Christians, Muslims and Jews. By authorising the existence of native justice within the framework of a Latin legal system, the city lord allowed each indigenous community to organise itself administratively and legislatively, and to judge cases according to its own laws providing that the juridical rights reserved to the *Cour des Bourgeois* were not infringed. To press hard the native populace would have proved counter-productive. Rather, granting them freedom of worship, coupled by and large with powers of justice, fostered a healthier sense of community. The *Cour des Syriens* was the court of native Christians probably in all the cities of the kingdom of Jerusalem, although we can only be certain of its existence in Jerusalem, Nablus, Tyre, Bethlehem, Nicosia and Famagusta.[196] Describing the founding of the *Cour des Syriens* in the twelfth century, John of Ibelin explained that it had been conceived during the reign of Godfrey of Bouillon to make judgements according to the 'usages of the Syrians',[197] that is those laws of the Syrian Christian communities which were enforceable with the approval of the city lord. Significantly, however, native jurisdiction in Acre differed somewhat in the thirteenth century, as the *Cour de la Fonde* of the city seems to have functioned in place of the *Cour des Syriens*. In inter-communal cases the authority of the *Cour de la Fonde* extended over Christians, Muslims and Jews, and we know that it heard cases of debt, pledge, the leasing of houses and commercial dealings.[198] It was made up of six jurors, four of whom were Syrian Christians and two Latins, and at its head was the *bailli* who was either a feudatory or a burgess.[199] John of Ibelin remarked that 'in one place in the kingdom there are jurors of the *Cour des Syriens* and no rays'.[200] John was perhaps referring to Acre where the *bailli* of the *Cour de la Fonde* carried out the responsibilities of the rays. There is, nevertheless, no existing evidence that the *Cour des Syriens* had been absorbed by the *Cour de la Fonde* in any other city where presumably these two courts existed alongside each other.

It has been argued that the existence of the *Cour de la Fonde* was indicative of

---

196 Riley-Smith, *The Feudal Nobility and the Kingdom of Jerusalem*, p. 90; Riley-Smith, 'Government and the Indigenous in the Latin Kingdom of Jerusalem', in D. Abulafia and N. Berend (eds), *Medieval Frontiers: Concepts and Practices* (Aldershot, Ashgate, 2002), p. 129; J. Chamberlayne (ed.), *Lacrimae nicossienses. Recueil d'inscriptions funéraires, la plupart française, existant encore dans l'île de Chypre* (Paris, 1894), I, pp. 31, 64; 'Bans et ordonnances', p. 377.

197 John of Ibelin, p. 55.

198 Kausler, pp. 270–73 (cf. Beugnot, 'Livre des assises', pp. 171–2). Riley-Smith, *The Feudal Nobility and the Kingdom of Jerusalem*, p. 90.

199 Kausler, p. 271 (cf. Beugnot, 'Livre des assises', p. 171).

200 John of Ibelin, p. 55. For an interpretation of this passage see J.S.C. Riley-Smith, 'Some Lesser Officials in Latin Syria', *EHR*, 87 (1972): 6–7.

a Latin society adapting to the needs of the native population; the Latin government, after initial wide-scale massacre, adopted the Muslim system of *dhimma* in order to cope with the religious and legal needs of an ethnically diverse society.[201] This led to the innovation of the *Cour de la Fonde* as a special small-claims court for inter-communal cases.[202] The formation of such a legal institution was essential if the economy, which depended on the interaction between neighbouring religious communities, was to function successfully. It has been suggested, however, that the separation of temporal and spiritual jurisdiction in the Latin legal system would have seemed artificial to non-Christians who were accustomed to having one court for the judgement of all cases according to their religious laws. For Muslims and Jews spiritual jurisdiction was reserved to the *qadi* (Muslim judge) or rabbinical court, respectively. But, if the 'Livre de la Cour des Bourgeois' is to be believed, besides the fact that native traditions and customs were not practised in the *Cour de la Fonde*, inter-communal cases were judged by the laws established in the *Cour des Bourgeois*.[203] This though may have been viewed as a fairer system which did not favour one community and its laws over another. It militated against legal confusion and disagreement. Only the laws of the *Cour des Bourgeois* were sufficient in disputes concerning 'selling, purchasing, leasing and other things', and in this law book 'est establie toutes raisons et toutes droitures pour toutes gens'.[204]

The *Cour de la Fonde* heard inter-communal cases of debt and pledges 'or whatever else' a Christian, Muslim or Jew has done. The underlying principle of the *Cour des Bourgeois* that a witness could not bear testimony against any person other than those of his own denomination existed in this court. A Jewish claimant took an oath on the Torah, the Muslim on the Quran, the Armenian, Greek and the Syrian on an image of the cross, and the Samaritan on the Pentateuch.[205] The court did not have competence over cases punishable with loss of life or limb that is murder, treason and larceny, and those that could be resolved by judicial duel.[206] The 'Livre de la Cour des Bourgeois' is the principal source for this court as a merchant's tribunal, although its function and purpose, along with the *Cour de la Chaine* – for example, the collection of tolls and market charges from Latins and

---

201 Riley-Smith, 'Government and the Indigenous in the Latin Kingdom of Jerusalem', p. 126. On the social and legal status of non-Muslims in a Muslim state, see C.E. Bosworth, '"The Protected Peoples" (Christians and Jews) in Medieval Egypt and Syria', *BJRL*, 62 (1979): 11–36.

202 Riley-Smith, 'Government and the Indigenous in the Latin Kingdom of Jerusalem', p. 130.

203 Kausler, p. 273 (cf. Beugnot, 'Livre des assises', p. 172). On the possible exercise of Byzantine law in the *Cour des Syriens*, see Edbury, 'The Lusignan Regime in Cyprus and the Indigenous Population', p. 5.

204 Kausler, p. 273 (cf. Beugnot, 'Livre des assises', p. 172).

205 Kausler, p. 272 (cf. Beugnot, 'Livre des assises', p. 172).

206 Kausler, p. 271 (cf. Beugnot, 'Livre des assises', p. 172).

non-Latins – is well known.[207] I should add though, that as a tribunal there is no suggestion in the 'Livre des Assises de la Cour des Bourgeois' that in Acre Latin merchants were subject to its jurisdiction, as opposed to the revenue collecting function it had. The emphasis was clearly on its legal authority over inter-communal cases involving native Christians, Muslims and Jews.[208]

A passage of the 'Livre de la Cour des Bourgeois' raises the possibility that certain laws of the law book of Acre were practised in the *Cour de la Fonde*. In his assessment of the jurisdictional duties of this court, one of the authors of the 'Livre de la Cour des Bourgeois' wrote:

> Bien sachés que les jurés de la fonde deivent juger cil qui mesferont l'un à l'autre, si come est de vente, ou d'achet, ou de luiement, ou d'autres choses, si les deivent enci juger coume establi est en ce livre, que devent faire les jures de la Cort des Borgeis, et non autrement.[209]

It was instructed that the jurors of the court base their judgements on those laws in the 'Livre de la Cour des Bourgeois' which contained right and reason regarding 'all men'.[210] Presumably, the cases heard in the *Cour de la Fonde* concerned disputes under a certain value, in the same way that the *Cours des Syriens* heard minor cases and referred more serious ones to courts of burgesses. Furthermore, the evidence of the 'Livre de la Cour des Bourgeois' casts light on the theory that in Acre the *Cour des Syriens* was absorbed by the *Cour de la Fonde*. There was apparently a fundamental difference between the *Cour de la Fonde* where natives were judged 'come les Frans', and the *Cour des Syriens* which, if John of Ibelin was right, was authorized to make judgements according to native Christian customs. In this respect, we must be cautious about drawing too many comparisons between the jurisdictional competence and function of both native courts.

The *Cour de la Fonde*, like the *Cour des Syriens*, did not have legal authority over *borgesies*, but did this mean that native Christian Syrians could not purchase such property? A formulaic proscription is repeated in the charters as evidenced in

---

207 Riley-Smith, *The Feudal Nobility and the Kingdom of Jerusalem*, p. 91. For examples of its tax levying powers, see Kausler, pp. 282–7 (cf. Beugnot, 'Livre des assises', pp. 178–81); G.L.F. Tafel, and G.M. Thomas (eds), *Urkunden zur älteren Handels und Staatsgeschichte der Republik Venedig: Mit besonderer Beziehung auf Byzanz und die Levante* (3 vols, Vienna, 1856–57), II, no. 299, p. 367; L. de Mas-Latrie (ed.), 'Quatre pièces relatives à l'Ordre Teutonique en Orient', in *AOL*, II (1884), no. 3, p. 167; A. Ferreto (ed.), 'Contributi alle relazioni tra Genova e l'Oriente. Una Lettera del pontifice Innocenzo III e un privilegio di Guido re di Gerusalemme e signore di Cipro', *Giornale Liguistico*, XXI (1896): 44. For Nicosia, Mas-Latrie, *Histoire de l'île de Chypre*, vol. 3, p. 206.

208 In Nicosia and Tyre, commercial matters were dealt with by the *mathesep* of the royal *Cours des Bourgeois*; 'Livre contrefais', p. 243.

209 Kausler, p. 273 (cf. Beugnot, 'Livre des assises', p. 172).

210 Kausler, p. 273 (cf. Beugnot, 'Livre des assises', p. 172).

a sale of 1186, when the Hospitallers conceded to John Poterius a house he had purchased from William Barbota. He was by the terms of the deed free to alienate his property to anyone 'exceptis ecclesiis, militibus, Surianis et aliis gentibus Romane ecclesie non hobedientibus'.[211] On the other hand, the 'Livre contrefais' defines those who were outside the Catholic faith and could not, therefore, purchase *borgesies* 'except by permission of the chief lord', as idolaters, Jews and Saracens – the prohibition against Muslims in the law book of Nicosia is evidence of their presence on the island[212] – for they are unable to carry out certain duties expected of them if they wish to buy *heritages*'.[213] It is interesting to note that native Christians were excluded from this latter proscription because unlike the people of other faiths they were permitted to swear the oath required of buyers in the *Cour des Bourgeois* – a buyer was obliged to swear on the Bible that he was purchasing a property for himself and no other person.[214] It is an omission further supporting the view that native Christians, both Greek and Syrian, did possess *borgesies*. There is reason to believe that there was a sizeable Syrian Christian community in Cyprus by about 1300 – apart from the well-established Maronites[215] – prospering from trade generated by the merchant communities.[216] This would warrant the reference to them made in the 'Livre contrefais' and in a royal ban of 1300 concerning tradesmen.[217] Syrian Christians were, after 1291, particularly important in trade with the Levantine coast, because as non-Latins they were not prohibited by the papacy from participating in commerce with Muslims.[218] In fact, the Syrian Christian population in Famagusta in the fourteenth century had its own rays,[219] as did Nicosia where the existence of this community leader may be traced back to 1210.

It was quite common for Syrian Christians on the mainland to hold *borgesies*. John of Ibelin describes the *Cour des Syriens* as having jurisdiction in all matters except 'carelle de sanc et carelle de quoi l'on pert vie ou membre, et *carelle de*

---

211 Delaville Le Roulx, *Cartulaire général*, no. 803, p. 503.

212 See also 'Bans et ordonnances', p. 365.

213 'Livre contrefais', pp. 254–5.

214 'Bans et ordonnances', p. 373.

215 J. Richard, 'Le Peuplement latin et syrien en Chypre au XIIIe siècle', p. 157; G.F. Hill, *A History of Cyprus in the Frankish Period* (4 vols: Cambridge, 1940–52), vol. 2, pp. 3–4.

216 Leontios Makhairas, *Chronicle*, ed. and trans. R.M. Dawkins, (2 vols, Oxford, 1932), vol. 1, p. 25; Edbury, 'The Lusignan Regime in Cyprus and the Indigenous Population', p. 4; Richard, 'Le Peuplement latin et syrien en Chypre au XIIIe siècle': 168–70.

217 'Livre contrefais', p. 365; D. Jacoby, 'Citoyens, et protégés de Venise et de Gènes en Chypre de XIIIe au XVe siècle', *BF*, V (1977), p. 160.

218 J. Richard, 'La Cour des Syriens de Famagouste d'après un texte de 1448', *BF*, XII (1987): 385.

219 Richard, 'La Cour des Syriens de Famagouste', pp. 387–8; Hill, vol. 2, pp. 1–2.

borgesie'.[220] The latter exception seems to suggest native Syrians could possess *borgesies* and as tenants were subject to the *Cour des Bourgeois*. There is further corroborating evidence. The 'Livre de la Cour des Bourgeois' stresses that a witness could not bear testimony against any persons other than those of his own denomination: '... ne le Samaritan contre le Jacobin, ne le Jacobin contre le Surien, por dette, *ne por heritage*'.[221] The word *heritage* is used throughout the law book as the alternative name for a *borgesie* situated inside a city.[222] Again, the suggestion is native Christians did possess this type of property, and that prohibition against them in charters was theoretical, because ultimately it was the seigneur's decision whether to permit non-Latins to lease *borgesies*.[223] Nowhere is this interpretation better illustrated than in a charter of 1143 granting a man called Arnulf houses and shops in Jerusalem and stipulating that as tenant he was entitled 'to sell (his *borgesies*) to whomever he wishes either burgesses or Syrians'.[224] There are in fact several other examples. Theoderic 'the Syrian' possessed a house in Tyre.[225] Brainus (Ibrahim?) Syrianus possessed a house in Jerusalem (1177),[226] and Theoderus Grecus a house in Acre (1255).[227] A royal charter in 1144 records that King Fulk purchased from a Syrian Christian an area of land and a vineyard located in the vicinity of Acre.[228] In the suburb of Montmusard, in 1241,[229] Farag, *syriacus*, was in possession of a house, and Nassarus, son of Henof, leased an area of land from the abbey of Notre Dame for five and a half besants a year, in return for rights of alienation and inheritance.[230] In an inventory of houses belonging to the Holy Sepulchre in Jerusalem and owing *cens*, two tenants, Seyr, described as a

220 John of Ibelin, p. 55.

221 Kausler, p. 92 (cf. Beugnot, 'Livre des assises', p. 56).

222 'Livre contrefais', p. 287.

223 It is not always clear in the charters to whom *Syriens* referred. James of Vitry associated *Suriani* with Greeks; James of Vitry, 'Historia Hierosolymitana', in J. Bongars (ed.), *Gesta Dei per Francos* (2 vols, Hanau, 1611), p. 1089ff.. Peter Tudebode, however, distinguished between Greeks and Syrians; Peter Tudebode, *Historia de Hierosolimitano Itinere*, eds J.H. Hill and L.L. Hill (Paris, 1977), pp. 55, 64, 68, 72, 76. It has even been suggested that *Suriani* had a narrower sense and was applicable only to Syriac-liturgising members of the native Christian churches; G. Every, 'Syrian Christians in Palestine in the Early Middle Ages', *ECQ*, 3 (1946): 365. However, in his account of the *Cour des Syriens*, John of Ibelin referred generally to the *peuple des Suriens*.

224 Delaville Le Roulx, no. 68, p. 165.

225 Strehlke, no. 24, pp. 21–2.

226 Delaville Le Roulx, *Cartulaire général*, no. 508, p. 349.

227 Delaville Le Roulx, *Cartulaire général*, no. 2732, p. 780.

228 Marsy, no. 3, p. 124.

229 For a topographical study of the suburb of Montmusard, see, D. Jacoby, 'Montmusard, Suburb of Crusader Acre: The First Stage of its Development', in B.Z. Kedar, H.E. Mayer and R.C. Smail (eds), *Outremer. Studies in the History of the Crusading Kingdom of Jerusalem Presented to Joshua Prawer* (Jerusalem, 1982), pp. 205–17.

230 *ROL*, VII, p. 178.

surianus, and Bulfarage (Abu al Farrag), a doctor, leased houses in St Martin Street, which bordered the Armenian quarter, for four besants and two besants respectively.[231] In the 'vicus de Repoes', a place probably near the church named *La Repos* and located in the Syrian quarter, Brain, a *drugoman*, possessed a house owing five besants a year,[232] and Selam (Salam) Mazun a house owing half a besant.[233] The Holy Sepulchre also possessed houses on Mount Sion Street which bordered the Armenian quarter: the tenants were Turoz (three besants *ad censum*) and Mahafe (two besants).[234] A patriarchal charter refers to the 'house of a certain Syrian', possibly situated in the patriarchal quarter,[235] and in a list of tenants owing *cens* to the Hospitallers, Jacobus Surianus is mentioned as leasing a house in Jerusalem.[236] In 1207, a charter of Acre concerning *borgesies* owing *cens*, mentions that Johannes Daht possessed a house in the 'catena Acconensis', as did his daughter and Tortosa, all of whom were it seems from their names native Christians.[237] In 1273, in a document recording the alienation of a property in the royal *Cour des Bourgeois* in Acre, Set Lehoue with the approval of her husband, Jorge le Haneisse, and her son, Faet, sold a *borgesie* in Montmusard to *dame* Ysabiau. Her native Christian neighbours are also revealed as being tenants of *borgesies*: Lorens,[238] son of Houdeir, possessed a *heritage*, and Josej le Grifon, the moneylender, possessed a garden.[239]

Syrian Christians could, like their burgess counterparts, alienate, bequeath and pledge their *borgesies*, and were subject to the *Cour des Bourgeois* in all matters pertaining to their property. But apart from such legal dependency, native Christians rarely came into contact with the court of burgesses unless they were charged with an offence which came under its jurisdiction. In short, they lived their lives, plied their trade and worshiped within their community. They respected their own laws and were subject to a *Cour des Syriens*. In almost every respect they were distinguishable from their burgess neighbours. This is not to say, however, that native Christians were completely excluded from the class of burgesses. On the contrary, some did qualify because they were uniate Catholics like the Maronites, who formally accepted Roman authority in around 1180, and whose identity became more distinct in the eyes of European Latins.[240] They could not be

231 Bresc-Bautier, no. 168, p. 321.

232 Bresc-Bautier, no. 168, p. 322; Boas, p. 24.

233 Bresc-Bautier, no. 168, p. 322.

234 Bresc-Bautier, no. 168, p. 321.

235 Delaville Le Roulx, *Cartulaire général*, no. 483, p. 333.

236 *RRH* no. 483, p. 127.

237 Delaville Le Roulx, *Cartulaire général*, no. 1276, pp. 78–9. (*RRH* no. 824, p. 221).

238 Judging from his name Lorens was perhaps a Catholic convert.

239 Favreau-Lilie, 'The Teutonic Knights in Acre after the Fall of Montfort (1271): Some Reflections', 'appendix', pp. 282–3.

240 On the communion of the Maronite Church with the Roman Catholic Church, K.S. Salibi, 'The Maronite Church in the Middle Ages and its Union with Rome', *Oriens*

excluded because they fulfilled all criteria: they were Catholics, tenants of *borgesies* and subject to a *Cour des Bourgeois*. The fact that they were of non-European origin was of no relevance because in the kingdom race was never used to define burgess status. The Maronites were resident in Jerusalem in the twelfth century[241] and evidence that they were a thriving community in Acre can be found on an inscription carrying the name of Abu'l-Fadl – a wealthy *magister* – and commemorating his building of a church in the city.[242] In theory, they would have enjoyed the same standing as other burgess inhabitants, most notably the right to represent the interests of their community – whether to attend general assemblies and give advice – or to serve as jurors and officials in the *Cour des Bourgeois*. In terms of property possession, although there is no concrete evidence of Maronites possessing *borgesies* – besides a charter of 1280 recording that Humphrey of Beirut granted a Maronite a fief[243] – there are examples of other native Catholics holding this type of property. One of these was Arnulf, 'son of Bernard the Syrian', who was a Catholic, as is suggested by his name and the name of his father.[244] In the thirteenth century, a man called Saliba was a wealthy burgess of Acre and a *confrater* of the order of St John. The family name of Saliba is Greek Orthodox and the fact that in his will he left some money to the hospital of St Catherine, a dependency of Mount Sinai, may suggest he was originally of the Orthodox faith. There are many indications, however, that he was a Latin Christian, particularly as he left the bulk of his estate to Latin churches and religious orders, including the Hospital to whom he bequeathed his house he had bought for 475 besants. Saliba was also a slave owner and requested that his baptised slaves Ametum and Sofia be manumitted.[245] Possibly another Latin Christian was 'Morage' rays,[246] who sold part of his house, with the consent of the king, to the canons of the Holy Sepulchre[247] – rayses were generally-speaking Latin Christians.[248] Leo of

Christianus, 42 (1958): 94; and on the union of the Armenian Church, E. Rey, *Les Colonies franques de Syrie au XIIe et XIIIe siècles* (Paris, 1883), pp. 84–8. The Maronites were mentioned by William of Tyre, p. 1018.

241 K.M. Salibi, *Maronite Historians of Mediaeval Lebanon* (Beirut, 1991), p. 48, note 1; Delaville Le Roulx, *Cartulaire général*, no. 3105, pp. 91–2.

242 C. Enlart, *Monuments des croisés* (Paris, 1928), II, p. 32; C. Cahen, 'Un Inscription mal comprise concernant le rapprochement entre Maronites et croisés', in S.A. Hanna (ed.), *Medieval and Middle Eastern Studies in Honor of Aziz Suryal Atiya* (Leyden, 1972), pp. 62–3.

243 C. Clermont-Ganneau (ed.), 'Deux chartes des croisés dans les archives arabes', *Revue d'Archéologie Orientale*, VI (1905): 4, 9–11.

244 Bresc-Bautier, no. 68, p. 165.

245 Delaville Le Roulx, *Cartulaire général*, no. 2105, pp. 191–2.

246 Riley-Smith, 'Some Lesser Officials in Latin Syria', p. 5.

247 Bresc-Bautier, no. 111, p. 232.

248 Riley-Smith, 'Some Lesser Officials in Latin Syria', p. 6.

Jerusalem – who it has been argued was a native of Syria[249] – was a Catholic resident in the Venetian quarter in Acre, tenant of a shop in 1283 and described in 1277 as a 'burgensis ac fidelis Veneti'.[250] In Jerusalem, Nicholas Manzur (Mansur) was, judging from his transaction with the Hospitallers in the royal *Cour des Bourgeois* (1179), a wealthy native Catholic tenant.[251] At around the end of the thirteenth century, a Syrian burgess by the name of Manuel Zaphet lived in Famagusta, and his son, Joseph, a wealthy trader on the island, became a citizen of Montpellier and died in the city in c. 1381.[252] Other wealthy Syrian burgesses of Famagusta were Farag of Bethlehem, whose business dealings were recorded by the Genoese notary Lamberto di Sambuceto (fl. 1300), and Simon, son of Joseph of 'Lezia' (Laodicea), 'burgensis Famagoste', who in 1301 was trading between Cyprus and Ancona.[253] These men and women could buy and sell *borgesies*, and as Latins of native origin they were not subject to the *Cour des Syriens* but to the *Cour des Bourgeois* in civil and criminal matters.

In theory, any Catholic could qualify as a burgess, a principle which the Church was eager to uphold as an incentive to natives who wished to convert to the Latin faith and to enjoy rights of inheritance and alienation of *borgesie*. The most obvious example of this kind of inducement was the religious conversion of slaves. It was a general custom that a person baptised was automatically granted freedom – baptism was not merely a prerequisite for manumission[254] – and a document of enfranchisement served as written confirmation of a person's new status.[255] In his position, the freed man, or *batié* as he was known, enjoyed some of the privileges of Latin non-feudatories, and the law was keen to emphasise that he was free even to inherit the *borgesie* of his former master.[256] Apart from loss of slave service, this right of property possession may have been the basis of some Latin opposition to the conversion of Muslims and Jews. In a letter to the patriarch of Jerusalem

---

249 D. Jacoby, 'L'Expansion occidentale dans le Levant: Les Vénitiens à Acre dans la seconde moitié du treizième siècle', *Journal of Medieval History*, 3 (1977): 246–7.

250 R. Cessi (ed.), *Deliberazioni del Maggior Consiglio* di Venezia, (3 vols, Bologna, 1931–50), vol. III, p. 40; Tafel and Thomas, III, no. 370, p. 257; Jacoby, 'L'Expansion occidentale dans le Levant', pp. 246–7.

251 Delaville Le Roulx, *Cartulaire général*, no. 554, p. 376.

252 J. Combes, 'Un Marchand de Chypre, bourgeois de Montpellier', in *Etudes médiévales offertes a M. Le Doyen Augustin Fliche* (Montpellier, 1952), pp. 35–9.

253 R. Pavoni (ed.), *Notai genovesi in oltremare: atti rogati a Cipro da Lamberto di Sambuceto (6 Luglio–27 Ottobre 1301)* (Genoa, 1982), pp. 234–5; D. Abulafia, 'The Anconitan Privileges in the Kingdom of Jerusalem and the Levant Trade of Ancona', in G. Airaldi and B.Z. Kedar (eds), *I Comuni italiani nel regno crociato di Gerusalemme* (Genoa, 1986), p. 548; Richard, 'Le Peuplement latin et syrien en Chypre au XIIIe siècle', 168–9.

254 B.Z. Kedar, *Crusade and Mission: European Approaches Toward the Muslims* (Princeton, 1984), pp. 76–7.

255 Balard, *Notai genovesi in oltremare: atti rogati a Cipro da Lamberto di Sambuceto (11 Ottobre 1296–23 Giugno 1299)*, no. 145, p. 170.

256 Kausler, pp. 225–6 (cf. Beugnot, 'Livre des assises', pp. 139–40).

(1237), Pope Gregory IX expressed concern that many slaves who desired conversion to the Catholic faith were being denied manumission. He advised that those slaves who promised to remain serving their Latin masters be granted freedom.[257] But as far as slaves enfranchised by religious conversion were concerned, their freedom was conditional in the eyes of the law. They were not of equal status to other Latin Christians. In Acre, a *batié* who acted criminally against his former master, his wife or children, could be returned to his status of servility if found guilty by the *Cour des Bourgeois.*[258] Indeed, the *borgesie* of a *batié* who died intestate and without children escheated to his former master, or, if he had been predeceased by his former master, to the lord of the domain.[259] The *Cour des Bourgeois* could further guarantee the inheritance rights of a convert's children, but prohibited his relatives from right of escheat. In this instance, the law safeguarded against the possibility of property passing into the hands of non-Christians.[260] By legal definition, the freedom only of children born of a free mother was permanent and unconditional,[261] a description which recalls to mind Philippe de Beaumanoir's assertion that a person could be judged free from birth, *franc naturelment.*[262] In the kingdom of Jerusalem, irrespective of the wealth or standing of a *batié* in the community, his status remained conditional throughout his lifetime. His freedom was curbed to such an extent – he was not permitted to plead in a *Cour des Bourgeois* on behalf of others[263] – that he could not have fulfilled all criteria of burgess status. Only his children qualified unconditionally.

It was mentioned above that neither the *Cour des Syriens* – nor the *Cour de la Fonde* had jurisdiction over *borgesies*, but in thirteenth-century Acre the latter did oversee the lease of certain properties, including houses specially set aside for non-Latin residents. This is significant proof of a secular court other than the *Cour des Bourgeois* with jurisdiction over the lease of city property. In a passage of the 'Livre de la Cour des Bourgeois', the reference to the jurisdictional competence the *bailli* and the jurors of the court of the *fonde* had over the leasing of houses, may help answer two important questions: Where in the city of Acre did the indigenous live? And what was the legal status of their properties? The emphasis that has hitherto been placed on the *Cour de la Fonde* as a commercial tribunal has diminished its status as a court which dealt with cases concerning the tenancy of native peoples in Acre. The relevant passage in the 'Livre de la Cour des Bourgeois' sets out the duties of the *bailli* and the jurors of the court. 'Et ses sont

[257] Gregory IX, *Acta (1227–1241)*, ed. A.L. Tautu (Vatican City, 1950), no. 228, pp. 307–308.

[258] Kausler, pp. 223–4 (cf. Beugnot, 'Livre des assises', p. 139).

[259] Kausler, pp. 222–3 (cf. Beugnot, 'Livre des assises', p. 138).

[260] Kausler, pp. 222–3 (cf. Beugnot, 'Livre des assises', p. 138).

[261] Kausler, pp. 223–4 (cf. Beugnot, 'Livre des assises', p. 139).

[262] Philip of Beaumanoir, *Les Coutumes du Beauvoisis*, ed. A.A. Beugnot (Paris, 1842), pp. 232–3.

[263] Kausler, p. 55 (cf. Beugnot, 'Livre des assises', p. 28).

tenus de juger tous les clains qui verront devant le bailly', it is written, 'si com est de dette, ou de gages qui perdus ou enpirés, ou si come est de luiement de maisons'.[264] The court had jurisdiction over the lease of houses by Christians, Muslims and Jews. But where in the region of the *fonde* were these houses located? Richard believes the *fonde* (Lat. *fondicum*; Arab. *funduk*), the marketplace, was located in the eastern part of Acre near the house of the Teutonic Order and the cathedral church of St Cross. He suggests the area *en amont*, the 'upper' part, was situated to the north and east of the *fonde*, and the area *en aval*, the 'lower' part, was nearer the port of the city and the Street of the Chain. In an opposing theory, it has been argued the reference in the 'Livre de la Cour des Bourgeois' was to two *fondes*: the *fonde en aval*, describing the Italian markets in the *Porte de la Chaine*; and the *fonde en amont*, that is the royal *fonde* or group of markets situated in the vicinity of the *Funda Regis*.[265] Besides the difficulty of establishing where exactly the houses of the natives were situated, it is unknown whether the jurisdictional authority of the *Cour de la Fonde* extended over native leasehold in the whole of Acre or just in a specific part of the city. In a law concerning the *fonde*, it was stipulated that indigenous inhabitants should live around the *fonde en amont* and not the *fonde en aval*,[266] so the lord in their quarter could collect the taxes that he was rightfully owed.[267] And yet this law seems to contradict the evidence we have of indigenous people living in various parts of Acre. The north of Acre, the suburb of Montmusard, was inhabited by Syrian Christians; in the examples earlier discussed, the native inhabitants were tenants of houses in the 1240s.[268] And as also pointed out, there were native Christians living in the *catena Acconensis*, the quarter of the Chain. These examples were *encensive* tenures whose tenants were either under the authority of the royal *Cour des Bourgeois* or, if held 'in alms', the jurisdiction of a Church Court. In the light of this evidence it was perhaps the case that the indigenous inhabitants who wished to trade in the *fondes*, and who as a consequence were subject to the commercial authority of the *Cour de la Fonde*, had to reside near the *fonde en amont*.

The question that remains unanswered is what status were these houses under the jurisdiction of the *Cour de la Fonde*. We are not helped by the law books

---

[264] Kausler, p. 273 (cf. Beugnot, 'Livre des assises', p. 171).

[265] J. Richard, 'Colonies marchandes privilégiées et marché seigneurial. La Fonde d'Acre et ses "droitures"', *Le Moyen Age*, LIX (1953): 334–6; J.S.C. Riley-Smith, 'The Government in Latin Syria and the Commercial Privileges of Foreign Merchants', D. Baker (ed.), *Relations Between East and West in the Middle Ages* (Edinburgh, 1973), p. 116.

[266] Kausler, p. 282 (cf. Beugnot, 'Livre des assises', p. 178): 'Suriens et Grifons et Nestourins et Jacobins et Samaritans et Judes et Mosserins, toutes ycés gens devent maner de la fonde en amont; et de le fonde d'Acre en aval ne deit nus estre, par dreit ne par l'assise'.

[267] On the royal system of taxation, see Riley-Smith, 'Government in Latin Syria and the Commercial Privileges of Foreign Merchants', p. 121.

[268] Jacoby, 'Montmusard, Suburb of Crusader Acre: The First Stage of its Development', pp. 205–17; Benvenisti, p. 112; Boas, pp. 41–2.

which for obvious reasons do not pay much attention to native city properties. One argument is that certain houses in Acre were not *borgesies* but properties specially set aside for habitation by non-Latins. Perhaps these were villeinage and their residents, like their rural counterparts, were attached to the properties with which they were sold. It is known that villeins lived in Nicosia[269] and traded in Acre,[270] and in the principality of Antioch in 1175, Bohemond III granted the Hospitallers 'in alms' a Syrian living in Jabala, named Bon Mosor, with his children and all his belongings, and a Jewish villein living in Laodicaea.[271] Villeins also lived in the cities of the kingdom of Jerusalem. A 'wealthy villein living in Nablus', for instance, was granted with all his properties to the Hospitallers sometime before 1154.[272] However, it is more probable that these houses were *borgesies* sub-leased by native Christians, Muslims and Jews on a temporary basis, and came under the jurisdiction of the *Cour de la Fonde*. As an inter-communal tribunal, the *Cour de la Fonde* could authorise a rental agreement between a Christian lessor and a non-Christian lessee. The general rule of the kingdom of Jerusalem was that Muslims and Jews could not purchase *borgesies*, and in Nicosia the laws of sale and purchase as practised in the *Cour des Bourgeois* disqualified those considered to be outside the 'Law of Rome' from possessing burgess property. Neither could they rent *borgesies* in perpetuity under terms of *encensive* as this type of tenancy entitled the lessee to right of sale of the property.[273] But this, notwithstanding, *borgesies* in Acre, Jerusalem and Nicosia could be leased temporarily by a tenant 'to whomever he wishes', under terms of *rente*.[274] Tenancy of this kind was agreed usually on a year-to-year basis. The lessee of *rente* property, as opposed to *encensive*, did not have right of alienation or inheritance, although in Acre as a temporary tenant he was protected against eviction by a lessor wishing to sell his house before completion of the period of tenancy.[275] In Nicosia a *rente* agreement was not a matter for the *Cour de Bourgeois* and as such could simply be drawn up in private before witnesses.[276] It is, therefore, not inconceivable that in terms of *rente* tenancy the law did not discriminate against Muslims and Jews. Ibn Jubayr's account of his travels in the kingdom in 1184 confirms this point. During a visit to Acre he remained in the city two days and leased a house from an indigenous Christian (*nasrani* as opposed to *ifranji* meaning Frank). The house was in the

269 'Livre contrefais', p. 259; 'Bans et ordonnances', p. 361.

270 'Livre contrefais', p. 179.

271 Delaville Le Roulx, *Les Archives*, no. 35, p. 121.

272 *RRH*, no. 293, p. 74.

273 'Livre contrefais', p. 254.

274 'Livre contrefais', pp. 287, 287–91.

275 Kausler, pp.115–16 (cf. Beugnot, 'Livre des assises', p. 71).

276 'Livre contrefais', p. 288: 'La tierce maniere de louage ce peut faire sans court et sans garens'. As I have argued, a sub-tenancy agreement could also take place in the High Court.

harbour area facing the sea.[277] This account is important for two reasons: first, it is further evidence that native Christians possessed city property which they were permitted to sub-lease; and, secondly, it is confirmation that Muslims could indeed lease property on a temporary basis.

Jurisdiction in the Italian Quarters

The following outlines the foundation of European merchant communities in the coastal cities of the kingdoms of Jerusalem and Cyprus. It is principally an inquiry into the legal status of men and women who resided in these quarters and the types of properties which they possessed. The term merchant communities describes generally settlers who originated from the coastal cities of Italy and France – including Amalfi, Ancona, Marseilles, Messina, Montpellier and Narbonne – but the most important commercial quarters were those of the Venetians, Pisans and Genoese in the royal cities of Acre and Tyre. Dependent on maritime trade and organised into close-knit communities, residents were subject to their own laws and customs and judged in their own courts of arbitration. The quarters were divided into *borgesies* although there may have existed, as in other parts of a city, properties which were legally defined as belonging to native non-Latin Christians. It is relevant to add that there probably existed no freehold tenure in the merchant communities, because all forms of property alienation were subject to the lord of the merchants' domain. Tenants were described as burgesses, swore an oath of loyalty to the commune and, according to the terms of their residency, were distinguished not only from native non-Latin Christians but also from other Europeans.

The creation of a merchant quarter was motivated by the commercial and jurisdictional needs of a city. Its boundaries were defined by the relationship of its residents to the overlord in whose domain their community was located.[278]

277 Muhammad Ibn Jubayr, *Rihlah*, ed. W. Wright (Leyden, 1852), p. 306.

278 See, in particular, M.-L., Favreau-Lilie, *Die Italiener im Heiligen Land: vom Ersten Kreuzzug bis zum Tode Heinrichs von Champagne (1098–1197)* (Amsterdam, 1989); D. Jacoby, 'The Venetian Privileges in the Latin Kingdom of Jerusalem: Twelfth and Thirteenth-Century Interpretations and Implementations', in B.Z. Kedar, J.S.C Riley-Smith and R. Hiestand (eds), *Montjoie: Studies in Honour of Hans Eberhard Mayer* (Aldershot, 1997), pp. 155–75, M.H. Chehab, *Tyr a l'epoque des croisades*: *Histoire sociale, economique et religeuse* (Paris, 1979). For evidence of the presence of smaller trading nations in Syria, Palestine, Cyprus and Cilician Armenia, see D. Abulafia, 'The Levant Trade of the Minor Cities in the Thirteenth and Fourteenth Centuries', in B.Z. Kedar and A.L. Udovich (eds), *The Medieval Levant. Studies in Memory of Eliyahu Ashtor* (Haifa, 1988), pp. 183–202; D. Abulafia, 'Crocuses and Crusaders: San Gimignano, Pisa and the Kingdom of Jerusalem', in B.Z. Kedar, H.E. Mayer and R.C. Smail (eds), *Outremer. Studies in the History of the Crusading Kingdom of Jerusalem Presented to Joshua Prawer*

Generally speaking, the courts of the merchant communities were authorised by the king or city lord to judge cases in all matters except high justice. In the Venetian quarters, the doge of Venice enjoyed jurisdiction over fief-holders and burgess tenants of property in his domain. And all residents swore to him an oath of fealty.[279] The doge enforced his own laws, and in the thirteenth century in their quarter in Beirut, the Venetians exercised jurisdiction 'according to the custom of Venice'.[280] The Genoese also enjoyed law-making powers. In their quarter in Acre legal cases were dealt with 'iuxta consuetudinem'.[281] And in King Henry I's general concessions to the Genoese in Cyprus (1232), they were permitted to judge cases 'secundum consuetudinem Ianue'.[282] It seems, therefore, that in some cases at least, the privileges granted the Italians as incentive to settle in the kingdom included rights to formulate laws in their quarters.

As a mark of their privileged status, merchant communities could be exempted from the services owing to the lord in whose domain their quarter was situated. In 1123, Patriarch William, acting on behalf of Baldwin II who was a captive of the Muslims, granted Dominico Michiel, the doge of Venice, a quarter in certain cities. In Acre the Venetians were 'free from all exactions', meaning that their quarter was service-exempt and held of the king in perpetuity.[283] The Venetians were further promised a quarter in Tyre if they helped in its capture.[284] The city was finally taken in 1124, but according to Baldwin II's concessions to the Venetians in 1125, they were required to provide some form of military service in return for their grant which constituted one-third of the city and its domain.[285] Concessions continued to be made to the Venetians in the latter decades of the twelfth century. In 1192, Conrad of Montferrat confirmed Venetian 'lands, possessions, fiefs (*honores*), liberties and courts', in Tyre and other cities.[286] In his report, written between 1242 and 1244, the *bailo* Marsiglio Zorzi gives details of the 'lands, possessions, *honores* and jurisdiction which the commune of Venice has in the city of Tyre and its districts'.[287] Other Italian communities were made similar concessions. In 1156, Baldwin III confirmed the concessions his predecessor Baldwin II had made to the Pisans, including the grant of 'five houses free from all tribute or returns in perpetuity with right of inheritance', and the freedom of

---

(Jerusalem, 1982), pp. 227–43; D. Jacoby, 'The Anconitan Privileges in the Kingdom of Jerusalem and the Levant Trade of Ancona', pp. 525–70.

279 Berggötz, pp. 141–2.

280 Tafel and Thomas, II, no. 262, p. 233.

281 Müller, no. 63, p. 440.

282 Puncuh, 1/2, no. 351, p. 180.

283 Tafel and Thomas, I, no. 40, p. 85.

284 Tafel and Thomas, I, no. 40, pp. 84–8; and the confirmation of the *pactum Warmundi* by Baldwin II in 1125 (I, no. 41, pp. 90–93).

285 Tafel and Thomas, I, no. 41, p. 93.

286 Tafel and Thomas, I, no. 76, p. 213.

287 Berggötz, p. 142.

alienation.[288] Baldwin III's concessions further added to this five carrucates of land near Tyre and an oven in the city. He also granted the Pisans a court over their properties and their nationals. In 1187, Conrad of Montferrat confirmed the right of the Pisans to a quarter in Tyre 'free from all tribute and exaction', and in this royal charter the community was described as a *honor* – as were their quarters in Jaffa and Acre[289] – a fief he had exempted from service, in other words a *franc fié*, also known as a *feudum honoratum*.[290] It was usually the case that a *franc fié*, like the *franc borgesie*, was conceded *pro bono servicio*, and the Pisans received their fief in Acre as reward for their help in the siege of Alexandria (1167),[291] while Conrad of Montferrat confirmed Pisan possessions in Tyre in return for their assistance in holding out against Saladin's forces (1187). The Genoese enjoyed similar privileges in 1104 when in return for their help in the capture of Antioch and Jerusalem, they received a street in Jerusalem and a third of Acre, Arsuf and Caesarea.[292] In 1187, it was also decided at a *parlement* held in Tyre, to concede to the Genoese a marketplace, houses and the right to establish a court over those living in their quarter in the city in return for their promise of military defence.[293] The Genoese seem to have been exempted from service for their fiefs. The communities of Marseilles, Montpellier, St Gilles and Barcelona, moreover, received a court 'in their *honores*' in Tyre from Conrad of Montferrat in 1187.[294] Although service-exemption was an incentive to settle, it was not necessarily the case that all merchant communities enjoyed this status.

Not much is known about the composition of the courts in the Italian lordships. The 'Livre de la Cour des Bourgeois' mentions only the Venetians, Genoese and Pisans as having their own courts in Acre exercising jurisdictional competence over their own citizens.[295] In a royal confirmation of 1156, Baldwin III granted the Pisans a court in their quarter in Tyre, and approved of a viscount who 'ought to judge Pisans in this court'.[296] Similarly, in a charter of 1187, Conrad of Montferrat granted the Pisans property in Jaffa when recaptured, and approved a viscount or consul 'pro regenda curia et eorum honore'.[297] With regard to the Genoese, William di Bulgaro and Simon Mallocello refer in their inventory to an 'old palace of the commune' in Acre where a court was regularly convened.[298] We know from

288 Müller, no. 5, p. 7.

289 Müller, no. 24, p. 29, and no. 32, p. 38.

290 Müller, no. 23, p. 27. For a discussion of the *feudum honoratum*, see Richardot, 'Francs-fiefs. Essai sur l'exemption totale ou partielle des services de fief', p. 229ff.

291 Müller, no. 11, p. 14.

292 Puncuh, nos 59–61, pp. 97–102.

293 Puncuh, no. 330, pp. 135–7.

294 H.E. Mayer, *Marseilles Levantehandel und ein Akkonensisches Fälscheratelier des 13. Jahrhunderts* (Tübingen, 1972), p. 182.

295 Kausler, pp.162–3 (cf. Beugnot, 'Livre des assises', pp. 100–101).

296 Müller, no. 5, p. 7. See also no. 31, p. 37.

297 Müller, no. 24, p. 29.

298 Desimoni, 'Quatre titres des propriétés des Génois à Acre et à Tyr', no. 2, p. 215.

a document of 1204 that a viscount presided over the Genoese court in Acre,[299] whilst in Tyre an officer known as a *capitaneus*, or a consul, fulfilled a similar jurisdictional role.[300] In an agreement between Philip of Montfort and the Genoese (1264) it was confirmed that the *capitaneus* or the consul had the authority to judge the Genoese in the court of the commune.[301]

The Venetian court in Acre was presided over by the *baiulus* or *baiulo* – first mentioned in Acre in 1187[302] – and his authority extended over lower *officiales regiminis* called *vicecomites*.[303] A *baiulus* or a *vicecomes* was head of the court in Tyre and the officer to whom jurors swore to make their judgements (*consilium*) in c. 1243.[304] According to the oath of fealty sworn by all tenants of the Venetian commune in Tyre, the *baiulus* was responsible for passing laws and exercising justice.[305] In a noteworthy case of 1283, the burgesses of the Venetian quarter in Beirut appealed against their *baiulus* whom they accused of abusing his position. It is not known what wrongs he had committed, but the *maggior consiglio* instructed the *baiulus* and *conscilliari* of Acre to investigate these accusations, and if they were found to be true to remove the man from his office. This demonstrates how representatives of burgesses in the Venetian quarter in Beirut were organised enough to appeal to the doge over matters of disagreement, especially when it was considered that the interests of the whole community were being undermined.

The *baiulus* was responsible for the lease of Venetian *borgesies* both inside and outside the boundaries of the quarter.[306] The officials of the *camera*, the chamberlains, were responsible for renting out the property of the commune and for collecting payments owed to the treasury. Others who were under the authority of the *baiulus* included a sergeant, a squire (*scutiferus*), an official notary and a *placierius* who besides policing duties was employed by the court and received one quarter of a besant for the transaction of each *borgesie*.[307] The treasure chest (*capsella*) was kept in the house of the *baiulus*, suggesting that like the royal seneschal, he fulfilled both a legal and financial role.[308] Moreover, just as a royal

[299] Müller, no. 63, p. 439.

[300] On the organisation of the Genoese commune in Tyre, M.H. Chehab, *Tyr a l'epoque des croisades*, pp. 220–22.

[301] Desimoni, 'Quatre titres des propriétés des Génois à Acre et à Tyr', no. 4, p. 226.

[302] D. Jacoby, 'The Venetian Privileges in the Latin Kingdom of Jerusalem: Twelfth and Thirteenth-Century Interpretations', p. 163; D. Jacoby, 'Conrad Marquis of Montferrat and the Kingdom of Jerusalem (1187–1192)', in L. Balleto (ed.), *Atti del Congresso Internazionale 'dai Feudi Montferrini e dal Piemonte ai Nuovi Mondi Oltre gli Oceani'*, (Alessandria, 1993), pp. 216, 224.

[303] Cessi, II, p. 357.

[304] On the governance and organisation of the Venetian communes, Chehab, *Tyr a l'epoque des croisades*, pp. 186–97.

[305] Berggötz, p. 141.

[306] Cessi, II, p. 357.

[307] Berggötz, p.142.

[308] Cessi, II, p. 357.

viscount was expected to appear in an ecclesiastical court whenever a burgess of the king was in dispute with a churchman, the *baiulus* represented Venetian interests outside the scope of his jurisdiction. His role as representative of the commune was demonstrated in 1290 in Acre, when a dispute arose between the Venetians and the order of St John over the possession of certain *borgesies*. The Hospitallers had purchased the houses – already church properties under the jurisdiction of the bishop of Acre – from the descendants of a man called Paul David. The dispute arose out of Venetian concern over the military threat that these houses being fortified by the Hospitallers posed. In the court of the bishop it was agreed that the order would sell the houses to the patriarch of Jerusalem, and in return the Venetians, represented by the *baiulus*, Nicholas Quirini de St Juliano, and the *conscilliari*, Henry Ferri and Johannes Barbarini, would give the patriarch 1000 besants to assist with the purchase.[309]

Further information can be gleaned from the sources that the Italian courts, like the royal or seigneurial *Cours des Bourgeois*, were made up of burgess *jurati*. A document of 1204, concerning the disputed tenancy of a *borgesie* in the Genoese quarter, makes reference to the *iurati curiae* of the Genoese in Acre, and gives the names of four *jurati*: Otto Fulcher, Jacob de Angla, Obertus Astalibeta and Jacob de Roduan;[310] a possible descendant of the latter appears in an inventory of Genoese possessions in Acre (1249) as a tenant of a *borgesie* in the quarter.[311] The jurors of the Venetian court were also described as *jurati* in Marsiglio Zorzi's inventory, and were required to swear an oath of office which according to the text had long been established, and was like that sworn by their counterparts in the royal *Cour des Bourgeois* of Nicosia. These men, who were knowledgeable of law and custom, promised to maintain the confidentiality of the court, to make fair and honest judgements 'according to the custom of the land', to deal with claim (*clamor*) and response (*responsum*), and to set precedent in cases not covered by law.[312]

What though was the jurisdictional competence of Italian burgess courts? In Acre in 1123, the Venetians were conceded the basic right of 'justice and taxation over all burgesses living in the quarter and the houses of the Venetians (outside the quarter)'.[313] The court had authority over all Venetians resident in the quarter in matters pertaining to the burgess laws of the commune which were outside the scope of royal jurisdiction. It heard cases concerning Venetians and others with the exception that when a Venetian brought a case against a non-Venetian the matter

---

309 Delaville Le Roulx, *Cartulaire général*, no. 4084, pp. 556–7.

310 Müller, no. 63, pp. 439–440.

311 Desimoni, 'Quatre titres des propriétés des Génois à Acre et à Tyr', no. 2, p. 220.

312 Berggötz, p. 141. See 'Livre contrefais', pp. 237–8.

313 Tafel and Thomas, I, no. 40, p. 88 and no. 41, p. 92. See Jacoby, 'The Venetian Privileges in the Latin Kingdom: Twelfth and Thirteenth-Century Interpretations and Implementations', p.164. On general aspects of Italian jurisdiction inside and outside their quarters, Richard, *The Kingdom of Jerusalem*, pp. 272–4; Mayer, *The Crusades*, pp. 180–82.

was heard in the royal *Cour des Bourgeois*.[314] In the Venetian quarter in Tyre, the *curia*, which judged commercial matters, also collected the taxes it was due both from burgesses and non-Latins, and in so doing adopted the financial practices of the *Cour des Bourgeois* which itself had adopted some practices of pre-existing Muslim administration.[315] Marsiglio Zorzi complained that pork butchers in the Venetian quarter had been compelled to pay *tuazo* to the royal *Cour des Bourgeois*. This had now ceased to be the case although the Venetian court continued to levy the tax.[316] Significantly, sometime after 1225, the court of the Venetians had gained jurisdiction over 'Syrians and all others who live' in the quarter. Furthermore, it was to the Venetian court that the Jews were subject, and every Jewish male over the age of fifteen was obliged to pay the court a poll tax of one besant a year; nine persons are named as being of this age or over.[317] Evidently, the court's authority like that of the *Cour des Bourgeois* was wide-ranging, inasmuch as it exercised jurisdiction over native Christians and non-Christians living in its quarter.

It was generally the case that when a king or a lord granted a merchant community jurisdiction over its inhabitants, he reserved to his *Cour des Bourgeois* justice over offences punishable by loss of life or limb.[318] There were exceptions. In 1264, Philip of Montfort, lord of Tyre, permitted the Genoese a criminal court over citizens in their quarter in the city, defining high justice as 'penalty of blood' including the right to pillory and to flog,[319] and in 1277, John of Montfort conceded the Venetians the right to administer criminal as well as civil justice in their quarter[320] – it is unlikely that the Venetians had been granted high justice either in Acre or Tyre in the concession of 1123.[321] When Conrad of Montferrat granted Marseilles, Montpellier, St Gilles and Barcelona each a court in their quarter in Tyre (1187), high justice, which he reserved to the royal *Cour des Bourgeois*, was described as jurisdiction over criminal assault resulting in the spilling of blood.[322] In Acre in the thirteenth century, the Venetians, Genoese and Pisans were not permitted *cort de sanc* in matters of *cop aparant*, murder, larceny, treason and heresy, all cases which came under the royal *Cour des Bourgeois*.[323]

---

314 Tafel and Thomas, I, no. 40, p. 87.

315 J.S.C. Riley-Smith, 'The Survival in Latin Palestine of Muslim Administration', in P.M. Holt (ed.), *The Eastern Mediterranean Lands in the Period of the Crusades* (Warminster, 1977), pp. 12–13.

316 Berggötz, p. 141.

317 Berggötz, p. 140.

318 Müller, no. 11, p. 14; Mayer, *Marseilles*, p. 182 and pp. 185–6; Richard, *The Kingdom of Jerusalem*, pp. 272–3.

319 Desimoni, 'Quatre titres des propriétés des Génois à Acre et à Tyr', no. 4, p. 226.

320 Tafel and Thomas, III, no. 369, p. 152.

321 Jacoby, 'The Venetian Privileges in the Latin Kingdom of Jerusalem: Twelfth and Thirteenth-Century Interpretations and Implementations', p. 159.

322 Mayer, *Marseilles*, p.182.

323 Kausler, pp.162–3 (Beugnot, 'Livre des assises', p. 101).

Indeed, it is possible a burgess would have stood trial in the court of his quarter, before being turned over to the lord for him to administer corporal or capital punishment. Philip of Montfort, for instance, stipulated that non-Genoese living in the Genoese quarter should be first judged in the court of the Genoese, and if found guilty of a crime and sentenced to death or mutilation, they should be turned over to the lord of the domain for him to administer punishment.[324] Admittedly, this rule only applied in cases involving subjects of the lord, but in more general terms, Conrad of Montferrat granted the Genoese in 1190 jurisdiction in their quarter in Tyre except in criminal cases, but stated that anyone accused of committing a crime should first be judged in the court of the Genoese before being turned over to the royal *Cour des Bourgeois* for punishment.[325]

The Genoese consul in Tyre was though representative of the whole Genoese community irrespective of whether its members lived inside a quarter or were tenants of the king. Their legal status was recognised in spite of the fact that their property came under the jurisdictional authority of the city's *Cour des Bourgeois*. In 1211, for instance, the consuls Jacobus de Marino and Lanfrancus de Mari appeared as witnesses to a dispute between the Teutonic Order and Martin Rozia, who in 1189 had been conceded a *franc borgesie* in Tyre by Conrad of Montferrat.[326] By 1211 the house had been given to the order 'in alms', but was being reclaimed by Martin Rozia. As the property had passed under ecclesiastical jurisdiction the disputing parties came before the patriarch in Acre in an effort to find a resolution. Interestingly, the case was not heard in the court of the archbishop of Tyre. The Teutonic Order was exempted from his authority, being under papal jurisdiction, and the patriarch heard the case as papal legate. It was agreed that Martin Rozia would no longer challenge the right of the order to possess the property, and the knights would in return pay him sixty besants. The Genoese consuls were there as witnesses to approve and confirm the agreement.[327]

The Italian burgess court, finally, may be compared to the *Cour des Bourgeois* in terms of its jurisdiction over the transfer of *borgesies*. The Italian *borgesie* was a similarly alienable and hereditary property which if changed hands required legal consent. The court conferred legitimacy and permanency on a transaction, as typified in 1266 when Matteo Marmora sold his house in the Venetian quarter in Acre to the Hospitallers in the presence of the *bailo* Michael Doro.[328] In Tyre it was 'custom' that the purchase of a house in the Venetian quarter take place in the

324 Desimoni, 'Quatre Titres des Propriétés des Génois à Acre et à Tyr', no. 4, p. 226. As far as heresy was concerned, it may be assumed that the royal court reserved the right to judge whether a man should stand trial for it in an ecclesiastical court.

325 Puncuh, 1/2, no. 331, pp.137–40.

326 Strehlke, no. 24, pp. 21–2.

327 Strehlke, no. 45, pp. 36–7.

328 Delaville Le Roulx, *Cartulaire général*, no. 3207, p. 132; Jacoby, 'L'Expansion occidentale dans le Levant', p. 229.

court which received from the purchaser three besants in sales tax.[329] The Genoese court fulfilled a similar role legitimising the transactions of *borgesies* and guaranteeing the terms of tenancy. In a dispute of 1204, Agnes Gastaldi, tenant of a house in the Genoese quarter in Acre, had sold part of her property to Lucensis wife of Bartholemew de Dominis 'without permission of the viscount and of his jurors'. The Genoese viewed this unauthorised sale as a blatant violation of their jurisdictional rights over the *borgesie*. The procedure of sale did not differ to that in the royal *Cour des Bourgeois* of Acre, and Agnes, 'just as other burgesses', was obliged to appear before the viscount and jurors of the community when wishing to transfer seisin of part of her *borgesie* to Lucensis. Agnes, who leased the property *ad censum*, repudiated any legal obligations claimed by the Genoese, since she argued that they had had no jurisdiction over her house for a long time. She also maintained that the Genoese constituted *seigneur de l'encensive* but not *seigneur justicier*. Had she, therefore, sought the consent of the royal *Cour des Bourgeois* when selling her house? The dispute was eventually resolved and Genoese jurisdiction over the *borgesie* vindicated. The sale was approved and the property divided between the two tenants; Agnes owed *cens* of nine and a half besants a year and Lucensis half a besant. The condition of this agreement was that Agnes would recognise the jurisdiction of the Genoese court over her tenancy.[330] This type of dispute is unique in the charters, but in view of the general disagreements that may have arisen over whether certain properties fell within the boundaries of European merchants' quarters and the authority of their courts, it was probably not uncommon in the twelfth and thirteenth centuries.

---

[329] Berggötz, p. 142.

[330] Müller, no. 63, pp. 439–40.

Chapter 5

Church Courts

In this chapter, I propose to look beyond purely secular Frankish legislation and jurisdiction. There is reason to believe that ecclesiastical institutions played a vital role in defining the status of *burgenses* and in shaping the terms of *borgesie* tenure. In the history of the kingdom the Church's influence was constant. In the eleventh century it had preached to non-feudatories the ideals of armed pilgrimage and remission of the sins of participants. On the First Crusade, at a time when Christian suffering could be interpreted as God's punishment for men's immorality, Church leaders helped establish a court to judge acts of impiety. And in the first decades of Frankish settlement, at assemblies such as the one held at Nablus in 1120, churchmen dispensed canons regarding various matters including marriage and miscegenation, for general application in the secular and ecclesiastical courts of the kingdom. In these early years the Church was instrumental in defining the rules under which Europeans were to live and work alongside indigenous Syrians, laying down the principle that Latin Christians were superior to all other religious communities. In its efforts to reinforce the ideals of a middle class composed of Latin Christians with legal privileges and property rights, the Church hoped to encourage the conversion of non-Latin natives to the Catholic faith. From the early existence of the kingdom, moreover, ecclesiastical institutions became wealthy and powerful landowners. Churchmen, such as the bishop of Lydda, were *seigneurs justiciers* who issued laws over burgesses living in their domains and had their own *Cours des Bourgeois*. There is reason to believe even, that in the context of burgess jurisdiction, the authority of churchmen extended beyond secular burgess courts. The intention of the following discussion is to demonstrate how the competence of Church courts over burgesses and *borgesies* in the cities and the Latin rural settlements went beyond the parameters of purely ecclesiastical jurisdiction. These judicial bodies helped uphold burgess written laws and unwritten customs. Richard and others who proposed the theory that in every city and village in the kingdom where there existed a Frankish population there was established a *Cour des Bourgeois*,[1] did not acknowledge sufficiently the influence of Church courts.

In order to understand precisely the system of jurisdiction in the kingdoms of Jerusalem and Cyprus, it is necessary to examine the competence of Church courts. A bishop's court heard all cases of canon law involving burgesses in his diocese. And when *borgesies* were conceded to an ecclesiastical institution 'in alms', issues

1 Richard, *The Latin Kingdom of Jerusalem*, p. 127; La Monte, *Feudal Monarchy*, pp. 104–105.

relating to the properties as a whole were subject to the bishop's court in whose diocese they were located. A bishop also dealt with the secular issues in his diocese regarding properties given to the Church 'in alms'. In some cases, however, ecclesiastical institutions created special courts to deal with issues concerning tenants in their *borgesies*. The patriarch of Jerusalem, for example, had a secular court to deal with the cases concerning tenants of *borgesies* in his lordship. The patriarch's lordship was situated in the north-west of the city, with at its centre the church of the Holy Sepulchre. Its boundaries ran along the western and northern walls of Jerusalem and the street stretching from David's Gate to St Stephen's Gate. The ecclesiastical quarter had been granted to the Church 'in alms' by Godfrey of Bouillon, and thus the patriarch, unlike the bishops of Nazareth and Lydda, was neither subject to the High Court nor burdened by any service other than prayers for his benefactor. The patriarch does not appear in John of Ibelin's list of persons required to furnish a contingent of knights to the kingdom's army, which further explains why John did not include the ecclesiastical quarter in his list of lordships.

The patriarch stood over the whole judicature, although in his absence the prior of the church had authority in the diocese.[2] In the lordship the *curia patriarchae*, which was composed of churchmen and burgesses, exercised secular jurisdiction over the tenants of *borgesies* located within the ecclesiastical quarter. In terms of approving the transfer of property or endorsing the permanency of an alienation or a donation, the court of the patriarch functioned in a similar way to the royal *Cour des Bourgeois* of the city. For instance, when in 1137 Patriarch William approved the sale of a house in his lordship to Robert Medicus, the transaction was witnessed by the court of the patriarch to whom Robert was to pay one besant a year in rent.[3] The sale, subsequently, of the same property to the Hospitallers in 1167, was sanctioned by a court composed of two canons of the Holy Sepulchre and eleven burgesses including Geoffrey of Tours, the patriarch's seneschal.[4] In his capacity as head of the court and representative of the patriarch, the *seigneur justicier*, the standing of the seneschal seems to have resembled that of a royal viscount. Appointment to the patriarchal seneschalcy, however, was not made exclusively from the class of feudatories. Burgesses could aspire to this highest office, in the same way that non-nobles acted as *judices* in secular burgess courts, or as *baillis* in *Cours de la Fonde*. The career of Geoffrey of Tours demonstrates how a juror of the royal *Cour des Bourgeois* could serve at the same time as a seneschal in the *curia patriarchae*. Geoffrey first appears in a confirmation of Baldwin III among the list of burgess witnesses (1155).[5] In 1158, he was a 'burgess of the king'.[6] By 1167, he was 'seneschal of the lord Patriarch Amalric' and of the *curia patriarchae*

2 Bresc-Bautier, no. 150, p. 296.

3 Delaville Le Roulx, *Les Archives*, no. 5, pp. 73–4.

4 Delaville Le Roulx, *Les Archives*, no. 25, pp. 107–108.

5 Bresc-Bautier, no. 41, p. 115.

6 Bresc-Bautier, no. 47, p. 131. See also no. 51, p. 138.

when authorising the sale and exchange of certain houses and land in the lordship to the order of St John.[7] Significantly, Geoffrey's acceptance of the seneschalcy did not disqualify him from remaining a juror of the royal *Cour des Bourgeois*. In 1163 and 1175, he was a juror of the court authorising the sale of land in the city to the Hospitallers and the purchase of houses and vineyards in the Frankish village of Casale Sancti Egidii by the Holy Sepulchre.[8] Also in 1175, he was one of fourteen jurors, the *jurati civitatis*, granting permission to Peter de Caors to sell houses and land to his brother Clarembald.[9] Evidence that he retained the patriarchal seneschalcy until at least 1177 is found in a charter of that year.[10] Previously, in c.1169, he had appeared as seneschal along with Guido de Beteras, a knight, and nine jurors of the royal *Cour des Bourgeois*, to witness the confirmation of houses belonging to Bonus Johanus.[11]

Some of the burgesses who appeared as witnesses in the court of the patriarch were also jurors in the royal *Cour des Bourgeois*. William Norman was a witness in the patriarchal court when Patriarch Amalric conceded to the Hospitallers the lease of certain houses in his lordship (1167).[12] Previously, his name appeared in a charter of 1158 among those of the *burgenses regis*,[13] while in 1163 he was a juror of the royal *Cour des Bourgeois*.[14] Lambert the money-changer was a witness in the patriarchal court in 1167 and in 1163 and 1179 he was a juror in the royal court of burgesses.[15] Peter of Perigueux was a member of the royal court in 1149, and often appeared in the ecclesiastical court to witness transactions involving the Church of the Holy Sepulchre.[16] This degree of interdependence is not only illustrative of the duties of jurors in both courts, it is also indicative of parallel developments in the royal and patriarchal systems of justice which enabled jurors to serve in both. The procedure for alienating *borgesies* seems, from the documentary evidence, to have been similar in the two courts.[17] It was probably the case that the *curia patriarchae* made use of the customs of the royal *Cour des Bourgeois*, and vice versa, to deal with matters such as tenancy.

---

7 Bresc-Bautier, no. 88, p. 202; Delaville Le Roulx, *Les Archives*, no. 25, p. 108, no. 26, p. 109.

8 Bresc-Bautier, no. 160, pp. 311–12; Delaville Le Roulx, *Cartulaire général*, no. 312, p. 226.

9 Delaville Le Roulx, *Les Archives*, no. 34, p. 120.

10 Bresc-Bautier, no. 162, p. 315.

11 Delaborde, no.3, pp. 185–6.

12 Delaville Le Roulx, *Les Archives*, no. 25, p. 108.

13 Bresc-Bautier, no. 51, p. 138.

14 *RRH*, no. 391, p. 103.

15 Delaville Le Roulx, *Cartulaire général*, no. 312, p. 226 and no. 554, p. 376.

16 Bresc-Bautier, no. 35, p. 103, no. 41, pp. 114–15, no. 46, p. 129, no. 50, p. 136, no. 102, p. 222, no. 110, p. 231, no. 117, p. 239, no. 124, p. 251.

17 Compare, for example, alienation of *borgesies* in the patriarch's lordship (Delaville Le Roulx, *Les Archives*, no. 5, pp. 73–4 and no. 25, pp. 107–108) with alienation in the royal *Cour des Bourgeois* (Delaville Le Roulx, *Les Archives*, no. 34, pp. 119–21).

A question which arises with regard to the ecclesiastical lordship in Jerusalem relates to the extent of the jurisdictional competence of its patriarchal court. Of course it had authority over the property of tenants within its domain, but how did it resolve cases of high justice? It is possible that any person caught committing a criminal offence in the patriarch's lordship was sent to the royal *Cour des Bourgeois* to be sentenced and punished. [18] Alternatively, the patriarchal court may have sentenced a burgess before turning him over to the *Cour des Bourgeois* for punishment. The Council of Nablus in 1120, laid down the basic rules of secular and ecclesiastical jurisdiction, and in the decree concerning sodomy, it was stipulated that if a man was found guilty by a Church court and sentenced to burn, he had to be turned over to a secular court for punishment.[19] Perhaps the jurisdictional framework of the papal state serves as a relevant model. The pope claimed powers of civil and criminal jurisdiction over his subjects which were exercised on his behalf by court officials he appointed.[20] It may be argued, therefore, that the patriarch in Jerusalem could have exercised criminal justice in his lordship through his secular officials.

Jurisdictional Competence of Church Courts

The system of justice in the kingdoms of Jerusalem and Cyprus differentiated between secular and ecclesiastical law. The king, his lords, the Church and the courts were agreed as to the parameters of ecclesiastical jurisdiction. Cases of heresy, sodomy, marriage, adultery, usury, simony and illegitimacy were always heard in a Church court. At the Council of Nablus it was agreed that the Church could judge in its courts clergymen who committed heresy as well as Christians accused of adultery, sodomy or marriage to Muslims.[21] Accordingly, the *Cour des Bourgeois* in Acre was obliged to send before the bishop's court any cases of heresy.[22] In terms of community property law, the *Cour des Bourgeois* could not fine a husband for committing an offence against his wife or vice versa, because

---

18 See, for instance, Kedar, 'On the Origins of the Earliest Laws of Frankish Jerusalem', 'appendix', p. 334.

19 Kedar, 'On the Origins of the Earliest Laws of Frankish Jerusalem', 'appendix', p. 334. See also Kausler, pp. 53–4 (cf. Beugnot, 'Livre des assises', pp. 27–8).

20 D. Waley, *The Papal State in the Thirteenth Century* (London, 1961), p. 75; T.F. X. Noble, *The Republic of St Peter: The Birth of the Papal State, 680–825* (Philadelphia, 1984), pp. 236–7: 'During the eighth century virtually all civil jurisdiction seems to have passed into the courts of the Church'. Beneath the pope 'were civil and criminal judges and other court officers'.

21 Kedar, 'On the Origins of the Earliest Laws of Frankish Jerusalem', 'appendix', pp. 333–4; Mayer, *The Crusades*, pp. 74–5; Richard, *The Latin Kingdom of Jerusalem*, p. 107.

22 Kausler, p. 343 (cf. Beugnot, 'Livre des assises', p. 219); Richard, *The Latin Kingdom of Jerusalem*, p. 107.

their possessions were owned jointly. It was left to a Church court to make judgement. In other cases of matrimony, where the jurisdictional competence of the *Cour des Bourgeois* and the Church overlapped, it was expected that the viscount and jurors of the court of burgesses would be present in the ecclesiastical court for the trial.[23] As the Church had also a right to levy tithes on the revenue of rural properties, disputes concerning the collection of this tax were heard in ecclesiastical courts.[24] Dowry was also a matter for Church jurisdiction. In 1135, in the court of the patriarch, Maria of Bethany gave her consent to her first husband's gift of dowry to her daughter and son-in-law Bernard. She had initially objected to this dowry of 100 besants (this may have been a *dos profecticia*, so described when given by a bride's parent), although her disapproval may have been because as the widow she believed this money to be part of her dower. Her husband also bequeathed to his daughter the share of a house in Jerusalem. It was agreed that this share of the property would not pass into the hands of Bernard until after the death of Maria, her husband and their son. The terms of this agreement were witnessed by the patriarch in the presence of viscount Anschetinus and two jurors of the royal *Cour des Bourgeois*, Rainald de Pontibus and Gaufridus Acus. The house concerned was under the jurisdiction of the *Cour des Bourgeois*, but as the dispute was over a will and a dowry resolution was reached in the court of the patriarch.[25]

A secular *Cour des Bourgeois* did not have jurisdiction over *borgesies* granted to the Church 'in alms'. The tenants of these *borgesies* were subject to the jurisdiction of a Church court as regards their properties, but in other civil and criminal matters not relating to the tenements, including high justice, they remained subject to a *Cour des Bourgeois*. The donors of an eleemosynary gift required first the permission of a *Cour des Bourgeois*,[26] and in Nicosia the right of the king to authorise eleemosynary grants was reinforced in a law issued by Henry II in May 1305.[27] There was obviously concern at the number of *borgesies* passing out of secular justice and a need to regulate more closely the conveyance of property. By comparison to an eleemosynary grant, the donor of a *post obit* gift or a deferred donation – which delayed the transfer of a *borgesie* to the Church – retained possession of his property in his lifetime and the court of burgesses had jurisdiction, but after his death the property passed under Church jurisdiction. The bequest, furthermore, of a property located in secular domain to the Church was subject to an ecclesiastical court and witnessed by the viscount.[28] For example, the will of Bernard of Béziers and his wife Ahoys was drawn up in the court of the

---

23 Kausler, pp. 196–7 (cf. Beugnot, 'Livre des assises', p. 121).

24 Ellenblum, *Frankish Rural Settlement*, pp. 145–56; Strehlke, no. 112, pp. 91–4.

25 Bresc-Bautier, no. 102, pp. 220–22.

26 'Livre contrefais', p. 269.

27 'Bans et ordonnances', p. 366.

28 'La Clef des assises de la Haute Cour du Royaume de Jérusalem et de Chypre', in *RHC Lois*, I, p. 579.

patriarch in c. 1130. Bernard promised to leave his house to the canons of the Holy Sepulchre on the condition that if either he or his wife died, the remaining spouse could enter the confraternity of the Church while retaining a third of the house. A final third of the *borgesie* belonged to their daughter for her lifetime. The testament was witnessed by viscount Anschetinus, first, to signify that the bequest of the property had required the permission of the *Cour des Bourgeois*, and secondly, to recognise the *borgesie* would remain under the jurisdiction of the burgess court until Bernard, his wife and their daughter were deceased. Once the canons inherited the house it would become subject to ecclesiastical jurisdiction.[29] This example demonstrates that in Jerusalem when a *borgesie* was granted to an ecclesiastical institution 'in alms', the patriarch's court had authority over cases relating to the property as a whole.

A Church court functioned in much the same way as a *Cour des Bourgeois* when leasing property. The status of the *borgesie* and the discernible features which set it apart from other types of property did not alter once it passed into Church possession. A *borgesie* was subject to the same basic customs of tenancy as those of the domain in which it had been located. An important function of an ecclesiastical court was to legitimise the transfer of property to its tenants. When in 1242 the bishop of Acre leased to the Teutonic Order in perpetuity two gardens close to the city for seventy-five besants a year, he promised to defend and guarantee the legitimacy of the lease 'according to the custom of the city of Acre'. In other words, in spite of the different secular and ecclesiastical courts which existed in the city, basic rules of tenancy were enforced uniformly. The legal procedure accompanying the transfer took place in the episcopal court, and as it was Church property the consent of the king was not required.[30] In 1239, when the Church of Mount Sion leased to the Teutonic Order a piece of land for twenty besants a year, the terms of the leasehold were agreed in the court of the bishop of Acre in whose diocese the property was located, and the Church of Mount Sion was committed to defend the agreement according to the custom of Acre.[31]

Ecclesiastical jurisdiction was of course not confined to the cities. In the thirteenth century the village *borgesie* of Saphoria passed into the possession of the archbishop of Nazareth. It had been subject to the royal *Cour des Bourgeois*, and in c.1155, the Church of the Holy Sepulchre had leased the property from the king.[32] But since then it must have been granted to the Church 'in alms'. In 1255, Henry, the archbishop of Nazareth, leased Madius de Marino, a Pisan of Acre, two carrucates of land and two small buildings described as *borgesies* in Saphoria, as well as a house and some land in Nazareth. Rather than lease the whole village as a *borgesie*, individual holdings were instead rented out. The lease was drawn up in

---

29 Bresc-Bautier, no. 98, pp. 215–16. See also no. 97, pp. 214–15.

30 Strehlke, no. 91, pp. 72–3.

31 Strehlke, no. 86, pp. 68–9.

32 Bresc-Bautier, no. 130, pp. 256–7.

the court of the archbishop in whose diocese and jurisdiction Saphoria was now located.[33]

The military orders, and in particular the order of St John, acquired most of their lands by eleemosynary grants, and in the thirteenth century the Hospitallers, being exempt, enjoyed a degree of freedom from episcopal authority. But did this mean that because of its privilege of exemption the tenants of the order of St John were exempt from the authority of the episcopal courts?[34] In Bethgibelin the Hospitallers exercised *justicia*, this being the right to create a secular court to deal with the cases involving tenants of their *borgesies*.[35] There are examples of the Hospitallers witnessing the lease of their *borgesies*. In 1173, the order leased to Arionus Jacobinus a house and a plot of land in Jerusalem for four besants a year reserving for itself right of pre-emption.[36] And in 1219, the order leased to Guy de Ronay a house in Acre for four besants a year.[37] In the witness lists are included the names of the brethren of the order, to which in the charter of 1173 are added the names of three lay men. A document of 1175 sheds further light on the secular jurisdiction exercised by the order of St John over tenants of its *borgesies*. In an exchange of properties between Patriarch Amalric and the order, it was stated that the order held *borgesies* in Jerusalem 'cum omni justicia que super his (properties) ad eos pertinebat'.[38] In fact, the exemption from episcopal courts applied also both to the Teutonic Order and the Church of the Holy Sepulchre. It was pointed out previously that when in 1211 a dispute arose between the order and Martin Rozia over the possession of a house in Tyre it had received 'in alms', the case was not heard in the court of the archbishop of the city because the order was exempted from his authority. The order was under papal jurisdiction and the patriarch heard the case as papal legate. Finally, I would highlight the distinction which was made between the jurisdictional authority of the patriarch and of the Holy Sepulchre. On the one hand, the canons played a part in the patriarchal court overseeing his lordship, and on the other, they had jurisdiction over their own properties both in the cities and in rural settlements such as Magna Mahumeria.

Jurisdiction in Latin Villes Neuves under Ecclesiastical Control

John of Ibelin does not mention in his list those villages in the kingdom which did not have a *Cour des Bourgeois* but were under the jurisdiction of a Church court.

---

33 E.G. Rey (ed.), *Recherches géographiques et historiques sur la domination des latins en Orient* (Paris, 1877), pp. 36–8.

34 Riley-Smith, *The Knights of St John*, pp. 75, 378.

35 Delaville Le Roulx, *Cartulaire général*, no. 399, p. 273; Hamilton, *The Latin Church*, p. 106.

36 Delaville Le Roulx, *Cartulaire général*, no. 450, pp. 311–12.

37 Delaville Le Roulx, *Cartulaire général*, no. 1656, pp. 261–2.

38 Delaville Le Roulx, *Cartulaire général*, no. 483, pp. 332–3.

Their existence may, however, be proven. The following discussion focuses attention on available evidence regarding the composition and function of the secular courts of a number of Latin rural villages under ecclesiastical control. This legal phenomenon should be considered as a significant aspect of the overall process of Latin settlement in the rural territories of Palestine and Syria. The Church court had authority over the tenancy of property and even judged certain criminal cases which, in principle, were outside the parameters of ecclesiastical justice. This legal assembly was made up of churchmen – although burgesses are also known to have been members – who were knowledgeable of common law and custom. It was a court which was endorsed by the local lord and bishop, and afforded the ecclesiastical institution concerned jurisdictional autonomy and control over its tenants. To explain more fully, when a village was conceded to an ecclesiastical institution 'in alms', cases relating to the ownership of the village as a whole were subject to the bishop's court in whose diocese it was situated. However, ecclesiastical institutions such as the Church of the Holy Sepulchre and the order of St John, who were granted settlements 'in alms', also set up secular courts with jurisdiction over their tenants, alongside the diocesan court which dealt with cases of Church law involving settlers, such as heresy, marriage and illegitimacy.

Magna Mahumeria (al-Bira)

The charters concerning Latin Christian settlement in Magna Mahumeria in the twelfth century, provide evidence of the existence of a Church secular court in this village. It is known that Godfrey of Bouillon granted the Church of the Holy Sepulchre twenty-one *casalia* 'in alms' which meant that, henceforth, the indigenous villages became subject to ecclesiastical jurisdiction.[39] This gift was confirmed by Baldwin I in 1114 following the request of Arnulf of Chocques, patriarch of Jerusalem.[40] And Baldwin III's confirmation in 1155 was made in the form of an eleemosynary donation: 'pro salute mea et meorum, tam vivorum quam defunctorum'.[41]

A document of 1168 records that the Holy Sepulchre settled the *casalia* of Magna Mahumeria – a settlement located sixteen kilometres north of Jerusalem – Parva Mahumeria and Bethsuri – both located north-west of Jerusalem – with burgesses, and as they grew in size and population the settlements came to be described as *villae*.[42] In 1168, furthermore, Amalric of Nesle, the patriarch of Jerusalem, confirmed that the canons of the Holy Sepulchre in Magna Mahumeria

---

39 Bresc-Bautier, no. 26, p. 87; Ellenblum, *Frankish Rural Settlement*, pp. 73–7.

40 Bresc-Bautier, no. 26, p. 87. Further royal confirmations followed in 1155, 1160 and 1164 (no. 42, p. 116, no. 45, p. 125 and no. 135, pp. 262–3).

41 Bresc-Bautier, no. 42, p. 116.

42 Bresc-Bautier, no. 150, p. 295.

possessed 'a church, entire jurisdiction and parish rights'.[43] What we understand from this is that the canons could exercise jurisdiction over tenants of *borgesies* within their village. The court of the Holy Sepulchre was composed of the prior, sub prior and canons of the Church in Jerusalem, together with the 'men of Mahumeria', these being burgesses who lived in the village.[44] In a charter of c.1158, the lease of vineyards to new settlers was witnessed by the court of canons and eight burgesses of the village.[45] However, judging from other witness lists, burgesses did not have to be present in court when *borgesies* were being alienated. When Robert Porcher, a canon of the Church, gave 'in alms' houses and land in the village, the *curia* approving the benefaction consisted solely of the canons of the Holy Sepulchre.[46] Similarly, the canons alone witnessed the sale of a house in 1160.[47] The court was just as valid without the attendance of burgesses.

Reinforcing the idea that this special court of the Holy Sepulchre was secular in character but composed primarily of churchmen, the *dispensator*, who was a canon, sat as a witness[48] and, according to one charter, determined where the *curia Sancti Sepulcri* should assemble in the village.[49] There is evidence in fact to suggest the *dispensator* – an official in western Europe employed as a steward or a bursar of a bishop in his diocese[50] – fulfilled a similar role managing ecclesiastical property elsewhere in the kingdom,[51] including responsibility for the collection of tithe and the issuing of fines against negligent farmers.[52] This court was, it seems, the hub of the community in Magna Mahumeria, in much the same way that a *domus*, whose existence has been identified in other Latin villages, was the centre of Church administration.[53] The court administered the land and judged all cases in the village pertaining to its jurisdiction. Importantly, the nature of this evidence disproves the argument that there existed a purely secular *Cour des Bourgeois* in Magna Mahumeria. Apart from information regarding the 'entire jurisdiction' of the court of the Holy Sepulchre,[54] there is little evidence to suggest a *Cour des Bourgeois* was established in the village. The 'curie Sancti Sepulcri de Mahumeria',[55] which was composed of clergy as well as burgesses, could not

---

43 Bresc-Bautier, no. 150, p. 295.

44 Bresc-Bautier, no. 123, p. 250.

45 Bresc-Bautier, no. 123, pp. 249–50. Experienced jurors are even known to have served in the royal *Cour des Bourgeois* of Jerusalem; Bresc-Bautier, no. 130, p. 257 and no. 160, p. 312.

46 Bresc-Bautier, no. 115, pp. 235–6. The gift was later confirmed, no.121, p. 246.

47 Bresc-Bautier, 125, pp. 251–2.

48 Bresc-Bautier, no. 123, p. 250.

49 Bresc-Bautier, no. 123, p. 249.

50 *Dictionnaire de droit canonique*, ed. R. Naz (Paris, 1949), vol. 4, pp. 1285–8.

51 Ellenblum, *Frankish Rural Settlement*, pp. 47–8.

52 Bresc-Bautier, no. 123, p. 249.

53 Ellenblum, *Frankish Rural Settlement*, pp. 47 and 153.

54 Bresc-Bautier, no. 150, p. 295.

55 Bresc-Bautier, no. 123, p. 249.

function as a court of burgesses with right of high justice without infringing canon law. Its primary function was the administration of land coupled with the authority even to lease property and increase the size of the village without the approval of the villagers.[56] It may be argued, however, a *Cour des Bourgeois* was established in the village in the same way that *Cours des Bourgeois* were established in the episcopal seigneuries of Lydda and Nazareth. But John of Ibelin makes no mention of a court in his text, and although, as has been pointed out, his list of courts is not totally reliable, no other document mentions a viscount of the village or an officer of equal standing. The *dispensator* was a churchman and could be found in other church villages administering the farming of land. There is no evidence that in the kingdom of Jerusalem he presided anywhere over a *Cour des Bourgeois*.

An understanding of the principles of eleemosynary donation provides further explanation of the system of justice in Magna Mahumeria. It has been argued that ecclesiastical institutions set up secular courts to deal with cases involving their tenants. In Jerusalem the court of the Holy Sepulchre, which was composed of canons and burgesses, had jurisdiction over *borgesies* donated the Church 'in alms'. Significantly, in civil and criminal cases not pertaining to property, the tenancy remained subject to the royal *Cour des Bourgeois*. It seems probable, therefore, that in Magna Mahumeria matters concerning tenants were heard in the secular court of the Holy Sepulchre, but in aspects of criminal law and certainly high justice, the settlers remained subject to royal jurisdiction. This seems to have been the understanding of the settlers who swore an oath of fealty to the Holy Sepulchre in c.1155, 'except for the fealty (which they owed) the king of Jerusalem'.[57]

It is interesting to add some points regarding the jurisdictional rights of the canons of the Holy Sepulchre over the whole village of Magna Mahumeria. When in c.1158 the authority of the Church to possess Magna Mahumeria was disputed by Robert de Retest, lord of the neighbouring Muslim-inhabited *casale* of Salemiya, and disagreement arose between the two sides over the boundaries of both villages,[58] the canons were able to prove, with the testimony of witnesses, that they had been granted the village 'in alms'.[59] Although issues relating to the ownership of the settlement granted to the Church 'in alms' as a whole were usually subject to the bishop's court in whose diocese it was situated, in the dispute over Magna Mahumeria the patriarch of Jerusalem did not participate in this arbitration. Witnesses to the final agreement were the canons of the Holy Sepulchre, Robert de Retest and his son and burgesses of Jerusalem and Magna Mahumeria. It seems, therefore, that the canons had a certain autonomy in jurisdictional matters concerning their village. By comparison, when in 1161 the Holy Sepulchre was in disagreement with the abbey of St Mary of Josaphat over

---

56 Bresc-Bautier, no. 123, p. 250.

57 Bresc-Bautier, no. 117, pp. 237–8.

58 Bresc-Bautier, no. 121, p. 247.

59 Bresc-Bautier, no. 122, pp. 247–8.

land near Castrum Feniculi, the dispute was resolved by the archbishop of Caesarea in whose diocese this settlement was situated.[60]

Parva Mahumeria (Qubeiba)

Another reference to the jurisdiction that the canons of the Holy Sepulchre had in certain *villes neuves* is found in a patriarchal confirmation (1168) of the Church's property in the kingdom.

> Viginti et unum casalia que dux Godefridus cum pertinentiis suis ecclesie vestre dedit; villas etiam quas edificastis, ut Magnam Mahomeria et Parvam et Bethsuri, et alias omnes quas edificaturi estis, ubi Latini habitabunt, cum ecclesiis et omni integritate justicie.[61]

Apart from hinting at future Latin settlements, it is recorded that the church had 'entire jurisdiction' in Parva Mahumeria (Qubeiba) – a village located on the ecclesiastical estate of Beit Suriq (Beitsurie), lying north-west of Jerusalem – as well as Bethsuri. Ellenblum has pointed to the existence of a *domus* in Parva Mahumeria,[62] and it may be assumed that from this place a *dispensator* managed, as in Magna Mahumeria, the property of the Holy Sepulchre. Over and above this, Parva Mahumeria and Magna Mahumeria seem also to have had in common the jurisdictional rights of the Holy Sepulchre. In theory, the whole village of Parva Mahumeria, which had been granted to the canons 'in alms', was subject to the court of the patriarch of Jerusalem. The Church, however, may have been granted a degree of jurisdictional autonomy in matters concerning the whole village similar to that which they enjoyed in Magna Mahumeria. The Church had 'entire jurisdiction' in Parva Mahumeria and established a secular court to deal with issues concerning burgesses living in the village. Again, any legal matters outside the competence of this court would have gone before the royal *Cour des Bourgeois* of Jerusalem.

Bethgibelin (Bait Jibrin)

In 1136, Hugh of Hebron conceded the fortress of Bethgibelin to the order of St John 'in alms', probably at the direct request of King Fulk. As it was a gift 'in alms' the fortress passed under ecclesiastical jurisdiction, and the grant was witnessed by William, patriarch of Jerusalem. The acquisition by the order of

---

60 Bresc-Bautier, no. 57, pp. 148–9.

61 Bresc-Bautier, no. 123, p. 250. Ellenblum, *Frankish Rural Settlement*, pp. 86–7; Benvenisti, pp. 224–7.

62 Ellenblum, *Frankish Rural Settlement*, pp. 88–90 and 92.

estates *en bloc* rather than being built up over years was not untypical. The same was certainly true of Hospitaller acquisition of lands around Crac des Chevaliers, Belvoir, Margat and Mount Thabor.[63] As for the fortress of Bethgibelin, it was situated halfway between Gaza and Hebron, and the grant to the order included ten villages in the vicinity of the fortress: two places by the name of Beithsur, Irnachar, Irrasin, Charroubete, Deirelcobebe, Meimes, Hale, Bothme and Helhtawahin. The king further gave the order four villages: Fectata, Sahalin, Zeita and Courcoza.[64] Sometime between 1153 and 1160, thirty-one Latin settlers and their families were granted land by Master Raymond of Le Puy (d. 1160). This *charte de peuplement* was later confirmed by Master Gilbert of Assailly in 1168.[65] From 1136 to 1154 legal affairs appertaining to the ownership of the settlement as a whole were probably heard in the court of the patriarch as the *castrum* was within the diocese of Jerusalem. After 1154, however, the order of St John was exempted from episcopal jurisdiction and as a consequence came directly under the authority of Rome.[66]

In Bethgibelin the order managed the tenancy of *borgesies* in the same way the Church of the Holy Sepulchre managed property in Magna Mahumeria. The order's right of *justicia* was mentioned in the *charte de peuplement* of 1168,[67] although there is conflicting evidence as to whether the Hospitallers had their own *Cour des Bourgeois*. The *Hospitalis justicia* was the right of the order to govern the tenants of *borgesies*, for example to authorise the alienation of property. But was this necessarily a reference to a *Cour des Bourgeois* which John of Ibelin mentioned in his treatise as belonging to the Hospitallers in Bethgibelin? As the settlement was so briefly in Christian hands after Saladin's conquest (1192 and 1240–44), it can be safely assumed that a *Cour des Bourgeois* was established in the first period of Hospitaller ownership. It is, however, puzzling why John believed the court to be subject to the lord of Hebron. The evidence perhaps reveals the existence of a seigneurial *Cour des Bourgeois* in Bethgibelin before the settlement was acquired by the Hospitallers, but this seems improbable as the process of settling Latins in the town was begun by the Hospitallers. Alternatively, the lord of Hebron may have had a settlement nearby to Bethgibelin with its own *Cour des Bourgeois* or Bethgibelin may have been divided – as was Parva Palmarea – with a court for the lord of Hebron's burgesses.

What is known for certain is that in Bethgibelin the order of St John set up a secular court to deal with cases concerning its tenants, just as the canons of the

---

63 Riley-Smith, *The Knights of St John*, p. 424.

64 Delaville Le Roulx, *Cartulaire général*, no. 116, p. 98; S. Tibble, *Monarchy and Lordships in the Kingdom of Jerusalem, 1099–1291* (Oxford, 1989), p. 11.

65 Delaville Le Roulx, *Cartulaire général*, no. 399, p. 273. See also, F.M. Abel, 'Les Deux "Mahomerie" el-Bireh, el Quobeibeh', *RB*, 25 (1926): 272–83; B. Baggati, 'Il Cristianesimo ad Eleuteropolis (Beit Gebrin)', *LA*, 22 (1972): 109–29.

66 Riley-Smith, *The Knights of St John*, pp. 376–85.

67 Delaville Le Roulx, *Cartulaire général*, no. 399, pp. 272–3.

Holy Sepulchre had set up a court in Magna Mahumeria. The Hospitallers formulated laws: for example, any man or woman caught committing adultery would be flogged in public or otherwise expelled from Bethgibelin. Furthermore, *Hospitalis justicia* was used in the context of leasehold, meaning the order had jurisdiction over issues concerning tenants. The settlers had the right to alienate their properties, except for the services and exactions owed to the order which were passed on to the new tenants.[68] The emphasis was understandable given that in the charter of 1168 the Hospitallers relinquished the right of pre-emption in order to attract new settlers. With this in mind the phrase 'atque justiciam et consuetudinem, servabunt judicia Jerusalem', may be interpreted as follows. It did not mean the Latin settlement was subject to the court of the patriarch or to the royal *Cour des Bourgeois* in Jerusalem. A more plausible explanation is that the 'custom' of the patriarch's court or the royal *Cour des Bourgeois* had been adopted by a special Hospitaller court in Bethgibelin, in the same way that the rules of plunder were based on the 'custom' of the *Cour des Bourgeois* in Lydda.

There is enough evidence to suggest that a lord in his domain could grant ecclesiastical institutions jurisdiction over property donated to them 'in alms', without diminishing his authority over tenants in matters civil and criminal, but the reference in the charter of 1168 to *Hospitalis justicia* suggests the Hospitallers dealt with certain criminal cases through their secular court. In the charter it was stipulated that brigands who were caught in Bethgibelin should be placed under the 'authority of the master of the Hospitallers'.[69] This kind of justice exercised by a religious military order whose principal concerns were the defence of its community and the law and order of Latin settlers, was perhaps what Philip of Novara had in mind when he stated that quite often the Church judged secular cases which were outside its scope of jurisdiction.[70]

The charter of 1168 highlights the extent of jurisdiction which the Hospital exercised in Bethgibelin. This is important because in those places where the Hospitallers did receive feudal lordship, for example Crac des Chevaliers and Margat, it is not always fully clear what these rights of *dominium* were and whether the administration of justice included authority over a *Cour des Bourgeois*. It has been suggested that at Crac des Chevaliers (1144) the Hospitallers were granted lordship over burgesses and authority over the local *Cours des Bourgeois*.[71] This was probably the case, but as the evidence of Bethgibelin demonstrates, it cannot be automatically concluded that *Hospitalis justicia* necessarily implied control of a secular *Cour des Bourgeois*.

---

68 Delaville Le Roulx, *Cartulaire général*, no. 399, p. 273.

69 Delaville Le Roulx, *Cartulaire général*, no. 399, p. 273.

70 Philip of Novara, 'Le Livre de forme de plait', p. 522.

71 Riley-Smith, *The Knights of St John*, p. 464; J. Richard, *Comté de Tripoli sous la dynastie toulousaine, 1102–1187* (Paris, 1945), pp. 63–4; Delaville Le Roulx, *Cartulaire général*, no. 144, pp. 116–18 and no. 391, pp. 266–8.

Parva Palmarea

The question of sub-infeudation and the extent of jurisdictional authority which rear-vassals had over the inhabitants of their estates, arises with regard to the village of Palmarea. There were two places called Palmarea in the kingdom of Jerusalem.[72] The first was in the lordship of Haifa, near which Vivian lord of Haifa granted land to the Church of the Holy Sepulchre in 1164.[73] In a confirmation of this concession (1168) the Holy Sepulchre was described as possessing property 'inside and outside the city of old Haifa'.[74] The other Palmarea was situated near Lake Tiberias in the principality of Galilee. It was also known as Parva Palmarea presumably to differentiate it from its namesake in the lordship of Haifa.[75] Parva Palmarea, 'otherwise known as Solinum', appears in a document of 1180 which outlines the eleemosynary concessions made by Lady Ahuhisa and her husband Rainald to the Cluniac monks of Mount Thabor. The monks were given land and houses 'in alms', and the burgesses in their *familia* had the exclusive right to use an oven in the town. The monks were accorded jurisdiction over their tenants caught committing criminal injury on the condition that the fines they imposed went to the lord of Parva Palmarea.[76] The jurisdictional framework of Parva Palmarea can thus be drawn. The whole community was held by its lord as a fief of the prince of Galilee, and although it does not appear in John of Ibelin's list as having its own *Cour des Bourgeois*, Rainald, its lord, is mentioned in the charter of 1180 as having jurisdiction over the local inhabitants, including the right to collect fines. It was a mark of his authority that he was able to concede jurisdictional rights to the monks.[77] Furthermore, the property given to the monks 'in alms' passed under ecclesiastical jurisdiction, and thus matters pertaining to the ownership of the Cluniac settlement were subject to the episcopal court of Nazareth in whose archdiocese Palmarea was situated.[78] This explains the presence of the archbishop of Nazareth as witness to the donation, as well as his archdeacon Gerald, who assisted the archbishop in Church administration and was responsible for the judicial business of the see. The other notable witness was Bernard, bishop of Lydda and formerly abbot of Mount Thabor.[79]

In all probability there did exist a *Cour des Bourgeois* in Parva Palmarea under

---

72 It was erroneously suggested by Prawer that there existed only one Palmarea, *Crusader Institutions*, pp. 136–8.

73 Bresc-Bautier, no. 137, p. 269.

74 Bresc-Bautier, no. 146, p. 285.

75 *RRH*, no. 522, p. 139 (1174); B.Z. Kedar, 'Palmarée, Abbaye Clunisienne du XIIe Siècle, en Galilée', *RBe*, 93 (1983): 260–69.

76 Delaville Le Roulx, *Cartulaire général*, no. 19, pp. 908–909.

77 Delaville Le Roulx, *Cartulaire général*, no. 19, p. 909.

78 It is odd that in this period the Cluniac monks were not exempted from episcopal jurisdiction.

79 Hamilton, *The Latin Church*, pp. 116 and 122.

the authority of Rainald. In addition, the monks established a secular court to deal with cases involving their tenants. A relevant question to ask is whether the court of the Cluniacs exercised any form of criminal justice similar to the court of the Hospitallers in Bethgibelin. According to the document of 1180, the lord of Parva Palmarea granted the monks justice over certain criminal offences committed by their burgesses on the condition that he collected any fines they imposed. These criminals, however, were not subject to the lord's court 'sed a baiulo ecclesie, qui steterit ibi'.[80] Therefore, an ecclesiastical bailiff, a presiding head of a secular court set up by churchmen, was present in Parva Palmarea and exercised jurisdiction over the tenants of the monks in matters of property and certain criminal cases.

Palmarea

The jurisdiction of an ecclesiastical settlement near the other Palmarea, in the lordship of Haifa, may be ascertained from an eleemosynary grant of property which Vivian lord of Haifa made to the canons of the Holy Sepulchre in 1164. Palmarea does not appear to have had a *Cour des Bourgeois* although it was here that in 1148 the High Court of Jerusalem assembled.[81] Vivian conceded to the canons land in a 'deserted village' located between Haifa and Palmarea, as well as a garden in the latter place. The village property passed under the jurisdiction of the court of the archbishopric of Caesarea and, as a consequence, archbishop Henry was witness to the concession. This was a straightforward gift 'in alms' and there is no suggestion that as in Magna Mahumeria the canons of the Holy Sepulchre had their own court. If this were the case, probably the leasing of land to Latin settlers was administered by the archbishop's court, whilst jurisdiction over burgesses in civil and criminal cases was reserved to the *Cour des Bourgeois* of Haifa. Vivian further stipulated that the canons could not buy or receive property donations in the vicinity of Palmarea without his express permission.[82]

Buria (Dabburiya)

Relatively little is known about the Galilean village of Buria which was situated at the foot of Mount Thabor. In 1101, Tancred, lord of Galilee, conceded Buria along with twenty-five other *casalia* in the vicinity of Mount Thabor to abbot Gerard and the Cluniac monastery there. Buria was described as uninhabited due to the devastation of war.[83] In 1103 and 1107, the possessions of the Cluniacs were

80 Delaville Le Roulx, *Cartulaire général*, no. 19, p. 909.

81 *RRH*, no. 250, p. 63.

82 Bresc-Bautier, no. 137, p. 269.

83 J. Delaville Le Roulx (ed.), 'Chartes du Mont-Thabor', in *Cartulaire général*, II, no. 1, pp. 897–8; Benvenisti, p. 358.

confirmed by Pope Paschal II and King Baldwin I, respectively.[84] Buria was still described as a *casale* which suggests that a Latin settlement had not yet been established. Latins did eventually settle and archaeology has revealed the existence of a parish church situated in the centre of the village.[85] Buria was not included in John of Ibelin's list of places with *Cours des Bourgeois*, although its significance as a settlement is apparent in the charter of Parva Palmarea (1168) where it is stated that the 'custom' of Buria, which allowed settlers to sell, pledge or alienate in other ways their properties, was adopted.[86] As the village was conceded to the Cluniac monks 'in alms' it passed under ecclesiastical jurisdiction. Thereafter, legal matters concerning the whole village were subject to the episcopal court of Nazareth in whose diocese the settlement was situated. It is possible that in Buria as in Parva Palmarea, the Cluniacs established a secular court to deal with issues relating to their tenants.

Conclusion

Analysis of the system of jurisdiction prevailing in the rural Latin settlements under ecclesiastical or secular control, and the evidence presented proving the existence of special Church courts which besides the *Cours des Bourgeois* administered *villes neuves* like Magna Mahumeria and Bethgibelin, point to the conclusion that John of Ibelin provided only a basic outline of justice in the kingdom of Jerusalem. He sought only to list the *Cours des Bourgeois* with which he was familiar. He did not undertake to record the other courts which had authority to exercise burgess jurisdiction. Within an expanded picture of settlement in the kingdom of Jerusalem, which included Latin rural villages of varying sizes hitherto unaccounted for, one finds a complex system of burgess jurisdiction. In the secular lordships, as well as in the ecclesiastical lordships of Lydda and Nazareth, the seigneurs had rights of *cours et coins et justise*, including the right to establish a *Cour des Bourgeois* with the authority of high justice in their domain. They could sub-infeudate their lands, create rear-fiefs, which either like Castellum Regis[87] had their own burgess courts, or like Casale Sancti Egidii had no court, so that burgesses were subject to the jurisdiction of the *Cour des Bourgeois* in the overlord's domain. Secular lords could also concede whole settlements 'in alms' to

---

84 Delaville Le Roulx, 'Charte du Mont-Thabor', II, no. 2, p. 898. From 1187 to 1239, Buria was in Muslim hands; P. Deschamps (ed.), 'Etude sur un texte latin enumérant les possessions musulmanes dans le Royaume de Jérusalem vers l'année 1239', *Syria* (1942–43), p. 98; Delaville Le Roulx, *Cartulaire général*, no. 2832, pp. 826–8.

85 D. Pringle, *The Churches of the Crusader Kingdom of Jerusalem. A Corpus*, I, A-K (excluding Acre and Jerusalem) (Cambridge, 1993), pp. 192–3.

86 Delaville Le Roulx, *Cartulaire général*, no. 19, p. 909.

87 R. Ellenblum, 'Colonization Activities in the Frankish East: The Example of Castellum Regis (Mi'ilya)', *EHR*, 111 (1996): 104–22.

ecclesiastical institutions which subsequently established their own special secular courts. In all of these examples, it is most striking how the secular courts of churchmen both incorporated the legal functions of the *Cour des Bourgeois* and adapted to the secular needs of the community. That is to say, the jurisdictional competence of these courts extended beyond the usual parameters of Church law. Thus, ecclesiastical institutions not only exercised laws of leasehold over tenants of their *borgesies*: in Bethgibelin a thief was placed 'under the authority of the master of the Hospital', and the property he had stolen confiscated by the secular court of the order;[88] and in Parva Palmarea the episcopal court of the archdiocese of Nazareth – with the approval of lord Rainald – appointed a *baiulus* to hear cases of criminal justice concerning burgess tenants of the Cluniac monks.[89] It can be clearly seen that to settle a village, an ecclesiastical institution was required to meet the secular and spiritual needs of its residents. More than anything else, it looked for a degree of self sufficiency both as a landowner, able to attract to its settlement immigrant farmers, and, importantly, as a legal authority with powers to deal with as many cases which did not require outside interference.

---

88 Delaville Le Roulx, *Cartulaire général*, no. 399, p. 273.

89 Delaville Le Roulx, *Cartulaire général*, no. 19, p. 909.

Conclusion

I have attempted in this book to trace the history of burgesses from their origins in Europe in the early decades of the eleventh century, by way of their involvement in the First Crusade and the creation of the kingdoms of Jerusalem and Cyprus, up to the fall of the Latin states in 1291 and beyond. Throughout I have focused on areas of significance. In the pre-crusade period consideration was given to the growth of European population and agrarian expansion, in particular the construction of *burgi* undertaken by secular and ecclesiastical landowners away from centres of overpopulation. These villages were in certain respects, including their administrative and juridical structure, similar to the *villes neuves* in the kingdom of Jerusalem. The free inhabitants of *burgi* were granted rights centred round the freedom and alienability of their properties in return for rent and often military service. The origin of the term *burgenses* was also considered, and it was argued that this generic term came to denote in the eleventh century the status of a class of people who lived in all manner of places including *burgi*. Furthermore, *burgagium* was defined as a type of alienable property which was widely found in Europe in *burgi* as well as cities and other types of rural settlement.

The laws and customs of property and person prevailing in the burgess communities of the kingdom of Jerusalem were also traced back to Europe in the eleventh century. It was observed that although regions such as Brittany, Anjou, Poitou and Berry had their own *consuetudines*, or unwritten customs, there began to evolve, in spite of local and regional differences, essential similarities in basic rules governing inhabitants of *burgi*. It was explained that certain well-known customs, for example, those of Breteuil and Cormeilles in Normandy, had far-reaching influence. This pan-European phenomenon may account for the development in this period of a more cohesive definition among European legal writers and lawmakers of the status of *burgenses* and *burgagium*.

Having considered the social position of the burgess class in Europe, attention was focused on the involvement of all non-nobles, free and unfree, rich and poor, in the First Crusade. In the eyes of contemporary writers, non-noble crusaders were moved to join partly out of a need to escape hardship, but more so out of a spiritual desire to take the cross. Heading East and ill-prepared for what awaited them, they suffered the privations of a long and arduous journey. They quickly succumbed in battle or starved slowly to death, and many, so tortured by the whole ordeal, returned home if they had the means to do so. For contemporary historians, however, crusade encapsulated the Christian principles of suffering and redemption. The infliction of suffering on crusaders was manifestation of God's anger, punishing those who engaged in illicit sexual acts – particularly with Muslims – or other forms of criminality. In clamping down on disorder the crusade leaders issued a set of laws and condign punishments, and established ad hoc courts of justice with authority over the ranks of non-feudatories in their armies.

During the period of crusade propaganda, the colourful rhetoric employed by chroniclers and annalists suggested an overwhelming response from non-feudatories, both serfs and freemen, to crusade preaching. There seems little doubt though that crusade was a popular movement and propagandists of the time were eager to characterize it as an event of unequalled magnitude. I have described the *commotio* or *transmigratio*, the mass movement of people which followed crusade, whilst refuting the unsubstantiated theory which incorporates the kingdom of Jerusalem within the greater context of European migration. There is evidence of notable emigration in the eleventh and twelfth centuries, for example, from Aquitaine, Massif Central and Catalonia to Languedoc, and even from England and Spain to cities in the south-west regions of France. But there is no similar evidence of significant migration East between crusades, as the long journey and the greater dangers of living in the kingdom when compared to more secure regions in Europe, would have deterred potential migrants. There was of course the *passagium* and pilgrimage with some people choosing to remain permanently in the kingdom. However, there were significant numbers who visited for short periods of time, and as discussed, many houses in the Italian communes in Acre were reserved for lease *ad passagium* for between one month and a year.

The immediate achievement of the First Crusade in capturing Jerusalem was ideological. The fall of the Holy City represented Latin Christian dominion over Islam, and signalled God's favour for their enterprise. The Muslim population thus displaced a Latin kingdom was created under the hegemony of its first ruler Godfrey of Bouillon. And by some form of common agreement, a new social order was contrived based in part on religious discrimination, and on a fundamental legal system which held firm that all Latin Christians of European origin were of free status. There would be no class of Latin Christian serfs, although native Latin Christians were not entirely excluded. Created was an environment conducive to settlement. To take Jerusalem as an example, freemen were encouraged to trade and to this end they were granted their own markets and exempted from certain taxes. What is more, as a nascent community they were accorded permission to establish their own court and to be judged by their peers. And in all likelihood, as was a commonly stated condition of settlement in west European cities, men of a certain age belonged to a garrison which the king could call upon in time of need to bolster his army or to carry out defensive duties. In European cities it was usually expected that able men between the ages of sixteen and sixty perform some form of military service. An army could thus be mobilized whenever a lord so wished.[1]

From early on in the new kingdom, necessity dictated the imposition of laws to strengthen the hand of Latin freemen, to define their status as legally distinct from that of the local population, and in turn help to shore up a heavily depleted knightly contingent which in the long term could not hope to prosper merely as an

---

1 Vercauteren, 'Marchands et bourgeois dans le pays mosan', pp. 665, 670.

occupying force. Viewed from this perspective, the emergent class of burgesses was intended to support or complement rather than counter-balance what was at certain times in the history of the kingdom a relatively weak knightly class. In reality, from the outset, the position of the burgess class was more to subdue the native population, and to control through legal institutions who could and could not possess *borgesies*. Burgesses were politically organized insofar as they were established into communities of influence in all the major cities and rural villages under Latin control. Forced to settle in groups geographically isolated and vulnerable to Muslim attack, they were an essential part of the apparatus of occupation and government that was the judiciary, administration and economy. It is a description of burgesses which dispenses with the commonly held view that their influence was marginal or that their political participation was no more than a 'formality'.[2] The traditional and symbolic duty of burgesses to serve food at the coronation banquet at the Temple of Solomon,[3] has oft been cited as evidence of their 'indispensable' but – when compared to the knightly class – less significant involvement in political life. The history of the kingdom suggests otherwise.

Political influence was further related to the concept of public power. It was explained that in the latter half of the eleventh century in Europe, freemen were granted increasing privileges and greater powers to control the affairs of their own communities. Ideally, there existed in each community a balance between the authority a lord enjoyed and the powers of its inhabitants. Increasingly, communities could choose or elect their own representatives, help formulate and enforce their laws or customs, administer their economy and run their judiciary. In the kingdom of Jerusalem these principles of public power were no less scrutinized. Greater freedom meant greater influence not merely to advise but also authorize. It was seen how in Acre the burgess community expected to give approval to royal legislation which directly affected its members. By the latter decades of the twelfth century, the burgess class had public power, political influence and commercial importance. Particularly, after the devastation of 1187, the well organized burgess community in Tyre could not be ignored by the ambitious Conrad of Montferrat.

The 1180s and 1190s was a time of unprecedented turmoil for the kingdom's burgess communities. In Ascalon, Guy of Lusignan, prisoner of Saladin after the defeat at Hattin, acted as intermediary and convinced a burgess delegation to relinquish the city. They agreed and the Frankish inhabitants were permitted to leave unharmed.[4] Soon after, burgess envoys of Jerusalem came to Saladin to

---

2 Mayer, *The Crusades*, p. 156.

3 John of Ibelin, pp. 575–6; Richard, *The Latin Kingdom of Jerusalem*, pp. 63–4.

4 'L'Estoire d'Eracles Emperuer et la conqueste de la terre d'outremer', pp. 78–9; 'Imad al-Din al-Isfahani, *Sana al-barq al Shami*, abridged by Fath.b. 'Ali al-Bundari, pt. 1, ed. R. Sesen (Beirut, 1971); see also, "A Critical Edition of the Abridgement by al-Bundari of the *Kitab al-Barq al-Shami* by Imad al-Din', by F. El-Nabarawy, unpublished thesis, Cambridge University Library, pp. 361–4.

request quarter for their city.[5] He offered them generous terms and the option to surrender peacefully. They refused. Saladin moved on Jerusalem and after a fierce encounter with an army made up largely of burgesses, terms for surrender were agreed.[6] The iron grip of the Ayyubids was as much a psychological blow to the Latin Christians as a military one, confined as they were to the densely populated coast – stretching from Tyre to Jaffa – and surrounded by a Muslim enemy of unprecedented power. Hence, the residual strength of the kingdom became centred in Tyre, and with the kingdom in disarray and King Guy in captivity, the strategically important city under the leadership of Marquis Conrad of Montferrat held out vigorously against Saladin's forces. It became a refuge for Latin Christians fleeing other devastated cities, and after the fall of Acre it became the commercial centre of Latin trade in the Levant. In Tyre a prosperous and well-organized burgess community guarded jealously its own interests. We cannot be certain that Conrad established a commune in the city in 1187, but judging from the charters which he issued over the next two years, burgesses played a very important role both commercially and militarily in his plans.

The size and strength of the kingdom of Jerusalem had been reduced sharply, and Saladin's systematic occupation of cities meant that several thousands at any one time had been displaced. Many were sold into slavery, whilst others sought refuge in cities still in Christian hands before they returned in 1191 to reclaim their properties. Importantly, these events further stimulated migration to the island of Cyprus where burgess society was considered, in this study, parallel to the history of the kingdom of Jerusalem. Property was distributed to the knights as well as the burgesses who had been driven out of Palestine and Syria. If Acre and Tyre were vulnerable to attack, Famagusta was stable and an increasingly important port along the eastern trade routes. Among a rapidly growing population it had its own wealthy class of merchants and burgesses. It is possible to build up a picture of city life from the registers of notaries like Lamberto di Sambuceto and Giovanni di Rocha who reveal to us the opportunities which existed for trade and commercial contracts. There were the ever popular investments in *commenda*, and one may discern the various kinds of business associations and acquaintances.

Throughout the thirteenth century the coastal cities of Cyprus were important centres of commerce as well as places of refuge for immigrants. On arriving they were absorbed into an exclusively urban society whose basic laws and juridical institutions were generally familiar to them. As a class of burgesses they were legally superior to native inhabitants. In theory, they could advise the lord of their city in the drawing up of legislation directly affecting them. And in every burgess community of notable size there was a *Cour des Bourgeois*, a legal body which in its basic composition and competence was modelled on the typical burgess court of justice existing in many of the cities of the kingdom of Jerusalem. I would conclude further, that in Cyprus, as on the mainland, there was no common law

---

5 'L'Estoire d'Eracles Empereur et la conqueste de la terre d'outremer', p. 79.

6 'L'Estoire d'Eracles Empereur et la conqueste de la terre d'outremer', pp. 80–81.

book, no single authority. But the 'Livre contrefais' is an invaluable source. It is revealing of how in a city like Nicosia legislative agreement jointly involved the king and members of the burgess community. Law, it is also apparent, arose from the setting of court precedent. In conjunction with this legislative activity was an eagerness to consult the law books of cities in the kingdom of Jerusalem, in order to determine the relevance of legislation practised in other communities. There was above all else an ardent interest in law and its preservation.

Apparent is the interconnectedness between burgess societies in Cyprus and the kingdom of Jerusalem. Migration of Latin Christians to the island was accompanied by a conveyance of certain legal practices. But as this study has proven, the translation of law from one place to another was not something unique in the East. The practice whereby cities or rural settlements adopted each other's rules concerning property and person is attested in charters. The Church, in particular, played a part in defining tenancy of *borgesies*, and in the twelfth century, in their settlements, ecclesiastical institutions established laws and customs which were repeated in other communities. This meant that *borgesie* tenancy in Latin cities and villages developed along similar lines. A *borgesie* could be commonly characterised as a house or area of cultivated land leased in perpetuity or temporarily by a burgess, feudatory, churchmen, member of a merchant community, or native Christian. A tenant had the freedom to alienate his property, but never privately, and always before a *Cour des Bourgeois* from whom he had to seek authority. A transaction could only become legitimate and permanent if authorised by the court of the *seigneur justicier* in whose territory of jurisdiction the property was located. The same basic rules of tenancy of *borgesies* were exercised in Church courts as in *Cours des Bourgeois*.

Whilst evidently most *borgesies* were subject to *Cours des Bourgeois*, a significant percentage of properties in the kingdom were not. But was the decentralisation of burgess jurisdiction a positive or negative development? Did it strengthen or weaken the burgess class? Did it hinder or enhance the development of burgess institutions? One may argue that certain developments were inevitable. The merchant communes would have insisted on their own courts to deal with burgesses living in their quarters. Equally, the Church would not have countenanced any attenuation of its jurisdictional rights not least over properties which were transferred 'in alms'. The system had also to adapt, thus minor inter-communal cases were dealt with by the *Cour de la Fonde*. But the disadvantage of such a system was that it accentuated divisions and underscored the notion that burgesses were always their lord's men. It further undermined the authority of the *Cour des Bourgeois* as the court with full competence over all burgesses. On the other hand, it is testimony of the strength of non-noble jurisdiction. It was a flexible legal system, certainly, and a consistent one. The fact, for example, that a *heritage de fié* was subject to a seigneurial court, did not alter its defining features as a *borgesie*, and in the hands of a tenant it was alienable and hereditary.

In the final assessment, a *Cour des Bourgeois* was a court for burgesses in civil and criminal cases. It was also a court of the native population in matters of high justice. The development of the *Cour des Bourgeois* can be summarised into three broad stages. In the first stage, the twelfth century, the evidence of royal and seigneurial charters is rather patchy, and there is a natural propensity to either overstate or understate the formation of the court. In my opinion, the essential features of the court were already in place in this period, and by this is meant the judgement-making powers of burgess jurors, and the standing of the viscount as legal head of the court and the burgess community. I am inclined to think, however, that the laws of the thirteenth century shaped most significantly the *Cour des Bourgeois*, in Acre and Nicosia at least. In this second important stage of its development, it began keeping for the first time records of the legal business which it carried out. In matters of dispute, the court could use its registers to refer back to judgements it had made and, where necessary, to establish the unequivocal right of a tenant over a particular *borgesie*, and the services he was owed by a sub-tenant. By the third stage of its development, the fourteenth century, the basic functions of the court and the duties of its officials were well established. The author of the 'Livre contrefais' could define the broad duties of the viscount and jurors. We are able, finally, to perceive with greater clarity the jurisdictional competence of the court. The first book of the 'Livre contrefais' reaffirms the position of the court as a legal conduit for the alienation of *borgesies*. It legitimised, publicised and symbolised the act of transfer. The second book is an important indication of how complex judicial procedure had become. In fact, the complex nature of court affairs had been commented on as early as the Acre *parlement* of 1250; a chief criticism of the participants was that drawn-out cases leading to adjournments, and detailed judgements regarding claimants and defendants, could no longer be simply committed to memory. In response to this, not only were written records introduced, but also a rigid set of rules was applied in order to ensure the court functioned efficiently when dealing with litigation; that it adhered uniformly to legal procedure when deferring or reconvening cases; and that it made fair judgements based on the evidence presented to it.

This summary of the function of the burgess court leads to the final objective of this study: a definition in the clearest terms of the status of burgesses. First, one should explain who for one reason or another could not belong to this class. The line separating burgesses from native peoples was scored most heavily by legal distinctions. Natives had their own courts in the shape of the *Cours des Syriens* – in Acre the *Cour de la Fonde* – to deal with inter-communal cases. Of these people the lowest class were Muslims and Jews who were tied to their properties in the rural *casalia* – and in some cases in the cities – and were expected to pay *kharaj*, a tax levied on their land. The same status was reserved for indigenous Christians who were tied to the land and like non-Christian peasants did not pay Church tithe.[7] All could not be considered burgesses because of their non-Latin faith and

7 Riley-Smith, 'Government and the Indigenous in the Latin Kingdom of Jerusalem', p. 127; Ellenblum, *Frankish Rural Settlement*, pp. 235–6; Gregory IX, *Registres*, ed. L. Auvray (4 vols, Paris, 1896–1955), II, pp. 841 and 1149.

not, it should be reiterated, their economic status. According to the Muslim traveller Ibn Jubayr, writing in the second half of the twelfth century, villeins in the rural villages had 'possession of their own houses and control of their own affairs'.[8] Indeed, some wealthy villeins possessed more than one house or plot of land,[9] whilst others living in the vicinity of Acre, had permission to trade in the *fonde*.[10] In general, villeins were non-Latin Christians, but this did not mean that all Catholics of native origin belonged to the class of burgesses. In the principality of Antioch in 1183, Bohemond III conceded to the Hospitallers 'in alms' Greek, Armenian, Jewish and 'Latin' villeins.[11] These Latin villeins may have been Maronites who were reconciled with Rome by 1183. This was not unusual, considering that Maronites of the county of Tripoli – who constituted the main native element in this region of northern Syria[12] – were rural villeins.[13] Evidence of this nature supports the view that a person could not be defined as a burgess merely because he was a Latin Christian.

Merely being subject to a *Cour des Bourgeois* was not sufficient to define a person as a burgess either, since that court's jurisdiction was reserved to all the more serious cases affecting inhabitants who were not knights. We learn from John of Ibelin that disputes concerning native Christian tenants of *borgesies*, as well as issues of high justice involving native peoples, were heard in the *Cour des Bourgeois*.[14] In addition, there were Latin Christians who were subject to the *Cour des Bourgeois* in civil and criminal matters, but were not tenants of *borgesies*. A comparison with the jurisdiction of seigneurial courts is here relevant. In the kingdom of Jerusalem and Cyprus a fief-holder was a Latin Christian liegeman who owed service to a lord and was permitted to sit in a seigneurial court. There were, nevertheless, mercenaries (*chevalers sodoiers*) or *milites ad terminum*[15] who possessed no land, but were subject to this seigneurial court in civil and criminal

---

8 Ibn Jubayr, p. 305.

9 Delaville Le Roulx, *Cartulaire général*, no. 225, p. 172.

10 The 'Livre de la Cour des Bourgeois' refers to the villeins who, 'living in our lordship, that is the diocese of the archbishop of Acre', traded in the *fonde en aval* and from whom the *Cour de la Fonde* levied a sales tax; Kausler, p. 282 (cf. Beugnot, 'Livre des assises', p. 179).

11 Delaville Le Roulx, *Cartulaire général*, no. 648, p. 437.

12 Richard, *Le Comté de Tripoli*, p. 86.

13 K.S. Salibi, 'The Maronites of Lebanon under Frankish and Mamluk Rule (1099–1516)', *Arabica*, 4 (1957): 291.

14 John of Ibelin, p. 55. See also, Kausler, p. 278 (cf. Beugnot, 'Livre des assises', p. 173). Riley-Smith, 'Some Lesser Officials in Latin Syria', p. 4.

15 For a discussion of mercenary soldiers, see J. Richard, 'The Political and Ecclesiastical Organisation of the Crusader States', in N.P. Zacour and H.W. Hazard (eds), *A History of the Crusades: The Impact of the Crusades on the Near East* (Wisconsin, 1985), vol. V, p. 226; Riley-Smith, *Knights of St John*, pp. 324–6.

matters.[16] As far as non-feudal Latins were concerned, a similar distinction was made between permanent settlers, described as *habitatores*, *burgenses* or *cives*, and visiting *mercatores* and pilgrims, all of whom were subject to a *Cour des Bourgeois* in civil and criminal matters.[17]

Nor was mere possession of a *borgesie* enough for a person to belong to the class of burgesses. In a charter of 1143, detailing the rights of a tenant of Jerusalem to sell his *borgesie*, it was stipulated that he could alienate his property to 'burgesses or Syrians'.[18] So although Syrian Christians could be tenants of *borgesies* and were answerable to the *Cour des Bourgeois* for their properties, they were not burgesses because they were not Latin Christians. In all matters not relating to burgess laws of tenancy they were probably subject to a *Cour des Syriens*, and their social and legal status was defined by their accountability to this court.

In conclusion, in the kingdoms of Jerusalem and Cyprus in the twelfth, thirteenth and fourteenth centuries, the status of burgesses was defined by three factors: religion, jurisdiction and property. It was not enough to be a Latin Christian in order to belong to the class of burgesses and nor was it enough to be a tenant of a *borgesie*, or to be subject to a *Cour des Bourgeois*. A person had to be a Latin Christian of European or native origin, subject to a *Cour des Bourgeois* in civil and criminal matters or in certain cases to other courts, such as Church courts, vested with authority over him, and a tenant of a *borgesie* in a city or rural settlement in order to qualify as a burgess. These characteristics combined defined his status.

---

16 The 'Livre au roi' states that a mercenary accused of assaulting a fief-holder should be judged in the High Court, and if found guilty banished from the kingdom; Greilsammer, 'Livre au roi', p. 251.

17 Jacoby, 'Citoyens et protégés de Venise et de Gènes en Chypre du XIIIe au XVe siècle', pp. 159–60. The residents, who were sometimes called *polains* or *pullani*, were either born in the kingdom of Jerusalem or had been settled there for a long time. See M.R. Morgan, 'The Meanings of Old French *Polain*, Latin *pullanus*', *Medium Aevum*, 48 (1979): 40–53.

18 Bresc-Bautier, no. 68, p. 165.

Bibliography

Primary Sources

'Abrégé du livre des assises de la Cour des Bourgeois', in *RHC Lois*, II.

Albert of Aachen, 'Historia Hierosolymitana', in *RHC Occ.*, IV.

Alexander IV, *Registres*, ed. C. Bourel de la Roncière *et al.* (Paris, 1895–1959).

Alishan, L.M. (ed.), *Assises d'Antioche* (Venice, 1876).

'Annales Magdeburgenses', *MGH SS*, 16.

Athir, al-, Ibn , *al-Kamil fi'il ta'rikh* , ed. C.J. Tornberg, (12 vols, Beirut reprint: Dar Sáder, 1965–67).

Balard, M. (ed.), *Notai genovesi in oltremare: atti rogati a Cipro da Lamberto di Sambuceto (11 Ottobre 1296–23 Giugno 1299)* (Genoa: Università di Genova, Instituto di Medievistica, 1983).

——— (ed.), *Notai genovesi in oltremare: atti rogati a Cipro. Lamberto di Sambuceto e Giovanni de Rocha (3 Agosto 1308–14 Marzo 1310)* (Genoa: Università di Genova, Instituto di Medievistica, 1984).

'Bans et ordonnances des rois de Chypre, 1286–1362', in *RHC Lois* II.

Berggötz, O. (ed.), *Der Bericht des Marsilio Zorzi: Codex Querini – Stampalia iv3 (1064)* (Frankfurt: Lang, 1991).

Bernold, 'Chronicon', *MGH SS*, 5.

Bresc-Bautier, G. (ed.), *Le Cartulaire du chapitre du Saint-Sépulcre de Jérusalem* (Paris: P. Geuthner, 1984).

Canciani, P. (ed.), *Barbarorum Leges Antiquae* (5 vols, Venice, 1781–92).

Cessi, R. (ed.), *Deliberazioni del Maggior Consiglio di Venezia* (3 vols, Bologna: N. Zanichelli, 1931–50).

Chamberlayne, T.J. (ed.), *Lacrimae nicossienses. Recueil d'inscriptions funéraires, la plupart françaises, existant encore dans l'île de Chypre* (Paris: Imprimeries Réunies, 1894).

Clermont-Ganneau, C. (ed.), 'Deux chartes des croisés dans les archives arabes', *Recueil d'Archéologie Orientale*, VI (1905): 1–30.

Colette, W. (ed.), *Les deux rédactions en vers du Moniage Guillaume* (2 vols, Paris: Firmin-Didot/Société des Anciens Textes Français, 1906–11).

'Cronica S. Petri Erfordensis Moderna', *MGH SS*, 30.

Delaborde, H.F. (ed.), *Chartes de la Terre Sainte provenant de l'Abbaye de Notre-Dame de Josaphat* (Paris: E. Thorin, 1880).

Delaville Le Roulx, J. 'Titres de l'hopital des Bretons d'Acre', in *AOL*, I (1881).

——— (ed.), *Les Archives, la bibliothèque et le trésor de l'Ordre de Saint-Jean de Jérusalem à Malte* (Paris: Bibliothèque des Ecoles Française d'Athènes et de Rome, 1883).

——— (ed.), *Cartulaire général de l'Ordre des Hospitaliers de St.-Jean de Jérusalem (1100–1310)* (4 vols, Paris: E. Leroux, 1894–1906).
——— (ed.), 'Inventaire des pièces de Terre Sainte de l'Ordre de l'Hôpital', in *ROL*, III (1895).
——— (ed.), 'Chartes du Mont-Thabor', ed. J. Delaville Le Roulx, in *Cartulaire général*, vol. 2.
——— (ed.), 'Chartes de Terre Sainte', in *ROL*, IX (1905–1908).
Deschamps, P. (ed.), 'Etude sur un texte latin enumerant les possessions Musulmanes dans le Royaume de Jérusalem vers l'année 1239', *Syria* (1942–43): 86–104.
Desimoni, C. (ed.), 'Actes passés à Famagouste de 1299–1301 par devant le notaire Génois Lamberto di Sambuceto', in *AOL*, II (1884).
——— (ed.), 'Quatre titres des propriétés des Génois à Acre et à Tyr', in *AOL*, II (1884).
'Documents relatifs à la successibilité au trône et à la régence', in *RHC Lois*, II.
Ekkehard of Aura, 'Hierosolymita', in *RHC Occ.*, V.
Ernoul, *Chronique d'Ernoul et de Bernard le Trésorier*, ed. L. de Mas-Latrie (Paris: Mme Ve J. Renouard, 1871).
'L'Estoire d'Eracles Empereur et la conqueste de la terre d'outremer', in *RHC Occ.*, I–II.
Evans, A. (ed.), *Francesco Balduci Pegolotti: La pratica della mercatura* (Cambridge, Mass.: The Medieval Academy of America, 1936).
Ferreto, A. (ed.), 'Contributi alle relazioni tra Genova e l'Oriente. Una Lettera del pontifice Innocenzo III e un privilegio di Guido re di Gerusalemme e Signore di Cipro', *Giornale Liguistico*, XXI (1896).
Fitting, H. and Suchier, H. (eds), *Lo Codi. Eine Summa Codicis in Provenzalischer Sprache aus der Mitte des XII Jahrhunderts* (Halle: M. Niemeyer, 1906).
Foucher, V. (ed.), 'Assises du Royaume de Jérusalem', part 1, 'Assises des bourgeois', part 2, 'Le Plédéant et le plaidoyer' (Rennes: Blin, 1840).
Fulcher of Chartres, *Historia Hierosolymitana (1095–1127)*, ed. H. Hagenmeyer (Heidelberg: Carl Winters Universitatsbuchhandlung, 1913).
Geoffrey Le Tor, 'Livre', in *RHC Lois*, I.
Gregory IX, *Registres*, ed. L. Auvray, (4 vols, Paris: Boccard, 1896–55).
———, *Acta (1227–1241)*, ed. A.L. Tautu (Vatican City: Typis polyglottis vaticanis, 1950).
Greilsammer, M (ed.), *Le Livre au roi*, (Paris: Académie des Inscriptions et Belles-Lettres, 1995).
Guibert of Nogent, 'Historia qua dicitur Gesta Dei per Francos', in *RHC Occ*, IV.
Hill, R. (ed.), *Gesta Francorum et aliorum Hierosolimitanorum* (London: T. Nelson, 1962).
Halphen, L. and Poupardin, R. (eds), *Chroniques des comtes d'Anjou et des seigneurs d'Amboise*, (Paris: Auguste Picard, 1913).
'Historia Peregrinorum euntium Jerusolymam', in *RHC Occ.*, III.

Honorius III, *Acta (1216-1227)*, ed. A.L. Tautu (Vatican City: Typis polyglottis vaticanis, 1950).

Ibn Jubayr, Muhammad, *Rihlah*, ed. W. Wright (London: E.J. Brill, 1852).

Isfahani, al-, Imad al-Din, *Sana al-barq al Shami*, abridged by Fath. b. 'Ali al-Bundari, pt. 1, ed. R. Sesen (Beirut: Dar al-Kitab al-Jadid, 1971). See also, 'A Critical Edition of the Abridgement by al-Bundari of the *Kitab al-Barq al-Shami* by Imad al-Din', by F. El-Nabarawy, unpublished thesis, Cambridge University Library.

James of Ibelin, 'Livre', in *RHC Lois*, I.

James of Vitry, 'Historia Hierosolymitana', in J. Bongars (ed.), *Gesta Dei per Francos* (2 vols, Hanau, 1611).

———, *Lettres*, ed. R.B.C. Huygens (Leyden: E.J. Brill, 1960).

John XXII, *Lettres communes*, ed. G. Mollat, vol. 1 (Paris: A. Fontemoing, 1904).

John of Ibelin, *Le Livre des assises*, ed. P.W. Edbury (Leyden: E.J. Brill, 2003).

John of Joinville, *Histoire de Saint Louis*, ed. M. Natalis de Wailly (Paris, 1868).

Kausler, E.H. (ed.), *Livre des assises de Jérusalem* (Stuttgart: A. Krabbe, 1839). Also the edition by A.A. Beugnot, 'Livre des assises de la Cour des Bourgeois', in *RHC Lois*, II.

Kohler, C. (ed.), 'Chartes de l'abbaye de Notre-Dame de la Vallée de Josaphat en Terre Sainte (1108–1291). Analyse et extraits', in *ROL*, VII (1899).

——— (ed.), 'Documents inédits concernant l'orient latin et les croisades (XIIe–XIVe siècle)', in *ROL*, VII (1899).

'La Clef des assises de la Haute Cour du Royaume de Jérusalem et de Chypre', in *RHC Lois*, I.

La Monte, J.L (ed.), 'A Register of the Cartulary of the Cathedral of Santa Sophia of Nicosia', *Byzantion*, V (1930): 439–522.

Legrand, L. (ed.), 'Relation du pèlerinage à Jérusalem de Nicolas de Martoni, notaire italien (1394–1395)', in *ROL*, III (1895).

Leontios Makhairas, *Chronicle*, ed. and trans. R.M. Dawkins, (2 vols, Oxford: Clarendon Press, 1932).

Mansi, G.D (ed.), *Sacrorum conciliorum nova et amplissima collectio*, (31 vols, Florence and Venice: Expensis Antonii Zatta, 1759–98).

Marchegay, P. and Mabille, E (eds), *Chroniques des églises d'Anjou* (Paris: J. Renouard, 1869).

Marsy, A. de (ed.), 'Fragment d'un cartulaire de l'Ordre de Saint-Lazare, en Terre Sainte', in *AOL*, II (1884).

Mas-Latrie, L. de (ed.), 'Documents et mémoires servant de preuves à l'histoire de l'île de Chypre sous les Lusignans', in *Histoire de l'île de Chypre sous le règne des princes de la maison de Lusignan*, vols 2–3 (3 vols, Paris: Impremerie Impériale, 1852–61).

——— (ed.), *Nouvelles preuves de l'histoire de Chypre sous le règne des princes de la maison de Lusignan* (Paris: J. Baur et Détaille, 1873).

——— (ed.), 'Commerce et expéditions militaires de la France et de Venise au Moyen Age', in *Collection des documents inédits sur l'histoire de France. Mélanges historiques. Choix de documents*, (Paris, 1880).

——— (ed.),'Quatre pièces relatives à l'Ordre Teutonique en Orient', in *AOL*, II (1884).

Michelet, M. (ed.), *Procès des Templiers* (2 vols, Paris, 1841–51).

Morgan, M.R. (ed.), *La Continuation de Guillaume de Tyr (1184–1197)* (Paris: Librairie Orientaliste P. Geuthner, 1982).

Morozzo della Rocca, R and Lombardi, A (eds), *Documenti del commercio veneziano nei secoli XI–XIII* (2 vols, Rome and Turin: Instituto Storico Italiano per il Medio Evo, 1940).

Müller, J. (ed.), *Documenti sulle relazioni delle città toscane coll'oriente cristiano e coi Turchi fino all' anno 1531* (Florence, 1879).

'Notitiae duae Lemovicenses/De Praedicatione Crucis in Aquitania', in *RHC Occ.*, V.

Orderic Vitalis, *The Ecclesiastical History of Orderic Vitalis*, ed. and trans. M. Chibnall (6 vols, Oxford: Clarendon Press, 1969–80).

Pauli, S. (ed.), *Codice diplomatico del sacro militare ordine geresolimitano oggi di Malta* (2 vols, Lucca: Per Salvatore e Giandomenico Marescandoli, 1733–37).

Pavoni, R. (ed.), *Notai genovesi in oltremare: atti rogati a Cipro da Lamberto di Sambuceto (6 Luglio–27 Ottobre 1301)* (Genoa, 1982).

Peter Tudebode, *Historia de Hierosolymitano Itinere*, eds J.H. Hill and L.L. Hill (Paris: Paul Geuthner, 1977).

Philip of Beaumanoir, *Les Coutumes du Beauvoisis*, ed. A.A. Beugnot (Paris: Renouard, 1842).

Philip of Novara, 'Le Livre de forme de plait', in *RHC Lois*, I.

———, 'Mémoires', in G. Raynaud (ed.), *Les Gestes des Chiprois* (Geneva, Imprimerie Jules-Guillaume Fick, 1887).

Puncuh, D. (ed.), *I Libri iurium della Repubblica di Genova*, (4 vols, Rome: Ministero per i beni culturali e ambientali, Ufficio centrale per i beni archivistici, 1992–98).

Raymond of Aguilers, *Le 'Liber' de Raymond d'Aguilers*, eds J.H. Hill and L.L. Hill (Paris: Librairie Orientaliste Paul Geuthner, 1969).

Raynaud, G. (ed.), *Les Gestes des Chiprois* (Geneva: Imprimerie Jules-Guillaume Fick, 1887).

Recoura, G. (ed.), *Les Assises de Romanie* (Paris: H. Champion, 1930).

Recueil des Historiens des Croisades, ed. Académie des Inscriptions et Belles-Lettres (Paris: 1841–1906).

———*Historiens Occidentaux* (5 vols, 1844–95).

———*Historiens Orientaux* (5 vols, 1872–1906).

———*Lois. Les Assises de Jérusalem* (2 vols , 1841–43).

Rey, E.G. (ed.), *Recherches géographiques et historiques sur la domination des latins en Orient: Accompagnées de textes inédits ou peu connus du XIIe au XIVe siècle* (Paris: Daupeley, 1877).

Robert the Monk, 'Historia Iherosolimitana', in *RHC Occ.*, III.

Roberto, C. (ed.), *Deliberazioni del Maggior Consiglio di Venezia* (3 vols, Bologna: N. Zanichelli, 1931–50).

Röhricht, R. (ed.), *Regesta regni Hierosolymitani, 1097–1291* (Innsbruck: Libraria Academica Wageriana, 1893). *Additamentum*, 1904.

'Rosenfeld Annals', *MGH SS*, 16.

Salloch, M. (ed.), *Die Lateinische Fortsetzung Wilhelms Von Tyrus* (Liepzig: M. Salloch, 1934).

Strehlke, E. (ed.), *Tabulae Ordinis Theutonici*, (Berlin, 1869).

Tafel, G.L.F and Thomas, G.M (eds), *Urkunden zur älteren Handels und Staatsgeschichte der Republik Venedig: Mit besonderer Beziehung auf Byzanz und die Levante* (3 vols,Vienna: Hof- und Staatsdruckerei, 1856–57).

Tardif, E.J (ed.), *Coutumiers de Normandie*, vol. 2: *La Summa de legibus normannie in curia laicali* (Rouen and Paris, 1896).

Thomas, G.M. and Predelli, R. (eds), *Diplomatarium Veneto-Levantium* (2 vols, Venice: Sumptibus Societatis, 1880–99).

Tobler, T. (ed.), Theoderic, *Libellus de Locis Sanctis*, (Paris: Librarie A. Frank, 1865).

Usamah Ibn Munqidh, *Kitab al-i'tibar,* ed. P.K. Hitti (Princeton: Princeton University Press, 1930).

Villehardouin, *La Conquête de Constantinople*, ed. E. Faral (2 vols, Paris: Belles Lettres, 1961).

William, Archbishop of Tyre, *Chronique*, ed. R.B.C. Huygens with H.E. Mayer and G. Rösch (Turnhout: Brepols 1986).

Secondary Works

Abel, F.M., 'Les deux "Mahomerie" el-Bireh, el Quobeibeh', *Revue Biblique*, 25 (1926): 272–83.

Abulafia, D., 'Crocuses and Crusaders: San Gimignano, Pisa and the Kingdom of Jerusalem', in B.Z. Kedar, H.E. Mayer and R.C. Smail (eds), *Outremer. Studies in the History of the Crusading Kingdom of Jerusalem Presented to Joshua Prawer* (Jerusalem: Yad Izhak Ben-Zvi Institute, 1982).

———, 'The Anconitan Privileges in the Kingdom of Jerusalem and the Levant Trade of Ancona', in G. Airaldi and B.Z. Kedar (eds), *I Comuni italiani nel regno crociato di Gerusalemme* (Genoa: Università di Genova, Istituto di Medievistica, 1986).

———, 'The Levant Trade of the Minor Cities in the Thirteenth and Fourteenth Centuries', in B.Z. Kedar and A.L. Udovish (eds), *The Medieval Levant. Studies in Memory of Eliyahu Ashtor* (Haifa: Gustav Hienemann Institute of Middle Eastern Studies, University of Haifa, 1988).

Althoffer, B., *Les Scabins* (Nancy, 1938).

Asbridge, T.S., *The Creation of the Principality of Antioch, 1098–1130* (Woodbridge: Boydell Press, 2000).

Baggati, B., 'Il Cristianesimo ad Eleuteropolis (Beit Gebrin)', *Liber Annus*, 22 (1972): 109–29.

Balard, M., 'L'Activité commerciale en Chypre dans les années 1300', in P.W. Edbury (ed.), *Crusade and Settlement. Papers Read at the First Conference of the Society for the Study of the Crusades and the Latin East and Presented to R. C. Smail* (Cardiff: University College Cardiff Press, 1985).

Benvenisti, M., *The Crusaders in the Holy Land* (Jerusalem: Israel Universities Press, 1970).

Beugnot, A.A., Introduction to *RHC Lois*, II.

Blake, E.O. and Morris, C., 'A Hermit Goes to War: Peter and the Origins of the First Crusade', *Studies in Church History*, 22 (1985): 79–107.

Boas, A.J., *Crusader Archaeology: The Material Culture of the Latin East* (London: Routledge, 1999).

Boase, T.S.R., 'The History of the Kingdom', in T.S.R. Boase (ed.), *The Cicilian Kingdom of Armenia* (Edinburgh: Scottish Academic Press, 1978).

Bonduard, E., 'Lo Codi, ancien livre de droit provençal', *Revue du Midi*, 13 (1899): 458–66.

Bongert, Y., *Recherches sur les cours laïques du Xe au XIIIe siècle* (Paris, A. & J. Picard, 1949).

Bosworth, C.E., '"The Protected Peoples" (Christians and Jews) in Medieval Egypt and Syria', *Bulletin of the John Rylands Library*, 62 (1979): 11–36.

Bourin-Derrau, M., *Villages médiévaux en Bas-Languedoc: Genèse d'une sociabilité Xe–XIVe Siècle* (2 vols, Paris: L'Harmattan, 1987).

Brooke, C.N.L., *The Medieval Idea of Marriage* (Oxford: Oxford University Press, 1989).

Brundage, J.A., 'Marriage Law in the Latin Kingdom of Jerusalem', in B.Z. Kedar, H.E. Mayer and R.C. Smail (eds), *Outremer. Studies in the History of the Crusading Kingdom of Jerusalem Presented to Joshua Prawer* (Jerusalem: Yad Izhak Ben-Zvi Institute, 1982).

———, 'Concubinage and Marriage in Medieval Canon Law', *Journal of Medieval History*, 1 (1975): 1–17.

Byl, R., *Les Jurisdictions scabinales dans le duché de Brabant des origines à la fin du XVe siècle* (Brussels: Presses Universitaires de Bruxelles, 1965).

Cahen, C., *La Syrie du nord à l'epoque des croisades et la principauté franque d'Antioche* (Paris: Paul Geuthner, 1940).

———, 'Notes sur l'histoire des croisades et de l'orient latin', II: 'Le Régime rural syrien au temps de la domination franque', *Bulletin de la Faculté des Lettres de l'Université de Strasbourg*, 29 (1950–51): 286–310.

———, 'Un Document concernant les Melkites et les latins d'Antioche au temps des croisades', *Revue des Etudes Byzantines*, 29 (1971): 285–92.

———, ‘Un Inscription mal comprise concernant le rapprochement entre Maronites et croisés’, in S.A. Hanna (ed.), *Medieval and Middle Eastern Studies in Honor of Aziz Suryal Atiya* (Leyden: E.J. Brill, 1972).

Caillemer, R., ‘Lo Codi et le droit provençal au XIIe siècle’, *Annales du Midi*, 18 (1906): 494–507.

Chehab, M.H., *Tyr à l’époque des croisades: Histoire sociale, economique et religieuse* (vols 31–32, Paris: Bulletin du Musée de Beyrouth, 1979).

Chénon, E., *Histoire générale du droit français public et privé des origines à 1815* (2 vols, Paris, 1926–29).

Clanchy, M.T., *From Memory to Written Record. England 1066–1307* (London: Edward Arnold, 1979).

Combes, J., ‘Un Marchand de Chypre, bourgeois de Montpellier’, *in Etudes médiévales offertes à M. Le Doyen Augustin Fliche* (Montpellier: Presses universitaires de France, 1954).

Cowdrey, H.E.J., ‘Pope Urban II’s Preaching of the First Crusade’, *History*, 55 (1970): 177–88.

Darlington, R.R., ‘The Early History of English Towns’, *History*, 23 (1939): 141–50.

Delisle, L.V., *Etudes sur la condition de la classe agricole et l’état de l’agriculture en Normandie au Moyen Age* (Evreux: Impr. Hérissey, 1851).

Devailly, G., *Le Berry du Xe siècle au milieu du XIIIe. Etude politique, religeuse, sociale et economiqué* (Paris: Mouton, 1973).

Dictionnaire de droit canonique, ed. R. Naz, vol. 4 (Paris: Letouzey et Ané, 1949).

Dodu, G., *Histoire des institutions monarchiques dans le Royaume de Jérusalem, 1099–1291* (Paris: Librairie Hachette, 1894).

Donahue, C., ‘What Causes Fundamental Legal Ideas? Marital Property in England and France in the Thirteenth Century’, *Michigan Law Review*, 78 (1979): 59–88.

Douglas, A.W. ‘Tenure *in Elimosinam*: Origins and Establishment in Twelfth-Century England’, *The American Journal of Legal History*, 24 (1980): 95–132.

Duby, G., *La Société aux XIe et XIIe siècles dans la région mâconnaise* (Paris: S.E.V.P.E.N, 1971).

——— *Medieval Marriage: Two Models from Twelfth-Century France*, trans. E. Forster (Baltimore: John Hopkins University Press, 1979).

Duesberg, J., *Les Jurisdictions scabinales en Flandre et en Lotharingie au moyen-âge* (Louvain, 1932).

Duncalf, F., ‘The Peasants’ Crusade’, *American Historical Review*, 26 (1920–21): 440–53.

Edbury, P.W., *The Kingdom of Cyprus and the Crusades, 1191–1374* (Cambridge: Cambridge University Press, 1991).

———, ‘Law and Custom in the Latin East: *Les Letres dou Sepulcre*’, *Mediterranean Historical Review*, 10 (1996): 71–79.

———, *John of Ibelin and the Kingdom of Jerusalem* (Woodbridge: Boydell Press, 1997).

———, 'The Lusignan Regime in Cyprus and the Indigenous Population', in *Kingdoms of the Crusaders. From Jerusalem to Cyprus* (Aldershot: Ashgate, 1999).

———, 'The Franco-Cypriot Landowning Class and its Exploitation of the Agrarian Resources of the Island of Cyprus', in *Kingdoms of the Crusaders. From Jerusalem to Cyprus* (Aldershot: Ashgate, 1999).

———, 'Famagusta Society ca. 1300 from the Registers of Lamberto di Sambuceto', in *Kingdoms of the Crusaders. From Jerusalem to Cyprus* (Aldershot: Ashgate, 1999).

——— and J.G. Rowe, *William of Tyre: Historian of the Latin East* (Cambridge: Cambridge University Press, 1988).

Ellenblum, R., 'Colonization Activities in the Frankish East: The Example of Castellum Regis (Mi'ilya)', *English Historical Review*, 111 (1996): 104–22.

———, *Frankish Rural Settlement in the Latin Kingdom of Jerusalem* (Cambridge: Cambridge University Press, 1998).

Enlart, C., *Monuments des croisés* (2 vols, Paris: P. Geuthner, 1925–28).

Esmein, A., *Le Mariage en droit canonique* (Paris: Larose et Forcel, 1891).

Every, G., 'Syrian Christians in Palestine in the Early Middle Ages', *Eastern Churches Quarterly*, 3 (1946): 363–72.

Favreau-Lilie, M.-L., 'The Teutonic Knights in Acre after the fall of Montfort 1271): Some Reflections', in B.Z. Kedar, H.E. Mayer and R.C. Smail (eds), *Outremer. Studies in the History of the Crusading Kingdom of Jerusalem Presented to Joshua Prawer* (Jerusalem: Yad Izhak Ben-Zvi Institute, 1982).

———, *Die Italiener im Heiligen Land: vom Ersten Kreuzzug bis zum Tode Heinrichs von Champagne (1098–1197)* (Amsterdam: Hakkert, 1989).

Flori, J., *Pierre l'Ermite et sa croisade* (Paris: Fayard, 1999).

Fossier, R., *La Tenure et les hommes en Picardie jusqu'à la fin du XIIIe siècle* (Paris: B. Nauwelaerts, 1968).

Ganshof, F.L., 'Les Transformations de l'organisation judiciaire dans le comté de Flandre', *Revue Belge de Philologie et d'Histoire*, 18 (1939): 43–61.

Génestal, R., *La Tenure en bourgage: Etude sur la propriété foncière dans les villes normandes* (Paris: Rousseau, 1900).

———, *Le Rôle des monastères comme établissement de Crédit. Etudié en Normandie du XIe à la fin du XIIIe siècle* (Paris: Librairie Nouvelle de Droit et de Jurisprudence, 1901).

Glasson, E., *Histoire du droit et des institutions de la France* (6 vols, Paris: Durand et Pedone-Lauriel, 1882–83).

Grandclaude, M., *Etude critique sur les livres des assises de Jérusalem* (Paris: Jouve, 1923).

———, 'Liste d'assises remontant au premier Royaume de Jérusalem 1099–1187', in *Mélanges Paul Fournier* (Paris: Société d'Histoire du Droit, 1929).

Greilsammer, M., 'Structure and Aims of the Livre au Roi', in B.Z. Kedar, H.E. Mayer and R.C. Smail (eds), *Outremer. Studies in the History of the Crusading*

Kingdom of Jerusalem Presented to Joshua Prawer (Jerusalem: Yad Izhak Ben-Zvi Institute, 1982).

Hagenmeyer, H., *Peter der Eremite* (Leipzig: Otto Harrassowitz, 1879).

Hamilton, B., *The Latin Church in the Crusader States: The Secular Church* (London: Variourum, 1980).

Hayek, D., *Le Droit franc en Syrie pendant les croisades: Institutions judiciaires* (Paris, 1925).

Herlihy, D., 'The Agrarian Revolution in Southern France and Italy, 801–1150', *Speculum*, 33 (1958): 23–37.

Higounet, C., 'Structures sociales: Castra et castlenaux dans le sud-ouest Aquitain (Xe–XIII siècles)', in *Structures féodales et féodalisme dans l'occident mediterranéen (Xe–XIIIe siècles)* (Rome, 1980).

———, 'Mouvements de population dans le Midi de la France du XIe au XVe siècle', in *Paysages et villages neufs du Moyen Age* (Bordeaux: Féderation Historique du Sud-Ouest, 1975).

Hill, G.F., *A History of Cyprus in the Frankish Period* (4 vols, Cambridge: Cambridge University Press, 1940–52).

Hitti, P.K., 'The Impact of the Crusades on Moslem Lands', in N.P. Zacour and H.W. Hazard (eds), *A History of the Crusades: The Impact of the Crusades on the Near East*, vol. V (Wisconsin: The University of Wisconsin Press, 1985).

Jacoby, D., 'Les Archontes grecs et la féodalité en Morée franque', *Traveaux et Mémoires du Centre de Recherche d'Histoire et Civilisation Byzantines*, 2 (1967): 421–81.

———, *La Féodalité en Grèce médievale. La 'Assises de Romanie': Sources, application et diffusion* (Paris: Mouton, 1971).

———, 'The Encounter of Two Societies: Western Conquerors and Byzantines in the Peloponnesus after the Fourth Crusade', *The American Historical Review*, 78 (1973): 873–906.

———, 'Citoyens, et protégés de Venise et de Gènes en Chypre du XIIIe au XVe siècle', *Byzantinische Forschungen*, V (1977): 159–88.

———, 'L'Expansion occidentale dans le Levant: Les Vénitiens à Acre dans la seconde moitié du treizième siècle', *Journal of Medieval History*, 3 (1977): 225–64.

———,'Montmusard, Suburb of Crusader Acre: The First Stage of its Development,' in B.Z. Kedar, H.E. Mayer and R.C. Smail (eds), *Outremer. Studies in the History of the Crusading Kingdom of Jerusalem Presented to Joshua Prawer* (Jerusalem: Yad Izhak Ben-Zvi Institute, 1982).

———, 'The Rise of a New Emporium in the Eastern Mediterranean: Famagusta in the Late Thirteenth Century', *Meletai kai Ipomnimata*, I (1984): 145–79.

———, 'Conrad Marquis of Montferrat and the Kingdom of Jerusalem (1187–1192)', in L. Balleto (ed.), *Atti del Congresso Internazionale 'dai Feudi Montferrini e dal Piemonte ai Nuovi Mondi oltre gli Oceani'* (Alessandria, 1993).

———, 'The Venetian Privileges in the Latin Kingdom of Jerusalem: Twelfth and Thirteenth-Century Interpretations and Implementations', in B.Z. Kedar, J. Riley-Smith and R. Hiestand (eds), *Montjoie: Studies in Crusade History in Honour of Hans Eberhard Mayer* (Aldershot: Variorum, 1997).

———, 'From Byzantium to Latin Romania: Continuity and Change', in B. Arbel, B. Hamilton and D. Jacoby (eds), *Latins and Greeks in the Eastern Mediterranean after 1204*, (London: The Society for the Study of the Crusades and the Latin East, 1989).

Johns, C.N., 'The Crusader Attempt to Colonise Palestine and Syria', *Journal of the Royal Central Asian Society*, 21 (1934): 288–300.

Joset, C.J., *Les Villes au pays de Luxembourg (1196–1383)* (Brussels: J. Vermaut, 1940).

Kedar, B., 'The General Tax of 1183 in the Crusading Kingdom of Jerusalem: Innovation or Adaptation?', *English Historical Review*, 89 (1974): 339–45.

———, 'Palmarée, abbaye clunisienne du XIIe siècle, en Galilée', *Revue Bénédictine*, 93 (1983): 260–69.

———, *Crusade and Mission: European Approaches Toward the Muslims* (Princeton: Princeton University Press, 1984).

———, 'On the Origins of the Earliest Laws of Frankish Jerusalem: The Canons of the Council of Nablus, 1120', *Speculum*, 74 (1999): 310–35

Kimball, E.G., 'Tenure in Frank Almoign and Secular Services', *English Historical Review*, 43 (1928): 341–53.

La Monte, J.L., *Feudal Monarchy in the Latin Kingdom of Jerusalem, 1100–1291* (Cambridge, Mass.: Medieval Academy of America, 1932).

———, 'Three Questions Concerning the Assises de Jerusalem', *Byzantina Metabyzantina*, I (1946): 201–11.

Latouche, R., 'Un Aspect de la vie rurale dans le Maine au XIe et au XIIe siècle: l'Establissement des bourgs', *Moyen Age*, 8 (1937): 214–64.

Legras, H., *Le Bourgage de Caen: Tenure à cens et tenure à rente* (*XIe–XVe Siècles*) (Paris: Rousseau, 1911).

Longnon, J., *L'Empire latin de Constantinople et la principauté de Morée* (Paris: Payot, 1949).

Magnou-Nortier, E., *La Société laïque et L'église dans la province ecclésiastique de Narbonne de la fin du VIII à la fin du XIe siècle* (Toulouse: Association des Publications de l'Université de Toulouse-Le Mirail, 1974).

Mas-Latrie, L. de (ed.), *Histoire de l'île de Chypre sous le règne des princes de la maison de Lusignan* (3 vols, Paris: Impremerie Impériale, 1852–61).

Mayer, H.E., *Marseilles Levantehandel und ein Akkonensisches Fälscheratelier des 13. Jahrhunderts*, (Tübingen: M. Niemeyer, 1972).

———, 'Latins, Muslims and Greeks in the Latin Kingdom of Jerusalem', *History*, 63 (1978): 175–92.

———, 'The Concordat of Nablus', *Journal of Ecclesiastical History*, 33 (1982): 531–43.

———, 'The Double County of Jaffa and Ascalon: One Fief or Two?', in P.W Edbury (ed.), *Crusade and Settlement. Papers Read at the First Conference of the Society for the Study of the Crusades and the Latin East and Presented to R.C. Smail* (Cardiff: University College Cardiff Press, 1985).

———, *The Crusades*, trans. J. Gillingham (Oxford: Clarendon Press, 1988).

———, 'The Origins of the Lordships of Ramla and Lydda in the Latin Kingdom of Jerusalem', in *Kings and Lords in the Latin Kingdom of Jerusalem* (Aldershot: Variorum, 1994).

Monier, R., 'L'Administration et la condition juridique des habitants de la ville d'Arras au XIIe siècle', in *Mêlanges Paul Fournier* (Paris: Société d'Histoire du Droit 1929).

Morgan, M.R., 'The Meanings of Old French *Polain*, Latin *Pullanus*', *Medium Aevum*, 48 (1979): 40–53.

Morris, C. 'Propaganda for War. The Dissemination of the Crusading Ideal in the Twelfth Century', *Studies in Church History*, 20 (1983): 79–101.

Musset, L. 'Peuplement en bourgage et bourgs ruraux en Normandie du Xe au XIIIe siècle', *Cahiers de Civilisation Médiévale*, IX (1966): 177–205.

Nersessian, S. der, 'The Kingdom of Cilician Armenia', in R.L. Wolff and H.W. Hazard (eds), *History of the Crusades: The Later Crusades*, vol. II (Wisconsin: The University of Wisconsin Press, 1969).

———, 'The Armenian Chronicle of the Constable Sempad', *Dumbarton Oaks Papers*, XIII (1959): 143–68.

Noble, T.F.X., *The Republic of St Peter: The Birth of the Papal State, 680–825* (Philadelphia: University of Pennsylvania Press, 1984).

Perat, C., 'Un Diplomate gascon au XIVe siècle: Raymond de Piis, nonce de Clément V en Orient', *Mélanges d'Archéologie et d'Histoire de l'Ecole Française de Rome*, XLIV (1927): 35–90.

Patterson, R.B., 'The Early Existence of the *Funda* and *Catena* in the Twelfth-Century Latin Kingdom of Jerusalem', *Speculum*, 39 (1964): 474–77.

Pollock, F., and Maitland, F.W., *The History of English Law* (2 vols, 2 edn Cambridge: Cambridge University Press, 1968).

Prawer, J., *The Latin Kingdom of Jerusalem. European Colonialism in the Middle Ages* (London: Weidenfeld and Nicolson, 1972).

———, *Crusader Institutions* (Oxford: Clarendon Press, 1980).

———, 'Social Classes in the Crusader States: The "Minorities"', in N.P. Zacour and H.W. Hazard (eds), *A History of the Crusades: The Impact of the Crusades on the Near East*, vol. V (Wisconsin: University of Wisconsin Press, 1985).

———, 'Social Classes in the Latin Kingdom: The Burgesses', in N.P. Zacour and H.W. Hazard (eds), *A History of the Crusades: The Impact of the Crusades on the Near East*, vol. V (Wisconsin: University of Wisconsin Press, 1985).

———, *Histoire du royaume latin de Jerusalem* (2 vols, Paris: Editions du Centre National de la Recherche Scientifique, 1969–71).

Pringle, D., 'Magna Mahumeria (al-Bira): The Archaeology of a Frankish New Town in Palestine', in P.W. Edbury (ed.), *Crusade and Settlement. Papers*

Read at the First Conference of the Society for the Study of the Crusades and the Latin East and Presented to R.C. Smail (Cardiff: University College Cardiff Press, 1985).

———, *The Churches of the Crusader Kingdom of Jerusalem. A Corpus*, I, A-K (excluding Acre and Jerusalem) (Cambridge: Cambridge University Press, 1993).

Prutz, H., *Kulturgeschichte der Kreuzzüge* (Berlin: E.S Mittler und sohn, 1883).

Recoura, G., 'Les Assises de Jérusalem. A propos d'un livre récent', *Le Moyen Age*, 26 (1924–25): 151–66.

Rey, E., *Les Colonies franques de Syrie aux XIIe et XIIIe siècles* (Paris: A. Picard, 1883).

Reynolds, S., *Kingdoms and Communities in Western Europe, 900–1300* (Oxford: Clarendon, 1984).

———, *Fiefs and Vassals: The Medieval Evidence Reinterpreted* (Oxford: Oxford University Press, 1994).

Richard, J., *Le Comté de Tripoli sous la dynastie toulousaine, 1102–1187* (Paris: P. Geuthner, 1945).

———, 'Colonies marchandes privilégiées et marché seigneurial. La Fonde d'Acre et ses "droitures"', *Le Moyen Age*, LIX (1953): 325–40.

———, 'Le Statut de la femme dans l'orient latin', *Recueils de la Société Jean Bodin*, XII, *La Femme*, 2e partie (1962): 5–58.

———'Le Peuplement latin et syrien en Chypre au XIIIe siècle', *Byzantinische Forschungen*, VII (1979): 157–73.

———, *The Latin Kingdom of Jerusalem*, trans. J. Shirley (Amsterdam, New York and Oxford: North-Holland Publishing Co., 1979).

———, 'The Political and Ecclesiastical Organisation of the Crusader States', in N.P. Zacour and H.W. Hazard (eds), *A History of the Crusades: The Impact of the Crusades on the Near East*, vol. V (Wisconsin: The University of Wisconsin Press, 1985).

———, 'La Cour des Syriens de Famagouste d'après un texte de 1448', *Byzantinische Forschungen*, XII (1987): 383–98.

Richardot, H., 'Francs-fiefs. Essai sur l'Eexemption totale ou partielle des services de fief', *Revue Historique de Droit Français et Etranger,* 27 (1949): 28–63 and 229–73.

Riley-Smith, J.S.C., *The Knights of St John in Jerusalem and Cyprus, c.1050–1310* (London: Macmillan, 1967).

———, 'The Assise sur Ligece and the Commune of Acre', *Traditio*, XXVII (1971): 179–204.

———, 'A Note on Confraternities in the Latin Kingdom of Jerusalem', *Bulletin of the Institute of Historical Research*, XLIV (1971): 301–08.

———, 'Some Lesser Officials in Latin Syria', *English Historical Review*, 87 (1972): 1–26.

———, *The Feudal Nobility and the Kingdom of Jerusalem, 1174–1277* (London: Macmillan, 1973).

———, 'The Government in Latin Syria and the Commercial Privileges of Foreign Merchants', in D. Baker (ed.), *Relations Between East and West in the Middle Ages*, (Edinburgh: Edinburgh University Press, 1973).

———'The Survival in Latin Palestine of Muslim Administration', in P.M. Holt (ed.), *The Eastern Mediterranean Lands in the Period of the Crusades* (Warminster: Aris and Phillips, 1977).

———, 'The Motives of the Earliest Crusaders and the Settlement of Latin Palestine, 1095–1100', *English Historical Review*, 98 (1983): 721–36.

———, *The First Crusade and the Idea of Crusading* (London: Athlone, 1986).

———, 'Government and the Indigenous in the Latin Kingdom of Jerusalem', in D. Abulafia and N. Berend (eds), *Medieval Frontiers: Concepts and Practices* (Aldershot: Ashgate, 2002).

Russell, J.C., 'The Population of the Crusader States', in N.P. Zacour and H.W. Hazard (eds), *A History of the Crusades: The Impact of the Crusades on the Near East*, vol. V (Wisconsin: The University of Wisconsin Press, 1985).

Salibi, K.S., 'The Maronites of Lebanon under Frankish and Mamluk Rule (1099–1516)', *Arabica*, IV (1957): 288–303.

———, 'The Maronite Church in the Middle Ages and its Union with Rome', *Oriens Christianus*, 42 (1958): 92–104.

———, *Maronite Historians of Mediaeval Lebanon* (Beirut: American University of Beirut. Oriental Series, no. 34, 1991).

Schneider, J., 'Les Origines des chartes de franchises dans le Royaume de France (XIe–XIIe siècle)', in *Les Libertes urbaines et rurales du XIe au XIVe siècle. Colloque international* (Brussels: Pro Civitate, 1968).

Setton, K.M. (general ed.), *A History of the Crusades* (6 vols, Wisconsin, 1955–89).

Smail, R.C., *Crusading Warfare 1097–1193* (Cambridge: Cambridge University Press, 1956).

Spufford, P., *Money and its Use in Medieval Europe* (Cambridge: Cambridge University Press, 1988).

Tabuteau, E.Z., *Transfers of Property in Eleventh-Century Norman Law* (Chapel Hill, London: University of North Carolina Press, 1988).

Tait, J., *The Medieval English Borough. Studies on its Origins and Constitutional History* (Manchester: Manchester University Press, 1936).

Tardif, J., 'Une Version provençal d'une somme du code', *Annales du Midi*, 5 (1893): 34–70.

Thorne, S.E.,'Livery of Seisin', *Law Quarterly Review*, 52 (1936): 345–64.

Tibble, S., *Monarchy and Lordships in the Latin Kingdom of Jerusalem, 1099–1291* (Oxford, Clarendon Press, 1989).

Topping, P., 'The Formation of the Assizes of Romania', *Byzantion*, XVII (1944–45): 304–14.

Toubert, P., *Les Structures de Latium médiéval. Le Latium méridional et Sabine du IXe siècle à la fin du XIIe siècle* (2 vols, Rome: Ecole Française de Rome, 1973).

Vercauteren, F., 'Marchands et bourgeois dans le pays mosan aux XIe et XIIe siècles', in *Mélanges Félix Rousseau. Etudes sur l'histoire du pays mosan au Moyen Age* (Brussels: La Reneissance du Livre, 1958), pp. 655–72.

———, 'Les Libertés urbaines et rurales du XIe au XIV siècle', in *Les Libertés urbaines et rurales du XIe au XIV siècle. Colloque international* (Brussels: Pro Civitate, 1968).

Vital Chomel, M., 'Francs et "rustiques" dans la seigneurie dauphinoise au temps des affranchissements', *Bulletin Philologique et Historique* (1965): 285–308.

Waley, D., *The Papal State in the Thirteenth Century* (London: Macmillan, 1961).

Wolf Hemmeon, M. de, *Burgage Tenure in Mediaeval England* (Cambridge, Mass.: Harvard University Press, 1914).

Yver, J., *Les Contrats dans très ancien droit normand (XIe–XIIIe siècles)* (Domfront: Imprimerie du 'Publicateur', 1926).

———, 'Le Droit privé des villes de l'ouest de la France, spécialement des villes normandes', *Recueils de la Société Jean Bodin*, VIII (1957): 133–61.

Index